Sweating the Small Stuff
Inner-City Schools and the New Paternalism

Sweating the Small Stuff

Inner-City Schools and the New Paternalism

David Whitman

Thomas B. Fordham Institute
June 2008

Published by the Thomas B. Fordham Institute Press
1016 16th Street NW, 8th Floor
Washington, D.C. 20036
www.edexcellence.net
letters@edexcellence.net
(202) 223-5452

The Thomas B. Fordham Institute is a nonprofit organization that conducts research,
issues publications, and directs action projects in elementary/secondary education reform
at the national level and in Ohio, with special emphasis on our hometown of Dayton.
It is affiliated with the Thomas B. Fordham Foundation. Further information can be found
at www.edexcellence.net, or by writing to the Institute at 1016 16th St. NW, 8th Floor,
Washington, D.C. 20036. The report is available in full on the Institute's website; additional
copies can be ordered at www.edexcellence.net. The Institute is neither connected with nor
sponsored by Fordham University.

ISBN: 978-0-615-21408-5

Text set in Adobe Garamond and Scala
Design by Alton Creative, Inc.

Printed and bound by Chroma Graphics in the United States of America

9   8   7   6   5   4   3   2   1

For Lynn and Lily

Contents

Foreword ix

Introduction 1

Chapter One: The Achievement Gap and Education Reform 10

Chapter Two: The Rise, Fall, and Rise of Paternalism 34

Chapter Three: The American Indian Public Charter School 68

Chapter Four: Who Are We, Proud to Be, Amistad Academy 96

Chapter Five: Cristo Rey Jesuit High School — The School That Works 122

Chapter Six: Kipp Academy — "Kipp-Notizing" through Music 152

Chapter Seven: The SEED School and the Custodial Culture 192

Chapter Eight: University Park's Mission Possible 224

Chapter Nine: The Habits of Highly Effective Schools — and
How to Create More of Them 252

Chapter Ten: Obstacles and Alternatives to Radical Paternalistic Reform 284

Endnotes 312

Index 342

Tables

Table 3-1, Page 83
Academic achievement at American Indian Public Charter School and nearby schools

Table 4-1, Page 113
Academic achievement at Amistad Academy and nearby schools

Table 5-1, Page 140
Graduation and college-going rates at Cristo Rey Jesuit High School and nearby schools

Table 5-2, Page 141
Academic achievement at Cristo Rey Jesuit High School and nearby schools

Table 6-1, Page 176
Academic achievement at KIPP Academy and nearby schools

Table 6-2, Page 183
Test scores of incoming students at KIPP Network schools

Table 7-1, Page 216
Academic achievement at the SEED school and nearby schools

Table 8-1, Page 246
Academic achievement at University Park Campus School and nearby schools

Table 8-2, Page 248
SAT and AP test scores and college-going rates at University Park Campus School

Foreword

by Chester E. Finn Jr. and Marci Kanstoroom

This book tells the story of six remarkable inner city secondary schools that have eliminated the achievement gap…or at least come close. They are living proof that poor, minority kids can learn as much as middle class white kids—and that great schools can make an enormous difference in their lives, thus giving the lie to defeatists, determinists, and apologists who insist that this isn't really possible in today's America.

But they are also proof that it isn't easy.

By the time youngsters reach high school in the United States, the achievement gap is immense. The average black twelfth grader has the reading and writing skills of a typical white eighth grader and the math skills of a typical white seventh grader. Graduation rates are low and college-going rates lower. At the schools profiled in this volume, however, inner-city black and Hispanic students surpass not only the average white student but even students attending high-performing suburban schools. These remarkable urban schools insist that narrowing the achievement gap is not enough; they declare that it must (and can) be closed—and their students must be set on a course to college graduation and later success in American society.

While many observers have written off urban secondary schools as beyond hope, while Washington dithers about "high school reform" and major foundations pour tens of millions of dollars into conferences, studies and pilot programs, these six schools—the American Indian Public Charter School in Oakland, Amistad Academy in New Haven, Cristo Rey Jesuit High School in Chicago, KIPP Academy in the Bronx, the SEED school in Washington, D.C., and University Park Campus School in Worcester—are already showing just how different things can be.

Some of those names are likely familiar to readers. Some have been featured in earlier reports on "no excuses" schools. But it's important not just to name and praise them but also to walk through their doors and see what makes them tick. In this ambitious book, veteran journalist David Whitman takes the reader inside their corridors and classrooms. The buildings are often cramped, old, and unlovely. Once inside, however, Whitman found inspiring principals, high academic standards, long school days and years, and a special ingredient that flavors everything about them, though many education experts wince when they hear it and few journalists have paid attention to it: a healthy, forceful, modern version of paternalism.

Like firm parents, the principals, teachers and other staff in these gap-busting schools are engaged in explicit character training aimed at creating a culture of kindness, decency, integrity and hard work. But the adults in these schools don't just mouth vague instructions like "be kind" and "work hard"; they translate abstract goals into concrete benchmarks and rules, check constantly to see how everyone is measuring up—and intervene whenever necessary. As Whitman reports, all of them "sweat the small stuff."

The schools are preoccupied with fighting disorder; they fix the proverbial broken windows quickly to deter further unruliness. Students are shown exactly how they are expected to behave—how to sit in a chair without slumping, how to track the teacher with their eyes, how to walk silently down the hall, how to greet visitors with a firm handshake, and how to keep track of daily assignments. Their behavior is closely monitored at all times and the schools mete out real rewards for excellence and real punishments for rule-breaking.

This close supervision might sound like a teenager's worst nightmare, but it is an atmosphere in which students thrive and that many come to appreciate. The orderly environment makes learning easier. Youngsters feel valued and respected by their teachers; many report that their school is a second home. They learn new habits and develop new attitudes that pay off in small and large ways: they earn special privileges at school as they prepare to take their place in college and the world beyond.

And college is where most are headed. The three high schools featured in this book send 85+ percent of their graduates to college, while only 31 percent of low-income 18-24 year olds nationwide ever enroll in college. (Among affluent young people, the college-going rate is about 75 percent.) Students attending the three middle schools score in the 80th and 90th percentiles on nationally normed tests. Data tables included in each chapter show exactly how these six schools compare with others in their neighborhoods, districts, and states.

To the keen eye of David Whitman, who has written on social policy for many years at *U.S. News and World Report* and other publications, the clear standards and close supervision of students at these schools are manifestations of paternalism of a benevolent sort—which he takes pains to distinguish from less welcome kinds.

Paternalistic policies, broadly understood, are those in which the government interferes with the freedom of individuals for their own good, requiring them to wear motorcycle helmets, for instance, or save money for retirement, even if they would prefer not to. In the United States, paternalism has often been controversial because it has frequently involved government imposing its values on poor or minority people in particular, and trying to change the way they live.

Educational paternalism is not new—and Whitman recounts its mixed history, including some ugly chapters. In the late 19th century, for example, thousands of Native American children were sent off, often against their parents' will, to attend Indian boarding schools that sought to eradicate their native culture, which was viewed as degenerate. Students were forced to undergo haircuts, give up their native clothing, speak English, and answer to Anglo names while they were lectured on monogamy, temperance, chastity and other Christian virtues.

In the early 20th century, many urban schools took on the task of assimilating millions of school-aged immigrants into American society. Teachers and curricula undertook not only to teach the children English and hygiene but also to wean them from the ways of the "old country." Some parents objected, but many welcomed the schools' help in turning their children into good,

English-speaking Americans who would succeed on these shores—and who often helped older members of their families to succeed as well. While the history of Indian boarding schools is generally regarded as shameful, the verdict on the paternalism of immigrant high schools is decidedly more mixed.

Paternalism was in the doghouse for much of the 20th century, but beginning in the 1990s, New York University professor Lawrence Mead and others began to rehabilitate it as an approach to social policy challenges. The "new paternalism" involves much more than telling poor people how to live. The best way to help the poor overcome social problems and make their way out of socio-cultural cul-de-sacs, Mead and others argue, is to create policies that set clear expectations and then closely supervise beneficiaries to ensure that they meet those expectations. The key to such policies is not the behavioral requirements themselves but the monitoring and assistance provided to people to help them meet those expectations and, ideally, change their lifestyles for the better. In the best known example of the "new paternalism" in successful operation, post-reform welfare policies do not simply require individuals to work in return for government assistance ("work-fare," it used to be called); they provide case managers who meet regularly with recipients and show them exactly how to get and keep a job, even as the terms by which cash assistance (and food stamps, health care, day care, etc.) are provided give them strong incentives to break free from dependency. New paternalists say that such policies merely enforce and reinforce values that the clients already embrace but are unable to live up to because of lack of support or personal problems. (Opponents argue that such policies treat low-income adults like children.)

The founders of the schools portrayed in this book don't much like the label of paternalism, nor will many of the schools' supporters. And indeed, there is something odd about labeling a *school* paternalistic. If it treats its clients like children, telling them to sit up straight and tuck in their shirts—well, they *are* children and good schools have always sought to teach them good values and acceptable behavior along with the three R's. If the term "paternalistic" didn't make people queasy, they would immediately recognize that schools and teachers, along with parents, are supposed to civilize, incentivize and nurture children. It's just that schools serving inner-city kids may need to do more of that and do it more intensively. Indeed, giving disadvantaged adolescents a full and fair shot at success in life may require a period of close supervision and explicit instruction in how to learn and how to live. If this makes the schools paternalistic, many education reformers will have no objection to the practice even if they're nervous about the terminology—and even if they reject paternalist policies aimed at adults.

Founders of these highly effective inner-city schools also reject any suggestion that their schools condescend to students or their parents, which some feel is implied by the paternalism label. The schools, say their leaders, don't substitute their moral judgments for those of their clients; they simply take advantage of every possible opportunity to inculcate and habituate children to values that are endorsed, if not always acted upon, by their own families.

Still and all, it's undeniable that these schools aim to change the lifestyles of those who attend them. They teach inner-city teenagers to embrace middle-class values, to aspire to college, to behave properly, and to reject the culture of the street, and they do all this by offering explicit instruction in how to behave, what to aim for, and how to get there.

The schools seek to support low-income families in raising their children well, but they do this by taking on some of the responsibilities normally assumed by parents—and by enveloping their pupils from dawn to dusk (and, in one case, all night). They work tirelessly to nurture a work ethic and high academic goals (as well as politeness, neatness, and respect for elders) because they see that many poor families can't pull this off alone. Nor do they see parent participation in the school as key to closing achievement gaps; while it's always welcome and sometimes encouraged, the main thing the schools ask of parents is that they get their children there on time each day and provide a quiet place for homework to be completed.

This stands in stark contrast to the conventional wisdom that we cannot expect inner-city schools to succeed without tons more parental support. In a debate among Democratic presidential aspirants in January 2008, for example, candidates were asked "To what do you attribute the disproportionately high dropout of black males at every level in our educational process, and what would you do to stem the tide of black men exiting the educational system?" Hillary Clinton responded "You know, this has to start in the families. This is what I've done for 35 years. We've got to do more to give families the tools and the support that they should have so that they can be the best parents." Barack Obama added that "We have to have our parents take their jobs seriously." To be fair, in a later speech Obama argued that the most important determinant of academic achievement is the teacher, not the parents.

The schools depicted in these pages aren't waiting for parents to change—nor excusing lackluster results by saying that parents aren't doing their part. On the contrary. They're working successfully with kids today. Yet taking on more of the parents' role is not the only thing that makes them unconventional. Their approach to teaching is also out of favor among conventionally trained educators. In most of today's colleges of education, aspiring principals and teachers learn to embrace progressivism and constructivism over behaviorism and instructivism. The ed school credo says that learning is natural and should be given freedom to unfold, with the teacher functioning as "a guide on the side, not a sage on the stage." Progressives eschew teacher-directed instruction, memorization, assessment, rewards, and the like; in short, just about everything that makes the schools profiled here work. It is hard to avoid the conclusion that progressive educators are turning their back on the most effective ways of closing the achievement gap.

It is perhaps no surprise that the schools in this book are mostly outside the reach of the long arm of the education establishment—the ed schools, the district bureaucrats, and the teacher unions, among others. Only one of the paternalistic schools described here is a district-operated neighborhood school (and it's an extraordinary exception within its district); four are public charter schools, and one is a Catholic school. Whatever their governance, all are break-the-mold schools; their founders all rejected conventional ways of doing things, beginning with progressive theories about child development, constructivist pedagogy, and teachers trained by schools of education (though students at one school, University Park, take part in a good deal of group work in addition to teacher-directed instruction).

Schools like these may, in fact, only be able to succeed when their leaders are unconstrained by bureaucratic rules and union contracts. Principals of successful paternalistic schools must be free to hire promising teachers who have a passionate commitment to the mission of the school, not state-certified teachers assigned by district headquarters. They must also be free to deploy and compensate their teams as they see fit—and to terminate anyone who performs poorly. These principals also need the power to set and revise their own curriculum and calendar, to control their budgets and to ask everyone to work long hours in single-minded support of the mission. It is hard—though surely not impossible—to recreate these conditions in a traditional district school that is subject to central-office rules and collective bargaining agreements, which is why most efforts to create paternalistic schools are taking place under the umbrella of charter schooling.

It is extremely difficult to read this book without wanting to create many more such schools for all the children in America who could benefit from them. Yet figuring out how to scale up highly effective schools in large numbers has been the Achilles heel of every sort of effective schools analysis of the past forty years. We can spot them, we can describe them, we can celebrate them, but we've not been sure we can replicate them. We're learning now.

The founders of all of the schools profiled here have embarked on serious efforts to replicate their models. Advocates say there are about 200 achievement-gap-closing charter schools nationwide today. The largest network of paternalistic schools, run by KIPP, includes 57 schools serving more than 14,000 students, and the KIPP network has plans to dramatically expand its operations in Houston, alone, to 21,000 students in the next decade. This would mean educating 10 percent of all the kids in Texas's largest city in paternalistic schools. We don't see any compelling reason that couldn't become 20 percent in 20 years and 30 percent in 30 years. And there's no reason Los Angeles and Philadelphia and Chicago couldn't also aim for 10 percent in the foreseeable future. We may never get to 100 percent, but 30 percent would be transformative for the country, and 70 percent would be incredible.

This book shows what it would take to make this kind of expansion happen (including courage, perseverance, amazing people, sleepless lives, and some extra money from forward-thinking philanthropists or the public fisc). These things may not be easy to come by at scale but, for those who are inspired to pursue this path, Whitman shows what they can do to break down barriers to radically expanding the number of paternalistic schools. Those barriers range from caps on the number of charter schools that may be opened in various states (a battle to be fought in legislative halls) to potential shortages of principals and teachers with the passion and talent to close the achievement gap (which must be addressed through creative recruitment, training and compensation strategies).

Everybody across the political spectrum likes a great school. Whitman explores whether growing recognition of just how successful these schools are—and acknowledgment of their paternalistic ways—could prompt a grand political compromise to foster more of them: if liberals agree to grant principals the autonomy they need to run effective schools, perhaps conservatives can kick in the extra money that it takes for schools to operate extended days and years. Whitman himself isn't wildly optimistic. Given the intransigence of unions and bureaucrats, he concludes, a more likely outcome is that we'll continue to see reforms pursued in piecemeal fashion within school districts, with principals granted somewhat greater autonomy here, extended days and years offered there, and a demanding college prep curriculum gradually installed in more inner-city secondary schools. Those aren't bad things to do but they don't add up to a formula for thousands of high-performance schools such as those profiled here.

Perhaps incremental changes within districts will help set the table for more radical reform, but there is something seriously frustrating about incrementalism when applied to inner-city education. If Americans are serious about changing the lives of disadvantaged kids through schooling, we need to embrace super-schools with the power to do that, and not pretend that the schools we have today, with a minor makeover and a few new fillips, will get the job done. The surest way to change a poor child's life prospects is to get him into and through a high-quality high school and into and through college. And to do that we need schools with a whole lot more horsepower than the overwhelming majority of what we have today. If we don't supply that horsepower, we won't produce the results.

This is a substantial book, longer than most Fordham studies and reports. But it tells a story worth telling in full. In the first two chapters, Whitman describes how paternalism works and what it is up against. Chapters 3 through 8 supply the school-specific case studies. In the two concluding chapters Whitman draws lessons and generalizations from the school profiles and examines the prospects for replicating these schools by the hundreds. The pages turn quickly, though, for Whitman is a gifted writer as well as a keen-eyed observer and shrewd analyst. That's why we asked him to tackle this important project—which at earlier stages we called "Schools on Steroids" and "Culture-transplant Schools." From the Fordham standpoint, it compellingly knits together four strands of education reform that have long inspired us: higher standards, quality choices, school autonomy, and high-performing teachers and school leaders.

Besides David Whitman, we owe sincere thanks to the Koret Foundation and the Searle Freedom Trust for helping to underwrite this project; to Aspire Consulting (and in particular Larry Maloney and Meagan Batdorff) for assisting with the analysis of school performance; to MaryJo Thomas for her keen and speedy copy editing; and to Fordham's Martin A. Davis, Jr. and Christina Hentges for pulling all of the pieces together.

Introduction

One Monday morning in the spring of 1989, Donna Rodrigues was teaching her first period Spanish class at South High School in Worcester, Massachusetts, when a student bolted into her classroom with an urgent announcement. Two South students were fighting in the corridor, and one boy had slashed the other with a knife. Before Rodrigues could move, several excited students darted out of her class to watch the fight. Rodrigues charged after the students to haul them back to class, just in time to see a sixteen-year-old knifing victim lying on the ground, drenched in blood. Blood was everywhere—the boy was cut so badly that his dark red blood had spattered the ceiling. Rodrigues, a couple of teachers, and the school nurse did their best to help the boy and quiet the crowd. But it was of no use. The boy was bleeding to death.

Awash with grief and covered in blood herself, Rodrigues left the police station later that day to ponder her future. Did she still really want to be a teacher? Rodrigues was no naïf. She had grown up in the rough neighborhood that surrounded South and lived just a few blocks from the school. Nor was she a stranger to the raucous world of urban high schools—she had taught in Worcester's public schools for nearly 20 years and was South's department chair for foreign languages. South High itself was a cavernous comprehensive high school with a soulless open-school design—the students met in classroom "pods" that had sliding walls as dividers that stopped short of the ceiling. Yet for all of her classroom savvy and experience, Rodrigues was shocked by the pettiness of the schoolyard murder she had witnessed. A carnival had been in town the weekend before, and somehow, in between the rides and the cotton candy, a teenager had complained about a boy making a comment about his girlfriend. And now the boy was dead.

During the months-long court case that followed the boy's murder, Rodrigues mulled over her future. Finally she reached a decision. She would keep teaching. But if she ever had a chance to run her own school, things would be different. "Seeing one of my students murdered made me acutely aware of the costs of chaos and unstructured environment," Rodrigues recalls. "I realized the importance of clear expectations and behavioral norms—I wanted my kids to know where they were going *all* the time." Given an opportunity to plan a new school, Rodrigues vowed her "number one decision would be that there was going to be a code of behavior based on professional norms—no swearing, no fighting, no street talk."

In fact, Rodrigues did get the chance in 1997 to design and open her own public school in Worcester, not far from South High School. And true to her word, the University Park Campus School (UPCS) is a school that has zero tolerance for street talk or displays of disrespect, even in student-to-student banter. By pushing rigorous academic standards and guaranteeing that every student would be accepted at college, Rodrigues succeeded in creating a culture of achievement within UPCS that is the antithesis of the learning environment at South and the culture of the street that captures so many of the neighborhood's disadvantaged youth. Although UPCS students are selected by lottery from the same inner-city neighborhood where South students live, the two schools could not be more different. In its decade of operation, UPCS students have compiled a nearly flawless record on Massachusetts' achievement test, a record that rivals some of the state's elite prep schools. The school has a *zero* percent dropout rate—and nearly every graduate has been accepted at a college. In effect, University Park has eliminated the costly and pervasive achievement gap between whites and disadvantaged black and Hispanic students.

This book tells the story of University Park Campus School and five other secondary schools that have succeeded in eliminating or dramatically shrinking that achievement gap. It is a hopeful book—in a field that is riddled with tales of disadvantaged teens whose lives are crippled by the schools, families, and communities that fail them. In addition to UPCS, the chapters that follow recount the stories of the American Indian Public Charter School in Oakland, Amistad Academy in New Haven, the Cristo Rey Jesuit High School in Chicago, the KIPP Academy in the Bronx, and the SEED school in Washington, D.C. Each of these secondary schools is an educational gem that is at odds with the notion that the achievement gap cannot be closed, or can only be meaningfully narrowed by the provision of massive new social programs to raise the income and change the living circumstances of poor families.

These half-dozen secondary schools are not all alike: three of the six are charter middle schools, one is a parochial high school, one is a traditional neighborhood public school and yet another is the only urban public boarding school in the nation for low-income students. Yet the schools have much in common. All of the schools have gifted, deeply committed teachers and dedicated, forceful principals. They also all have rigorous academic standards, test students frequently, and carefully monitor students' academic performance to assess where students need help. "Accountability," both for teachers and students, is not a dirty word but a lodestar. Students take a college-prep curriculum and are not tracked into vocational or non-college-bound classes. At the same time, none of the six schools practices "social promotion," a common policy in inner-city high schools that allows students to be promoted automatically to the next grade. Most of the schools have uniforms or a dress code, an extended school day, and three weeks of summer school.

Above all, however, these schools share a paternalistic ethos supporting a common school culture that prizes academic achievement. By paternalistic I mean that each of the six schools is a highly prescriptive institution that teaches students not just how to think but how to act according to what are commonly termed traditional, middle-class values. Much in the manner of a responsible parent, these schools tell students that they need an "attitude adjustment." Like secondary schools elsewhere, paternalistic schools can value freedom, curiosity, and self-expression, too — but not at the expense of inculcating diligence, thrift, politeness, and a strong work ethic. These paternalistic schools go beyond just teaching values as abstractions; the schools tell students exactly how they are expected to behave and their behavior is closely monitored, with real rewards for compliance and penalties for noncompliance. Students are required to talk a certain way, sit a certain way, and dress a certain way. Even minor infractions are not tolerated. These schools thus *require* and *teach* students to meet high expectations for behavior and academic achievement—rather than just encouraging them to aim high. These six schools stand out because they refuse to accede, in George Bush's phrase, to the "soft bigotry of low expectations" that public schools often display toward low-income minority students. In the loose parlance of education reform, they are "No Excuses" schools.

While these "no excuses" schools have demonstrated remarkable results, the notion of reintroducing paternalism in inner-city schools is deeply at odds with the conventional wisdom of the K–12 education establishment. For a host of reasons, teachers unions, school board members, ed school professors, big-city school administrators, multicultural activists, bilingual educators, and progressive education proponents do not embrace the idea that what might most help disadvantaged students are highly prescriptive schools that favor traditional instructional methods. And even the many parents who are foursquare in favor of what paternalistic schools do cringe at labeling schools in those terms. In 2008, paternalism remains a dirty word in American culture. As Chester E. Finn Jr. noted a decade ago, "although nearly all parents would run screaming from schools that *call* themselves paternalistic, in practice paternalism seems to be what many want: institutions with explicit standards for skills, knowledge, and behavior, and with the gumption to hold both teachers and pupils accountable for achieving those norms." [1]

In the chapter that follows, I begin by examining the disturbing and stubborn achievement gap that exists between white adolescents and black and Hispanic teenagers and recent attempts to close that gap. Chapter two recounts the history of paternalistic social policies in the United States, particularly as they have played out in schools. Chapters three through eight then provide a view from inside the classroom of the six "no excuses" schools. In the concluding chapters, I assess the lessons that policymakers and parents can draw from these extraordinary schools–and consider whether these new paternalistic schools can be scaled up dramatically to reshape inner-city education.

What these highly structured schools do seems like common sense, if perhaps a bit strict. Indeed, during the course of reporting this book, I was bemused to find that many middle-class parents whom I told about the project thought the need for rigorous, authoritative schools for disadvantaged adolescents was all too obvious, even when they sent their own children to less traditional institutions. I myself attended a private, progressive Quaker school in a gritty neighborhood in Philadelphia during the 1960s and early 1970s. It was an outstanding school and provided a first-rate education. But decades later, having spent time in urban schools as a reporter, I can see that a progressive pedagogy would have been ill-suited to many inner-city schools. Today, it is no coincidence that many of the founders of the new paternalistic schools are young white liberals—notwithstanding the schools' seemingly conservative culture.

What is the take-away conclusion about these schools? The new breed of paternalistic schools appears to be the single most effective way of closing the achievement gap. No other school model or policy reform in urban secondary schools seems to come close to having such a dramatic impact on the performance of inner-city students. Successful "no excuses" schools use many strategies for raising achievement that are widely recognized as important, such as assessing students regularly and setting rigorous standards. But these schools follow one additional practice that is not discussed much: they teach students exactly how to live. Their paternalism is an essential, if often overlooked, aspect of education reform, and of growing importance in social policy today. Done right, paternalistic schooling provides a novel way to remake inner-city education in the years ahead.

It Depends on What "Success" Is

During the last two decades, I have had many opportunities as a reporter to visit a variety of model programs. Almost without fail, I have been struck by the gulf between what social scientists deem a "successful" program and the far more ambitious expectations of the public. A job training program for welfare recipients that, say, raises the earnings of women by 10 percent or trims the welfare rolls by 5 percentage points would be hailed by researchers as a great success, even though most Americans would deem those outcomes modest at best.

By contrast, the schools profiled in these pages stand out because they are a success by anyone's standards. They dramatically raise the achievement of disadvantaged students. They have low dropout rates—though they sit next to schools where more than half of the students fail to graduate on time. They rapidly ratchet up student achievement several grade levels and level the playing field between white and minority students—even as nearby neighborhood schools fail miserably.

How robust is the evidence of success? It is clear that these schools sub-stantially boost student achievement—and the individual schools profiled here were selected in part because they have better data on achievement over a longer period of time than many schools. Each of the six chapters devoted to a school and its education model compares the performance of its students with their peers in nearby public schools. At the request of the Thomas B. Fordham Foundation, Aspire Consulting used a relatively simple methodology to identify appropriate comparison schools. It located all public schools within a three-mile radius of the paternalistic school and then sifted out schools that lacked a high percentage of minority and low-income students, or were oth-erwise atypical because they served special student populations (e.g., magnet schools, vocational academies, special education schools, schools for students with disciplinary problems, and the like). [2]

To accomplish this sifting and matching of comparison schools, Aspire de-veloped a composite index of similarity that factored in the percent of minority enrollment in a school in 2005–2006, the percent of students eligible for the federal free and reduced price lunch program, and the percent of limited-Eng-lish proficient and bilingual education students. In a few chapters, additional comparison schools have been included in the data tables. These schools are located close to the profiled schools and draw students from the same neigh-borhood, though their student bodies may not match the profiled schools as closely. The reader will find that these school-to-school comparisons show not only the poor quality of inner-city education today but the life-changing impact that a great school can have in closing the achievement gap.

Despite the strong evidence that these schools dramatically boost student performance and college enrollment, their record of accomplishment is not near-ly as well documented as it could be. No researcher, for example, has ever done a controlled experiment using random assignment of students to a control group and treatment group to evaluate the impact of a particular school on academic performance. Nor has any of the six schools been evaluated in a rigorous "quasi-experimental" study in which researchers attempt to match school students with a comparison group before and after the fact. But it is worth noting here, too, an ironic secret of K–12 research: Few education reforms are ever field-tested in randomized experiments, the gold standard of program evaluation. As a result, definitive proof of "what works" in schools can be surprisingly elusive.

The record of education researchers is every bit as sorry when it comes to evaluating the types of whole-school reforms described in the chapters that follow—and particularly so for middle schools and high schools. In a 2006 review, the American Institutes for Research screened nearly 1,500 studies and documents on 18 widely implemented whole-school reform models in middle school and high school. Fewer than 200 of the studies were of sufficient quality to merit review, and only 41 were judged to be rigorous enough to evaluate the impact of the schools upon academic achievement.[3]

Despite these caveats about the data, an overarching consensus among researchers about closing the achievement gap might be summed up as follows: Early intervention in preschool and elementary school can be effective but secondary school interventions by and large are not. "The biggest question of all," states a recent report by the Mass Insight Education and Research Institute, is whether closing the achievement gap can "be done at the high school level…Few—in fact, hardly any—traditional urban high schools today are bringing most of their high-poverty students to true college-readiness."[4] Peer pressure, street culture, and years of growing up in a disadvantaged family and neighborhood take a cumulative toll that is all but impossible to reverse in high school—or so the argument goes. This skepticism about closing the achievement gap in secondary schools makes the success of the paternalistic academies all the more important.

Skeptics of the new paternalistic schools, including education analysts Richard Rothstein[5] and David Armor[6], acknowledge that these schools appear to boost academic achievement. But they contend that the success of schools like the KIPP Academy in the Bronx may be due largely to the "self-selection" of the students—meaning that the students who apply for the KIPP admission lottery are already more motivated and have more supportive parents than students who fail to enter the lottery and enroll in nearby neighborhood schools. The problem of self-selection or so-called creaming is a longstanding flaw in many program evaluations, and some self-selection undoubtedly does occur at these six paternalistic schools, particularly after they have established a record of success. Nonetheless, all six of the schools (with the exception of Cristo Rey Jesuit High School in Chicago) have an open, nonselective admissions process that minimizes creaming and adds credence to the claims that the schools dramatically raise minority achievement. Certainly none of the six schools is a thinly disguised magnet school, much less an elite prep school or competitive-exam school.

Despite the shortcomings of education evaluation, it is worth remembering, too, that 2008 remains a propitious and exciting moment in the history of K–12 school reform. It is hard to think of a time when closing the achievement gap has taken on such national prominence or when so much experimentation in inner-city schools is flourishing. For the first time in American history, closing the achievement gap is now the explicit objective of the federal government, enshrined in the 2002 No Child Left Behind law. Not long ago, new high schools, reconstituted schools, inner-city schools divvied up into smaller schools, schools run by private firms, charter schools, and school improvement models were all rarities. Today, by contrast, the nation has more than a million students attending 4,000 charter schools—and hundreds of thousands more pupils attend the thousands of urban schools that have adopted school-wide improvement models in the last decade.

Even as researchers continue to founder in their attempts to evaluate urban secondary school reforms, a pop wisdom of sorts has quietly emerged about how to fix inner-city high schools, fed by an unlikely source: Hollywood. In the last two decades, a string of movies has dramatized the true stories of tenacious teachers and principals who turned around failing urban schools and sullen students. The string of movies began with the 1988 hit *Stand and Deliver,* which recounted the triumph of Jaime Escalante's AP Calculus class at Garfield High School in East Los Angeles. Soon after *Lean on Me* (1989) spotlighted Joe Clark, the baseball bat-wielding principal at Eastside High School in Paterson, New Jersey, with Clark immortalized by actor Morgan Freeman. In 1995, in *Dangerous Minds,* Michelle Pfeiffer portrayed English teacher LouAnne Johnson, an ex-Marine who wrote *My Posse Don't Do Homework* about her experiences teaching at-risk teens in California. Three years later it was Meryl Streep's turn in *Music of the Heart* to portray Roberta Guaspari, a prickly but inspirational violin teacher in three of East Harlem's elementary schools. And in 2007, Hilary Swank starred in *Freedom Writers,* adapted from the book, *The Freedom Writers Dairy.* Like its "ed flick" predecessors, *Freedom Writers* tells the tale of Erin Gruwell's efforts to transform a class of disadvantaged and disinterested students at Woodrow Wilson High School in Long Beach, California into engaged and gifted writers.

For all of the inevitable Tinseltown embellishment of the facts in these films, this genre of "tough love" ed flicks implanted, or perhaps reinforced, several important lessons about inner-city schools. They showed that driven teachers and principals could successfully promote high academic and behavioral standards in impoverished neighborhoods and that, with the right exhortation and guidance, poor black and Hispanic teenagers will excel. The films also tended to underscore that the education establishment itself was an impediment to improving inner-city schools, particularly teachers unions and administrators in the school superintendent's offices.

Nonetheless, the ed flicks may have had a less salutary effect on public expectations of school reform. The message of these films—that extraordinary teachers can transform indifferent students—is readily recognized both by parents and policymakers. But the implicit flip side of that message—that *only* extraordinary teachers can rescue disadvantaged students—made successful school reforms seem like one-of-a-kind miracles that could not be replicated in other schools that lacked charismatic teachers and principals. That high-achieving schools for poor and immigrant students have existed in past decades is no secret. But both parents and policy analysts have been quick to dismiss successful urban schools in the past as *sui generis* phenomena that could not be reproduced elsewhere.

The notion that inner-city schools can only succeed when heroic educators are at the helm gives too little credit to the shift in pedagogy and academic culture that animates the new paternalistic schools. Each of the six schools portrayed in the pages that follow adheres to a reform model, and each of the schools is seeking to replicate itself, sometimes locally and sometimes in distant cities. To be sure, these six schools still require talented and committed teachers to succeed. But they do not need Socrates or Jaime Escalante to take roll.

The modern-day "no excuses" schools are thus unlike most of the high-achieving, one-of-a-kind urban schools of earlier decades. They consciously seek to copy themselves and spread a reform gospel, a message that runs counter to the defeatist view that underlying social inequalities have to be redressed before low-income minority students can do well. It is too early to say definitively whether the copycat schools will flourish. Yet the preliminary results, spelled out in subsequent chapters, are extremely encouraging. This potential—to replicate successful inner-city schools—provides a rare reason for optimism about education reform in the nation's ghettos and barrios.

Chapter One
The Achievement Gap and Education Reform

A little over a hundred years ago, W.E.B. DuBois famously predicted that "the problem of the Twentieth Century is the problem of the color-line." For all of DuBois's prescience about the last century, the problem of the color line seems to have faded in this century. Through court rulings, new laws, and executive orders, the federal government has put an end to segregation in the armed forces, discriminatory housing covenants, and legal segregation in schools, public accommodations, and the voting booth. To help blacks ward off the legacy of slavery and centuries of discrimination, the government created affirmative action programs, minority set-asides, busing, Head Start, Title I, and other compensatory programs. Black mayors and congressmen rose to power and took over political patronage machines in many cities. Interracial marriages and friendships blossomed to a degree unthinkable 50 years ago, and a variety of black figures became national icons—Muhammad Ali, Oprah Winfrey, Colin Powell, Michael Jordan, Condolezza Rice, and now Barack Obama. A thriving black middle class developed and sent millions of their sons and daughters to colleges and graduate schools. Hispanic immigrants, especially those from Mexico and Puerto Rico, also received a hand-up in the form of affirmative action, bilingual education, and the like.

Yet for all the progress of the last century, the central problem facing American high schools in 2008 is still the problem of the color line—and the premier civil rights issue of the day is arguably the achievement gap. In the modern era, when college is often a prerequisite for obtaining a decent job in the global economy, education is more critical than ever to ensuring equal opportunity for disadvantaged black and Hispanic students. A school record that was good enough to land a well-paid factory job a quarter century ago is no longer good enough. Today, nearly three out of four young black men who have dropped out of high school are jobless. And even as urban crime rates have plunged during the last 15 years, incarceration rates among young black males have soared—so much so that a staggering 60 percent of black male dropouts now have served time in prison by the time they are in their mid-thirties.

This ongoing failure to deliver equal educational opportunities to poor black and Hispanic youth is not just an economic and personal tragedy but a moral problem as well. In few areas of American life are the country's professed ideals so at odds with reality. As Gunnar Myrdal observed as far back as 1944 in *An American Dilemma,* his landmark study of race relations, "Education has always been the great hope for both individual and society. In the American Creed it has been the main ground upon which 'equality of opportunity' and 'free outlet for ability' could be based."[1]

The gulf in academic achievement between white high school seniors and their black and Hispanic counterparts is loosely familiar but nonetheless shocking. To summarize briefly, the National Assessment of Educational Progress (NAEP) shows that in twelfth grade the average black student has the reading and writing skills of a typical white student in eighth grade and the math skills of a white student in seventh grade. On average, black high school seniors also test four to five years behind white students in U.S. history and geography. This well-documented four-year achievement gap is not simply a reflection of the fact that proportionately more blacks than whites live in poverty, since poor whites handily outscore poor blacks on achievement tests and middle-income white students outscore middle-income black students. In percentile terms, the average black student is at the 27th percentile in academic achievement nationally and the average non-Hispanic white is at the 61st percentile, according to a 2005 study by Richard Rothstein and Tamara Wilder. Considering the case of Latinos separately, the average Hispanic high school senior has the same level of math skills as a white eighth grader, too, though they score a few points higher in reading than white thirteen-year-olds.[2]

As Stephan and Abigail Thernstrom pointed out in their 2003 book *No Excuses*, the Hispanic-white achievement gap is mitigated by the fact that native-born Latino students have substantially stronger reading and math skills than Latino immigrant students. Like the Italians who flocked en masse to the United States at turn of the last century, the second and third generations of Latinos are doing much better in school than their predecessors. Yet so long as large numbers of Hispanic immigrants continue to arrive in the U.S. from Mexico and Central American nations, Hispanic educational achievement will likely remain depressed for decades to come.

Closing the achievement gap is a priority not just for a select group of school reformers but for many Americans today. The 2006 Phi Delta Kappa/ Gallup Poll of attitudes toward public schools reported that two in three Americans felt that closing the achievement gap is "very important." At the same time, the public is of two minds about how to do this. Only about 20 percent of Americans believe that the achievement gap is due mostly to the "quality of schooling" that minorities receive, as opposed to other factors like poverty and family background. But a majority of Americans (57 percent) nonetheless believe that even if public schools don't cause the achievement gap, they should be responsible for closing it.

Is the Gap Closing? The Impact of No Child Left Behind

Somewhat surprisingly, the notion that academic achievement of all students should be the chief goal of K-12 education only started to take hold in the last half-century, after the Soviet Union launched the Sputnik satellite in 1957. Before the Sputnik launch, American schools commonly offered numerous "life adjustment education" courses on home economics, vocational training, and social guidance rather than concentrating primarily on boosting student achievement in math, reading, science, and foreign languages. A half-century ago, a comparatively small, elite group of students went on from high school to attend four-year colleges.

Academic achievement did not ultimately become the fulcrum of education policy until the enactment of the No Child Left Behind Act (NCLB) in 2002. NCLB is a rare example of an aptly titled piece of legislation. For the first time, the federal government called upon every state to have all of its students—black, Hispanic, disabled, American Indian, and limited-English speakers—"proficient" in reading and math by the 2013–2014 school year. As the NAEP test results illustrate, NCLB's requirement for universal proficiency in math and reading almost certainly cannot be attained by 2014—unless states water down their standards of proficiency to the point where they become meaningless. (Less than 15 percent of black and Hispanic eighth graders are currently "proficient" in reading or math, according to the NAEP.) Yet NCLB's noble if naïve requirement for universal proficiency is not just boilerplate rhetoric. The law requires each state to set academic standards and implement an assessment system to monitor progress toward the goal of universal proficiency. Each year, schools must show that they are making sufficient progress toward that destination, and the state must have sanctions in place for schools that fail to show adequate yearly progress (AYP).

The requirement of universal proficiency puts the achievement gap at the very core of NCLB. How well are states doing in closing the achievement gap? The evidence on national tests is mixed. The good news is that black and Hispanic eighth graders and twelfth graders appreciably narrowed the achievement gap in math and reading between 1971 and 2004 on the NAEP "Long-Term Trend Assessment." The bad news is that the achievement gap is still huge and thus continues to dwarf the real gains that minority students have made, especially at a time where the job market places a high premium on education.

In 2006, Secretary of Education Margaret Spellings announced that the nation's schools were "well on [their] way to every child learning on grade level by 2014."[3] But halfway to NCLB's 2014 deadline, Spellings' optimism seems wildly premature. Professor David Armor of George Mason University has calculated how long it would take whites, blacks, and Hispanic students to reach 100 percent proficiency under the NAEP standards if eighth-grade students in the nation continued to raise their achievement levels at the same pace as they have for the last decade. If recent progress continues, he found, white students would become 100 percent proficient 61 years from now. Black students would all achieve proficiency in about 180 years.[4]

Compounding the difficulty of low achievement in high school are two problems that bookend the K-12 experience of black and Hispanic students and make closing the achievement gap an even more formidable challenge. One of the most disturbing aspects of the achievement gap is that it exists before blacks and whites enter kindergarten. Richard Rothstein cites data indicating that four- to five-year-old black students score 16 percentile points below white children in reading tests and 23 percentile points below white children in math skill tests.[5] As both Rothstein and his conservative critics acknowledge, minority students start school behind white students partly because they are more likely to be poor than whites. But a complicated mix of family and child-rearing culture also plays a role in generating the achievement gap. Black parents, for example, are somewhat less likely than white parents to provide toddlers with cognitive stimulation in the form of exposure to books and vocabulary. Christopher Jencks, editor of an authoritative volume on the black-white test score gap, has written that "the cognitive disparities between black and white preschool children are currently so large that it hard to imagine how schools alone could eliminate them."[6]

The existence of an achievement gap prior to kindergarten means both that schools do not create the achievement gap and that they face substantial obstacles outside their control in trying to equalize achievement. On the other hand, the K-12 system, particularly middle schools and high schools, fails to do much to shrink the gulf in achievement either. In secondary school, the achievement gap typically widens further.

The second factor feeding current disparities in achievement—this time at the end of the educational pipeline—is the high dropout rates of black and Latino students. During much of the last century, black educational attainment rose dramatically. But in the last 15 years, the black high school dropout rate stopped plummeting. In fact, by some measures black and Latino students are less likely to graduate from high school in a timely fashion today than in 1990. *Education Week's* June 2007 "Diplomas Count" report shows that, while nearly eight out of ten white students graduate with a high school diploma in four years, only 58 percent of Hispanics and 53 percent of blacks graduate on time. These dropout rates are even worse in urban schools in high-poverty neighborhoods, where 60 to 80 percent of students typically fail to get a diploma in four years.

These inner-city schools have been likened to "dropout factories," and they remain the locus of the nation's dropout problem. About 2,000 of the more than 20,000 high schools in the United States produce almost half of the nation's dropouts. Nearly half of black students nationwide and about 40 percent of Hispanic students attend those 2,000 failing high schools. High school dropouts have a particularly devastating impact in poor black communities, where many black male dropouts eventually turn to crime. A disheartening 30 percent of African-American males in their mid-thirties who did not attend college now have prison records. But a stunning 60 percent of all black male high school dropouts in their mid-thirties have prison records—a grim measure, if ever there was one, of the costly toll of the achievement gap.

The Inner-City Secondary School Experience

Many books and journalistic accounts have chronicled the daily struggles that minority students face in inner-city middle schools and high schools. These anthropological accounts provide a gritty look into a world that few white Americans (and even fewer education researchers) have ever personally witnessed. As a body of literature, the coverage of inner-city schools tells a consistent tale—and offers a profile of urban schools in high-poverty areas that is squarely at odds with that of the new paternalistic schools depicted in ensuing chapters.

Indulge in a brief thought experiment and imagine what a typical public school is like for a low-income black or Hispanic teenager—let us call him Johnny—in the inner city. Johnny will typically go to a large, aging neighborhood school with 1,500 students or more. When Johnny shows up for the first day of ninth grade, he finds that the vast majority of his fellow students are also poor, minority adolescents and that many if not most of them come from single-parent families. Once inside the school, he soon realizes that virtually every aspect of the school bespeaks its lack of academic rigor. Many students are tracked into vocational education or life-education courses like home economics, retail merchandising, and sewing. In place of algebra and trigonometry instruction, students take courses in consumer math and practice how to use a cash register. The library is a good place to gab, but not to study or do research. College is a nice goal in principle—but the reality of how and what it takes to get there remains largely mysterious. Ultimately, it does not even matter whether students fail courses or not; they still get promoted to the next grade. Unlike more affluent neighborhoods, where some special needs students can afford to attend private schools, Johnny's classes have a disproportionate number of students with learning disabilities and limited English proficiency. All told, more than three out of five students who start ninth grade with Johnny will drop out of school before he reaches twelfth grade.

While gang shootings and fights periodically erupt near the school, violence per se is not a big problem inside the school. With its metal detectors and security officers, periodic sweeps for drugs and weapons contraband, and security cameras, the school is often safer than the surrounding neighborhood. Yet Johnny soon discovers that turmoil at the school takes a subtler form: disorder, rather than violence, haunts the hallways and classrooms. At lunch and during breaks, students use street language, show off tattoos, flash gang colors, curse, boast, answer their beepers, dish the dirt, talk on their cell phones, "diss" each other, and get in spats. Like teens elsewhere—only more so—some students sport saucy outfits, do-rags, bare midriffs, baggy pants, and gold chains. Graffiti adorns the walls and bathroom stalls, and the maintenance staff is slow to fix running toilets, broken or vandalized classroom equipment, and crumbling ceilings.

To be sure, Johnny's school has a few bright lines delineating unacceptable behavior. No student can openly bring a gun, other weapons, or drugs to school or assault a teacher without getting expelled or suspended. But Johnny's teachers and principal have pretty much abandoned any serious effort to teach character or train students to "act right." Students get away with using street language in class rather than proper English. Being tardy, calling out in class out-of-turn, swearing, drifting off task, teasing other students, failing to turn in homework, tuning out on an iPod, chatting on a cell phone, or talking disrespectfully to other students rarely brings serious or consistent consequences. When teachers do punish students for acting disruptively or failing to do their work, the consequences for misbehavior differ from teacher to teacher. Before long, Johnny realizes that the school's code of conduct is not really a code after all.

In class, the discussion often veers from indifference to chaos, forcing teachers to discipline students more regularly than their counterparts in suburban schools. One journalist who spent a year teaching eighth-grade math in a Brooklyn middle school recalls that students told her to "fuck off," called her "cuntface," spat in her face, played radios during class, and hurled chairs at one another.[7] In fact, to Johnny his teachers sometimes seem more like policemen or proctors than educators. Another reporter who spent a year as a teacher in a rough Puerto Rican neighborhood in north Philadelphia remembers teachers who "screamed at the students all day," creating a "climate of fear [and] abuse."[8]

As his classes manically bounce back and forth in a cycle of disruption and discipline, Johnny realizes that his teachers have low expectations for him and his fellow students. He is face-to-face with what educator Theodore Sizer calls the "conspiracy of the least." Not surprisingly, Johnny grows bored and puzzled. He begins to wonder if there is much point in school. He starts thinking that maybe he should drop out, too, like some of his friends.

An outstanding teacher can make all the difference to a disadvantaged kid, and inner-city schools have their share of dedicated and talented teachers. Nonetheless, top-notch teachers are more the exception than the rule at Johnny's high school. With so many other students on hand, Johnny finds it hard to make a personal connection with a teacher or coach. He starts to feel more like a number—anonymous in the midst of the school's vast student body. Teacher turnover is high, and highly qualified instructors often drift away when they can to low-poverty schools with few minority students. Johnny has no way of knowing it but the collective bargaining rights and seniority privileges secured by teacher unions give exceptional instructors an easy exit to teach at less disruptive suburban schools, closer to home. In the highest-poverty schools, meanwhile, students have novice teachers almost twice as often as do pupils in low-poverty schools. And Johnny is substantially more likely to have a core academic class taught by an "out of field" teacher with little expertise in the subject or be led by a teacher who failed her licensing exam at least once.[9] What happens when Johnny gets a terrible teacher? Not much. Principals are frequently prevented from firing woeful instructors by tenure rules and procedural restrictions in collective bargaining contracts.

A July 2007 analysis by the New Teacher Project of more than 36,000 teacher evaluations in Chicago's public schools helps to put some numbers on the odds that the principal at Johnny's school will even try to dismiss an incompetent teacher. From 2003 through 2006, just three out of every 1,000 teachers in Chicago's public schools received an "unsatisfactory" rating in annual evaluations. Even at failing schools—with below-average test scores that dropped from 2003 to 2005—a teacher with an unsatisfactory rating was rare, indeed. Of 87 failing schools in the city, 69 did not issue *one* unsatisfactory teacher rating during the three-year study period. A total of just nine teachers in the entire city of Chicago managed to accrue two or more unsatisfactory ratings between 2003 and 2006—and not one of them was dismissed.[10]

Johnny's classes are not unusually large. Nor does his school spend much less on his education than other schools around the state. Horror stories about overcrowded classrooms and under-funded, dilapidated schools where rats dart across hallways make for riveting copy. Yet they distort the typical high school experience of low-income, minority students. For all of the warnings about the digital divide, federal statistics show that central city schools today are about as likely as suburban ones to have a library media center. (On average, those library media centers have 13 workstations with Internet access, compared to an average of 14 workstations in suburban schools).[11] Nevertheless, a number of liberal commentators, notably Jonathan Kozol, have argued for decades that there is little seriously wrong with inner-city schools that money cannot help fix. It is true that some inner-city schools receive significantly less funding per pupil than schools in wealthy suburbs, particularly in localities that rely heavily on property taxes to fund the public school system. But large funding disparities are not characteristic of urban education. Overall, states spend slightly more per pupil in central city and minority-dominated schools than elsewhere in the state—though once the higher cost of living in urban areas is taken into account, state officials probably spend a bit less on inner-city students.[12] Even so, gross disparities in spending and the lore of the wildly under-funded inner-city school are more myth than fact.

The most recent data on urban school spending come from the Council of the Great City Schools, a coalition of 66 of the nation's largest urban public school systems. During the 2002–2003 school year, the current expenditure per pupil in the Council's member districts was $8,608, compared to a national average of $8,003. Spending per pupil (not adjusted for inflation) had risen by almost 20 percent in urban schools since 1999–2000, a bit faster than expenditures have risen nationwide. In fact, three out of four urban school systems spent as much or more per pupil in 2003 than the state average while a quarter of urban school districts spent less. Student-teacher ratios in big city school systems do turn out to be higher than the national average but only by a whisker: urban schools averaged 17 students per teacher, compared to a nationwide average of 16.[13]

Given the economic and personal toll of the achievement gap, a strong case can be made that inner-city schools *should* be better funded and should receive more aid than other districts where schools are not failing. Yet there is little reason to believe that money alone is the root of the achievement gap or that more money per se will necessarily narrow it. After adjusting for inflation, spending per pupil in the United States has more than doubled since 1970.[14] Inner-city schools appear to have received a significant share of the added funding. At the same time, class size has shrunk dramatically, with the average ratio of students per teacher falling from 26.9 in 1955, to 17.9 in 1985, to 15.5 today.

America has long been renowned for spending less on social welfare programs than most western industrialized nations. Yet it spends more per pupil on secondary education than all but a handful of small, wealthy countries. The Organization for Economic Cooperation and Development (OECD) reports that the United States spends more per pupil in secondary schools than 33 of its 36 industrialized member states. Only Luxembourg, Switzerland, and Norway spend more per pupil in middle school and high school. Social welfare bastions like France, Denmark, Germany, and Sweden spend less on their secondary school students than the supposedly stingy United States.[15]

Breaking the Mold: The New Paternalistic Schools

Johnny's inner-city high school differs dramatically from the new paternalistic high schools—except for the shared racial and ethnic origins of its students, and its aging, deteriorating facilities. Unlike Johnny's school, all six of the paternalistic secondary schools depicted in these pages are small, generally with fewer than 400 students. All are academically rigorous institutions with carefully structured college-prep curricula dominated by reading, writing, math, science, and foreign language study. Students are tested regularly—and encouraged from the first day of school to start planning for where they will attend college. Social promotion does not exist, and schools offer no vocational training and home education courses.

Inside the school, students wear uniforms or follow a dress code. The schools generally have an extended day and mandatory summer sessions, though a couple of them have been forced to scale back to a regular school season and hours. Teachers and principals regularly rebuke and may punish students who resort to street talk, profanity, disrespectful language, or are simply inattentive. For their part, teachers are hired not on the basis of seniority, teaching credentials, or central office assignments but rather because they are committed to educating poor kids and have themselves succeeded in school. Many instructors are young, ex-Teach For America graduates who bear more resemblance to the idealistic Peace Corps volunteers of the 1960s than to veteran teachers with ed school degrees. Even when it means bending union rules, teachers often work extra hours at paternalistic schools, sometimes taking calls on their cell phones late into the night from students with homework queries. And unlike many of their peers at other inner-city schools, principals are not handcuffed most of the time by the central office or local teacher unions. Principals hire teachers to raise student achievement—and will fire a teacher who fails in his or her mission. As journalist Paul Tough summarized in a November 2006 *New York Times Magazine* cover story, these no-excuses schools provide a "counterintuitive combination of touchy-feely idealism and intense discipline."[16]

Two features of the new paternalistic schools bear underscoring because they go to the heart of what makes such schools distinct—and what makes them so hard for the K–12 education establishment to emulate. First, the new paternalistic schools are preoccupied with keeping order. They teach character and middle-class virtues like diligence, politeness, cleanliness, and thrift because they believe that adolescents learn best in schools that minimize disorder and that students who are diligent and polite are more likely to succeed later in life. Second, the paternalistic schools portrayed in subsequent chapters (with the exception of the University Park Campus School) are not traditional neighborhood public schools to which pupils are assigned on the basis of where they live—nor do no-excuses schools place the high premium on parental involvement that colors many local efforts to reform schools.

To be sure, none of the six actively discourages parental involvement, and several of their school principals are now seeking to expand it. Still, boosting parental involvement is not a Holy Grail at any of them. Rather, successful paternalistic schools create a culture of achievement within the school that is at odds with the culture of adolescents' peers and high-poverty neighborhoods. Such a school culture can also sometimes be at odds with a student's home environment, particularly in families where no adult speaks English or has graduated from high school, much less attended college. Thus, by their very nature, the new paternalistic schools for teens tend to displace a piece of parents' traditional role in transmitting values, serving at times in loco parentis. Parents' chief role at no-excuses schools is helping to steer their children through the door—paternalistic schools are typically schools of choice—and then ensuring that their children get to school on time and do their homework.

The emphasis on curbing disorder springs from an understanding of urban schools that owes much to James Q. Wilson and George L. Kelling's well-known "broken windows" theory of crime reduction. Wilson and his colleague discovered that signs of public disorder—graffiti, prostitutes and gangs hanging out on street corners, homeless alcoholics loitering in alleyways—are more important in establishing public perceptions of safety than actual changes in the crime rate. Disorder also emboldens potential criminals to break laws, since nobody seems to be in charge or taking care of public spaces. Wilson hypothesized that when disorder is visible, people stay inside, leaving the streets to criminals. But if the graffiti and gangs are cleaned up, people feel safe outside. Criminals are less bold—and find it hard to attack law-abiding citizens in public. In Wilson's terminology, when policymakers fix one broken window at the factory, the other windows stay intact. But if the broken window goes unfixed, soon all of the windows will be broken.

The founders of the new paternalistic schools similarly believe that disorder, not violence or poverty per se, is the fatal undoing of urban schools in poor neighborhoods. That is why their schools devote inordinate attention to making sure that shirts are tucked in, bathrooms are kept clean, students speak politely, gang insignia is banned, trash is picked up, and youngsters are trained to follow teachers with their eyes during the course of class. A favorite slogan at Amistad Academy is "We Sweat the Small Stuff"—just the opposite philosophy of most inner-city schools where teachers and administrators are advised to "pick their battles." This concentration on minimizing disorder also helps explain why these paternalistic schools are long on rituals, including school-affirming chants at assemblies, hallways of academic fame with photos of student honorees plastered on the wall, public recognition and awards for students who have done well scholastically, and activities that build a sense of teamwork and esprit de corps. Time and again, students say that one of the features of paternalistic schools that they most prize is that they feel "safe" there.

At first glance, the character training and rituals of these paternalistic institutions give the schools a decidedly traditional feel. The schools teach old-fashioned virtues, simply put. They presume that young people who grow up in poor neighborhoods, surrounded by street culture, may well embrace middle-class virtues in theory but will often fail to hew to these values in practice, so they show their pupils exactly what it means to behave in accord with these values. Yet there is an implicit subtext of paternalistic institutions that is also surprisingly consistent with an emerging group of left-leaning school reformers, too. For every conservative who praises the value of teaching "character," a liberal now extols the virtues of strengthening disadvantaged students' "noncognitive skills"—abilities like persistence, self-discipline, leadership, and cooperativeness.

Bolstering noncognitive skills is appealing to liberals because success in the workplace often hinges on such competencies as much (or more) than on cognitive achievement, per se. The belief that hard work and discipline pay off in school and life is a persistent American ideal, in keeping with Thomas Edison's observation that genius is "1 percent inspiration and 99 percent perspiration." As it turns out, a number of studies suggest that character traits like self-discipline and persistence do play an outsized role in determining student achievement.

The recent resurgence of interest in noncognitive skills can be traced back to the landmark 1966 "Coleman Report," whose take-away message, to paraphrase a modern-day campaign slogan, was "it's the family, stupid." Coleman found that differences in families' socioeconomic backgrounds mattered more than school quality and variations in school resources in explaining the persistent differences in achievement between white and black students and between rich and poor kids. Soon after Coleman's report was released, a small cottage industry of researchers sprung up to review and debunk his unwelcome findings.

One team of researchers, led by Christopher Jencks, concluded in 1972 that family background was indeed the strongest predictor of adult economic success. But Jencks and his colleagues also found that test scores played a relatively small role in determining economic success—noncognitive abilities like leadership had a bigger impact.[17] Jenck's modern-day liberal heirs include Richard Rothstein of the Economic Policy Institute and James Heckman, the Nobel laureate in economics at the University of Chicago. Heckman, for example, has argued that expanded investment in mentoring programs among at-risk adolescents could help narrow the achievement gap.[18] The noncognitive abilities that Heckman wishes to build are precisely the skills that paternalistic schools develop.

As *New York Times* reporter Paul Tough pointed out, two of the left-leaning cofounders of paternalistic schools—Dacia Toll of Amistad Academy and

Dave Levin of the KIPP Academy—specifically designed their school culture to bolster noncognitive traits like persistence, thrift, and politeness.[19] Both Levin and Toll are believers in the practice of "learned optimism" promoted by University of Pennsylvania professor Martin Seligman and have adopted some of its basic tenets in their schools' character training. Seligman allows that adversity in life is inevitable but argues that the "explanatory style" and the responses that people take toward adversity are anything but inevitable. His workplace studies found that IQ and SAT tests alone did a poor job of predicting who would be successful workers. By contrast, employees' optimistic explanatory style explained much of the variation in who succeeded and who fell short. Being successful, Seligman concluded, requires persistence in the face of failure.

In recent years, Seligman has begun to expand his research into secondary schools. Seligman and his colleague Angela Duckworth found much the same pattern in schools as in the workplace in a longitudinal study of 304 eighth graders at a magnet school in northeast Philadelphia in 2005. Roughly half of them were white, and all were admitted to the school based on their grades and test scores. Yet despite the selective nature of the student body, the more impulsive students with higher IQs did worse in school than self-disciplined students with lower IQs. In fact, the self-discipline of students accounted for more than twice as much of the variance in final grades at the end of eighth grade as student IQ. "Underachievement among American youth is often blamed on inadequate teachers, boring textbooks, and large class sizes," Seligman and Duckworth concluded. "We suggest another reason for students falling short of their intellectual potential: their failure to exercise self-discipline... Programs that build self-discipline may be the royal road to building academic achievement."[20] With a mix of ideological motivations, paternalistic schools like KIPP and Amistad have already started down that royal road—and may, paradoxically, be more optimistic institutions about the potential of inner-city students than more permissive and progressive urban schools.

The Enduring Appeal of Neighborhood Schools and Parental Involvement

With the exception of the University Park Campus School, the schools studied here are not traditional neighborhood public schools. They do not, in other words, just recruit students from the surrounding neighborhood and oblige students from nearby neighborhoods to justify an "out-of-boundary" placement. Nor are they the automatic default option of area students; students and their parents have to choose to apply to a paternalistic school. Finally, paternalistic schools feel less like community-run institutions than traditional neighborhood schools because they are more likely to have been founded by outsiders—and less likely to be come-one, come-all community and parent-driven institutions.

The neighborhood public school is such a fixture in American life today that many parents consider it an inalienable right of all youngsters to receive a free quality education in the community. The demands of minority activists for community control of local schools during the 1960s in New York, Detroit, Chicago, and other cities solidified the image of neighborhood schools as community institutions that amplified the power and voices of blacks and Hispanics. Today, the neighborhood school holds a quasi-monopoly on the provision of public education.

Parents often remain loyal to the neighborhood high school, even when—as is the case in many inner-cities—it is dreadful. This loyalty stems partly from human nature. Like everyone else, parents suffer from "optimistic bias," the belief that conditions are better close at hand than in the impersonal elsewhere seen on television. Thus, Americans consistently think their congressional representative is okay but Congress is a sewer, their street is safe but violent crime is exploding elsewhere, and their local school works well while public education overall is a mess.

This "I'm OK-They're Not Syndrome"[21] is a powerful impediment to urban school reform. In 1987, then-Secretary of Education William Bennett cited Chicago as the "worst" public system in the nation. The following year, the Illinois legislature passed a radical reform law that created local councils at every Chicago school. Each council was dominated by elected parents with the power to hire and fire principals and with substantial control over state education funds previously routed through a central bureaucracy. But local councils and neighborhood-based reforms proved curiously ineffective at bringing about change in Chicago education. Parents, it turned out, were chiefly upset about *other* people's schools, not those their own children attended. A survey of white, black, and Hispanic public school parents in Chicago, the results of which are summarized in Dan Lewis and Kathryn Nakagawa's 1995 book *Race and Educational Reform in the American Metropolis*, showed that "in the eyes of the parents, the Chicago public schools were adequately educating their children." Coauthor Lewis marveled that "80 percent of parents in Chicago are satisfied with their kid's school even when the public school system is a disaster on wheels."[22]

The persistent appeal of lousy neighborhood schools has continued to undermine urban school reform efforts since the 2002 passage of the No Child Left Behind Act. Consider the history of a key provision of NCLB, the so-called Title I choice provision. As was the case with other public schools, NCLB obliged Title I schools, which have large numbers of poor students, to make adequate yearly progress (AYP) toward universal proficiency in reading and math. If a Title I school fails to make AYP two years in a row, districts had to provide parents with the option of transferring their child to another school in the district that did make AYP—and foot the bill for the student's transportation. The Title I choice program was thus supposed to be an escape hatch for poor kids stuck in failing inner-city schools.

A funny thing happened, though, on the way to education reform. In 2003–2004, 2.75 million students attended some 5,600 Title I schools that failed to make AYP two years in a row. At least two out of three of those schools were located in big-city or high-poverty school districts. Yet nationwide, just 32,000 students—1 percent of those eligible to transfer—switched out of their failing schools. In Illinois, parents of 390,000 students could have transferred their sons and daughters to another school, but only 1,313 did so. In Connecticut, a grand total of 260 students transferred out of troubled local schools.[23]

The reluctance to transfer students out of failing schools was due partly to a design flaw in NCLB. Under the new law, school districts with failing schools were responsible for informing parents of their option to transfer to better schools, assuming the district had some. It was not in the self-interest of districts to advertise that students in local, faltering schools could attend other schools. Not surprisingly, many school districts did a poor job of informing parents of their rights, despite repeated appeals and directives from the U.S. Department of Education. In many cities riddled with failing schools, the number of students eligible to transfer to higher-performing institutions also far outnumbered the number of seats available to transfer students.

But if the school districts were part of the problem, parents themselves were also a stumbling block. National surveys taken in 2004 confirmed that parents overwhelmingly supported neighborhood schools: 85 percent favored keeping students in faltering local schools while just 14 percent supported giving them the right to transfer to a better-performing school.[24] Case studies and news reports documented the same parental reluctance to move students, particularly when children might be obliged to take a bus to school (rather than walk) or attend a different school than their sibling. When a *Washington Post* reporter set out to investigate why only 612 students transferred out of Prince George's County's troubled Title I schools in 2006–2007, Maryland assistant superintendent of education Ann Chafin told him that the "neighborhood school concept is a very, very big deal."[25]

The reluctance of inner-city parents to leave faltering neighborhood schools stems partly from fear of the unfamiliar and logistical concerns about the inconvenience of attending a more distant school. But it also reflects the belief that neighborhood schools are more receptive to parents and that parental involvement benefits both the school and the student. The idea that children do better in school when their parents are involved seems like common sense and is bolstered by a slew of studies. Yet the positive impact of parental involvement on student performance is modest at best in secondary school. The impact of programs designed to stimulate parental involvement in secondary schools is more modest still.[26]

The failure of poor black and Hispanic parents to transfer their children out of failing neighborhood schools suggests that their limited participation in inner-city secondary schools is due to a number of economic, historic, and cultural factors. Not surprisingly, parents in general tend to be less involved with their child's education in high school than in elementary school. But poverty, being a single mother, and working full-time in a low-wage job also makes it harder for parents to stay involved with their child's high school. A final possible factor—that poor black and Hispanic communities may place less value on academic achievement—was a taboo subject not long ago. Today, however, commentators on both sides of the political aisle are beginning candidly to assess the educational impact of black and Hispanic lower-class culture.

One popular theory on the left is that poor blacks have been forced to develop an "oppositional identity" to fight back against a legacy of racism and poverty. As a result, low-income black youths develop a cultural identity that is not merely different from the position of the white majority but actively opposed to it. That identity is reflected in news reports about studious black students in inner-city schools being mocked for "acting white" when they earn good grades and in tales of failing black students being admired because they have the ability to rap. "For black males especially, there seems to be a correlation between a high drop-out rate and a deep attachment to Black English," Bill Cosby and Harvard psychiatry professor Alvin Poussaint observe in their new book, *Come On People*. Cosby and Poussaint add that "these kids often feel pressured to know how to rap in black dialect. They feel they 'own' Black English and use it with a certain bravado and arrogance. Those who don't or won't speak the dialect are considered not 'hip' enough or even 'black' enough and may face rejection."[27]

Today, few civil rights leaders anymore sing the praises of oppositional identity and sticking it to "The Man." In a 2007 speech commemorating the 42nd anniversary of the Selma to Montgomery civil rights march, Senator Barack Obama urged black parents to do a better job of "instilling a sense in our young children that there is nothing to be ashamed about in educational achievement. I don't know who taught them that reading and writing and conjugating your verbs was something white."[28]

It is far from clear whether this anti-achievement ethic is more powerful or pervasive in inner-city schools than in other schools (some research suggests otherwise).[29] But while the cultural origins of black and Hispanic underachievement remain unsettled, policy analysts of various stripes have documented a series of cultural differences that contribute to the achievement gap.[30] It is clear, for example, that poor black and Hispanic families have fewer books than their white peers, read less to their children, and allow kids to watch more television.

Some of the harshest critics of poor black and Hispanic parents have themselves been upwardly mobile blacks and Hispanics. In his 2006 book *One Nation, One Standard*, Herman Badillo, the nation's first Puerto Rican congressman, writes that in his experience "Hispanic parents rarely get involved with their children's schools." Badillo contends that Latino parents "seldom attend parent-teacher conferences, ensure that children do their homework, or inspire their dream of attending college."[31] In 2004, Bill Cosby spoke even more harshly about low-income black parents at an NAACP gala marking the 50th anniversary of *Brown v Board of Education*. "People marched and were hit in the face with rocks to get an education, and now we've got these knuckleheads walking around," Cosby observed. "The lower-economic people are not holding up their end in this deal. These people are not parenting. They are buying things for their kids—$500 sneakers, for what? And [they] won't spend $200 for 'Hooked on Phonics'." Harvard professor Henry Louis Gates Jr. recently made much the same point, albeit in less pointed terms. "The sad truth," Gates wrote in the *New York Times*, "is that the civil rights movement cannot be reborn until we identify the causes of black suffering, some of them self inflicted. Why can't black leaders organize rallies around responsible sexuality, birth within marriage, parents reading to their children and students staying in school and doing homework? Imagine Al Sharpton and Jesse Jackson...demanding that black parents sign pledges to read to their children."[32]

The new paternalistic schools may well ask parents to sign pledges to check that children have done their homework, and the schools relentlessly promote the importance of academic achievement. But the founders of these schools do not talk about or even hint that lower-class black and Hispanic culture may hinder student performance. Instead, they consistently attribute parental disengagement and disinterest in academic performance to economic and historic causes. Many of their students, they note, come from families where no one has attended college and no one speaks English. Under the circumstances, it is not likely that Mom or Dad will help Johnny study for his trigonometry test. Many parents, moreover, are single moms who struggle to make ends meet. And it is no surprise that they can't take off in the middle of the day from work to come cross town for a parent-teacher conference.

Most of the new paternalistic schools, in other words, are founded on the premise that minority parents want to do the right thing but often don't have the time or resources to keep their children from being dragged down by an unhealthy street culture. Taking on a piece of the parent's role, the school helps to reinforce middle-class mores by nurturing a work ethic and culture of achievement. To be sure, paternalistic schools usually encourage parental involvement. But unlike much of the public and a parade of politicians, they do not presume that boosting parental participation is a key to narrowing the achievement gap.

School-Level Reform: Then and Now

Overhauling individual schools in slums and barrios is nothing new in the United States although the movement to remake inner-city schools has grown enormously in the last 15 years. A half-century ago, urban high schools were thought of as immortal edifices that were rarely broken up into smaller schools, reconstituted, or outsourced to private sector management. An exceptional high school might develop in an urban slum but high-achieving secondary schools for poor kids tended to be one-of-a-kind phenomena that disappeared once a charismatic principal left for another job.

Educators did not begin concentrating on reforming schools for disadvantaged students until after Coleman's seminal 1966 report, which spurred school-level reform on two fronts. First, the report flipped the assumption that education research should primarily evaluate inputs (e.g., class size, school funding, teacher credentials) rather than outcomes (e.g., test scores, educational attainment). By forcing educators to focus on outcomes for minority students, Coleman's work presaged the development of the standards movement and redirected public attention to the achievement gap. Second, Coleman's unexpected finding that differences in school quality—at least the kinds of differences across schools that existed at that time—had little impact on student performance underlined the socioeconomic status of children's parents as the single most important determinant of academic achievement. Educators who wanted to challenge Coleman's research now needed to show that a different kind of school could narrow the achievement gap.

Magnet schools got their start in the 1960s and were perhaps the first manifestation of the growing concern about urban education for poor children. They were soon followed by experimentation with a host of school improvement models. The best-known reform prototypes included the Association for Effective Schools movement (known today as More Effective Schools, or MES), James Comer's School Development Program, Theodore Sizer's Coalition of Essential Schools, and the Success for All curricular program. These school improvement models differed significantly from one another. Sizer-inspired schools, for example, were distinctly not paternalistic. But all of the models shared two important assumptions: all sought to "reinvent" schools and all presumed that a good public school would enable low-income minority children to achieve at a high level.

The More Effective Schools movement, in particular, was a forerunner of today's paternalistic inner-city schools. MES was originated by Ronald Edmonds, a former director of the Center for Urban Studies at Harvard University. Edmonds and his colleagues set out to counter Coleman's work by searching out schools where most students succeeded academically despite being from low-income families. Edmonds and his team were thus arguably the first researchers who went into the field to systematically identify traits of successful schools for low-income students. He found that successful schools for low-income students were staffed by principals and teachers who believed that all students could meet high expectations of academic performance. In addition, effective schools tested students frequently to monitor their performance, spent extra time on classroom instruction, were safe and orderly, and had strong principals who served as the schools' instructional leaders. The effective schools research, in other words, suggested that what happened in the classroom mattered a great deal in determining student performance.

Edmonds' work was extended in a fashion in 2001 by Samuel Casey Carter in a Heritage Foundation monograph entitled *No Excuses: Lessons from 21 High-Performing, High-Poverty Schools.* Carter was the first researcher to coin the catchy tagline "no excuses schools" for the 21 high-performing schools for low-income students he identified, which included KIPP Academy of the Bronx, one of the six paternalistic schools depicted here. The schools he singled out shared many of the characteristics of paternalistic schools, including extra time spent on task and a rigorous culture of achievement. But his 21 schools differed in significant ways from those chronicled in this volume, making it easier for critics to attribute the high test scores achieved by the schools to "creaming."[33]

Carter's schools, for example, included institutions with selective admissions, private schools, and magnet programs. The vast majority were also elementary schools. (Only one was a traditional public high school.) Unlike the paternalistic schools profiled here, Carter found from his interviews with principals and site visits at the schools that active parental involvement was one of the key traits of high-performing, high-poverty schools. And character building, or teaching students how to behave, was not identified by Carter as a critical feature of high-performing schools.

The first study to identify the importance of schools that changed the culture and character of inner-city adolescents was the Thernstroms' 2003 book, *No Excuses*. In addition to providing a thorough and lucid analysis of the racial achievement gap, the Thernstroms visited and reported on several of the nation's top paternalistic inner-city schools, including KIPP Academy in the Bronx and Amistad Academy in New Haven. Although the Thernstroms did not write about paternalism per se, they did underscore that high-performing inner-city schools believed strongly in the importance of curbing disorder and carefully cultivating character and middle-class values.

Even as the Thernstroms and Carter began to identify "no excuses" schools, MES and other new urban school models continued to proliferate. Today, the Association for Effective Schools claims that it has trained more than 400 schools in the MES process; the Coalition of Essential Schools claims to have 600 schools in its network; and the Success for All Foundation reports that its curriculum is used in more than 1,300 schools. Nonetheless, these numbers may exaggerate the impact of the new urban school models since many schools adopt only part of a model—or quietly drop the pedagogical regimen. Thus, the problem of taking school improvement models to scale remains: The United States has more than 93,000 public elementary and secondary schools, over 29,000 low-income Title I school-wide schools, and roughly 51,000 Title I "eligible" schools.[34]

Only in the last decade have school reformers sought to reinvent secondary schools at scale. The effort dates to 1991, when Minnesota enacted a law authorizing the nation's first charter schools. At the same time, a number of prominent corporate CEOs established the New American Schools Development Corporation to create a series of school reform models that would "break the mold" and could be taken to scale. Under the direction of Chris Whittle, Edison Schools Inc. also took control in the late 1990s of numerous failing public schools in urban areas and tried to reinvent them under private management. Today, the nation has more than 4,000 charter schools, home to more than one million students. Edison Schools Inc. is managing 84 school sites with 48,300 students in 2007–2008, but only three high schools.

The whole-school reform movement peaked after Congress passed the Comprehensive School Reform Demonstration (CSRD) program in 1997, providing grants to schools to adopt research-based, school-wide reform models. In the last decade, more than 9,000 schools nationwide have implemented school-wide reform[35], chiefly through the CSRD program. CSRD helped open the floodgates to overhauling schools because it gave researchers and reformers the opportunity to work directly with schools, rather than operating only through the district bureaucracy. Several large cities, including New York, Miami, and Memphis, have mounted major efforts to implement whole-school improvement models, albeit primarily at the elementary level.

What, then, has been the impact of whole school reform on academic achievement in secondary schools? No one is entirely sure because studies of the new and remade schools are plagued by methodological shortcomings. A 2006 "consumer guide" review by the American Institutes for Research (AIR) of 18 widely used middle school and high school improvement models found that nearly half of the reform models could show no rigorous evidence of raising student achievement. Nor did any school model, in AIR's judgment, show either a very strong or moderately strong effect on student achievement, based on existing research evidence.[36]

Much the same pattern is evident in studies of charter schools. Since 2004, at least two rounds of dueling national studies have reached conflicting results regarding their impact on academic achievement. As the National Charter School Research Project recently reported, "two national evaluations concluded that charter schools collectively had lower academic performance, while two other analyses found that charter schools modestly boost academic achievement."[37]

Beyond these conflicting conclusions, it is plain that enormous variability exists both in charter schools and in public schools taken under private wings. Some new or reconstituted schools do an excellent job of closing the achievement gap; others fail abjectly. This variability and the general lack of scientifically demonstrable impacts of reform suggest that school improvement on the whole is no miracle worker. But the evidence shortfall does not mean that all whole-school reforms fail. AIR reviewed a number of studies that indicated that several school models can dramatically elevate student achievement.[38] One quasi-experimental study of whole-school reform efforts in elementary schools in New York City in the mid-1990s found that students in More Effective Schools with MES trainers raised their reading scores significantly. (By contrast, New York schools that used the Success for All curricula and James Comer's Social Development Program saw no such rise in reading scores.)[39]

To sum up, a reform movement involving thousands of urban schools is now underway in America. Its central aim is to close the achievement gap—and this movement will likely persist, even as researchers debate the data.

Meanwhile, far from the hallways of academe and think tanks, principals continue to face formidable real-life challenges in reforming, reinventing, or opening a new inner-city school. What teachers should they hire? What should the curriculum consist of—and how can it best be aligned with state standards? How can they foster a culture of achievement at the school—and should they try to mold students' character as well as their minds? The task of creating and remaking a school brings to mind Woodrow Wilson's quip about the difficulty of changing a college curriculum. To paraphrase Wilson, changing a school is like moving a graveyard. You never know how many friends the dead have until you try to move them. As the founders of the new paternalistic schools have discovered, failing inner-city schools still have a surprising number of friends.

Chapter Two

The Rise, Fall, and Rise of Paternalism

"Ben Hur didn't have to make himself keep rowing.
The man with the whip took care of that."

—Nobel laureate Thomas Schelling

What is paternalism and why does it have so few friends? *Webster's* defines paternalism as a principle or system of governing that echoes a father's relationship with his children. But government-directed paternalism does more than ape the father/child relationship. Paternalism is controversial because it contains an element of moral arrogance, an assertion of superior competence. Paternalistic policies interfere with the freedom of individuals, and this interference is justified by the argument that the individuals will be better off as a result. Individual A, in his official duties, is interfering with individual B in order to promote B's own good—though left to his own devices, B might choose another course of action. Dismayed libertarians believe that Social Security is a paternalistic government program since participation is compulsory, and some Americans might prefer to plan their retirement on their own. The government requires motorcyclists to wear helmets, even when the motorcyclist would prefer to feel like Dennis Hopper in *Easy Rider*, blasting down the highway with the wind rustling his hair.

34

In the last decade, paternalism has undergone something of a refurbishing. In a 1997 volume on "The New Paternalism," Lawrence Mead, the leading revisionist, explored the emergence of a new breed of paternalistic policies aimed at reducing poverty and other social problems by closely supervising the poor. These paternalistic programs try to curb social problems by imposing behavioral requirements for assistance and then monitoring recipients to ensure compliance. "Misbehavior is not just punished" in paternalistic programs, writes New York University professor Mead. "It is *preempted* by the oversight of authority figures, much as parents supervise their families."[1] A classic example of a paternalistic program is the welfare office that requires the able-bodied poor to work to receive benefits, rather than simply providing them with a check. Yet today's welfare programs do much more than simply require recipients to work; case managers in effective welfare offices combine "help and hassle," checking up on clients frequently to ensure that they are meeting all requirements and showing them how to align their lifestyle with the world of work.[2]

The schools profiled in this book are paternalistic in the very way described by Mead. They unapologetically tell children continually what is good for them. They also compel good behavior and keep adolescents off the wrong track using both carrots and sticks. The students who attend them are closely supervised in an effort to change their behavior and create new habits, and maybe even new attitudes.

Paternalistic programs, including paternalistic schools, survive only because they typically enforce values that "clients already believe," Mead notes. Rare is the parent who thinks it is a good idea for their child to be disruptive or do poorly in school. But many paternalistic programs remain controversial because they seek to change the lifestyles of the poor, immigrants, and minorities, rather than the lifestyles of middle-class and upper-class families. The paternalistic presumption, implicit in the schools portrayed here, is that the poor lack the family and community support, cultural capital, and personal follow-through to live according to the middle-class values that they, too, espouse.

As Mead points out, paternalism is neither conservative nor liberal per se; in some eras of American history, liberals have pressed for paternalistic programs while at other times conservatives have lobbied for them. He summarizes the limited political appeal of paternalism by observing:

35

Paternalism is distinct from the social policy traditionally favored by either the left or right in America. It is a conservative policy in that it focuses on changing how the poor live rather than on improving their benefits or opportunities. It seeks order rather than justice, and social critics might call it blaming the victim. But paternalism is also a liberal policy because it is pro-government. Far from reducing the welfare state, as conservatives usually ask, paternalism expands it. Now social agencies attempt not only to help those in need but to reorganize their lives.[3]

This paternalistic approach runs counter to the proclivities of most K–12 educators, who prefer to maximize freedom and opportunity for children. Students should be free to explore, to cultivate a love of learning, and to develop their "critical thinking" skills unencumbered by rote learning. By contrast, the new paternalistic schools are animated more by obligation than freedom, more by enforcement than entitlement. Mead argues that "the problem of poverty or underachievement is not that the poor lack freedom. The real problem is that the poor are *too* free." Paternalistic schools, he says, flip the freedom-maximizing prescriptions of educators by "making obligation the key to these kids' lives." Paternalistic schools assume that disadvantaged students do best when structure and expectations are crystal clear, rather than presuming that kids should learn to figure things out for themselves.

In the narrowest sense, all American schools are paternalistic. "Schooling virtually defines what paternalism means in a democratic society," the political scientist James Q. Wilson has written. "For a long time, children have been legally obliged to attend school because education, if it is acquired in schools, makes them better citizens, better workers, and better voters. The requirement is paternalistic because young people will not know what they must learn until after they acquire the benefits of learning."[4] Many schools are paternalistic in a more substantive sense as well. Elementary schools often attempt to teach values and enforce rules about how students are to behave and treat others. The thin paternalism of these schools is widely accepted because paternalistic programs for young children have traditionally been easier to sell than paternalistic programs for adults. The distinction between how society treats adults and children is also evident in the nation's secondary schools, where adolescents are patently not considered to be emancipated adults entitled to unabridged freedom from adult supervision. Still, as Wilson notes, schools in America are typically paternalistic only when it comes to procedure (e.g., mandating attendance, limiting in-school violence and/or drug abuse). At the same time, most schools are permissive about learning, instruction, and pedagogy. Students must attend school in the United States. But they are not required to learn anything while there.

For a secondary school today to be truly "paternalistic," it must do much more than compel attendance, ban weapons from campus, offer classes on "values," or require students to abide by a dress code. The truth is that hundreds of parochial and traditional public schools in the inner city are authoritarian institutions with pronounced paternalistic elements. Yet these traditional secondary schools do not rise to the level of a thoroughgoing paternalistic school.

The new paternalistic schools profiled in this book look and feel very different. They combine the core elements of paternalistic programs. They are highly prescriptive institutions that often serve in loco parentis; they are morally and culturally assertive schools, which unapologetically insist that students adhere to middle-class virtues and explicitly rebuff the culture of the street; they are rigorous both about academics and instilling character; and they are places where obligation trumps freedom—they compel students to act according to school standards and preempt misbehavior, much in the manner of a watchful parent.

The most distinctive feature of new paternalistic schools is that they are fixated on curbing disorder. To this end, they are extraordinarily prescriptive. They impose detentions for tardiness and being disruptive in class; require students to wear uniforms or conform to a dress code; bar students from using iPods, Walkmen, cell phones, and beepers during the school day; forbid pupils from cursing at or talking disrespectfully to teachers; and do not allow students to run down hallways between class. But that's not all: the new paternalistic schools go further than even strict Catholic schools in prescribing student conduct and minimizing signs of disorder.

Pupils are typically taught not just to walk in the hallway—they learn how to walk from class to class: silently, with a book in hand. In class, teachers constantly monitor whether students are tracking them with their eyes, whether students nod their heads to show that they listening, and if any students have slouched in their seats. Teachers repeatedly admonish students to sit up, listen, nod, and track the speaker with their eyes. Looking inattentive, or merely tapping a pen on the desk, can lead to students losing "scholar dollars" from virtual "paychecks" that can be used to earn special privileges at school.

Thus, teachers at the new paternalistic schools don't just provide "values education" and encourage students to become good citizens. They ceaselessly monitor student conduct and character development to assess if students are acting respectfully, developing self-discipline, displaying good manners, working hard, and taking responsibility for their actions. One paternalistic school even requires students to have teachers sign a note after each class assessing how the student performed on a list of 12 "responsible behaviors" and 12 "irresponsible behaviors."

Paternalistic schools are culturally authoritative schools as well. Their pupils learn—and practice—how to shake hands when they are introduced to someone until they give a firm handshake and look the other individual in the eye. At several of these schools, students take etiquette classes. They practice sitting down to a formal place setting typical of a restaurant and learn the difference between the dinner fork and the salad fork. The new paternalistic schools are cultural evangelists: they build up the "cultural capital" of low-income students by taking them to concerts, Shakespearean plays, college campus tours, and on trips to Washington, D.C. and national parks. They help students find white-collar internships—and teach them how to prepare resumes and comport themselves in an office.

At the same time that these schools reinforce middle-class mores, they also steadfastly suppress all aspects of street culture. Street slang, the use of the "n-word," and cursing are typically not only barred in the classroom but in hallways and lunch rooms as well. Merely fraternizing with gang members can lead to expulsion. One paternalistic school in Chicago suspends students if they doodle gang insignia on their notebooks and expels those who do so a second time. The school day and year are extended in part to boost academic achievement—but also to keep kids off the street and out of homes with few academic supports.

The prescriptive rigor and accountability of paternalistic schools extend not just to student character and conduct but to academics as well. Paternalistic schools push all students to perform to high standards. They spell out exactly what their pupils are supposed to learn and then ride herd on them until they master it. These schools have no formal tracking, no bilingual classes, provide almost no formal multicultural classes, minimize pull-out instruction for special-ed students, and do not practice social promotion. Instead the schools offer a demanding core curriculum aligned to state standards. They test students regularly and use the results from the assessments to retarget instruction and assist struggling pupils.

Far from treating tests as discriminatory or unfair to minority youngsters, paternalistic schools view state and national tests as invaluable measuring sticks of performance. The schools set explicit and ambitious performance goals for students, and they hold teachers accountable for producing dramatic gains in academic achievement. From the first day students walk through the door, their principal and teachers envelop them in a college-going ethos, with the goal that 100 percent of students will be admitted into college. Over time, paternalistic schools create a culture of achievement that is the antithesis of street culture. Students come to think it is cool to excel in school.

For all their strictness, the new breed of paternalistic schools bear no resemblance to correctional boot camps for juvenile offenders, spartan wilderness therapy camps for troubled youths, or prisons. Their paternalism is benevolent. They have classrooms where teachers share laughter with students, where students are regularly recognized and applauded for displaying good character, and where students record many triumphs of which they are justifiably proud. Teachers are deeply devoted to their students, often answering phone queries late into the night from students, showing up before school starts to help a struggling pupil, or staying late to help tutor.

Principals and teachers at such schools are surprisingly familiar with students' personal lives. As a result, students call on teachers and principals for advice and help. It is not uncommon for students to describe their schools as a "second home." The fact that school officials sometimes serve in loco parentis enables them to be both authoritative and caring figures.

Finally, the new paternalistic schools employ a kinder, gentler form of paternalism because parents, typically single mothers, choose to send their children to these inner-city schools. Paternalistic programs for disadvantaged adolescents have historically had both voluntary and involuntary aspects. A century ago, orphans had little choice but to go to an orphanage, where public or private authorities taught them how to live properly. Today, parents are choosing to send their teenagers to the new paternalistic schools — but they are also acting under a sense of duress. They believe their neighborhood schools fail to educate students and are breeding grounds for gang strife and drugs. They are often desperate for alternatives—and are particularly excited to find a no-nonsense public school committed to readying their children for college.

The Cultural Aversion to Paternalism

Americans of all stripes have long been suspicious of governmental paternalism, and the leaders who founded the schools profiled here are no different. With the notable exception of Ben Chavis of the American Indian Public Charter School in Oakland, most of the principals of the schools chronicled here were uneasy with having their schools described as paternalistic. Paternalism remains a loaded term for many educators. Matt Taylor, the Director of Amistad Academy, says he prefers to think of Amistad as a middle school that "empowers" students. Eric Adler, cofounder of the SEED School in Washington, D.C., argues that calling a school paternalistic implies that its staff is asserting that it "knows better than others—like the parents or the neighborhood"—which values schools should transmit. "I don't think SEED asserts that we 'know better,' we just assert that we have more resources with which to teach," Adler argued. For Adler, it did not help to say that his school was paternalistic in Mead's terms and the terms of this book—that SEED was a highly prescriptive institution that taught children how to behave and think. "I don't think there is a positive way to say a school is paternalistic," Adler asserted. Dave Levin, cofounder of the network of KIPP schools, shared Adler's reservations: "To say that a school is paternalistic suggests that we are condescending, rather than serving in the role of additional parents...Unfortunately, trying to re-brand paternalism is a very tough row to hoe and the label plays into the hands of critics. If we ever said to a parent 'do you want to send your child to a paternalistic school?' no parent would say yes."

Levin, Adler, and Taylor's skittishness illustrates the potent allergic reaction to the label of "paternalism" that infects American political culture. As James Q. Wilson puts it, "paternalism seems to have democracy as its enemy and bureaucracy as its friend."[5] In overwhelming numbers, Americans embrace the famous standard for government intervention that John Stuart Mill articulated in *On Liberty*: "The only purpose for which power can be rightfully exercised over any member of a civilized community, against his will, is to prevent harm from others." Mill also captured a corollary criticism of paternalism—namely that young men who let themselves be guided by others are doomed to become unthinking sheep. "He who lets the world choose . . . his plan of life for him, has no need of any other faculty than the ape-like one of imitation."[6]

It would appear, however, that K–12 educators bear a special animus toward paternalism and its instructional incarnations. This is evident in their dislike of teacher-directed instruction—"drill-and-kill" memorization, rote learning, and direct instructional methods that emphasize the importance of acquiring basic facts and skills at the expense of "critical thinking skills." The Romantic educational philosophy of Jean-Jacques Rousseau (and his American heir, John Dewey) continues to prevail in many classrooms, not the educational theories of John Locke. Locke believed that a student was a tabula rasa, a blank slate. Children, he acknowledged, might acquire language naturally. But only with the help of teachers and hard work could they become literate, self-disciplined, and develop virtuous habits. Rousseau, by contrast, argued in *Emile* that the chief aim of education should be to allow as much freedom as possible for the child to explore and evolve naturally. In Rousseau's view, experience was the best teacher. Neither teacher nor parent should lecture children, make them memorize facts, or even provide much exposure to books when children are young.

Rousseau's and Dewey's theories about learning and children remain at the core of modern progressive education, which emphasizes the value of hands-on learning and critical thinking, while rejecting the enforcement of universal and concrete academic standards. Critics such as E. D. Hirsch have contended that, for all its liberal patina, progressive education actually hurts poor children and fuels the achievement gap. "The Romantic idea that learning is natural, and that the motivation for academic achievement comes from within is an illusion that forms one of the greatest barriers to social justice imaginable," Hirsch argues. "The gravest disservice to social justice entailed by Romantic theories of education is the delusion that educational achievement comes as naturally as leaves to a tree, without extrinsic motivation, discipline, toil, and sweat."[7]

The idea that progressivism might be downright harmful to disadvantaged students was echoed by David Brooks in a December 2006 column that recapped a *New York Times Magazine* cover story on successful inner-city schools such as KIPP:

KIPP is taking skills that middle-class kids pick up unconsciously and it is rigorously drilling them into students with less fortunate backgrounds. KIPP Academies, like many of the best schools these days, don't just cram information into brains. They surround students with a total environment, a holistic set of habits and messages, and they dominate students' lives for many hours a day. A generation ago, the gods of education fashion ordained that children should be liberated from desks-in-a-row pedagogy to follow their "natural" inclinations. In those days, human beings were commonly divided between their natural selves, assumed to be free and wonderful, and their socially constructed selves, assumed to be inhibited and repressed. But now, thanks to bitter experience and scientific research, we know that the best environments don't liberate students. We know, or have rediscovered, that the most nurturing environments are highly structured...Many of today's most effective antipoverty institutions are incredibly intrusive, even authoritarian.[8]

The K–12 establishment's aversion to pedagogic paternalism is illustrated as well by the hostile response of many urban educators to military schools, junior ROTC programs, and instructional methods with any kind of militaristic whiff. Indeed, "militaristic" is almost as dirty a word as "paternalistic" in many urban school districts. A decade ago, not a single secondary school in New York City had a JROTC program.[9] Dave Levin nearly choked at the suggestion that KIPP schools use some quasi-militaristic rituals. "That doesn't describe any of our schools," he said. "There is structure. But I don't see any of our schools as militaristic and I don't see that harshness. There is strictness, but it is balanced off by teacher involvement."

It may seem a stretch to acknowledge that a school is structured, strict, and ritual-bound yet balk so viscerally at the suggestion that it is quasi-militaristic or paternalistic. In fact, descriptions of the Air Force Academy's acculturation of cadets sound similar in many respects to KIPP Academy—and recent research on military schools, JROTC programs, and the military youth corps finds that successful quasi-militaristic initiatives for disadvantaged adolescents share a number of the characteristics of paternalistic schools.[10] Nevertheless, Levin's response illustrates how paternalism remains the Rodney Dangerfield of social policy—it can't get no respect, inside school or out.

Consider the yawning gap in the key child development theory of the "good-enough" mother, which Donald Winnicott, the eminent pediatrician and psychoanalyst, first pioneered a half-century ago. The good-enough mother starts with almost complete adaptation to her infant's needs. But as the infant begins to mature, the mother adapts less and less, stimulating the child's ability to grapple with failure and develop a sense of independence. The "good-enough" mother is thus not "good enough" because she is a serviceable parent but rather because she has figured out a way to be close enough to her child to promote growth—without smothering the child in the manner of an ever-hovering, helicopter "supermom."

Like today's paternalistic schools, the good-enough father might be described as a guardian of adolescents who brings structure and discipline to their lives but ultimately encourages the development of a sense of mastery and self-sufficiency. This good-enough father thus provides rigorous supervision to adolescents at first, with the expectation that teens eventually will internalize an ethos of hard work and respect and a moral conscience. The good-enough father thus aims to preempt misbehavior and inculcate middle-class mores by teaching children to "act right," much as paternalistic schools do. He celebrates his children's hard-won accomplishments, without gushing over each and every step. As adolescents mature and show they have internalized their father's teachings, his supervision slowly diminishes, much as is the case at paternalistic schools. Yet the concept of a good-enough father does not exist in Winnicott's writings—or anywhere else in popular culture.[11] And urban schools do little to take on the role of the good-enough father, which is so vital to healthy adolescent development, particularly in poor communities.

Bill Cosby and Harvard psychiatry professor Dr. Alvin Poussaint warned recently that "there are whole blocks [in poor, black neighborhoods] with scarcely a married couple, whole blocks without responsible males to watch out for wayward boys, whole neighborhoods in which little girls and boys come of age without seeing up close a committed partnership." A home without a father "is a challenge," Cosby and Poussaint write. "A neighborhood without fathers is a catastrophe."[12] In high-poverty high schools, where the overwhelming majority of students are raised in single-parent families headed by women, adolescents desperately need a good-enough father to teach the value of work, self-discipline, and commitment. Paternalistic schools provide one.

The Paternalism Hall of Shame: More Gruel, Please

In fairness to Levin and Adler, government paternalism has a terrible reputation in American history, much of it well deserved. The heyday of such programs reaches back to the aftermath of the Civil War, when the nation faced an onslaught of war orphans and enormous waves of immigration. The new arrivals, particularly those from Ireland and Italy, were likely to have rural, peasant origins. They lived in poverty, and many of the children toiled at brutal jobs for long hours at little pay. Middle-class Americans treated the Irish, and later Italian, immigrants with much the same suspicion, fear, and prejudice that they displayed toward poor blacks. Irish and Italian slums were epicenters of crime, alcoholism, family breakdown, high school dropouts, and riots.

The public response was paternalism. But it was paternalism in its most intrusive form. Initially, this malevolent paternalism took the form of intrusion into family life by social workers and privately run religious charities, before expanding into institutions like orphanages, poorhouses, and asylums that usurped traditional family roles.

The most infamous paternalistic institution was the orphanage. American orphanages initially cared only for orphans—that is, children with no living parent. But during the unprecedented rush of European immigrants from 1890 to 1910, many impoverished immigrant parents turned their children over to orphanages for care, temporarily or permanently. A 1910 census report found that orphanages were rearing a huge number of American children—all in all, more than 110,000 dependent, neglected, and delinquent children lived in 1,151 orphanages, asylums, and congregate facilities.[13] Historian Michael Katz, a fierce critic of paternalistic institutions, notes that the proportion of children living in institutions in the U.S. doubled from 10 percent in 1900 to an astonishing 18 to 21 percent by 1904.[14] And orphanages were not just paternalistic because they served in loco parentis. Their paternalistic regimen, with their busy daily schedules and strict discipline, was designed to instill values like thrift, self-reliance, and sobriety.

The abuses of orphanages are legendary. With the exception perhaps of the insane asylum, no institution has come in for such opprobrium. The movie rendition of Charles Dickens's *Oliver Twist*, in which Oliver pleads for more gruel, is the iconic image that many Americans retain of orphanages even today. James Q. Wilson has said that mere mention of the word "orphanage" in polite company reverberates "like a hand grenade at a dinner party."[15]

The strength of this sentiment was illustrated little more than a decade ago when then-House Speaker Newt Gingrich was nearly eviscerated for suggesting that some children of welfare mothers might be better off in orphanages. The 1994 GOP Contract with America, promoted heavily by Gingrich, contained a provision that would have allowed states to use welfare savings to promote adoption, establish group homes for unwed mothers, and establish orphanages. Gingrich envisioned that orphanages might be expanded for children whose mothers could not stop using drugs, find jobs, or get off welfare within two years. But the "o" word and the lingering ghosts of Dickens's orphans doomed Gingrich's proposal. *Newsweek*'s pithy headline read "The Gingrich That Stole Christmas"; *Time* ran with "Uncle Scrooge." On *This Week with David Brinkley*, correspondent Sam Donaldson informed Gingrich: "A lot of people are afraid of you. They think you are a bomb thrower. Worse, you are an intolerant bigot. Speak to them."

Democratic politicians and liberal pundits could barely contain their glee. Stealing a page from Ronald Reagan, President Bill Clinton lectured Gingrich that "governments don't raise children, parents do." Columnist Molly Ivins declared "if Representative Newt Gingrich is for orphanages for kids on welfare, let us support concentration camps." White House aide George Stephanopolous announced plans to "mail all the Republicans and members of Congress a copy of *Oliver Twist*." Hillary Clinton, meanwhile, said Gingrich's suggestion was "unbelievable and absurd"—and would only lead to putting "thousands and thousands of people in our streets."[16]

Gingrich did his best to exorcise the ghost of Oliver Twist by summoning up Spencer Tracy's turn as the stern but loving real-life Father Flanagan in the 1938 melodrama *Boys Town*, the movie that made the Nebraska home for delinquent boys famous. He hosted a televised New Year's Eve showing of *Boys Town* and urged First Lady Hillary Clinton "to go to Blockbuster" to rent the movie. Ultimately, Gingrich's repeated invocations of *Boys Town* did little but spawn a new PR fiasco—this time among fiscal conservatives. Modern-day congregate care facilities turned out to be expensive and administratively complex—the average cost of housing a teen at Boys Town ran from $40,000 to $48,000 a year.[17] Finally, Gingrich and the GOP abandoned the orphanage provision altogether.

Paternalism in Schools

If the institutional paternalism of orphanages and asylums has a poor reputation, the record of paternalism in schools is not much better. Twice in U.S. history, paternalism has held sway in schools for low-income or minority students. The first major expansion of paternalistic schooling was the Indian boarding schools of the late 19th century, which sought to "civilize" American Indians. The second major expansion took place a century ago when urban schools sought to acculturate hordes of European immigrants to American society.

The largely disastrous experiment with Indian boarding schools had its roots in the government's professed desire to eradicate "savagism" among Indians. Federal officials viewed Indian children as products of cultures that failed to prize order and self-restraint and of parents who let their children "run wild." Monogamy, temperance, chastity, self-sacrifice, respect for the Sabbath, and other Christian virtues were thought to be alien to Indians. One superintendent of an Indian boarding school later remarked that the average Native American student had as much regard for education "as a horse does for the Constitution."[18] Regular schools could not close this chasm between Indians and whites, government officials concluded. Secretary of Interior Carl Schurz told Congress in 1879 that "it is the experience of the department that mere day schools, however well conducted, do not withdraw the children sufficiently from the influences, habits, and traditions of their home life, and produce for this reason but a . . . limited effect." His successor at Interior, Lucius Q. Lamar saw boarding school as a do-or-die choice for Native American children. The "only alternative now presented to the American Indian race," he declared, "is speedy entrance into the pale of American civilization or absolute extinction."[19]

From a slow start in the 1870s, Indian boarding schools grew rapidly so that by 1905 more than 21,000 Indians attended them, 9,700 at off-reservation sites and 11,400 at reservation boarding schools. From the start, the boarding schools proved controversial and unpopular with many parents. Agents from the Bureau of Indian Affairs rounded up Indian children—often against their parents' will—to attend the schools. On the reservation, children who boarded were gone from home for months at a time; at off-reservation schools, children were stuck at distant schools for three- to five-year stints. In his aptly titled history, *Education for Extinction,* David Wallace Adams writes that Indian parents "resented boarding schools, both reservation and off-reservation, because they severed the most fundamental of human ties: the parent-child bond."[20]

Once on campus, the schools obliged their students to commit a form of slow cultural suicide. Upon their arrival, children's hair was cut, Native American garb was replaced with school uniforms, and teachers forbade students to speak in their native tongue, often punishing students who failed to speak in English. Students with exotic or hard-to-pronounce Indian names were abruptly given Anglo surnames. Teachers and principals constantly informed students that their ancestors were savages. Many of the boarding schools, particularly off-reservation, organized students into army units with drill routines. More than a few of the boarding schools were hotbeds for contagious illnesses; one Public Health Service survey of 16,500 Indian students found that 30 percent had trachoma, an eye disease that can lead to blindness.[21] A number of homesick students tried to run away during the winter from off-reservation schools only to freeze to death before they made it home.[22]

Like the paternalistic schools of today—only more so—the Indian boarding schools tried to teach moral character. To impart the value of punctuality, for example, Indian students had to be familiarized with clock time, schedules, and the white man's calendar of holidays, weekends, and months, all of which were alien to native cultures. To teach the value of thrift, schools set up student savings programs and created opportunities to earn pocket change from the sale of beadwork and other products. To teach the importance of chastity, monogamy, temperance, and self-sacrifice, teachers constantly drilled into students the foreign concepts of sin and guilt. In 1915, students in all boarding schools wrote essays on the perils of alcoholism.[23]

Despite surface similarities, however, the Indian boarding schools of a century ago differ fundamentally from the paternalistic schools of today. Indian boarding schools sought to eradicate local culture and traditions and destroy the parent-child bond. As David Wallace Adams put it, "reformers had wanted to obliterate Indian lifeways, not modify them."[24] Paternalistic schools today are far less radical. They seek to boost already existing values that are often undermined in poor communities and beleaguered single-parent families. In effect, the new paternalistic schools provide a cultural booster shot instead of an amputation. And while today's no-excuses schools do take on some aspects of parental supervision, parents clearly remain in charge of their children. They actively choose to send their daughters and sons to the new paternalistic schools, and most of the schools profiled in this book have waiting lists of students who would like to attend.

The distinction between malevolent and benevolent paternalism was more evident early in the 20th century when urban schools took on the task of acculturating millions of Italian, Irish, and Polish children — many of whom came from peasant roots and had little familiarity with secondary school education or the English language. The so-called "Americanization" of impoverished immigrant children took on a feverish pitch after 1900, as urban schools tried to speed the acquisition of English by foreign-born students and acclimate immigrant children from rural areas to the schedules and expectations of city life.

In *The Great School Wars*, historian Diane Ravitch notes that the massive waves of immigrants prompted reformers to charge urban schools for the first time "with responsibilities which previously belonged to the family, the settlement house, and the community." [25] Public schools inaugurated a medical inspection for all children, and school facilities were opened to the community for after-hours recreation and academic programs. Urban schools, Ravitch writes, began to adopt the "social work concept of schooling" whereby the school became "an institution that 'takes charge' of children in lieu of an incompetent family and disintegrated community." [26]

Most teachers and school administrators fully supported aggressive assimilation of immigrant children, and urban schools soon took on the role of cultural evangelist. Teachers inspected children's heads for lice and lectured them about hygiene and nutrition. Students were taught how to speak proper English; Anglicizing of names was common. Education historian David Tyack reports that "textbooks for immigrants stressed cleanliness to the point of obsession, implying that the readers had never known soap, a toothbrush, or a hairbrush." [27]

Bilingual instruction continued up until the outbreak of World War I in several cities, but the ethos of Americanization was powerful, even within many immigrant slums. Time and again, when cities provided foreign language instruction, immigrants declined to enroll in classes taught in their native tongue. Like the paternalistic schools of today, schools for immigrant children also reinforced values that parents held but alone could not pass on to their children—namely, the desire that their children learn English and become Americans. During "the first half of the twentieth century," Jonathan Zimmerman reports, "Americans adopted ethnic identities but shunned ethnic languages."[28] President Theodore Roosevelt's attacks on "hyphenated Americanism" were particularly uncompromising. "We have room for but one language here, and that is the English language," Roosevelt declared. "We intend to see that the crucible turns our people out as Americans, of American nationality, and not as dwellers in a polyglot boarding house."[29] In 1902, after the Spanish-American war, federal appointees decided that classes must be taught in English even in Puerto Rico, though few students spoke the language or ever had the opportunity to hear it. School officials did not abandon the attempt to anglicize Puerto Rican children and reinstate Spanish as the basic language of instruction until 1948.[30]

On the mainland, both bilingual instruction and the influx of new immigrants ground to a halt after World War I erupted in 1914. The war prompted new doubts about the loyalties of immigrants who spoke foreign languages, particularly German. Teddy Roosevelt went so far as to urge that while every immigrant should be given the chance to learn English, if, after "five years, he has not learned English, he should be sent back to the land from whence he came."[31]

Like the paternalistic inner-city schools of today, urban educators a century ago sought to curtail parental and communal influence on poor immigrant children by lengthening the school day and year. William Henry Maxwell, the first citywide superintendent of schools in New York City, announced in 1904 that "our duty to the home, our duty to society, is to increase rather than diminish the number of hours per day during which the school will take charge of the child."[32] Diane Ravitch writes:

> The social reformers, appalled by the baleful influence of slum life, pressed the schools to lengthen the school day, week, and year. The longer the child was removed from the street and, although it was rarely admitted outright, the slum home, the more chance the school had [to] work right influences on him. These progressives looked to the school to do "preventive social work." In the school, the child was supposed to learn the attitudes, the values, and the skills that his home environment was too poor to provide.[33]

The record of urban schooling for poor immigrants is mixed, though far better than that of Indian boarding schools. Few immigrant students completed high school a century ago, and huge numbers of students were held back a grade, sometimes several years in a row. The zealous drive to Americanize impoverished immigrants also went too far at times, failing to respect the traditions and culture of newcomers. Children, for instance, who spoke little English were often labeled as mentally retarded and punished for using their native tongues. Nevertheless, within a couple of generations, the children of European immigrants generally performed well at school. On the whole, historians have judged the relatively rapid Americanization of millions of poor newcomers to be a qualified success. A more benevolent form of paternalism thus helped impoverished immigrants work toward achieving the national motto on the Great Seal of the United States, e pluribus unum — out of many, one.

The Death of Paternalism in Urban Schools and the Rise of Multiculturalism

From 1965 to roughly 1995, paternalistic education largely disappeared from inner-city schools in the United States. During that 30-year span, urban educators effectively stopped addressing issues of lower-class culture and family breakdown. At the same time, bilingual education and multicultural course offerings exploded, along with progressive pedagogy like whole language reading and invented spelling. A core premise of paternalistic schools — that they can transport students out of poor communities by providing a sustained injection of middle-class values — became politically taboo. For a quarter century after the controversial 1965 Moynihan report on "The Negro Family," urban school administrators abided by an unwritten gag rule that barred candid discussion of the impact of ethnic culture and family values on academic performance. Unlike the Coleman report, which would highlight the influence of impersonal socioeconomic factors (such as parental education and income) on scholastic achievement, Moynihan's report cast a spotlight on illegitimacy and lower-class culture as enduring sources of poverty.

Prior to the Moynihan report, black leaders were some of the staunchest proponents of a paternalistic pedagogical regiment. Some of the top civil rights leaders of the last century — men like Booker T. Washington, W.E.B. DuBois, and Malcolm X — constantly preached the importance of middle-class mores. Martin Luther King earned his doctorate in theology at Boston University in

1955, barely six months before he led the historic Montgomery bus boycott. One historian summed up Booker T. Washington's teachings by noting that his message could be reduced "to the familiar Protestant virtues: industry, frugality, cleanliness, temperance, order, decorum, and punctuality."[34]

Laments about the "culture of poverty" have a conservative ring today, but up until the Moynihan report, the notion that a separate culture held back poor blacks, ensnaring them in a vicious cycle of unemployment and underachievement, was very much promoted by white liberals. The culture-of-poverty thesis was first articulated in 1959 by Oscar Lewis, an American Marxist anthropologist who had studied poor Mexican families in Mexico City. Michael Harrington, the social democrat who reawakened America to the existence of poverty in the early 1960s, followed in Lewis's footsteps. Harrington almost single-handedly popularized the concept of the culture of poverty in the United States. His 1962 book, *The Other America*, was read by President Kennedy at the very onset of the War of Poverty, and, for a brief interlude, Harrington's book became a bible of sorts for Democratic policymakers. In it, Harrington famously argued that the poor constituted "a separate culture, another nation, with its own way of life." The failure of poor whites and blacks to get ahead was attributable in part to the "present-mindedness" and inability to "defer gratification" emblematic of "underclass" culture, rooted in their material deprivation. A key solution to the cycle of poverty, promoted by Harrington and other liberals at the Office of Economic Opportunity, was to "empower" poor blacks. Inner-city enterprise zones and school vouchers for poor parents are now thought of as conservative policy prescriptions. But in the 1960s, liberal thinkers like Christopher Jencks promoted vouchers. Indeed, when Matt Taylor talks today about how Amistad Academy schools "empower" students, he is unconsciously echoing the liberal rhetoric of the early 1960s.

The 1965 publication of the Moynihan report largely brought to a halt the work of education reformers who believed that urban schools should explicitly redress the culture gap between poor and middle-class children. Daniel Patrick Moynihan, then a young assistant secretary in President Johnson's Department of Labor, concluded in his controversial report that "most Negro youth are in *danger* of being caught up in [a] tangle of pathology,"[35] which was driven by the "deterioration of the Negro family." Moynihan attributed the high rate of family breakdown among poor blacks to centuries of slavery and discrimination. He urged, too, that the federal government take steps to bolster black families because "the present tangle of pathology is capable of perpetuating itself without assistance from the white world."[36] But Moynihan's liberal policy prescriptions were overshadowed by his rhetoric suggesting that lower-class black families and culture were dysfunctional.

The response of civil rights leaders and academia to Moynihan's prescient report was bitter and prolonged. A psychologist and civil rights activist named William Ryan cleverly crystallized the attacks on Moynihan by accusing him of "blaming the victim." The catchphrase "blaming the victim" soon took on a life of its own in schools of education, civil rights oratory, and popular culture. (A 2007 Google search for the phrase "blaming the victim" turned up 344,000 references.) For a quarter century after the Moynihan report, liberal critics and black leaders largely shut down debates about the impact of ethnicity, culture, family breakdown, and personal responsibility on minority achievement by warning against "blaming the victim." Education reformers and analysts who suggested that the underachievement of black youth was due to anything other than "structural" impediments like poverty, insufficient government spending, and a history of discrimination risked the charge that they were covert racists.

At the same time, the Moynihan report helped spur the spread of multiculturalism in urban schools and the rise of the "black pride" movement. In the decade that followed, a string of black academics, including Andrew Billingsley, Carol Stack, and Joyce Ladner, authored books celebrating the "strengths" of black female-headed families. "One must question the validity of the white middle-class lifestyle from its very foundation because it has already proven itself to be decadent and unworthy of emulation," Ladner wrote in 1972.[37] Before long, some urban school systems started teaching Ebonics or "black English" to minority students.

The glorifying of fatherless families and the teaching of black English started to fade by the mid-1980s. But the larger pedagogical shift toward multiculturalism—also fostered by postmodern and relativist mindsets among intellectuals and academics—continued to have a profound impact upon instruction in urban schools. In some ways, the explosion of multicultural secondary school courses that began in the 1970s was overdue, a corrective to the narrow historical record, patriotic pabulum, and racist and sexist stereotypes that dominated American high school textbooks in the 1950s and 1960s. In time, however, multicultural instruction generated its own excesses—from changing the sex of *The Little Engine that Could* from male to female to correct for "gender imbalance" to publisher guidelines that banned the use of the word "America" because it reeked of geographical chauvinism.[38] By the 1990s, the multicultural movement had spawned a well-documented and well-deserved backlash in the form of complaints about political correctness.

While many excesses of multiculturalism have been rolled back, its core premise—relativism—was also used to challenge many forms of traditional instruction. Multiculturalists did not merely believe that students needed to learn more about non-European cultures and history but rather that all cultures are created equal. Much the same ethos prevailed in the bilingual education community, where, beginning in the 1970s, activists asserted that it was just as valuable for students to be taught in their native tongue as in English. Relativism ruled the roost in urban public schools from the mid-1960s to the late-1990s, making it difficult to establish exacting academic standards or champion the teaching of "old-fashioned" virtues like studiousness, discipline, self-reliance, and thrift. In an era of identity politics, white principals who wished to specify what low-income, minority students should learn ran the risk of being dismissed as tools of "the establishment." Ronald Ferguson, a black Harvard economist who authored a review of the impact of schools on the black-white test score gap, candidly observed in a 2002 newspaper interview that it is "hard to talk about [these problems] in public. Black folks don't want white folks coming into their communities and saying 'You ought to be more like us'."[39]

The proliferation of multiculturalism and bilingual education in the schools between 1970 and 1995 dovetailed with the continued dominance of progressive teaching practices in the classroom, creating a double whammy for traditional-minded educators. Diane Ravitch has described the tenets of progressive education as emphasizing "active learning through experience rather than passive learning through systematic instruction; cooperative planning of classroom activities by teachers and pupils; cooperation among pupils on group projects rather than competitions for grades...Progressive teachers reject drill and memorization as teaching methods; [and] the teaching of traditional subject matter unrelated to functional, 'real-life' problems."[40]

By contrast, traditional educators favor "behaviorist" or "instructivist" teaching methods that are teacher-directed rather than student-centered.

Such classroom strategies include direct instruction, mastery learning, and curricula like the Success for All program, all of which emphasize the early development of basic skills, assess student's performance regularly, and set concrete, rigorous standards. While progressive instruction grew in popularity in inner-city schools, researchers often found that the methods that worked best in such classrooms were traditional ones. Writing in 1997, Chester Finn noted that

> any fair minded analyst of research into effective schools and productive teaching strategies [like direct instruction and Success for All] will be struck by the powerful role of—choose your word—instructivism, behaviorism, or paternalism. Success in strengthening student achievement generally accompanies the active use of goals, standards, expectations, assessments, and feedback, the persistent redoing of what is not yet done well and, perhaps especially, accountability for results.[41]

Traditional instruction, in other words, typically has a paternalistic flavor; students are told what to do and compliance is enforced. But a decade ago, Finn was not sanguine about the appeal of successful paternalistic instructional methods to the K–12 education establishment, despite their documented successes. "The most important thing to know about these proven and empirically tested instructional strategies is that they are little used in American schools," he noted. "This is because the educational philosophy that underlies them conflicts with the 'child-centered' or 'developmentalist' philosophy that has ruled the education profession throughout this century."[42]

The standards movement has grown considerably since Finn wrote. And with the passage of NCLB, many more teachers of low-income youngsters rely on behaviorist instruction today than a decade ago. State-level standards are broad, and teachers can help their students reach them using either traditional or progressive methods of instruction, but the pressure to demonstrate results has led many educators and school districts to embrace a more paternalistic approach to instruction. Still, the ongoing resistance to the standards movement in general and NCLB in particular by much of the K–12 education establishment highlights the tenacity of progressive thinking inside urban classrooms. Paternalistic instruction is still regularly dismissed by education critics like Jonathan Kozol as "Skinnerian,"[43] as if educational behaviorists treat children like rats in B.F. Skinner's box.

Yet one paternalistic type of high school did continue to thrive, even in the aftermath of the Moynihan report: the private boarding school. Boarding schools literally filled the role of surrogate parents for teens during their time away from home. And with their fusty rituals, uniforms, honor codes, academic rigor, and pedagogical prescriptiveness, boarding schools were thoroughgoing paternalistic institutions. To be sure, private boarding schools, like other traditional institutions, suffered their share of post-1960s' drubbing for being elitist and emotionally barren. One thinks of novels like *A Separate Peace* and *Catcher in the Rye*. Yet in an era where paternalism for the poor was scorned, rich parents kept vying to send their children to overtly paternalistic boarding schools. And during the 1960s and 1970s, when paternalism was scorned by the education establishment, low-income black students lined up as well to get coveted spots at elite boarding schools.

In 1963, 16 top independent schools founded the ABC (A Better Chance) program, which sent more than 5,000 disadvantaged minority students to the nation's elite day and boarding schools (e.g., Exeter, Andover, Choate, Hotchkiss) over the next quarter century.[44] From 1964 to 1975, more than 100 of the nation's top secondary schools (nearly all of them independent, private schools) provided scholarships to ABC students. The ABC program ended up with a sterling record of academic achievement—99 percent of its graduates attended college, and many went to Ivy League universities and other prestigious colleges.

The ABC program, especially during the 1960s, was also paternalistic. Like the paternalistic inner-city academies of today, it ran an eight-week summer school orientation/"boot camp" for minority students to get them acclimated to boarding school life and academics. During that orientation, inner-city teens were tutored in English and math as well as the folkways of upper-class white society. At the summer program at Mt. Holyoke College in 1966, teen girls visited Tanglewood to hear classical music, learned to swim, played field hockey, and took ballet.[45] The girls were taken out to restaurants and made to order their food, many for the first time. Once a week, they dressed for dinner in dresses; afterward they sipped coffee in demitasse cups. The summer program at Dartmouth obliged teen boys to attend Sunday evening symphony concerts and plays by local repertory theaters.

From the time students awoke at 6:50 A.M., until lights were turned off at 10:00 P.M., teachers and counselors ran them ragged. Most of the day was taken up with English, math, and study hall. In *Blacks in the White Establishment,* their careful account of the ABC program, Richard Zweigenhaft and G. William Domhoff write that the summer program's daily schedule "reveal[ed] all the features of what sociologists call a 'total institution,' one that controls every aspect of a person's life."[46] The ABC students, many of whom were used to being the stars of their class, found the academic competition intense. Francisco Borges, who later went on to be elected treasurer of the state of Connecticut, recalls that at the 1966 Dartmouth program, small groups of students were assigned to counselors to get extra tutoring at night. Borges's demanding counselor was a diminutive and droll Dartmouth College student named Robert Reich—who eventually became secretary of labor in the Clinton administration, and a prominent progressive thinker and critic of standardized testing. In 1966, the young Reich, Borges recalled, was "a real tough son of a bitch."[47]

The Revival of Paternalism and the Growth of the Avuncular State

In the last decade, government paternalism has made something of a quiet comeback, albeit in a softer form that is more palatable to the public. As in the past, the chief impetus to rethinking paternalism was a longstanding failure of government—not unlike the failure of inner-city schools to educate disadvantaged children. Most recently, paternalism has resurged due to the decades-long inability of federal and state welfare offices to curb dependency on the dole. The 1996 welfare reform law fundamentally reshaped public assistance in the United States by limiting cash aid to two years and compelling millions of welfare mothers to find work to retain their welfare checks. The new law soon led to massive reductions in the welfare rolls, without creating the nightmare "Calcutta in the street" scenarios that many analysts feared would arise as families lost their benefits.

The legislation conditioned government aid upon "good behavior" like seeking and holding a job, and staying off drugs. The new time limits on welfare and the imposition of a real work requirement changed the culture of welfare offices, too, so that they no longer were places where the primary job of caseworkers was to help process checks for eligible recipients. Instead, welfare offices became places where caseworkers cajoled welfare recipients into looking for work. Through a combination of "help and hassle" policies similar to those of paternalistic schools, caseworkers provided both help (e.g., finding child care so a mother could go to work) and hassle (calling people on the phone to hound them when they failed to show up for a job interview).

Apart from its work requirements, the new welfare law contained several paternalistic intrusions into the lives of poor families that would have never been endorsed by Congress a quarter century ago. The law, for example, authorized the creation of "second chance" homes for unwed teen mothers on welfare where older, more experienced mothers were supposed to tutor them in how to cook, clean, manage money, and abide by curfews. More memorably, the new welfare law was the first federal legislation to make marriage an explicit policy goal. It authorized new "marriage promotion" and "responsible fatherhood" programs. The federal Department of Health and Human Services is currently spending $150 million a year on such initiatives.[48] The programs are voluntary, but they teach relationship skills to low-income couples and provide help in solving money problems.

When welfare reform was enacted, most journalists and pundits snickered at the notion of Uncle Sam trying to get poor couples hitched. Numerous critics suggested that promoting marriage among low-income families was little more than a heavy-handed government attempt to impose middle-class values on low-income mothers. Skeptics claimed that marriage-promotion programs would either be ineffective or, worse, would prompt a rise in domestic violence. When the law came up for renewal in 2002, Avis Jones-DeWeever of the Institute for Women's Policy Research was still protesting that marriage-promotion programs in low-income communities were "the ultimate in big government, if not social engineering."[49] Yet as the *St. Petersburg Times* reported in 2007, marriage promotion programs are no longer even controversial in many quarters. The *Times* found that since passage of the welfare law and its subsequent reauthorization, "the government's marriage initiative has gone from a hot-button political issue to that rare social policy on which liberal academics and Bush administration officials can agree...Many who once opposed the policy now support it."[50]

It is still too early to say whether marriage-promotion programs are effective. But it is not too early to note that a little-noticed reassessment of orphanages has taken place in recent years with surprising results: orphanages for dependent and disadvantaged children turn out not to be so bad after all. The revisionist research on orphanages has been led by Richard McKenzie of the University of California at Irvine, who himself grew up in a North Carolina orphanage in the 1950s. McKenzie, a libertarian-leaning business school professor, was in some respects an unlikely defender of orphanages.

In 1999, however, he edited a scholarly volume reassessing orphanage research entitled *Rethinking Orphanages for the 21st Century*. As part of the reassessment, McKenzie himself oversaw the only known extensive survey of orphanage alumni/ae. He surveyed alumni/ae of nine all-white orphanages in the South and Midwest, all of which required orphans to work in shops or on farms and all of which served poor or dependent children exclusively (as opposed to severely troubled or delinquent children). Ultimately, McKenzie received survey responses from more than 1,800 orphanage alumni/ae age 45 and older. His results belie public beliefs about the horrors of such institutions: 76 percent of the alumni/ae gave their orphanages a "very favorable" rating and only 1 percent rated their orphanage very unfavorably.[51] Four out of five said they never wanted to be adopted; three in four said they preferred growing up in an orphanage to living with available members of their family. In fact, the longer that orphans stayed at orphanages, the happier they seemed to be. Former orphans, moreover, were significantly more likely to graduate from high school, attend college, and have a professional degree than their peers in the general white population.[52] As Richard Gelles, dean of the University of Pennsylvania School of Social Policy and Practice put it, "the key assumption that 'children always do best when cared for by their biological parents' must be revealed as a canard."[53]

These findings provide a reminder that paternalism and compassion need not be incompatible. Orphanages, too, can be staffed by compassionate teachers and mentors, much like today's no-excuses schools. Tom Monaghan, founder of Domino's Pizza, spent much of his childhood in an orphanage because his mother, a maid, made too little to support her children while studying to become a nurse. But Monaghan's life was changed forever by an orphanage nun named Mary Beralda, who shaped his conscience and spirituality. "She was very kind," Monaghan said later. "She was everything. She was our mother, and our father."[54]

Even as scholars like McKenzie, Lawrence Mead, and James Q. Wilson have started to reassess the historical record of paternalism, government paternalism has itself become both less intrusive and more acceptable. The newest push for paternalistic policymaking comes from lawmakers who seek to require Americans to purchase health insurance, an indirect outgrowth of state laws that require motorists to carry liability insurance. In 2006, Massachusetts, with Governor Mitt Romney at its helm, became the first state in the country to require individuals to purchase health insurance. Massachusetts mandated that residents purchase health insurance under penalty of fines, though the state agreed to provide hardship exemptions to 20 percent of uninsured adults who could not afford insurance. Then, in the 2008 presidential campaign, Democratic candidates Hillary Clinton and John Edwards both offered health insurance plans with individual mandates, while Barack Obama proposed that parents be required to purchase health insurance for children. On the GOP campaign trail, Sen. John McCain attacked the Massachusetts law signed by rival Romney as a "big-government mandate," and Barack Obama voiced similar criticisms of Hillary Clinton's individual mandate requirement.[55] Yet for the most part, the idea that Americans should be required to purchase health insurance—whether they wanted to or not—provoked much less controversy than it would have a decade ago.

At the same time, the rise of "soft paternalism," or what *The Economist* has dubbed "the avuncular state," introduces an element of choice that is missing from traditional paternalistic schemes.[56] To take one example, in 1996, Mississippi pioneered a plan, since adopted by Michigan and New Jersey, that allows gambling addicts to add their name to a blacklist that bars them for life from gambling in riverboat casinos. If they breach the gambling ban, the gamblers could be arrested for trespassing, and their winnings would be confiscated. More than 10,000 people have signed up voluntarily to ban themselves from the riverboats.[57]

Soft paternalism schemes thus rig the "default" option. They are typically promoted by a new breed of behavioral economists who argue that people left to their own devices often make bad choices and, therefore, need a gentle guiding hand from government or an employer. The 2006 pension reform law, for instance, allows employers automatically to enroll employees in the company 401(k) plan unless the employee specifically chooses otherwise, rather than requiring employees to sign up for such a plan; the law also empowers companies to boost employees' contribution levels up to 6 percent of pay following automatic enrollment. Companies that sign their workers up for pension plans are being avuncular; so are European governments that presume that citizens will consent to allow their organs to be used for the benefit of others after they die unless they specifically choose otherwise. In both instances, government or employer is deciding what's best for others, rather than simply throwing open the door to having them do whatever they wish.

Unlike traditional government paternalism, the avuncular state is aimed primarily at middle-class individuals, not at the poor or recent immigrants. And unlike the hard paternalism of the past, soft paternalism draws on the tradition of self-restraint demonstrated by Ulysses in *The Odyssey* when he orders his men to tie him to the mast lest he be tempted by the call of the Sirens. Such actions introduce an element of choice, making soft paternalism more acceptable to political moderates. As Glen Whitman of the Cato Institute has observed, "the old paternalism said, 'We know what's best for you, and we'll make you do it.' The new paternalism says, '*You* know what's best for you, and we'll make you do it."[58] One sign of the widening acceptance of soft paternalism is a hopeful paper, coauthored by University of Chicago law professor Cass Sunstein in 2003, titled "Libertarian Paternalism is Not an Oxymoron." "Libertarian paternalism," Sunstein and Richard Thaler wrote, "is a relatively weak and nonintrusive type of paternalism, because choices are not blocked or fenced off…Policies rooted in libertarian paternalism will often be a big improvement on the most likely alternative: inept neglect."[59]

Are the new "no excuses" inner-city schools examples of soft paternalism? Not exactly. While students and their families do choose to apply to them, they are still institutions that preach obligation and practice compulsion. Soft paternalism is also targeted primarily toward middle-class individuals, not at the poor or newly arrived immigrants, as with no-excuses schools. But neither are the new paternalistic schools mere revivals of traditional paternalistic policies, as Lawrence Mead pointed out in an interview. "The old paternalistic programs like the Indian boarding schools and orphanages were custodial in nature," Mead noted, "whereas the paternalism of today is temporary and limited. The old paternalism focused very much on family life — on how children behaved at home. The new paternalism focuses on how you behave outside the home." Today's paternalistic schools, says Mead, are not "focused on family behavior or taking children away from parents — the two things that were most sensitive about the old paternalism. It's not Dickens."

Mead emphasizes that government paternalism takes different forms. So does philosopher Robert E. Goodin, who argues that paternalistic policies can become "permissible" when they reinforce an individual's own value judgments, much as no-excuses schools reinforce the predilections of parents who want their children to strive academically and attend safe schools. "The charge of paternalism is typically taken to be a knock-down objection to any policy," writes Goodin. But, he adds, when one is "confronted with the charge of paternalism, it should always be open to us to say, 'sure this proposal is paternalistic—but is the paternalism in view permissible or impermissible, good or bad?'"[60]

The Slow-mo Rebound of Paternalism and "Militarism" in Urban Schools

In the last decade, paternalism has begun a slow return to the classroom too. The standards and accountability movement has pushed teaching methods to become more content-specific and pedagogy to become more directive. Traditional teaching methods and curricula such as Direct Instruction, Success for All, and CORE Knowledge are more widespread today in classrooms than ten years ago. Prescriptive instructional strategies have now spread to thousands of urban schools.

Multiculturalism has receded somewhat, too, particularly the use of bilingual education. Roughly a quarter of the nation's four million limited English proficient (LEP) students live in California.[61] But in 1998, California passed Proposition 227, effectively bringing an end to bilingual education in the state where it had flourished since the early 1970s. Within a few years, Arizona and Massachusetts followed suit, substituting English immersion programs for bilingual education.

It bears underscoring, too, that the half-dozen inner-city schools singled out here are by no means the only successful urban secondary schools to employ paternalistic teaching methods. The Uncommon Schools coalition (led by its well-known flagship school, North Star Academy Charter School of Newark), Aspire Public Schools (which serve nearly 4,000 students in California in Stockton, Modesto, Oakland, and East Palo Alto), and YES Prep Public Schools (serving 1,500 low-income students in Houston), all hew to a similar model, and all have opened in the last decade. Each of these school networks is making substantial progress in narrowing the achievement gap between low-income and other students.

The reappearance of paternalism in urban schools comes with a couple of important asterisks when it comes to high schools. First, the prescriptive teaching methods and curricula cited above are far more apt to be found in elementary than in secondary schools. Second, while paternalistic secondary schools in the inner city are more common than a decade ago, they still represent only a small fraction of the approximately 2,000 schoolwide Title I public secondary schools in the nation's 100 largest school districts.

Another sign of the increasing acceptance of paternalism is the resurgence of JROTC and other quasi-militaristic programs in inner-city schools. The military has long been viewed as an important ladder of upward mobility for low-income black and Hispanic teenagers. And it is easy to overlook the huge role played by the military services, particularly the Army, in providing opportunities to black males during the years of the peacetime draft. From 1953 to 1965, roughly 170,000 black males turned 18 on average each year—and about 65,000 joined the military annually, or nearly 40 percent of all black 18-year-old males.[62] Given those numbers, it is not surprising that a number of black leaders tout the virtues of an "Army education" for disadvantaged teens. Hugh Price, the former CEO of the National Urban League, recalls that in the 1950s, prior to the abolition of the draft,

> [s]ome of my disaffected [high school] classmates would drop out of school and out of sight. I recall encountering them years later. Somehow they had managed to enlist in the Army—or else they had been drafted. Either way, they strutted about proudly in their uniforms, with a discernible sense of purpose. The Army had turned them around by successfully instilling a basic lesson of military life: if you do a job well, you get ahead. Years ago, the Army worked wonders with aimless young men. What's the explanation? Beyond the armed forces' legendary discipline, my strong hunch is that the intricate system of ranks and incentives helped motivate young people who cannot see far over the horizon. Unfortunately, the military eventually went upscale and stopped accepting school dropouts. This shut off an important escape route and road to salvation for desperate inner-city and rural youngsters.[63]

While the Army today provides less of an open "road to salvation" for disadvantaged teens, it is still hands-down the most racially integrated organization in the country. It is also, as Charles Moskos and John Sibley Butler observe, "an institution unmatched in its broad record of black achievement."[64] Black soldiers, for instance, are less likely to get fired than their white counterparts, though just the opposite pattern prevails in the civil service.[65] And the homicide rate for black male civilians is 12 times that of black male soldiers.

What explains the secret of the Army's success with low-income youth? In rhetoric strikingly similar to that used by principals and teachers at the new paternalistic schools, Moskos and Butler noted a decade ago in *All That We Can Be*:

> Race relations can best be transformed by an absolute commitment to non-discrimination, coupled with uncompromising standards of performance. To maintain standards, however, paths of opportunity must be created—through education, training, and mentoring—for individuals who otherwise would be at a disadvantage…The Army does not lower its standards; it elevates its recruits and soldiers.[66]

Moskos and Butler note that, for all of the Army's success with young black males, the military elevates far fewer youth today than in the past due to the abolition of the draft and toughened screening standards for the all-volunteer force. In 1995, about 265,000 black males turned 18. But only 22,000 of them—8 percent—joined the armed services.[67]

The diminished role of military culture and discipline among black males was on General Colin Powell's mind when he visited Los Angeles to get a firsthand look at the carnage of that city's epic 1992 race riot. Powell himself had enrolled in Army ROTC at City College after high school and found it a useful introduction to the military. He thought that expanding Junior ROTC programs in high schools might give young black males in South Central Los Angeles and other cities a sense of hope and belonging to an organization other than a gang and cultivate discipline. Shortly after he returned from Los Angeles, General Powell proposed to the secretary of defense that the department should double the number of JROTC programs nationwide, from about 1,500 to 2,900, by the 1996–1997 school year.

In most high schools where it exists, the Junior ROTC provides a paternalistic but supplementary curriculum to required courses. Its name, in fact, is something of a misnomer, since JROTC does not develop Army reserve officers or serve as a military training corps. JROTC cadets, for example, are not obligated to serve in the military, nor are instructors typically active members of the military. The vast majority of JROTC graduates (71 percent in Chicago in 2004) go on to post-secondary education, though 18 percent of JROTC graduates in Chicago that same year joined the military, a substantially higher enlistment rate than among non-JROTC graduates.[68]

The JROTC program has retained some of its military structure, including uniforms, drill teams that use dummy weapons and sabers, and spit-and-polish discipline. Many programs include marksmanship training and have in-school firing ranges (although students do not use live ammunition and typically fire air rifles). But the program has largely abandoned explicit military instruction in favor of teaching technology, ethics, leadership, citizenship, teamwork, and self-discipline. Hugh Price reports in a recent study that

> the objective of military-inspired programs like [a military youth corps] and JROTC is not to whip youngsters into shape for combat...The goal is to negate the culture of the streets and instill in young people the skills and self-discipline needed to function in the workforce and life. For many youngsters who have disengaged from school or dropped out, the antidote for deeply ingrained behavioral problems and dysfunctional parenting is heavy doses of structure and regimentation."[69]

Still, the "demilitarization" of the JROTC program in the 1990s didn't keep a number of pundits and educators from being aghast at General Powell's proposal to expand it. *Washington Post* columnist Colman McCarthy dubbed Powell's plan "Operation Just More Guns." "America's schools are impoverished and violence-ridden," McCarthy wrote, "and the solution to these social problems is to militarize kids and cajole them into embracing the government's war plans? Teaching JROTC marksmanship and gun-handling to what the Pentagon calls 'at-risk' inner-city youth is the worst of efforts. The aim of some of these kids is deadly enough now."[70]

Despite such concerns, Powell's initiative did lead to a dramatic increase of JROTC programs in urban high schools during the next decade. In 2005, more than 3,400 secondary schools had JROTC programs, with an enrollment of more than 500,000 students. Several cities now have a significant JROTC presence in their high schools. In Chicago, JROTC expansion was driven by Mayor Richard Daley and Paul Vallas. More than 9,500 cadets are currently enrolled in JROTC programs in 43 Chicago high schools.[71] That means that one out of every eleven high school students in Chicago now shows up at school in military uniform at least one day a week. However, in most large cities, including New York, JROTC has a modest to negligible presence. To date, little research exists to show whether the program achieves the goals Powell laid out for it. (Preliminary data suggest that JROTC participation does not raise test scores but appears to improve student behavior, modestly boosts academic achievement, and reduces dropout rates.)

As JROTC programs have spread, quasi-militaristic residential programs for high school dropouts, modeled after Job Corps, have also expanded in urban areas. Residential corps programs like the National Guard Youth ChalleNGe Corps provoke less controversy among progressive educators. Job Corps has long been one of the most popular and effective social programs providing disadvantaged teens with a second shot at a diploma or a trade. Since President Johnson created it in the mid-1960s, some two million teens and young adults have passed through Job Corps residential training centers. These centers have zero tolerance policies toward violence, drugs, and harassment, set dress codes for enrollees, and bar students from bringing expensive video and audio equipment to their dorm rooms.

Some years after the draft ended, Hugh Price concluded that one way to help black high school dropouts gain skills would be to have them enroll in a Job Corps-like residential program run by the National Guard. Price approached the National Guard about the idea, and in 1993 Congress approved a 10-state pilot for the National Guard Youth ChalleNGe program.[72] The 17-month-long, coeducational corps is open only to high school dropouts, who spend five months living on a military base, followed by a year of intense mentorship that includes academic instruction, leadership training, and a minimum of 40 hours of required community service. Cadets in the program adhere to a dress code, must be drug free, and cannot be in trouble with the law.

In 1998, Congress made the National Guard youth corps program permanent. It is currently running at more than 30 sites in 28 states, and some 75,000 teens have graduated since its inception. Again, little scientific evaluation has been done, but time spent in the corps does appear to boost educational attainment and job prospects among the high school dropouts. In 2005, ChalleNGe graduates raised their math scores by 2.2 grade levels and lifted their reading scores by 1.5 grade levels during their residential stay at military bases. Two of three cadets who graduated in 2005 received their high school diploma or GED, nearly 60 percent joined the workforce, 12 percent joined the military, and just over a quarter of the graduates continued with their education.[73] All told, more than nine in ten graduates go on to college, the military, or start career-track jobs, according to National Guard Youth Foundation president Greg Sharp.[74]

JROTC and National Guard youth corps programs are still far from the norm, but they are far more common today than a decade ago. So is the use of school uniforms. Many parochial and boarding schools have long required students to wear uniforms, but uniformed public school students, especially at the secondary school level, were exceedingly rare. Progressive educators believed that requiring students to wear uniforms crimped free expression and was a reactionary attempt to impose conformity. Not until 1994 did an urban school district (Long Beach) impose a system-wide uniform requirement.

Two years later, President Clinton touted uniforms as a way to improve school safety in his 1996 State of the Union address. Public schools ought to be allowed to require students to wear uniforms, Clinton said, "if it means teenagers will stop killing each other over designer jackets." By 1999–2000, roughly 12 percent of all public school students and 4 percent of secondary students were required to wear uniforms.[75] But that included 40 percent of students who attended predominantly minority schools, or went to schools in high crime neighborhoods.[76] By 2003–2004, nearly 60 percent of principals at charter schools reported that their students were required to wear uniforms.[77] Today, schools in 21 states and the District of Columbia have some sort of uniform or other dress code requirements, and in Boston, Chicago, Cleveland, and New Orleans, two thirds or more of public schools require uniforms.

As the spread of uniform requirements and the growth of the National Guard youth corps illustrate, the politics of urban education have shifted in the last decade. Liberals like Clinton or Hugh Price can now promote paternalistic, quasi-militaristic institutions and dress codes for low-income youth without fear of being vilified. Indeed, many of the founders of today's paternalistic inner-city schools are white, liberal, and young. Growing up, they had little direct exposure to inner-city schools. Dave Levin of KIPP went to the Riverdale School in the Bronx, an elite and rather progressive private school before going on to Yale. Dacia Toll, president of Achievement First and one of the founders of Amistad Academy, attended the National Cathedral School in Washington, D.C., another venerable private school. Toll's father, John Toll, was the long-time president of the University of Maryland. After graduating from the National Cathedral School, Toll herself went on to the University of North Carolina at Chapel Hill, Oxford (where she was a Rhodes Scholar), and Yale Law School. Eric Adler, cofounder of the SEED School, graduated from Sidwell Friends a decade before Chelsea Clinton. From there he went to

Swarthmore and earned his M.B.A. at Wharton. Until he started looking for sites for the SEED school, Adler "had never been east of the Anacostia River," the dividing line that separates Congress and federal agencies from Washington's impoverished Anacostia neighborhood.

Not all founders of the paternalistic schools are children of privilege. But few grew up in poverty or knew what it felt like to be black or Hispanic. It is hard to imagine that Levin, twenty years ago, could have gone door-to-door in Houston's slums or the South Bronx to recruit poor minority kids for a new charter school and have parents entrust their kids to a fresh-faced twenty-something white kid from Yale — much less willingly sign a contract with Levin attesting that they would live up to their parental duties. But Levin, Toll, and Adler do not feel held back by their origins or fret that they are somehow inauthentic, disqualified by their race and upbringing from running schools for disadvantaged minority students.

The rise of these schools bears out a prediction that Lawrence Mead made a decade ago:[78] paternalism would soon become a postracial social policy, denuded of many of its racial overtones. Paternalism has taken on a more liberal hue at these schools because, while many of their leaders and teachers have little personal experience with poverty, few also have experience with the identity politics of the 1970s and 1980s. When Dave Levin was a sophomore in college, the Moynihan Report was already 25 years old. Levin, Toll, and Adler believe they are just doing their jobs, running schools as effectively as they can to tackle the achievement gap. They don't attach great importance to conforming to a political ideology. In a fashion, the new paternalists are like modern-day missionaries, ready to have a few doors slammed in their faces as they try to spread the gospel of transformational urban school reform.

Chapter Three

The American Indian Public Charter School

The new school had an inauspicious beginning. When the American Indian Public Charter School (AIPCS) first opened in Oakland, California, in September 1996, it was a multicultural dream that would soon become an educational nightmare. A 1996 newspaper account written by a high school student for the *Golden Gater Jr.*, a San Francisco State college newspaper sponsored by the Bay Area Multicultural Media Academy, neatly encapsulated the novel approach of the new middle school — and inadvertently foreshadowed the disaster to come. The paper reported that

> A new charter school emphasizing Native American culture will open this September …Richard Lavato, 34, a father of two children and chair of the parent committee [said] "my children, including other Native American children, have experienced problems in the public schools, including harassment and racism. The American Indian Charter School will help the children feel comfortable about themselves.". . . Carol Wahpepah, director of the Indian American Education Center in Oakland, said, "We want our children back. Children should be proud of who they are, public schools do not provide a good environment."[1]

How exactly would the new middle school teach Indian children to be "comfortable" with themselves? Not, apparently, by teaching them to read and write proficiently. The school's distinctive curriculum, the *Golden Gater Jr.* reported, was designed chiefly to build student pride in being Native American:

> The curriculum will integrate [Indian] culture in all subjects. Students will be involved in various ethnic-related projects from planting crops and learning traditional cooking to Native American storytelling and researching their individual tribes...Other activities students will participate in include pottery, making musical instruments, basket weaving, and cultural art...Parent participation will be important to the community-supported and run school. Parents will continually review the curriculum and help write the handbook that includes disciplinary rules. All parents are required to volunteer in school four hours a month.[2]

Cut to the summer of 2000, by which time the American Indian Public Charter School had become a caricature of almost everything that can go wrong with a parent-driven, multicultural school. During the previous four years, parents had squabbled incessantly over how to best teach Indian culture. Each fall, the school had a new principal, yet neither its board nor anyone else associated with the school ever seemed to be held accountable for its poor performance. The enrollment in grades six through eight had dwindled to 27 students, two-thirds of whom were Indian. Student achievement was pitiful. In 2001, American Indian Public Charter School (AIPCS) students scored a 436 out of 1000 on California's Academic Performance Index (API)[3]—one of the worst scores in a city already renowned for its dreadful public schools. Students roamed in and out of class at will. One school board member at the time said, "there were supposed to be sixty kids enrolled but you were lucky to find one kid in class" during school visits. AIPCS was also $80,000 in arrears on the modest two-floor building it leased from the Tongan Methodist Church in the Laurel neighborhood of Oakland's rough "flatlands." Finally, the Oakland School Board decided it had had enough: It was going to close AIPCS and revoke the school's charter. But then one member persuaded the district school board to give the school one last shot under the new leadership of Ben Chavis, a Lumbee Indian who had taught in the ethnic studies department at San Francisco State University.

Chavis was no stranger to poverty or poor schools. Though he had made a small fortune in real estate investments, he had also been superintendent of

education on an impoverished Indian reservation in Arizona. Yet when Chavis
arrived at AIPCS in July 2000, even he was outraged by the educational cha-
rade that school administrators had perpetrated on poor kids in the name of
developing their Native American identity. "What the school and students had
been doing was playing Indian," he recalls scornfully. The school day started,
Chavis says, at 9:00 or 9:30 A.M. with a "talking circle":

> The school believed in what it called "Indian Time"—students were sup-
> posed to show up when they showed up because Indians can't get up early. The
> students either stopped coming to school or they would turn the Talking Circle
> into a bitch session that lasted until 11:00 a.m. Then there was a culture class,
> where students would bang drums and were taught basket weaving and bead-
> making. The kids also got smoking breaks—I'm not making this shit up. The
> school had no dress code. The school was filthy, and the walls were covered with
> graffiti and gang markings. One member of the cafeteria and janitorial staff had
> been convicted of selling drugs. The teachers were paid lousy salaries. But the
> school had spent $90,000 to wire the school for 65 computers.

Within days of his appointment as principal, Chavis began to undo every
decision of his predecessors. He fired all but one member of the staff and
eliminated every curricular consultant. Chavis knew that students sometimes
broke computers to avoid having to complete assignments, so using a pair of
wire cutters, he snipped every computer connection and hauled all 65 of the
PCs out of the building himself. When Chavis discovered that students didn't
like the food in the cafeteria, he closed it—and told students to start bringing their own lunches. He eliminated every multicultural offering, requiring
instead that students have a minimum of three hours of English language arts
and math each morning that followed state-adopted textbooks, step-for-step.
Arriving one minute late to school would henceforth earn a student a guar-
anteed hour of silent detention after school; so would talking out of turn in
class or uniform violations of the new school dress code. Bypassing the local
union, he recruited new teachers by posting online ads on Craigslist—and
promptly hired three young teachers, none of whom had a teaching credential.
Using his own funds, he then paid the inexperienced, non-union teachers
$5,000 more a year than they would have received in Oakland's neighbor-
hood public schools. The $5,000 bonus both helped lure teachers from Ivy
League colleges to the faltering charter school and effectively ensured that

the local teachers union would never incorporate better-paid AIPCS teachers into the union.

Today, seven years later, Chavis's reforms have produced one of the great educational turnaround stories in recent history. American Indian Public Charter School is currently the highest performing middle school in the Oakland area. After raising its Academic Performance Index (API) scores each year for seven years running, in 2006 AIPCS' 196 students even bested the Piedmont Middle School, the school for the "rich kids" in the hills above Oakland's gritty "flatlands" neighborhoods. AIPCS students on average scored 920 out of 1000 on California's API in 2006, far above the 800 point target that California has set as a statewide goal (and more than double its 2001 API score).

In October 2006, AIPCS became the first public school in Oakland to win a coveted Blue Ribbon award from the U.S. secretary of education. That same year, 35 students participated in the prestigious Johns Hopkins Center for Talented Youth (CTY) summer programs at universities around the country. To be nominated for the program, students must score above the 95th percentile on any nationally normed test or score at advanced levels on state tests. To gain admittance to the CTY summer program, an eighth grader (for example) must take the SAT—and score above 600 on either the English or math portion at the age of 14. In 2006, AIPCS alone sent more students to the Hopkins program than the rest of Oakland's schools combined. It has made such a name for itself that families from other ethnic backgrounds, including low-income Asian-Americans and Latinos, have started seeking the school out. During a 2006 visit to AIPCS, California governor Arnold Schwarzenegger hailed it as "an educational miracle."[4]

Oakland's "flatlands" neighborhoods are known for their terrible schools, which makes AIPCS stand out all the more. In 2003, when only a third of district students graduated on time,[5] the state legislature stripped the school board of its powers, clearing the way for the state to assume control of the district. Today, 57 of Oakland's 130 public schools are designated "Schools in Need of Improvement," having failed to make adequate yearly progress (AYP) for at least two years under NCLB. As the *East Bay Express* notes, Oakland has "long operated two distinct systems: one for rich and primarily white kids in the hills, and another for the poor black and Latino kids in the flatlands. The shining hillside schools stood out for their top-notch test scores and savvy veteran teachers. The flatlands schools stood out for their broken toilets, noncredentialed instructors, and rock-bottom test results."[6] The first state-appointed administrator of the Oakland schools, Randy Ward, was even more brutal in his assessment of the district's inability to move forward with reform. "They have been sitting around singing kum-ba-ya for 30 years while kids are dropping out and shooting each other," he told one journalist. "That's what they do in Oakland."[7]

Not surprisingly, Oakland's inferior schools and the state takeover of the district have made the city something of a charter mecca, with everybody from former mayor Jerry Brown to the KIPP Foundation establishing schools in the city. All told, roughly 7,200 students now attend 29 charter schools in Oakland, representing 15 percent of district enrollment, tied for eighth in the nation for having the highest proportion of students in charter schools.[8] With the support of Ward (who left in 2006 to become superintendent of the San Diego County schools) and the backing of leading philanthropies like the Broad, Gates, and Dell foundations, Oakland has also moved aggressively to break up large schools and open more small schools.

Amid this reform ferment, what accounts for American Indian's rise to the top? One thing is certain: The school's transformation was not due to an infusion of resources. In fact, AIPCS spends about $2,000 less per student than the Oakland district (which currently spends about $9,000). The two-story building that houses the middle school has a small, ratty gym in the basement, and six classrooms, split by a corridor, on the top floor. For exercise, the physical education instructor sometimes has students run around the block. The school's new ninth and tenth grade classes meet, respectively, in a room up an outdoor metal stairwell at the back of the Tongan Methodist Church next door and in an apartment that Chavis gutted next to the school's modest blacktop playground.

AIPCS's resources and electives include nary a bell or a whistle. The school has no technology lab (or student computers), a nonfunctioning cafeteria (students still bring their own lunches), and a small library propped up on a stage, supplemented by a biweekly visit from a bookmobile. Students use their desks as lockers. AIPCS does not put on a school play because it has no drama instructor. Next to the middle school sits an abandoned, boarded-up building, also owned by the Tongan Methodist Church. In several classrooms, students get choice views of boarded-up houses nearby as they read their Steinbeck assignments. The school has no security guards. A janitor comes twice a week to clean the floors, but students are responsible every day for cleaning the grounds and maintaining the bathrooms. Governor Schwarzenegger, a supporter of AIPCS, visited the school twice in 2006 to promote his $10.4 billion school bond construction referendum. "No school should be in a building like this," Schwarzenegger sympathetically observed on his first visit. "Our children deserve better than run-down classrooms with sheets over broken windows."[9]

A Paternalistic School and Its "Dictator" Principal

"There's never any talent without a little stain of madness."

—Jean-Louis Trintignant, posted on a sign in the entryway to AIPCS

The secret of American Indian's success lies not in its resources but rather in its paternalistic blend of instruction and discipline. Yet more than any other school profiled here, AIPCS also reflects the contrarian passions of its self-described "control freak" and "dictator," mad-dog principal Ben Chavis. Unlike the architects of other paternalistic schools, Chavis grew up poor and attended segregated Indian schools in North Carolina as a child. He remains a deeply controversial figure among Oakland educators. In action, Chavis is more like the famed bullhorn-wielding principal Joe Clark—who transformed Eastside High School, one of the worst schools in Paterson, New Jersey, into a model school for a period in the early 1980s—than, say, Dave Levin, the curly-haired boy-wonder who cofounded KIPP. Chavis still retains the lean figure of a college track star, despite his salt and pepper hair and old-school crew cut. But on days when he's not sporting a business suit, Chavis will show up at school in jogging warm-ups with an air of restless intensity that makes him look like he is about to bolt out of the starting blocks. Proud, prickly, and hot-tempered, Chavis has a mouth that would make a longshoreman blush. He's not afraid to get into a profane shouting match with parents and will deliberately challenge students with ethnic stereotypes. He is shrewd, a quick judge of character—and a walking testament to political incorrectness. Unlike most principals, Chavis is a successful businessman who relishes competition and believes in creating mercantile incentives in the form of cold hard cash for students and teachers who perform well. And while students see "Dr. Chavis" as a no-nonsense disciplinarian, they also ultimately see him as "family"—a substitute father figure who cares about them, even as he wheedles, shames, and scolds. He is truly a "paternal" principal.

American Indian plainly shares many of the paternalistic policies of other no-excuses schools. Yet unlike the other schools, AIPCS's authoritarian policies have often evolved directly out of Chavis's own experiences of childhood poverty. AIPCS, for instance, requires students to attend three weeks of summer school, lengthening the year from 180 days to 200 days. American Indian has increased instructional time during the school day, too, by cutting down on electives, shortening the lunch hour to 20 minutes, and reducing classroom rotation. It is an academically rigorous institution and one of only two middle schools in Oakland to require every eighth grader—including special ed students—to take algebra I. Without doubt, it has the toughest detention rules of any of the six schools profiled in these pages. During detention, students must sit upright for an hour after school in absolute silence with nothing on their desks. By contrast, other schools allow students to do their homework, write notes of apologies, clean, or read during detentions.

Yet for all the school's strict discipline, American Indian is also infused with Chavis's personal sense of mission and his deep antipathy for the tenets of progressive education. Chavis was an illegitimate child reared in a dirt-poor family with six siblings in Robeson County, North Carolina. As a child, he had no electricity, used an outhouse, and had an illiterate mother who toiled as a maid. Chavis says his father "was a drunk who fit the stereotype of the alcoholic Indian." When Chavis was six or seven, his father was in a serious car accident and died shortly thereafter. But Chavis survived—and ultimately flourished because he grew up with an extended sense of family and tradition. Chavis's great-great uncle was Anderson Locklear, a pioneer Native American teacher for the Lumbee tribe who once met with President Teddy Roosevelt. And his stepfather, Henry Bell, was "wonderful," says Chavis. "He could not read. But he believed you could do what you wanted if you worked hard."

Chavis later went on to earn a doctorate from the University of Arizona, but he was an indifferent student for much of his youth in Lumberton, North Carolina. He repeated first grade. In third grade, teacher Helen Smith gave each student three dollars for having perfect attendance for the year. It was the only time Chavis had perfect attendance—and he maintained perfect attendance despite having to pretend that he hurt one leg, walking to school with a shoe wrapped in an old rag to conceal the fact that he had only one good shoe. "Poverty taught me to improvise," says Chavis. "I don't care if you have one shoe when you come here. We've had kids who were homeless, kids who didn't know who their daddy is. That motivates them."

Remembering his experience with Ms. Smith, Chavis decided that money motivates poor children, too. "I'm teaching my students to be capitalists," Chavis says with a grin. Using funds from his own salary, Chavis opted to pay sixth graders at AIPCS $50 if they did not miss a single day of class. Seventh graders receive $75 for perfect attendance and eighth graders $100. Three years of perfect attendance earns a $150 bonus. Today, AIPCS has the best attendance record of any secondary school in Oakland, with an average daily attendance rate north of 99.5 percent. In the 2005–2006 school year, Mr. Berniker's seventh grade class set the school record, racking up 180 days in a row of perfect attendance for the entire class, meaning that no student missed even one day—an almost unheard-of-feat in an urban secondary school. Pictures of the record-setting class adorn AIPCS classrooms, encouraging subsequent classes to vie to be the new attendance record-holders.

While Chavis didn't study hard in secondary school, he did find a new passion: track. Chavis was a star half-miler and miler—he ran the half mile in 1:53—and track provided a ticket to a college scholarship. Yet at college and during his postgraduate studies, Chavis's first-hand exposure to poverty left him deeply skeptical of progressive rhetoric about multicultural education and parental involvement. He came to believe that

> The whole concept of parental involvement in schools for poor kids is bullshit. You can have extended "family" involvement at school, with grandmothers and aunts involved. In fact, if you act out at American Indian, I will call your grandmother and your auntie and they will embarrass your ass. But focusing on parent involvement alone is the worst idea in the world in these schools, and I don't care whether you are talking about poor white parents in Kentucky or poor Mexicans in Oakland. My mom was a maid. She had six kids and couldn't read—how was she supposed to volunteer at school? Its fine for white, middle-class soccer moms to talk about the nuclear family and getting parents involved in school. But in schools for poor kids, "parental involvement" has become an excuse to blame somebody—Johnny can't read because his momma didn't work with him. I say, you get your kid to school dressed and on time. And we'll do our job to educate him.

Chavis was also disillusioned with multicultural education and bilingual instruction. In an August 2006 interview with National Public Radio, Chavis observed that progressive educators "have no standards for minorities. They're like, you know, let's give them freedom. Let's understand their learning style. Let's give them multiculturalism. And no discipline, no structure, no game plan. They've destroyed a whole generation."[10] Once again, Chavis's strong convictions stemmed largely from lessons he learned the hard way. He explained:

> We don't do bilingual education here. We throw the non-English speakers in with everyone else...I've got kids who arrived in the U.S. not able to speak a word of English, and they are outperforming the kids from every bilingual program in the state. I remember one Chinese boy who said he couldn't speak any English but after awhile I got suspicious. I pulled him aside one day and said privately "do you like boys?" "No!" he said. Well, he's speaking English now and is in the Johns Hopkins summer program for gifted students. You can't get into Berkeley if you can't speak English. Black students, Indian students, poor whites—they don't need a black teacher or an Indian teacher. They need a great teacher.

The metaphor of sports figures prominently in Chavis's educational philosophy. He noted that:

> When I ran the half-mile in track, I didn't get a head start because I was Indian. Sports create the most even playing field of all. And I run the school like it's a sports team. I love the No Child Left Behind law—it's the best thing the education establishment has done for minorities in decades. What I love about testing is that it is just like track. If you run a 1:50 half-mile in North Carolina you know how you would compare against a half-miler from California. I don't believe in all this self-esteem crap—telling students they are smart, even when they are doing a lousy job. I had a child who applied to the school and the mother said "my child doesn't take tests because they discriminate." I asked her "how is that test going to figure out that you are Jamaican? And how is your kid going to get in to Berkeley without an SAT score?"

Chavis's opposition to progressive education is not ultimately what most irks his critics. More controversial is his periodic use of unorthodox discipline and his willingness to challenge students to perform better by goading them with ethnic stereotypes. In 2006, NPR recounted the story of ninth grader Johnny Gonzalez, a Navajo Indian, who, along with a classmate, showed up at school without the mandatory belt for his pants. "Me and my [friend's pants] were sagging," Gonzalez told NPR, and the two were sent to the principal's office. Chavis promptly took a heat lamp from his office and tied the cord around Gonzalez's waist before tying the light cord from a light around the waist of Gonzalez's classmate. The two ninth graders dragged around a heat lamp and a light for the rest of the day to remind them to wear a belt in the future.[11] Neither of the students forgot his belt again—and Gonzalez has since received a scholarship to a private school.

In two well-publicized incidents several years ago, Chavis cut the hair of an eighth grader (with the father's permission) after the student stole a radio, and he allowed a sixth grade boy to be pinned with a note for a day that said "I'm a bitch" after the sixth grader called a girl in his class "a bitch." The sixth grader's mother subsequently withdrew her boy, saying "my child was really learning. But I can't deal with an administration that is a dictatorship."[12] Chavis defended his actions, explaining:

> The Chinese kid whose hair I cut off said he wanted to be in a gang when he first came here in sixth grade. I used to be a [petty] thief when I was a kid, too. So I told him if he did well and went through school, I'd pay for his first year of college. He told me at the time that his hair was an important thing to him, and that if he got caught stealing, to cut his hair off. In his third year here, he did get caught stealing and I brought him in front of the school and announced I was going to cut his hair off—which I did that night at my home. He looked like a dodo bird after going to Chavis's barbershop. ... [In the other incident], a black sixth grader called a girl in his class a "bitch." His teacher, who was also black, had him write "I'm a bitch" on a sign and wear it around his neck. I was not OK with that. But I believe in backing up my teachers. The mother came in the next day and said she wanted the teacher fired. I told her that her son was a fool and what she should have done was whip his butt...People don't like the use of shaming and embarrassment in middle-class society. But in tribal society, it is a very effective tool. My parents here know that. My methods are not for middle-class and upper-class schools. But they work well with this population of poor kids.

Chavis is not above giving himself a dose of his own medicine. He has a policy that any student who calls a girl a bitch is suspended for a day. But a couple of years ago, Chavis got in a heated argument outside the school with a mother about her daughter's repeated tardiness and mediocre school performance. Chavis told the mother that her daughter was going to repeat sixth grade because "she had 18 absences and excessive tardies." The mother disagreed and threatened to "tell the superintendent and the school board you sexually harassed me and they'll fire you." Infuriated by the mother's willingness to fabricate charges against him, Chavis told her to tell the superintendent that he had sexually harassed the superintendent's wife, too, and called her a "bitch." Afterwards, a couple of the girls stopped by his office to confront him. "Dr. Chavis, we heard you use the b-word," they said. "You know what, you're right," Chavis told them. Chavis suspended himself for a day, paid a fine of $600 to the school ($100 for each class of students) and wrote a letter of apology to school parents.

Even so, Chavis's use of unflattering stereotypes—he'll call students a "lazy Mexican" or a "dumb black"—would most likely be a firing offense in traditional public schools. But among AIPCS parents, Chavis's rhetoric seems to create surprisingly little controversy. There is a method of sorts to his madness, says Chavis:

> I'll tell students who are slacking off "now don't you be a lazy Mexican or a lazy Indian." But the truth is that the kids are going to be called half-breeds and lazy some day. And when my kids leave this school, and someone insults them like that, I want them to be able to say "that's nuthin. I can handle that." We're not preparing poor kids for the real world today. I am trying to condition them early so they can handle it. It offends a lot of people. I say outrageous things to the kids. I talk smack to them. I talk to them like their grandpa or grandma will talk to them. But their parents laugh because they know I'm saying what people are thinking but won't say.

It is striking how often AIPCS students describe the school as a substitute family—much like the extended family that Chavis extols. Many students think of Chavis as a stern surrogate father. When Governor Schwarzenegger appeared at American Indian in October 2006 to push his bond referendum, eighth grader Michael Gantt joined him at the podium to add student input about the state of the school's physical facilities. Chavis, Gantt told the governor, "is zero-tolerance. He does not play. But still he respects you and loves you like you were his own kid, and I love him for that."[13] The AIPCS Success Credo, plastered around the classrooms, similarly evokes the notion of the school as extended family in rhetoric that is hard to imagine at an affluent suburban school. The school credo states:

The Family:
We are a family at AIPCS.

The Goal:
We are all working for academic and social excellence.

The Faith:
We will prosper by focusing and working toward our goals.

The Journey:
We will go forward, continue working, and remember we will always be part of the AIPCS family.

It may sound like a contradiction in terms to talk about the soft, family side of zero-tolerance discipline. But beneath the surface of Chavis's persona as the mad-dog principal lies a close connection with disadvantaged students and a deep-seated commitment to closing the achievement gap. "I take my salary and give it back to the school in the form of bonuses and to help pay for resource teachers to tutor kids in math and spelling," says Chavis. In 2001, Chavis started at AIPCS with a $50,000 salary. He subsequently reduced his salary, first to $36,000 and then to $30,000, which he donates back to the school—making him probably the lowest paid school administrator in California. And though he is a multi-millionaire from his real estate business, Chavis insists that "this school is my dream: Taking low-income kids and just kicking butt on state exams and the SAT's—and kicking the ass of the rich kids." On the wall of his office, Chavis has posted a quote from Thomas Jefferson for inspiration. In 1782, Jefferson wrote that by including "the youths of genius from among the classes of the poor, we hope to avail the State of those talents which nature has sown as liberally among the poor as the rich, but which perish without use if not sought for and cultivated."

A Tale of Two Students

Just as the turnaround of AIPCS is a remarkable tale, so, too, is the transformation of individual pupils at AIPCS. Some of the top students were getting Ds and Fs prior to arriving at American Indian. Once there, Chavis considers any student with a C- average to be failing and automatically retains them. Failing students from other schools who become ace pupils at AIPCS may well have some hidden innate ability not evident at their previous schools. But they are hardly an example of selective recruiting or creaming from the top of the local academic pool. Armante Washington, a seventh grader who had the highest GPA in his AIPCS class in the spring of 2006, was getting Ds and Fs at his previous school. When he applied to AIPCS, Chavis told his unhappy mother that Washington would have to repeat seventh grade. "Hell, I was retained in first grade," Chavis explained to her. "It was the best thing that could have happened to me."

When Washington arrived at AIPCS, he goofed off at first like in his old school, talked to other students during class, and threw erasers. He started racking up after-school detentions and soon discovered that detention was more stultifying at AIPCS than at his old school. "Here you get detention for everything, for every little mistake," said Washington. "I didn't want to do detentions anymore. So I decided I had to do my homework." Washington now tells his rowdy street acquaintances from his old school, including a young drug dealer, that they should get better grades to make something of themselves. They tell him "be quiet." In 2006, Washington qualified for the Johns Hopkins CTY program in mathematics.

In his previous school, seventh grader Dean Vargas was not only failing his classes but had earned a reputation as a troublemaker. A Lakota Sioux from North Dakota, Vargas was in a predominantly African-American middle school and was getting into fights regularly. The principal threatened to send Vargas to a boys' home if he didn't stop fighting — prompting him to skip school for a week to test the principal's resolve. His first week back, Vargas got in two more fights. But school authorities "didn't do anything to discipline me, except to say that they were 'disappointed' in me," Vargas recalls. "I learned from that that I could basically do whatever I wanted at school." Vargas finished sixth grade with 3 Ds and a lot of Fs.

Outside school, Vargas and his buddies would commit petty crimes, breaking into cars to steal money and jewelry. His father had been deported to Mexico several years earlier for immigration violations. His mother, who supported five children on welfare, was having trouble making ends meet, says Vargas. At the end of sixth grade, she told Vargas that he was going to live temporarily with his aunt. Vargas was getting into too much trouble in school, she said, and would have to go through sixth grade again, this time at AIPCS.

When Vargas started sixth grade at AIPCS, he was often tardy and disruptive. But he soon discovered that American Indian was a very different institution:

> I came here thinking I could miss days sometimes. But Dr. Chavis would come to my house and pick me up on mornings when I didn't show. I thought he was crazy when he would show up—no principal ever did anything like that before. It was a shock. My aunt would open the door and Dr. Chavis would be standing outside, pissed off. He'd say "hurry the fuck up" and "you're the dumbass Indian that is making us look bad."

For the first four months of school, Vargas got detention almost every day, sometimes for failing to complete homework but usually for talking in class. During his frequent visits to monitor school classes, Chavis would tell Vargas "be quiet, you fool." But slowly the detentions began to wear on Vargas. "The detention was a whole hour and it was after school, not during lunch or recess," says Vargas. "You would just stare at the wall. And if you had books, pencils, or anything on your desk, it was another hour of detention." Finally, in January, Vargas decided he "couldn't take it anymore." He started to buckle down and stopped getting detentions. "American Indian changed me by making me focus on academics more than my street respect," says Vargas.

Teachers helped Vargas control his temper, too, instructing him to take a walk or punch something that didn't hurt anyone when he felt angry. His instructor informed Vargas that if he got in another fight, he would have 30 days straight of detention. Vargas stopped fighting. As of the spring of 2006, Vargas had not yet made the honor roll. But the 420 math score he earned on the SAT in seventh grade was enough to qualify him to apply to the CTY program for gifted students. "I was shocked and happy at the same time that I might get accepted to the Johns Hopkins programs," he says.

Academic Achievement at American Indian

By any standard, AIPCS's record of performance is extraordinary—and there is little evidence to suggest it is due to deliberate creaming. Ever since Chavis took over American Indian in 2001, he has been gunning to outperform Piedmont Middle School, the school in the hills that has long been the best performing school in the county. In 2006, American Indian students outscored their peers at Piedmont for the first time, scoring 920 out of 1000 on California's battery of Academic Performance Index (API) tests, while Piedmont's pupils scored 917.

If demographics are destiny, Piedmont should vastly outperform American Indian. It's in a wealthy community; its website features (under "School Trends") photos of a pink Polo shirt, iPods, a Tiffany sterling silver heart necklace, a Coach purse, and a Louis Vuitton handbag. Nine out of ten Piedmont students are white or Asian (70 percent white, 19 percent Asian), whereas 65 percent of AIPCS students are black, Hispanic, or Native American. None of Piedmont's students participated in the free or reduced-price federal lunch program for low-income children in 2006 while nine in ten pupils at AIPCS did so. Piedmont has a Scottish bagpiper as its school mascot. In fact, less than 1 percent of Piedmont students were English language learners last year, compared to 44 percent at American Indian (roughly equally split between Spanish and Cantonese native speakers). Unlike AIPCS's spartan facility, Piedmont has two computer labs, orchestra and band rooms, and provides electives in drama, filmmaking, and computer network management. In P.E. class, students can choose from rock-climbing, ultimate Frisbee, bocce ball, dance, and croquet. Nor does Piedmont lack qualified teachers. On average, they have taught at the school for 15 years, and 98 percent are fully credentialed. At AIPCS, teachers on average have two years of experience—and only 22 percent (i.e., two teachers) have full credentials.

The contrast between AIPCS's academic performance and that of other Oakland public schools is equally dramatic when the school's tests scores are compared to the four nearest comparable public schools in the area with reported data. Table 3-1 below shows the percentage of AIPCS seventh and eighth graders that were proficient on the California Standards Tests (CST), the chief determinant of a school's API (Academic Performance Index) score. The table provides both a sense of how poorly students perform in Oakland public schools generally and the vast gulf between AIPCS and its peers.

Are there hidden factors that might explain why American Indian students outscore students from nearby public schools by 50 percentage points or more? Certainly none that result from deliberate policy. Some local charter schools kick out problem students, and a few, like Mayor Jerry Brown's Oakland School for the Arts, screen applicants for talent or drive. Chavis does no screening of applicants, does not currently have a waiting list for applicants, and has never expelled a student—in fact, he takes a particular pride in taking

Table 3-1. Academic achievement at American Indian Public Charter School and nearby schools[14]

	Distance from AIPCS (miles)	2006–07 California Standards Tests (CST) • Percentage of Students Scoring Proficient or Advanced		
		8th grade English Language Arts	7th grade English Language Arts	7th grade Math
American Indian Public Charter School		87	96	98
Bret Harte Middle School	0.6	36	32	19
East Oakland Leadership Academy	1.6	15	5	10
Roosevelt Middle School	2.1	25	25	32
District Average (Oakland Unified)		24	29	23
State Average (California)		41	46	39

Source: California Department of Education, California Standardized Testing and Reporting (STAR) Program, http://star.cde.ca.gov/star2007/Viewreport.asp (accessed April 1, 2008).

Note: Eighth grade math scores are not reported because eighth graders may choose to take either an algebra test or a standard math test. Students at American Indian were more likely to take the former.

on tough cases, including students who have been on probation and come to schools with bracelets on their ankles.

Chavis reports that 7 percent of AIPCS pupils were special education students in 2006, a slightly lower proportion than at nearby Oakland public schools (8–12 percent). In seven years, Chavis has sought only once to enroll a student in a pull-out special ed program. AIPCS instead mainstreams special ed students and provides tutoring in reading and math for those who are below grade level. It is true that American Indian's classes are smaller than most Oakland schools, though the differences are not significant, except in eighth grade. (For the district as whole, the average class size is 27 students in sixth grade, 28 in seventh grade, and 26 in eighth grade. The corresponding numbers at AIPCS are 26 students per class in sixth grade, 23 in seventh, and 20 in eighth). Retention is not a problem at AIPCS and does not appear to figure prominently in the school's academic performance, though a small number of poorly performing students periodically leave the school of their own volition. According to Chavis, AIPCS loses about 10 students in a typical year, a 5 percent attrition rate. Most students who leave relocate out of the area, though a handful switches to less demanding schools. In the 2004–2005 school year (the last year with public data), not a single student dropped out of AIPCS.

As American Indian's academic reputation has spread, the school has attracted more low-income Asian students (who tend to enter AIPCS with higher scores on standardized tests) and proportionately fewer Native American students. In 2006, AIPCS had 29 Native American students, up from 23 in 2001, but the student body as a whole has grown from 27 to 181 students during the same time. The test scores of sixth graders today are significantly higher than when Chavis arrived, and some of this improvement may reflect the changing composition of the school. A third of AIPCS students are now Asian, and they scored a 945 on the API in 2006, helping to elevate the school's overall performance. Still, it is a testament to the school's ongoing impact that achievement levels rise substantially for all students as they move from sixth grade up through eighth no matter what level of skills they enter with. And it is also the case that few Asian students enrolled at AIPCS until after the school's API score had climbed past 800.

Not only Asian students excel at AIPCS; black, Hispanic, and Native American pupils all outstrip students at nearby schools. Some 83 percent of black seventh graders at AIPCS were proficient in English language arts in 2006, along with 91 percent of Latinos, and 94 percent of economically disadvantaged students (statewide, by contrast, just 41 percent of all students were proficient). The numbers for math are similar. By eighth grade, 92 percent of AIPCS black students, 91 percent of Hispanic students, and 90 percent of disadvantaged students were proficient on state tests. "We still have more Indian kids here than any school in the city, and the Indian kids here outperform the Indian kids in any school in the state," Chavis contends. In short, the American Indian Public Charter School has not just eliminated the achievement gap. It has also shown that a school composed of poor minority students can outperform their white, affluent peers.

The AIPCS Model

Ben Chavis's larger-than-life presence at American Indian makes it easy to overlook the fact that AIPCS has a distinctive educational model that is vital to its success. Like other paternalistic schools, it provides its pupils with extra instructional time during the school day and year, and it hews to a rigorous curriculum closely aligned with state standards. Yet unlike most no-excuses schools, American Indian has self-contained classrooms. Students do not rotate from teacher to teacher, as at most secondary schools. Instead, one instructor is responsible for teaching English language arts, math, history, and science to each class. In a practice known as "looping," teachers also remain with their classes from sixth grade until they leave AIPCS. Teachers new to the school thus usually start with sixth graders, and continue with their students until they graduate.

A visit to Isaac Berniker's seventh grade class in 2006 provided an illustration of the rigor of AIPCS curricula. Berniker, then a first-year teacher and Dartmouth grad with a degree in computer science, was teaching a class on Leonardo da Vinci. He and other teachers at American Indian follow carefully prescribed lesson plans, based on state-adopted textbooks. Teacher-directed instruction is typical, and on this particular afternoon, Berniker first asked students how da Vinci had used his scientific abilities to better humanity. A student pointed out that when da Vinci had studied the flow of water, he was thinking about how to use hydraulics for human benefit. Berniker noted that da Vinci had similarly studied a bird's flight to see if he could discern the dynamics of flight for humans.

Berniker next turned the discussion to da Vinci's painting, *"The Mona Lisa,"* and her iconic smile; why, he asked, was the painting famous? Because Mona Lisa's smile was enigmatic. Da Vinci had used a technique that made the viewer of the painting feel as though Mona Lisa's eyes were following them when they moved across the room. "Some day, when you go to Paris, I want you take a look at this painting," Berniker told his seventh graders. "It is in a museum called the Louvre." The room fell quiet, as students started to fill out a worksheet on da Vinci. Suddenly a puzzled student's hand shot up. "What's chiaroscuro?" she asked. Chiaroscuro, Berniker explained, was a technique in painting that alters light and shade to give a painting an illusion of depth. "The use of chiaroscuro contributes to Mona Lisa's elusive smile," Berniker added.

Berniker's class has none of the rowdiness commonly seen in middle school. Students don't speak unless they have been called on, and no one is whispering or giggling at the back of the room. No student is slumped over a desk. The seventh graders don't exactly sit upright with military rectitude, but their uniforms of white shirts and dark pants give the room a far more studious air than most middle school classrooms. None of the girls has on jewelry, make-up, or brightly colored hair ornaments. None of the boys sports baggy, drooping pants. The no-frills attire is matched by a no-frills schedule that allows extra time for English and math but only 20 minutes for lunch. "Mr. B's" seventh grade daily schedule, posted on the wall, reads as follows:

8:30–10:00: Language Arts
10:00–11:30: Pre-Algebra
11:30–12:00: Life Science
12:00–12:20: Reading
12:20–12:40: Lunch
12:40–1:25: History
1:30–2:10: PE
2:15–3:00: Elective

Students who aren't keeping up or who need extra help in English language arts or math have an even busier schedule. They receive two to four hours of additional instructional time each week at AIPCS, with two hours falling during PE classes and two hours with an after-school tutor. Saturday make-up classes and Mandarin classes plus three weeks of summer school create a powerful emphasis on academics.

The self-contained classroom and looping of teachers with their classes place a special burden on teachers. "It's a lot of work to be a teacher here," says Berniker. "Math was easy for me to teach. But then you have to teach science, history, and English, too, and you have to learn the curriculum all over again the next year." Yet Berniker notes that the self-contained classroom and the consistency of having the same teacher year after year also build a sense of class unity and extended family, turning each grade into its own little clan. On this particular day in March of 2006, Berniker had noted on the blackboard that his students had had 125 consecutive days of perfect attendance, a record in which his seventh graders took pride. One girl's parents had planned a trip around Christmas to visit relatives in Mexico that would have necessitated her missing class. But the girl said she "didn't want to let the class down." Working with the girl's grandmother, Chavis paid for the student to change the date of her plane ticket so she would not miss school. Berniker's class then went on to record 180 consecutive days of perfect attendance, an AIPCS record. To celebrate their achievement, Chavis arranged to have 10 billboards plastered around the city with a photo featuring the record-setting class. When the girl's grandmother passed away in February 2007, the student came to school anyway. "I am in school to honor my grandmother," she informed Chavis.

A perfect, or nearly flawless, attendance record can be surprisingly important to sustaining academic achievement. Leah Rose, a first-year sixth grade teacher in 2006 at AIPCS, had previously worked with foster youth and special ed kids at a number of Oakland schools. She found the comprehensive schools where she visited and worked to "be a disaster. There was no accountability—if a student missed a math class, the teacher just marked them down as tardy." From a teacher's perspective, she adds, "it makes a huge difference to always have the class present. You don't have to constantly retrace steps for kids who missed class."

As Berniker's and Rose's observations suggest, self-contained classroom and looping place a large premium on having first-rate teachers, lest students be stuck for three years with a lemon of an instructor. Here, too, Chavis' teacher recruitment strategies are somewhat unorthodox. He is no fan of ed schools and views a teaching credential as more of a minus than a plus for applicants because ed schools rarely attract top-caliber college students. Chavis believes instead in hiring the smartest young teachers without credentials that he can find, on the theory that a teacher who did well in school is likely to be a better teacher than a mediocre student with a teaching credential. The resumes of AIPCS's eight teachers of core subjects are, indeed, impressive, despite the fact that only one of them has a teaching credential. The 2005–2006 roster included three graduates from Wesleyan and one each from Harvard, Brown, Berkeley, Columbia, and Dartmouth.

Many AIPCS job applicants seek the school out precisely because Chavis does not require a teaching credential—and it doesn't hurt that Chavis offers novice teachers a starting salary in 2006–2007 of $44,000, roughly $7,000 more than they would get at Oakland's public noncharter schools. Chavis is constantly recruiting new teachers, partly because new teachers eventually decide to explore other careers or education jobs, and partly because when teachers finish cycling through a three-year commitment to teaching their class, some are not ready to make an extended commitment to a second time around. AIPCS teachers work hard, and Chavis can be an intense taskmaster. But unlike teachers at other paternalistic schools, such as KIPP, Chavis does not expect them to take phone calls at all hours from students who need help with their homework or home life.

The hiring of Jerry Mishkin illustrates Chavis's unorthodox recruitment methods. Mishkin, who served as on-site coordinator and acting principal for AIPCS in 2005–2006 when Chavis was busy opening AIPCS's high school classrooms, started off as a teacher at American Indian. At the tender age of 30 in 2006, he was already the old man of the teaching staff. Previously, after graduating from Duke summa cum laude with a degree in philosophy and working in Europe, Mishkin moved to San Francisco and started working for a tutoring program. "When I got out here," says Mishkin, "I went from public school to public school in San Francisco trying to talk to principals. And they would say, literally, 'I can't even talk to you until you have a teaching credential.' I had to teach at a charter school." So one day Mishkin came to a spring job fair and handed Chavis a resume. Chavis, Mishkin recalls, "barely looked at me. Then when I'm leaving, he comes running down the hall and hollers 'you went to Duke? I'm from North Carolina!' He says, 'I want you working here—you're smart.' That's how I got hired." Isaac Berniker's hire wasn't quite so speedy—he responded to Chavis's ad in Craigslist and stopped by Chavis's house for a real job interview. But like most charter schools, AIPCS does not have a union. Freed from the constraints of union hiring, Chavis can make a mistake and recover more quickly. At American Indian, teachers who fail to boost student achievement lose their jobs.

Expanding the Brand to High School

The latest chapter of the AIPCS story began to take shape in March 2007 when Chavis told the school's board that he intended to step down in July as principal to manage the expansion of the AIPCS model to other schools. During 2006–2007, Chavis had already opened the American Indian Public High School in several renovated rooms in an adjoining building, installing a former AIPCS teacher, Janet Shoeman, as the first principal. Starting out with 47 ninth graders and 20 tenth graders, the first-year achievement scores at Chavis's fledgling high school were every bit as extraordinary as those at his middle school. More than 70 percent of Chavis's high school students were Latino, American Indian, or black, and over 80 percent qualified for the federal subsidized lunch program. Yet on the California Standards Test (CST), American Indian Public High School was arguably the top performing high school in 2007 in the entire Bay Area, with AIPHS students doing as well as students at Lowell High, San Francisco's renowned selective high school.

Unlike AIPHS, Lowell High is a large and generously endowed exam school with six computer labs, 10 tennis courts, and a performing arts building with a 1,000-seat auditorium. Both *Newsweek* and *U.S. News* rank Lowell High as one of the top 100 high schools in the United States. Admission is based on standardized test scores, GPA, a writing sample, and extracurricular activities. Lowell's student body, unlike that of AIPHS, is two-thirds Asian. Only about a third of students are eligible to participate in free or reduced-price lunch.

In 2007, ninth and tenth graders at Lowell had higher English language arts scores than Chavis's ninth and tenth graders. But AIPHS's students outscored their peers at Lowell in world history, biology, and earth science, as well as math, once the more demanding nature of AIPHS's math program was taken into account. On average, more than 80 percent of AIPHS students had proficient or advanced skills in the seven subject areas tested by the state. Moreover, every single tenth grader passed the state graduation or exit exam on the first try, though half the tenth graders in Alameda County flunked it. "We were the only high school in the state where all the tenth graders passed on their first try," Chavis says with pride.

Ultimately, AIPHS students edged out Lowell for the highest API score in the Bay Area, totaling 940 to Lowell's 938.[15] In fact, among the 1,687 high schools in California, AIPHS had the fifth highest API score. Meanwhile, the middle school ranked tenth out of more than 1,200 middle schools.[16]

While Chavis was expanding AIPCS to a high school next door, he also received a charter to copy the American Indian model in a second middle school and high school in Oakland, both of which opened in 2007–2008. The two new schools are located at a modern, downtown facility, which Chavis has christened the Milton and Rose Friedman Campus, in honor of the famed libertarian economist and his wife, Chavis's friends. All told, Oakland schools using the American Indian model now enroll about 700 students. Chavis is the chief of educational programs at the umbrella organization overseeing the school expansion, tentatively titled CHESS.

Chavis formally stepped down as principal at AIPCS in July 2007 but not before setting off a new round of controversy. In March 2007, Sabrina Zirkel, a Mills College education professor and skeptic of Chavis's methods, brought a group of graduate students to American Indian to observe the middle school. One of the students, a 25-year-old African American named Unity Lewis, who taught in the Oakland public school system, arrived 15 minutes late bearing coffee. An angry confrontation with Chavis followed. Chavis yelled in Lewis's face, cursed him for being late and for reinforcing racial stereotypes, and called Lewis a "disgrace" to his race. Chavis later told the *Oakland Tribune* that Lewis has "acted like a fool" and had called Chavis a "homey."[17] Lewis initially refused to leave the school grounds, provoking a profanity-laced tirade from Chavis who said he would "kick [Lewis's] ass" if the graduate student didn't leave.

After the confrontation, Lewis wrote a letter of complaint to the Oakland Unified School District, which dispatched Kirsten Vital, the district's accountability chief, to visit the school in June 2007. In a letter the following month to AIPCS's governing board, Vital complained about, among other things, Chavis's repeated use of the words "whities and darkies" in front of students. Chavis defended his use of "darkies" to refer to black, Latinos, and Indians, saying that one of the students' slogans is "Darkies: smart and proud of it."[18] Chavis, however, did fine himself $700 for cursing Lewis out within earshot of students, a fine of $100 per class. But the controversy didn't end there. Local press coverage of Chavis's resignation as principal incorrectly reported that he was leaving American Indian behind and had moved back to Arizona to manage his real estate business and be near family. One such account in the *Oakland Tribune* with the erroneous headline "Charter's Notorious Chief Quits"[19] so annoyed Chavis, a Lumbee Indian, that he decided then and there to give himself the title "chief of educational programs" at the new organization overseeing the expansion of the American Indian model.

Chavis was succeeded as principal at AIPCS by Isaac Berniker, who believes in Chavis's educational model but lacks his fiery, finger-in-the-eye demeanor. Chavis, like the legendary principal Joe Clark, or perhaps like Indiana basketball coach Bobby Knight, achieved remarkable results at AIPCS and at AIPHS but not without thoroughly antagonizing the Oakland education establishment.

The Copycat Middle School

Chavis's combative and idiosyncratic persona makes it easy to dismiss American Indian's turnaround as a one-time fluke engineered by a charismatic principal. That conclusion would be a mistake. In fact, the second-highest performing middle school in the city of Oakland, Oakland Charter Academy (OCA), adopted Chavis's model in toto after principal Jorge Lopez did his graduate internship at AIPCS and became fast friends with Chavis. Like AIPCS, Oakland Charter Academy was, until a few years ago, a floundering multicultural school, founded and run by Mexican American parents who disapproved of Oakland's programs for English language learners. Unlike AIPCS, OCA provided bilingual education in Spanish, and virtually all of its 150 students were Hispanic. Lopez shares Ben Chavis's distaste for progressive education, multiculturalism, bilingual education, and parent-run schools. And like Chavis, he comes from humble roots. But Lopez does not share Chavis's penchant for the outrageous. He is a more understated provocateur.

Oakland Charter Academy was one of the first charter schools in Oakland, and at the time of its opening in 1993, it was hailed even by conservatives as an example of a charter school that was parent-driven and ready to buck the teachers union. Soon, though, the heavy emphasis on Spanish instruction and Mexican history proved a waste of instructional resources. The students were fluent in Spanish already—what they lacked was quality English instruction. The school's parental involvement requirement fizzled, too, except for a small group who micromanaged the school's affairs and a succession of principals.

When Lopez was hired as principal in June 2004, he says that only seven students out of 170 at the school were proficient in one subject area on state tests and hardly any were proficient in English. The school had four Spanish teachers, no English teachers, no library, and no English textbooks. Students rotated among portables to attend some classes, and the entryway hall was adorned with graffiti and holes. Lunch was served from a taco truck that pulled into the middle of the playground, rap music blasting away during a 55-minute lunch period. Not only had the school failed to make AYP, but it had excluded English language learners and special education students from testing to boost its mediocre test scores. Despite the school's poor performance and deteriorating facilities, staff development activities included boondoggles like an all-expense week-long retreat to a Napa winery.[20]

Just as Chavis had discovered school-sanctioned "bitch sessions" when he arrived at American Indian, Lopez found that students at OCA got to air their grievances to teachers during "community circle" class time. As he was readying to take over the school, Lopez sat in on a "70-minute-long community circle where a student said 'my dog didn't eat last night' and the teacher actually said 'let's talk about that'." In Lopez's view, the emphasis on bilingual education was particularly damaging to the students:

When I arrived at my charter school they didn't have any English textbooks. The former Oakland Charter staff said the kids couldn't read them because they were English-language learners. They used pamphlets from the Mexican consulate instead to teach American kids. The school essentially didn't have English Language Arts instruction. These immigrant students were already fluent in Spanish—many were more fluent than their teachers. But for Spanish class they would to go Starbucks to practice ordering in Spanish or watch "Shrek" in Spanish.

Like Chavis, Lopez scoffed at the notion that parental involvement was critical to a charter school for low-income Mexican students. OCA had required parents to put in 40 hours a year at the school, but most parents opted to pay the school $10 an hour for 40 hours in lieu of volunteering their time.[21] As a college undergraduate, Lopez had worked as a tutor in a Sacramento high school where the legendary high school calculus teacher Jaime Escalante, the subject of the film *Stand and Deliver*, taught. Escalante was a demanding dictator in his class and no democrat. For Lopez, the message of Escalante's pedagogy had been reinforced by his own upbringing. "My mom had four kids in three schools," Lopez says. "What was she supposed to do in terms of parental involvement? Should my mom have been expected to come in and make cookies for a bake sale?"

Shortly after arriving at OCA in the summer of 2004, Lopez decided to clean house. He fired all of the school's teachers and secretaries, prompting, he says, "nine lawsuits from fired employees" in 2005. When Lopez hired new teachers, he did not hire a single Spanish instructor. Lopez fired the janitor, too—and instituted a policy that the students would primarily be responsible for keeping the school clean. For the first time in the school's ten-year history, he opened a small library. Lopez knew the school administrators' joke about the surrounding Fruitvale neighborhood—that people would steal a computer but never steal a book. Lopez next ripped the school's computers out and gave them away to students. Lacking a gym, Lopez had students do wind sprints and run around the playground for P.E.; they learned that 19 laps equals a mile.

Ultimately, Lopez adopted AIPCS's curricular and teaching model in its entirety. First, Lopez purchased state-adopted textbooks that were aligned with state standards and made sure they formed the core of a prescribed curriculum with heavy emphasis on English language arts, math, and reading. Algebra I became a requirement for all eighth graders. He then created self-contained classrooms with no rotation from subject to subject in each grade; teachers would loop with their class through the entire three-year span of middle school. Like Chavis, he recruited teachers by posting want ads on Craigslist, hiring a series of instructors without full teaching credentials but from top-notch universities.

Lopez also instituted zero-tolerance disciplinary policies and a school uniform (white tops and khaki slacks) similar to American Indian's dress code. He insisted that all students attend three weeks of summer school and expanded instructional time during the day by cutting lunch back to 20 minutes and reducing electives. "I do one step for discipline that Ben doesn't do," says Lopez, with a grin. "Our students take turns with American Indian students on Saturday school for Mandarin classes or when they have to make up school work. But I've added Sunday school as well [for disciplinary infractions]. Sunday school is at my house. The kids come by and do yard work." Like Chavis, Lopez believes that his school should serve as a kind of extended family for low-income students.

Since Lopez became principal, the turnaround in performance by OCA students has been almost as dramatic as at American Indian. For the last two years, OCA has had the largest Academic Performance Index (API) gains in Oakland, raising its score from 650 in 2004 to 857 in 2006. The school's API scores are more than 100 points higher than four middle schools that all draw from the same predominantly Hispanic population and are located within a few blocks of OCA. In most head-to-head comparisons, OCA students are two to three times more likely to be proficient than low-income students at nearby neighborhood schools.

The API scores of OCA students also bested those of students from KIPP Bridge College Preparatory Academy by 110 points in 2006, despite the fact that former secretary of education Rod Paige singled out the KIPP school as one of the nation's "most amazing examples of how education and public schooling can work."[22] In 2007, OCAs score jumped an additional 40 points, to 896, enabling it to surpass Lincoln Middle School, the only nearby public school (in suburban Alameda) where students had previously outscored OCA students.

Just as important, the intensive English and math curriculum at OCA succeeded in dramatically boosting academic achievement among Hispanic students who were once thought to be unteachable English language learners.

In 2003, a mere 11 percent of eighth graders were proficient in English language arts and 9 percent in math, according to California's CST results. By 2006, 68 percent of eighth graders were proficient in English language arts and 66 percent in math. Like American Indian students, OCA students are qualifying for the first time for the Johns Hopkins summer programs for gifted students. In 2006, half of the 26 seventh and eighth graders tested for the Johns Hopkins program were accepted, as were six sixth graders. Pictures of the "Johns Hopkins Scholars" now adorn the entryway hall that not long ago was covered with graffiti and holes. Meanwhile, OCA's student body is still overwhelmingly Hispanic, and nearly 90 percent are poor enough to qualify for the federally subsidized lunch program. Just 1 to 2 percent of OCA students in 2006 were Asian—so the school's jump in academic achievement since 2004 cannot be attributed to an influx of high-scoring Asian students.

This year (2007–2008), Lopez has stepped down as principal of Oakland Charter Academy to serve as principal for two new schools, a middle school (American Indian Public Charter School II) and a high school (Oakland Charter Academy High School). Both will be housed downtown in American Indian's new Milton and Rose Friedman Campus, the expansion effort overseen by Ben Chavis. But over lunch with Chavis, prior to announcing his new appointments, Lopez said he expected to continue to make large test score gains at Oakland Charter Academy. He aimed to surpass not just Lincoln Middle School but Piedmont Middle School as well, for many years the highest performing school in the area. Unlike many principals, Lopez relishes competition. He has no qualms about focusing on raising test scores. "I'm shooting to beat Piedmont soon," Lopez said, before pausing. "And then I'm going to whup Ben's kids at American Indian, too." "I love it!" Chavis said with a laugh. "This guy wants to beat my school. Bring it on!"

Chapter Four

Who Are We, Proud to Be, Amistad Academy

I Don't Understand

I don't understand

Why we have homework

Why we have mean teachers

Why we have a lot of work

But most of all I don't understand

Why people are poor

Why kids play with guns

Why kids are in jail

What I understand most are:

Why I need an education

Why cows moo

Why kids scream

> —"Color Poem" by 10-year-old Aalihza, one of a dozen poems
> by fifth graders posted on a hallway bulletin board at Amistad Academy

I t's a late May morning, and all of Amistad Academy's 270 middle school students are sitting in chairs or milling around the edges of the school's basketball court, chatting with their classmates before the start of the 8:00 A.M. "Morning Circle." The 2005–2006 school year is almost over, and students are talking excitedly after having returned from class trips to Washington, D.C., Atlanta, and a camping excursion. But then the gym abruptly falls silent: Three student drummers have started thumping in time on large djembe drums, calling the morning circle to order. Students quietly stand and quickly fold up chairs and tables and stack them along the walls of the gym. Led by their teachers and school director Matt Taylor, the students then start to chant, sometimes with hand gestures or in a call-and-response format reminiscent of boot camp training:

People, people do you see?

Education is the key.

We work hard all day long.

Our REACH values make us strong.

Amistad reaching

Amistad achieving

Amistad succeeding!

Following the opening of morning circle, the school-wide meeting proceeds to recognize students who have distinguished themselves academically or shown outstanding character. Teachers step forward to acknowledge students, and the entire school cheers them with a series of chants, stomps, and claps. One student gets two hand claps, two foot stomps, and a round of hands raised to the roof. Another student gets a "home run"—the students collectively pretend to take a swing with a bat and click their tongues to simulate the noise of the bat hitting a home run. A third student gets the "roller coaster" recognition as the students go "woo-woo," simulating the wave of arms held aloft during an up-and-down roller coaster ride. Today, unlike some morning circles, no student has to step forward to apologize to the school community for his or her misbehavior. One enthused teacher even wants to recognize her whole sixth grade class for exemplary behavior on their trip. Students step forward to receive a school-wide salute, but school director Matt Taylor interrupts them.

"Hold it!" he calls out. "Let's do that again," he tells the class. "You didn't step forward clearly enough for your recognition." Finally, several chanters close the meeting with a quick call-and-response: "Who are We, Proud to Be?" And the roar comes back: "AMISTAD ACADEMY!"

Despite its multicultural trappings, Amistad's morning circle bears no resemblance to the talking circle "bitch sessions" that Ben Chavis did away with at American Indian Public Charter School. In fact, Amistad's morning circle is more like a Protestant-virtues pep rally than a multicultural celebration. All students singled out had distinguished themselves by hard work, citizenship, academic achievement, polite behavior, and other middle-class barometers of success. Much like the KIPP schools, Amistad Academy preaches the value of striving and moral character in sometimes unconventional ways. David Levin of KIPP describes the new paternalistic pedagogy practiced by KIPP and Amistad as "traditional education for the hip-hop generation."

By any measure, Amistad Academy is a remarkable success story; former Secretary of Education Rod Paige has called it "possibly the nation's best charter school." A little context helps explain his enthusiasm. New Haven's public schools are mostly forlorn institutions where half of all black students and two-thirds of Latino students drop out. During Amistad's first five years, parents deluged the school with applications — eight students for every available spot.

In 2007, Connecticut had the nation's largest achievement gap between rich and poor students[1] — white eighth graders outscored black students in the math NAEP by a staggering 38 points, and the gap was every bit as wide for Hispanic students.[2] Much the same educational chasm shows up on the state's CMT (Connecticut Mastery Test), a demanding, high-stakes test with open-ended writing and math questions. In 2006, 74 percent of white students in traditional public middle schools in Connecticut met state goals on the CMT — compared to a pitiful 30 percent of black students and 25 percent of Hispanic students.[3]

Amistad has succeeded in not only narrowing but eliminating the achievement gap. In 2007, 93 percent of its eighth graders were proficient in math on the CMT and 76 percent were proficient in reading, and 99 percent scored basic or above on the writing section of the test. Amistad students thus not only outperformed the average student in the state, they also did almost as well as the rich white kids from Greenwich and Madison. Amistad's students compiled this superior record despite being poor, black, and Hispanic—and despite having woefully inadequate skills when they entered in fifth grade.

Amistad Academy has no admissions standards and automatically enrolls all children who win spots in a lottery run by the New Haven public school system. Roughly two-thirds of its students are black, one-third Hispanic, and nearly 85 percent qualify for the free and reduced price lunch program. Three out of four come from single-parent households. When students arrive as fifth graders, the educational burden of poverty and family breakdown is painfully evident. A recent entering group of fifth graders scored on average at the 27th percentile in reading and the 25th percentile in math on nationally normed tests.

Yet once in the Amistad system, children make dramatic academic gains. In 2006, Amistad seventh graders had the largest single jump in academic performance of any of the 181 public middle schools in Connecticut with reported CMT scores; the percentage scoring within goal range jumped 20.4 percentage points from the end of sixth grade to the end of seventh.[4] And since the school opened in 1999, more than 40 of its students have won scholarships to elite prep schools like Taft, Choate Rosemary Hall, Hopkins, and Loomis Chafee. The current secretary of education, Margaret Spellings, has singled out Amistad as one of seven charter schools nationwide that is "dispelling the myth that some students cannot achieve to high standards." New York City school chancellor Joel Klein has enthusiastically embraced this education model, too, inviting Amistad's parent organization, Achievement First, to open a half-dozen schools in Brooklyn. Amistad's success, says Klein, "basically puts the lie to the excuse crowd."[5]

What explains the school's extraordinary record? In many ways, Amistad is much like other paternalistic schools, with extended instructional time, summer school, zero-tolerance discipline, uniforms, and an intense academic focus on a standards-based curriculum. But Amistad has also two distinctive features that help account for its success and differentiate it from more traditional institutions like American Indian Public Charter School. First, Amistad invests an enormous amount of time and effort in explicit character and values education. And second, Amistad employs distinctive instructional methods, including the use of mnemonics like chanting and clapping.

Amistad's beginnings were organic if a bit cerebral. In 1998, a 32-member committee composed of Yale law students, teachers, philanthropists, bankers, and parents seized on the achievement gap as the civil rights issue of the twenty-first century. Working from the premise that a first-rate school could close the achievement gap, a multiracial steering committee of five members helped Amistad's slate of cofounders raise funds and find a school site, an abandoned office equipment company which they purchased for $3.5 million. But repeatedly the idealistic founders heard the cautionary refrains from public school educators: "New Haven won't go for a young Yale law school graduate directing a local public school" and "Don't start with the middle school; it's the toughest nut to crack." Under the leadership of Dacia Toll and Doug McCurry, two Yale law school students, Amistad's founders plowed ahead undaunted.

Toll, now the president of Achievement First and Amistad Academy's director from 1999 to 2005, came by her can-do attitude early on and has never been much swayed by identity politics. Her father, a physics professor who served as president of the University of Maryland for a decade, counseled Toll to seek work that "has the greatest impact on people's lives." From the time Toll was at National Cathedral school in Washington, D.C., and through her Rhodes Scholarship and Yale law school years, she was active in community programs. While at the University of North Carolina at Chapel Hill, the 20-year-old Toll landed an internship with the Beethoven Project, a renowned preschool program in the Robert Taylor Homes in Chicago, perhaps the worst public housing project in the United States. Toll showed up on her first day, only to have the director come out to greet her and say "Oh, my God, it's a white woman." "They thought my name had sounded African American," Toll recalls. Toll was supposed to recruit families to enroll in Head Start programs but was informed that she couldn't go door-to-door in the projects. "Why not?" Toll asked. "You'll be killed," a staff member told her. Toll went anyway. As it turned out, drug dealers in the projects wanted to make sure Toll was not harmed since an attack on a white female college student would attract swarms of cops. "I came from a fairly privileged background," says Toll. "But I remember talking to someone at the time who said 'if you communicate your intentions, build relationships, and earn trust, it will work out'—and it did."

Toll took the same direct approach with disadvantaged black and Hispanic families at Amistad. During the first year of Amistad's operation, one of Toll's assignments was to visit some of the top-achieving urban schools in North America. "I just went around and found out what worked," says Toll. "My search wasn't terribly ideological." Everywhere Toll went, she cribbed shamelessly. From North Star Academy, an inner-city charter school in New-ark, New Jersey, Toll borrowed the concept of a school-wide morning circle. From Calgary Academy in Calgary—a successful private school for affluent white kids with learning differences—Toll adopted a modified version of the REACH behavioral rubric to promote character formation and boost academic achievement. (Indeed, in Amistad's first year, Calgary provided most of its teacher training.) From KIPP, Toll copied the use of mnemonic chants and claps, intensive teacher recruitment and selection strategies, and a number of disciplinary approaches. She is quick to credit others with educational innova-tions and continues to work closely with many of the schools she admires. "I've been to KIPP Academy in the Bronx probably 10 times," says Toll. Today, her work in helping build a coalition of like-minded schools has the potential to provide a kind of multiplier effect for paternalistic schools in the inner city. "We are part of what I call the 'no-excuses coalition,'" says Toll, a self-described "total liberal."[6] "Paternalism is such a loaded term," she adds. "But if you think that the job of education should be to create well-informed citizens, then skills and achievement are important but so are values. And I don't know how that became a bad thing. Teaching values is key to what we do at Amistad."

SLANT, REACH, Scholar Dollars, and Tipping Points

Amistad's values-and-character training is grounded firmly in James Q. Wilson's "broken windows" theory, the idea that if one broken window goes unfixed, more broken windows will soon follow. The key insight of broken-window theorists is that disorder, rather than violence or poverty per se, fatally undermines institutions like inner-city schools. A shirt left untucked leads more students to leave their shirts hanging out. The pupil who snickers at a teacher without serious consequence encourages other students to act disrespectfully. Noisy hallways and lunch rooms encourage rowdy behavior, cursing, and fights. Among other forms of training, Amistad teachers read a chapter on the broken windows theory in Malcolm Gladwell's book, *The Tipping Point*.

Amistad combats visible signs of disorder by scrupulously adhering to the motto "sweat the small stuff." Through a system of carrots and sticks, Amis-tad corrects students who act out and recognizes those who behave well. The indoctrination of students starts for fifth graders on the first day of school, when pupils must sign contracts agreeing that they will show up at school on time at 7:30 A.M., will complete their homework and reading every night, wear their uniform every day, will always make their best effort, will raise their hand to ask for help, and will live up to the school's REACH values (Respect, Enthusiasm, Achievement, Citizenship, and Hard Work). The contract is a tall order for most ten-year-olds, who often wonder when they arrive, as Aalihza does in the poem opening this chapter, why teachers at Amistad require so much homework and hard work and are so "mean."

As new students soon discover, the contract is only the beginning of an intense campaign to develop their knowledge, skills, and strength of character. Once inside the classroom, the students must learn a bevy of rules and procedures about how to record homework assignments, how to organize subject binders, how to participate in class, and how to pay attention to the instructor. Amistad teachers frequently tell students to "correct their SLANT"—an acronym borrowed from KIPP that stands for Sit Up. Listen. Ask and answer questions. Nod your head so people know you are listening and understanding. Track the speaker by keeping your eyes on whoever is talking. At the end of class, students line up quietly, in the same order, and proceed to the next class or to the lunchroom.

Students who fail to complete two homework assignments in one week usually end up in a two-hour detention session on Friday afternoon, during which they can finish their homework. More serious disciplinary infractions, like disrespecting a teacher or putting your hands on another student, earn suspensions. In such cases, students must not only apologize to their classmates but to the entire school for their behavior and often do some form of community service to compensate for their mistake. Suspensions are not rare at Amistad—school authorities handed out 41 in 2004–2005, roughly one for every seven students, though the number of suspensions declined appreciably thereafter. Students soon learn they have to constantly monitor their conduct in school and in the classroom. In numerous interviews, Amistad upperclassmen said that when they started in fifth grade they thought Amistad's many rules were "wack" and that REACH was "corny." Only after they had been at school for a year or two did they come to appreciate that the rules for student conduct created order and a sense of safety that they hadn't had at their previous schools.

What happens when a student is only mildly disruptive in class? Amistad still enforces a zero tolerance policy. Calling out in class, distracting other students, rolling your eyes at a teacher—all rather common occurrences in most middle school classrooms—result in students being sent to a "time out" desk or losing scholar dollars. During their stint at the time out desk, students have to review how their behavior fails to comply with the REACH values. And whether students are well behaved or not, every student—along with his or her teacher—fills out a REACH self-evaluation form every six weeks to keep tabs on each student's character development.

Like KIPP, Amistad's founders say their "culture revolves around the twin pillars of being nice and working hard," and teachers are encouraged to constantly "preach" these values to students. The REACH self-evaluation, which students use to grade their behavior for each component and sub-component on a scale of one to five, provides a sense of the Papa-does-Preach ethos of Amistad. In places, the REACH rubric reads like an inner-city Boy Scout manual:

Respect

—Treat Teachers Like PLATINUM: My teachers care about me and my future. I never talk back, roll my eyes, or suck my teeth. My teachers are here to help me be my best, so I treat them with TOTAL RESPECT.

—Be Nice: I treat my teammates as I wish to be treated. I never tease, laugh at, or put down others.

—Patience Pays: I raise my hand to speak during class. Calling out is disruptive.

—Keep It Clean: I keep my desk, my classroom, our bathrooms, and the rest of the school spotless. I pick up trash any time I see it.

Enthusiasm

—Jump to It: I follow all directions the first time.

—Focus: I commit two eyes, two ears, and one big brain to learning. I SLANT and participate actively in class.

—Bring an A+ Attitude: I'm excited to climb the mountain to college. I always bring a positive attitude. I never whine, pout, or act out when things don't go my way.

Achievement

—Top quality: I do my absolute best on all assignments. I never rush through my work. My homework and class work are always neat and complete.

—Achievement First: I am constantly mastering new standards. My grades and test scores show dramatic gains.

Citizenship

—No excuses: I take responsibility for my actions. I admit when I am wrong, and I apologize to the people I let down.

—Be Honest: I tell the truth at all times. I never lie.

—Help Others: I am part of the school's team and family. I celebrate the achievements of others and always look for ways to support my teammates.

Hard Work

—Bring My Tools: I come to class with all necessary materials. I come to school everyday, and I am never late. I wear my uniform properly at all times.

—Act like a college student today: Climbing the mountain to college is not easy. To get to college, I must do all my work and treat each class like a priceless gift.

The vast majority of students violate REACH values at some point during their years at Amistad. Lauren Okafor, one of the top students in her class, generally had a sterling record, but she found that Amistad really did "sweat the small stuff" when she started fifth grade. "I was overwhelmed when I got here," Okafor recalls from the vantage point of eighth grade. "I was like 'these people are not my mother!'" Okafor and a gaggle of girls tried to rebel one day in fifth grade, showing up at school with untucked shirts—only to be dragged promptly into the Dean of Students office and told to clean up their act. Okafor's elementary school had been untidy and allowed girls to be sloppily dressed and sport big hoop earrings. But at Amistad, she says, "they had a rule that your earrings could be no bigger than a quarter. And if the girls' bathroom was messy, they would pull us out of class to find out who made the mess—and have them clean it up."

Okafor soon learned not only that Amistad would monitor her behavior carefully but that the school would also insist that she publicly take responsibility for violating its values. The eighth-grade hallway has banners strung from the ceiling that say "No Excuses" and "MISTAKES: OWN THEM, FIX THEM"—and they're not there for show. The only time Okafor got suspended at Amistad was during fifth grade when she got into a fight with a seventh-grade boy after school. Okafor, a tall athlete and captain of the girls' basketball team, more than held her own in the fight with the older boy. But she was surprised at the time just how far the watchful eye of Amistad extended. During the bus ride home from school, the seventh grader had taunted Okafor, calling her mother "fat" and had sounded like he was using curse words to describe Okafor's mother. Understandably furious, Okafor got in a fight with the boy after she got off the school bus. But the bus driver halted the school bus, tried to break up the fight, and reported Okafor and the older student to the principal. "At my old [elementary] school, I don't think anyone would have done anything about seeing me get in a fight after I got off a school bus," says Okafor. "In my fourth-grade class, a boy brought a knife to school. The principal took it away from him — and sent him right back to class."

Amistad, however, didn't care that Okafor was defending her mother's honor at a healthy distance from school grounds. Toll suspended both Okafor and the seventh grader. Upon their return, both students had to stand up at morning circle and apologize to the entire school. Okafor went on to become an ace student and won a scholarship last year to the Hopkins School, an elite private academic powerhouse in New Haven. She says she's now even "pretty good friends" with her one-time seventh-grade tormenter. "I look back on what happened and think this wasn't doing anything for me," says Okafor. "If it wasn't for Amistad, I don't think I would be going to Hopkins."

Amistad does manage to soften the severity of its behavioral "sticks" by providing a wide range of "carrots." Toll and school director Matt Taylor believe in "recognition" incentives; to underscore the importance of character and citizenship, teachers regularly recognize students both for exemplary behavior and academic achievement. Like KIPP, Amistad has scholar dollars, a pseudo-paycheck that can rise or fall depending on a youngster's conduct and school performance that week. Students who accrue more scholar dollars win special privileges, like going on a field trip. Fifth graders with enough scholar dollars get to trade in their white Amistad tee-shirts for blue collared shirts, signifying that they are full-fledged members of the community. Older students can earn prized honors like the senior pin, for excelling in their conduct and citizenship. Academic performance, of course, is singled out for praise, too. Amistad had only eight straight A students in 2006. But these students, dubbed "Amistad Aces," all received special tee-shirts and had their pictures posted in the front hall to spotlight their achievements. Honor roll students, who earn all As and Bs, also receive special shirts. Some awards, like the Homework Champion Cup, are collective, going to the class with the highest homework completion rate.

The proliferation of awards and tee-shirts at Amistad might seem to cheapen their impact and run the risk of nurturing an exaggerated sense of self-esteem. But like Boy Scouts with merit badges, Amistad students remember their moments of recognition for years afterwards. Jose Torres, an eighth grader, says "my two proudest moments here were getting recognized for having one of the highest GPAs in sixth grade and getting my blue shirt in fifth grade the first time around. Most students don't get their blue shirts on their first try."

Perhaps the biggest incentive that Amistad offers students to work hard and do right is the promise of attending college. Amistad creates an unmistakable college-going culture from day one. Each class section is named after a college, and all students learn which year they are expected to graduate from a four-year college. When students are assembled to go to their next class, their teacher will call out "Tufts, line up!"—rather than "Mr. Sudmyer's class, line up!" The curriculum is unabashedly college-prep. College and university banners adorn the hallways, and eighth graders visit Washington College in Maryland for practice interviews in the admissions office. "When I arrived at Amistad in fifth grade," says Torres, "we talked right away about going to college. I had never heard anyone talk about me going to college—it encouraged me to think bigger and better."

Like Torres, fellow eighth grader Shamont Wright also started thinking about college because of Amistad. By his own admission, Wright was a disruptive student who was suspended frequently in elementary school. He earned three suspensions at Amistad during fifth grade alone—and reports that he entered Amistad performing at a third-grade level in reading and a second-grade level in math. In sixth grade, he continued to struggle academically, racking up a number of Cs and Fs. But in seventh and eighth grade, Wright began slowly to turn around. His teachers continued to ride him, and his mother warned him not to drop out of high school as his older brothers had. His father, who had remarried, told Wright that he was fortunate to be going to a good school and that "all these other kids are ending up in jail." Wright formed a rap group with two Amistad classmates and started writing songs about staying positive with titles like "We All in the Game." He started earning better grades, too, Bs, Cs, and even an occasional A. In eighth grade, he tested at a tenth-grade level in reading and writing, and he has raised his once-feeble math skills to grade level. "The happiest day of my life was in seventh grade when I got a 95 percent on my textual analysis on the [year-end] CBM, the practice test for the CMT," says Wright. "It would be good for me to go college...A lot of kids want to be gangsta and they say school is wack. But they don't think about the prospect that in ten years they'll be in prison."

Wright's elation at doing well on his end-of-year exam echoed sentiments expressed by other Amistad students who had initially disliked the school's strict rules and heavy homework loads. After a couple of years at Amistad, the vast majority of students buy into the school's system of high expectations, support, and accountability. Slowly, like Wright, they even become excited and proud of doing well academically. The average daily attendance at Amistad hovers around 98 percent. And excelling is cool, instead of a lonely pastime for nerdy eggheads. "The high expectations, rules, procedures, and apologies only work in a culture where kids know unambiguously that you care about them and want them to succeed," says Dacia Toll. "Kids have to really love coming to school," she adds. "Instruction has to be fun and engaging, and teachers have to have meaningful relationships with students and their parents. We call all of this 'the J-factor'—short for Joy Factor."

In fact, the J-factor—and the strong academic commitment of both students and teachers—is evident to visitors as soon as they enter the school. When Connecticut Governor M. Jodi Rell visited Amistad in September 2006, she marveled at the can-do attitude of the students. "I have never been in a school," Rell declared, "where there has been so much enthusiasm."[7] One consultant who works for an education venture capital firm was so moved by a recent visit to Amistad that she repaired to the bathroom at the end of the day—to weep in private.

Amistad Pedagogy: Rap, Rhythm, Rhyme, and Rigor

School director Matt Taylor started out at Amistad by teaching language arts and science in seventh and eighth grade. He recalls clearly the first time he walked into the school in 2003. Taylor, a magna cum laude graduate of Carleton College with a master's degree from the Harvard School of Education, was already a veteran teacher with stints in Boston and Miami. But at Taylor's previous schools, teachers expected a handful of students to go on to college and rejoiced when they reached just one student. Amistad, he says, "was the first school I had ever been in where it was not okay to have four of five kids in a class completely fail. Amistad works in the end because of the high expectations. The teachers here truly believe that every kid can go on to college."

While school culture plays a crucial role in Amistad's success, the school's novel instructional techniques are also critical. Borrowing liberally from KIPP and the Calgary Academy, Amistad has helped pioneer an unorthodox style of pedagogy that combines traditional curriculum with multi-modal mnemonic learning devices, like rap, rhythm, and rhyme. Particularly in lower grades, Amistad and other Achievement First schools use well-known, standards-based curricula, such as Direct Instruction, Saxon Math, Scholastic Guided Reading, Waterford Early Reading, and Core Knowledge materials. But teachers supplement the traditional course content by using claps, hand signals, countdowns, timers, chants, and songs.

In the space of a single sixth-grade social studies class last May, the teacher sent a restless student out into the hall to count to 50, told students to count down from 10 before handing back papers to each other for peer review, and gave a three-second countdown before students had to fall silent. Each class follows a general daily lesson format that starts with "quick questions" — usually easy questions that most students can answer, building confidence at the start of class. From there, the teacher lays out the aim and agenda for that day — and then moves rapidly back and forth between a series of different instructional techniques. Teaching at Amistad, in short, requires a good deal of nimbleness on the part of instructors. At prescribed points during the class, the teacher will use call-and-response exercises, have students read aloud, show a short video, or use other teaching techniques to engage students who tune out traditional instruction, such as teacher-led discussion with textbook, paper, and a blackboard.

One day in Joshua Sloat's fifth-grade English class, Sloat was diagramming sentences, asking the 11-year-olds to explain both the difference between helping verbs and linking verbs and to identify appositive phrases. Unlike at some inner-city schools, Amistad does not assume that students will largely intuit grammar or pick it up by ear. "How can you tell what a helping verb is?" Sloat asked the class. A helping verb "helps" another verb, Sloat explained — in the sentence "He was trying to remember," the word "was" is a helping verb. Next, Sloat had the class diagram a sentence from the book *Because of Winn Dixie.* He clapped five times and told them they had done "a good job" in deconstructing the grammatical elements of the sentence. The students promptly clapped back twice, unbidden. Sloat then made students take the lead. "What's an appositive phrase?" Sloat asked. A series of hands shot up. "It's an AKA phrase," a boy explained. Sloat smiled. "That's exactly right. One quick way to look for appositive phrases is to see if they mean 'also known as'."

Amistad adopted the use of countdowns, timers, clapping, rhythm, and rapping largely from the work of Harriett Ball, a legendary African-American teacher in Houston. David Levin and Michael Feinberg first studied Ball's teaching methods before copying them in KIPP classrooms, from which they have spread to Amistad. A typical motivational chant used in lower grades, first by Ball and now at Amistad, is a song called "Read Baby Read," replete with student hand motions and movement. The lyrics go:

Read, Baby, Read

[Stomps and Claps—4X].

You've got to Read, Baby, Read.

(Say What?)

You've got to Read, Baby, Read

The more I read, the more I know

The more I know, the more I grow

The more I talk, the less I know

Because knowledge is POWER

and POWER helps others

And I want to…Umph!

You've got to Read, Baby, Read

You've got to read!

The periodic use of rhymes and rap makes class far more entertaining for students, which is not altogether surprising given the soporific prose of most modern textbooks. But since mnemonic learning devices are only used intermittently, classes can still be academically rigorous. In Tamara Orput's fifth-grade literature class, Orput led a discussion of *Leon's Story,* a book about a black man born in 1936 who grew up in North Carolina under Jim Crow laws with a father who was a sharecropper. Orput took turns going around the room asking students to read parts of two paragraphs out loud. Then she asked students to characterize the tone of the writing. That question might have provoked puzzled stares in many fifth-grade urban classrooms, but in Orput's class, a half-dozen hands went up. One girl pointed out that the author of *Leon's Story* had used the word "whatever"—thereby suggesting that the author was adopting a casual or conversational tone with the reader. Why, Orput wanted to know, was it hard for the sharecroppers to keep track of their expenses at the store? Because, a student noted, many blacks then didn't know how to read or write—white overseers deliberately restricted their access to education. The theme of Orput's lesson—that getting a good education is invaluable—was not lost on her fifth graders.

Upstairs, in Jeff Sudmyer's eighth-grade history class, Sudmyer had tasked the class with evaluating the question "was Teddy Roosevelt actually a progressive?" Most textbooks simply presume that Roosevelt was a progressive. But Sudmyer's question forced the students to grapple with the historical meaning of being "progressive." After some teacher-guided discussion, the class settled on the idea that being progressive in Roosevelt's day meant using the government to benefit the "little people." The class then had a surprisingly spirited debate about whether Roosevelt's policy of establishing new national parks was progressive or not. A couple of students pointed out that setting aside land for new parks might reduce the number of jobs available to local residents. Other students countered that everyone from kids to the elderly could enjoy parks.

In fifth and sixth grade, Amistad groups students according to four skill levels, though such groupings fade out by eighth grade. Most students are a couple of years behind grade level when they arrive, and Amistad has found that they can catch up faster with more intensive, skill-appropriate instruction. However, Amistad's skill groupings differ from traditional tracking. Teachers do not have lower expectations or provide less attention to students with weaker skills. In fact, Amistad assigns its most talented and experienced teachers to the lowest skill groups, reversing the pecking order of teacher assignments at most urban public schools. Struggling youngsters gets lots of individualized help in before- and after-school tutoring sessions, Saturday classes, or during the three-week summer school session. Amistad even has a specifically designated group of teachers known simply as the "Whatever It Takes Team" to help struggling readers.

Since 98 percent of the students are black or Hispanic, skill groupings at the school do not have the same political freight that tracking minority students might have in a predominantly white school. "I'm not naïve about the fact that because we have almost no white kids we can do certain things that a magnet school might not be able to do," offers Dacia Toll. "We are able to do these skill groupings in a way that is depoliticized—the lowest-skill group has Black and Latino students—but so does the highest-skill group."

The second distinctive aspect of instruction at Amistad is the use of interim student assessments every six weeks—a testing model that was loosely inspired by Wendy Kopp, founder of Teach for America. At many inner-city schools, students take tests infrequently, or they may only be tested at year's end. At Amistad, learning is automatically assessed every six weeks to see whether students are mastering essential material and prepared for the state's year-end CMT test. The school has a structured process for analyzing the results of the year's five interim assessments. Teachers must both brief the principal on the status of each student in each subject every six weeks and use the data to re-teach problem concepts and/or target specific students for extra tutoring and support. For example, Matt Taylor learned from an interim assessment that 72 percent of his seventh-grade language arts pupils didn't know how to write a summary according to the state's seventh-grade standard. He had to go back and teach the unit on writing a summary a second time.

The youthful teachers at Amistad face frequent assessments of their own. Teaching here is not for the thin-skinned. Master teachers frequently drift in and out of class to observe their less experienced colleagues in action and critique their performance afterwards. Twice a year, each teacher undergoes a comprehensive evaluation. And unlike at traditional public schools, the most important factor in the evaluations is whether teachers are substantially raising student achievement. This ethic of accountability creates an intellectual restlessness at Amistad that prevents students and teachers from resting on their laurels. As Taylor describes it, "we have a culture of overachievers here and of never being satisfied with our accomplishments."

Amistad shares several features with other paternalistic, inner-city schools, including an extended school day and year. The school day essentially runs from 8:00 A.M. until 5:00 P.M., about two hours longer than normal, with a 20-minute break for lunch, short P.E. classes, and an art/music special period. The bulk of athletic and extracurricular arts activities (like orchestra practice) are reserved for the required after-school "Encore" program from 3:50 to 5:00 P.M. This longer day enables Amistad to schedule students for two reading and writing classes and an extended math class every day, allowing students to spend a total of three-and-a-half hours a day on reading, writing, and math. At night, all students have homework that includes independent reading. "I tell students that one day here is like three days in a typical school," says Taylor. The school's three-week mandatory summer program is also designed to accelerate learning (rather than remediate failing students). It effectively expands the school year from the national norm of 182 instructional days to 197.

Not surprisingly, Amistad's instructional techniques place a huge premium on hiring outstanding teachers. "If you teach here, it's a lifestyle," says Taylor. "It's more time, it's some time on the weekends, and you have to have an extremely high commitment to the kids." Early on, says Dacia Toll, Amistad's founders recognized that "teacher quality is the most important variable in student achievement" and mounted an unusually ambitious effort to recruit teachers. Achievement First (AF) dedicates two full-time staff members to recruiting teachers for AF's New Haven schools. To compensate teachers for extra hours on the job, Amistad pays instructors about 10 percent more than their peers in New Haven public schools. They also can earn a $1,500 attendance bonus if they are present every day, with pro-rata reductions based on the number of days they are out.

Under state law, teachers at Amistad have to be certified. But they are not unionized, which has allowed school administrators to recruit promising individuals outside of conventional district channels. Teach for America graduates have been a prime target. Toll, who oversaw the hiring of teachers for Achievement First's new schools in Brooklyn, says that when she went to talk to school principals in the borough she would invariably ask them "how do you hire your teachers?" The answer that usually came back was "I have to hire whomever the central office sends me." By contrast, says Toll, "50 percent of the teachers we hired in New York City were Teach for America alumni."

Amistad has wide leeway to screen and hire bright and committed teachers and has made it a priority to find teachers with a personal commitment to closing the achievement gap. Potential teachers write six short essays about their teaching philosophy and how they would handle hypothetical classroom situations. If they pass the initial screening, they are invited to guest teach a class and receive feedback afterwards. The competition for teaching jobs can be fierce—Achievement First picks fewer than one in ten applicants for teaching and leadership positions. When Amistad identifies a promising rookie teacher, the school will put him or her through a two-year professional development program to accelerate that teacher's learning. Still, unlike American Indian Public Charter School, which often recruits inexperienced and uncertified teachers, 85 percent of teachers at Amistad have more than two years of teaching experience, and roughly four in five classes at Amistad are taught by a "highly qualified" teacher, according to federal criteria.[8]

Student Achievement

By the time students reach eighth grade at Amistad, they have eliminated the achievement gap between minority students and white students. At the same time, they have opened up an even wider achievement gap between themselves and their black and Hispanics peers in New Haven's public schools. Table 4-1 below, comparing the proficiency levels of Amistad eighth graders on the CMT to students from nearby schools, gives a sense of the gulf.

Table 4-1. Academic achievement at Amistad Academy and nearby schools[9]

		2006-07 Connecticut Mastery Test (CMT) • Percentage of students scoring Proficient or Higher	
	Distance from Amistad (miles)	8th grade Reading	8th grade Math
Amistad Academy		**76**	**93**
East Rock Global Studies Magnet	0.4	56	59
John S. Martinez School	0.6	39	42
Fair Haven Middle School	0.7	23	35
Troup Magnet Academy of Science	2.0	68	73
Clemente Leadership Academy	2.1	34	48
King/Robinson Magnet School	2.2	42	42
District Average (New Haven)		47	55
State Average (Connecticut)		76	81

Source: Connecticut State Department of Education, CMT Assessment Data website, Performance Level Summary, http://www.cmtreports.com/CMTCode/chartselections.aspx (accessed April 1, 2008).

It is hard to explain away this huge gap in academic achievement by rounding up the usual suspects. Compared to students elsewhere in the New Haven school system, Amistad students are actually somewhat *more* likely to be black and Hispanic and eligible for the free lunch program. Smaller class size and teacher experience do not account for Amistad's performance either. Amistad had slightly more students per full-time equivalent (FTE) teacher (19) than the rest of the nearby comparison schools (which averaged about 15 pupils per FTE teacher). At the seven schools, teachers generally had comparable levels of experience.

Nor can Amistad's stellar performance be explained by a subtle shift in the school's population toward ethnic groups that tend to have higher test scores. Amistad has no Asian students and just eight non-Hispanic white students out of 270 pupils. Only 3 percent of Amistad students are white, compared to 11 percent of students in New Haven public schools. Within Amistad itself, Hispanic students have slightly higher average CMT scores than black students.

From the start, Amistad has made a deliberate effort to avoid being selective. It has no admissions standards and does not screen prospective applicants or expel bad students. The lottery to select incoming Amistad students is run by the New Haven school system. "When we were setting up Amistad," says Dacia Toll, "we said we wanted to be part of school reform for all of New Haven and not just for a few students. One way to make yourself irrelevant in that discussion is to skim or cream." Toll says that about "8 percent of our kids walking in the door have an IEP [Individual Education Plan for special ed students]. We also have a full-time director of special ed." During their time at Amistad, some students make such significant gains that they no longer qualify for special education, lowering the school's overall percentage of special needs students to about 3 percent. Over eight years, Amistad has expelled only two students; one was expelled for a year for bringing marijuana to the school, and the second was suspended for three months for aggressive behavior. Both students returned to Amistad with markedly improved behavior.

As Amistad's reputation for excellence has spread, the skills of entering fifth-grade students have risen slightly, suggesting that more talented students are entering the lottery. Nonetheless, once students arrive they still demonstrate dramatic gains in achievement. This ongoing and dramatic "value added" bump in student performance from sixth to seventh grade undermines the claim that Amistad's high test scores stem from creaming rather than the education the school provides.

Might Amistad students do well because the school has extra resources? Not really. The facility that Amistad purchased and renovated is a cheerful, modern building with adequate space for the middle school and a modest set of offices for Achievement First staff. Compared to the rundown American Indian Public Charter School, it looks like a palace, with a full-sized gym and a space for orchestra rehearsal. Still, the school lacks the spacious library, technology labs, and athletic fields typical of many middle schools. (Toll notes that the roughly $4 million Amistad spent to purchase and renovate the facility is a modest sum for a new school.) Amistad also spends less per student than traditional public schools in New Haven. State law limits the amount that charters can receive from the state to $8,650 per pupil while New Haven public schools receive roughly $11,850 per student in state and municipal operating funds. Amistad raises about $3,000 per student in private funds, bringing its total expenditure per student to around $11,700 per student. "In no situation," says Toll, "would we want to spend more than the New Haven public schools."

Some left-leaning skeptics of no-excuses schools have suggested that student achievement is elevated at institutions like Amistad because the schools attract unusually motivated parents. But since nearly 80 percent of Amistad students come from single-parent families, it is unlikely that large differences in family structure exist between Amistad students and nearby schools.

Still, Amistad students may benefit from more parental attention than students at nearby middle schools. More than most no-excuses schools, Amistad goes to some lengths to keep parents informed about their child's progress. Every Monday, students bring home their scholar dollar paycheck, which provides detailed information about a student's behavior, attendance, and school work. Each Wednesday, parents receive a school-wide update about upcoming events and schedule changes. And each month, the school requires parents to sign their child's REACH evaluation form, completed by both teachers and students.

Amistad does ask parents to sign a non-enforceable pledge agreeing to get their children to school on time (by 7:30 A.M.) dressed in the school uniform, to provide a quiet space for their child to study, to check homework, and to ensure that the child reads independently every evening. Each day, parents are supposed to sign their children's reading log, indicating that they did their required independent reading. If the school calls home about a student, parents are to make every effort to return the phone call within 24 hours.

These parent involvement provisions are not especially onerous—and have been scaled back from Amistad's initial contracts. Originally, Amistad also asked parents to contribute 10 hours of volunteer time to the school during the course of the year. But that requirement, says Toll, "proved a distraction for parents and keeping track of the ten hours was a nightmare for us. We realized we were creating makework and that the volunteer requirement had become silly."

More troubling to Toll was that relatively few parents were actively involved in the school—and a significant number failed to abide by the letter of the parent contract:

> I'd say that ten or fifteen percent of the parents, roughly 30 parents, would do anything for their kids and the school, and they totally get what the school is doing. They tell their kids "no, you cannot skip your reading tonight." These are the 30 parents who show up at a Parent Leadership Council meeting. On the other extreme, about five percent of the parents seem like they are actively undermining us. They think the day is too long. They lie on the reading log when they are asked to sign it when their child hasn't done the reading. They tell their kids to hit another kid if they disagree with them.

Between those poles, the vast majority of parents, Toll says, "believe that education is valuable and a path to college. But the attention to detail and follow through is not always manifested at home. I suspect that in 60 percent of our households, the kid is running out the door in the morning and says 'Mom, Mom, sign this'—and the parent doesn't really know whether the child has done their reading or not."

The disengagement of a significant number of parents from their child's education also shows up in the casual attitudes that some parents take toward attendance. Overall, Amistad has an excellent attendance record, but school administrators and teachers have to devote considerable effort to promoting the importance of attendance and punctuality. When students had mediocre attendance records, Toll used to give them an alarm clock or send a taxi to pick them up. "I have had unbelievable conversations with parents about attendance," says Toll. "A lot of kids struggle with asthma. But you have to figure out a way to make sure they show up at school regularly—you get them inhalers; you take them to the doctor to figure out a way that the child can manage the asthma. They can't miss 10 days of school." Toll added, "Don't even get me started on the menstrual cramps. I had one student who missed a couple of days a month for menstrual cramps—and her mother and I really fought about it. A pattern of attendance like that will really hold that young lady back in life."

One of Toll's biggest concerns about disengaged parents was the damage they could do to a student after the student graduated from Amistad and moved on to less-structured settings with fewer adult mentors. High school students tend to be more affected by street culture than middle schoolers, but high schools lack Amistad's paternalistic support system. To cite one example, Amistad's advisory system requires that a class of 22 to 27 students be co-advised by two teachers. These co-advisors, according to Achievement First's website, "serve in loco parentis while the students are at school, and they work hard to develop meaningful relationships with all the students in their advisory." After students are cut adrift from that support network, Toll has seen a number of promising graduates founder. "The parents," she has found, "wouldn't ask the kid to live up to their potential. And that was heartbreaking to watch."

Replication and Follow Up

Toll, Doug McCurry, and other founders of Amistad Academy intended from the start that the school would be a prototype that could be replicated elsewhere so as to have a broad impact on school reform. In June 2003, Amistad created Achievement First, a nonprofit organization that is responsible for spreading the school's gospel and for overseeing the opening of new Achievement First schools in New Haven and Brooklyn. In 2007–2008, Achievement First operated a total of 12 academies, half in New Haven and half in Brooklyn, with a population of more than 1,800 students. Over the next five years, AF plans to open 17 additional small college preparatory academies in New Haven, Bridgeport, Hartford, and Brooklyn, ultimately serving some 9,000 students. So far, AF has focused on opening middle schools (in 2008, AF operated six) and elementary schools (opening five to date).

AF currently operates only one high school, which currently consists of 96 ninth and tenth grade students. However, by 2014, AF expects to be running six high schools (three in Brooklyn, and one each in New Haven, Bridgeport, and Hartford). Essentially, AF has opted for a geographical cluster model, where each cluster will have two elementary and two middle schools feeding into one high school. A decade from now, when all 30 academies are at full capacity, AF expects to serve over 11,000 students.

The first AF academies to open after Amistad were the Elm City College Preparatory middle and elementary schools in New Haven, both of which started in 2004. In their first two years, they have already compiled a remarkable record of academic achievement. At the start of the 2004–2005 school year, 26 percent of kindergarteners and first graders at Elm City elementary read at or above grade level on the Developmental Reading Assessment, Connecticut's early reading test. By the end of the year, 96 percent were at or above grade level—and the proportion demonstrating advanced reading skills had gone from 1 percent to 56 percent.

Students at Elm City middle school made just as rapid progress—despite the fact that the school is also 99 percent black and Hispanic, close to 80 percent of its students are economically disadvantaged, and most are two grades behind when they enter Elm City. When Elm City students started fifth grade in 2004, just 18 percent had reading skills at or above grade level on the DRP (Degrees of Reading Power) test, a nationally normed reading assessment. At year's end, 56 percent of fifth graders read at grade level. By the time black and Hispanic Elm City students complete sixth grade, they have eliminated the achievement gap altogether, surpassing state averages in all three subjects on the CMT (reading, writing, and math.). In fact, Elm City middle school had the highest sixth grade CMT scores of any predominantly African-American Connecticut public school—and Elm City sixth graders did better on the math portion of the CMT than students in the affluent Greenwich, Madison, and Woodbridge districts.

It is still too early to assess definitively the three AF charter schools that opened in Brooklyn in the fall of 2005. Even so, the first-year results are striking. At the AF Crown Heights Charter Elementary School and the AF East New York Charter School, the percentage of elementary pupils reading at the proficient level doubled, from 43 to 87 percent, and the percentage of proficient math students in first grade jumped nearly five-fold. The one-year leap in achievement at the AF Crown Heights Middle Academy followed the same pattern. Fifth graders read at the 19th percentile on the DRP when they entered. By year's end, their reading scores as a group had jumped to the 47th percentile. In math, the Crown Heights fifth graders made an astonishing one-year jump, going from the 12th percentile on the Stanford 9 in September to the 58th at the year's end.

At each of its new schools, Achievement First seeks to replicate the essential practices of Amistad while leaving room for innovation and refinement of the basic model. A core premise of the replication effort is that it should *not* depend on hiring heroic, charismatic principals but rather that "mere mortals" can successfully eliminate the achievement gap using the Amistad model.

Unlike some urban school reform initiatives, Achievement First's replication efforts are largely centralized in the nonprofit organization's home offices in Brooklyn and New Haven. The AF central office has the lead responsibility for new school startup, developing the interim assessment system, recruiting teachers, establishing a school-wide intranet for AF curricula and documents, financing and renovating school facilities, setting up the budgeting system, and a dozen other critical administrative support functions. Assigning business and operational decision making to an on-site school manager and the central office is intended to free up the principal to focus on instructional leadership and eliminating the achievement gap.

Achievement First is unmistakably a child of the standards movement, and it clearly specifies its goals and outcomes for evaluating principals, teachers, and schools. AF's ultimate "outcome metric" is simple: college graduation. But Achievement First expects every AF school to close the achievement gap rather than narrow it. At minimum, AF expects all its schools to produce test scores that surpass the averages for full-price lunch students (which are higher than statewide averages) as well as "student achievement [gains] that increase at least five national percentiles (e.g., from 65th to 70th) in every subject at every grade level each school year." Achievement First plans as well to evaluate the performance of principals and schools each year in finely tuned "report cards" that calibrate student achievement by grade level. After one year at an AF school, at least half the students are expected to be proficient on the state assessment in all subject areas. After two and three years, the benchmark is raised; by the fourth year of an AF school, at least 95 percent of all students are to be proficient in all subject areas on state tests.

In addition, AF schools are supposed to meet demanding criteria that prevent schools from creaming more talented students or shedding less talented ones. AF schools, for example, are expected to keep student attrition to less than 5 percent a year (not counting youngsters who move out of the district), and generally to mirror the local population of disadvantaged students. At least 70 percent must qualify for the free and reduced lunch program. At the same time, AF schools can have no more than a 7 percent variance between their student body and the local district public school population in terms of minority representation, ELL, and special education participation.

In many schools, these performance benchmarks would sound hopelessly Pollyannaish. But they are benchmarks that Amistad is already well on its way to achieving. Now in its ninth year of operation, Amistad Academy finally has the luxury of fine-tuning parts of its program. Toll and Taylor believe the school faces two related problems that were not readily apparent in the early years. They are both concerned about what happens to students after they graduate from Amistad—particularly when they go on to New Haven public schools. Toll and Taylor feel that Amistad needs to track its graduates better to see what kind of academic problems they encounter after Amistad and to see if there is anything that Amistad can do to promote greater academic resilience among students. Toll explains that

> One-third of our eighth graders have gone on to private school and are gener-
> ally doing well. That said, it is telling that every single one of the kids who
> went to private school and came back to talk to our students here said that at
> some point they were called a racial slur or made in some other way to stick out
> at their private school. Of the two-thirds of students who are back in public
> school, half are doing "well" but the level of academic expectation in those
> schools is pitiful. The other half of public school students are getting caught
> up in the environments of New Haven high schools. So far, only two of our
> students have dropped out of school and gotten a GED. But more students
> have struggled in one way or another.

Taylor echoed Toll, saying that "most of our alumni are doing pretty well. But some students leave here getting As and Bs and then start getting Cs, Ds, and Fs in the traditional public schools. They don't have the strength of character to not emulate their peers."

For the most part, Amistad has found that the alumni most likely to backslide tend to be black males. That fact has stimulated more interest on the part of Amistad's African-American male staff in encouraging parental involvement, especially on the part of fathers, and a new effort to nurture a more positive middle-class identity among black males at the school. In 2006, Amistad sponsored its first Boys Night Out event with fathers, big brothers, pastors, and other male role models, as well as its first Latino Parent Night in Spanish. School officials expected that perhaps 25 parents would show up for Boys Night Out but were surprised when 100 people attended. The event opened with a half hour of sports in the gym — followed by dinner and a candid discussion of why the girls did better in school at Amistad than the boys. Fathers are still too often an erratic presence in the lives of their sons at Amistad. Yet the school recognizes the important role that the good-enough father fills for adolescent black males. "We've learned over the years," says Taylor, "that if the partnership is not there with the parents, it's really hard to reach the more difficult students.

Chapter Five

Cristo Rey Jesuit High School—
The School That Works

"I will now write about two days ago when the sun was glowing and the humidity was strong enough to make anyone feel as if they had asthma. It was also a fine day for a miracle. To my doggy it was going to be a day of extreme pain but also of extreme relief…My dog had puppies, seven little ones, but to our misfortune one of them came out lifeless…The ones that survived are so funny-looking: Though they are small, they look like baby rats…The [puppies] look just like their mom—white, small, good-smelling, and full of life. They're three days old now, and their eyes are just beginning to open."

—From Sergio Garcia's ninth-grade English journal, March 30, 2001

One September afternoon in 2003, a group of seniors from Cristo Rey Jesuit High School in Chicago piled out of their family cars at a cemetery to celebrate Sergio Garcia's eighteenth birthday. As Latin music played through an open car window, the students quietly assembled by Sergio's grave, Winnie the Pooh balloons in hand, to sing "Happy Birthday" in Spanish and English. It seemed so strange that it was Sergio who was gone. Unlike the inquisitive puppies he had once admired, Sergio's youthful eyes would never open again. Garcia, a lanky, easygoing adolescent, was smart and had a quirky sense of humor that endeared

122

him to his fellow classmates. He loved to watch both the History Channel and *The Simpsons* and had soaked up J. D. Salinger's classic, *The Catcher in the Rye*. Garcia had a knack for the English language, too, that eluded most of his Mexican-American peers. When he tutored elementary school students in math at the local public library, Garcia returned to Cristo Rey grandly to dub his inattentive pupils "little rapscallions." Not long before he died, Garcia recorded one of the highest PSAT scores in Cristo Rey's short history.[1] Days after his burial, a letter from Georgetown University arrived at the Garcia's home, inviting Sergio to apply to the prestigious Jesuit institution.[2]

Garcia was no gang member. But like most teenagers in the Pilsen and Little Village area, Garcia knew boys who ran with one of the half-dozen Latino gangs that vied for turf in the neighborhood. In March of 2003, a spate of gang shootings erupted in Little Village. And late one weekend night, just as spring began, Garcia was riding home with a couple of friends from a gathering at another buddy's house. A bullet fired by an unknown assailant whizzed through the car window and hit Garcia, seated alone in the back seat. Twenty-two minutes later, Garcia was pronounced dead at Mt. Sinai Hospital.[3]

Garcia was not the first seventeen-year-old to be gunned down in the Little Village neighborhood. In 2005, the police district that is home to Cristo Rey had thirteen gang-motivated murders, one of the highest tolls in Chicago. But Garcia's senseless murder shocked Cristo Rey students and teachers, nonetheless. Students at the Jesuit school honored him with special masses and created commemorative tee-shirts; at the school's Day of the Dead celebration, the seniors sang a song dedicated to the honor-roll student and danced with his photograph.

In the decade since Cristo Rey Jesuit High School (CRJHS) opened, Garcia remains the school's only homicide victim. Yet the murder of such a promising pupil serves both as an ongoing reminder of the hazards that lurk in Chicago's barrios and the formidable obstacles that CRJHS educators face in nurturing a culture of Latino achievement. Shortly after Garcia's death, Cristo Rey administrators felt compelled to expel five students—not because the boys were gang members but simply because they had fraternized with gang members. CRJHS president, Father Jim Gartland, told an interviewer from the BBC in 2006 that "the worst thing I had to do as a priest is to go with the mother of a [fourteen-year-old] or [sixteen-year-old] kid to the morgue to identify him, and then bury the kid, and then ask the question, why?"[4]

As Father Gartland can attest, the poverty, ignorance, and alienation of Mexican-American immigrant youth in Chicago help to explain the appeal of Latino gangs—and it is those very conditions that Cristo Rey seeks to redress. CRJHS sits in Chicago's near southwest side in the middle of the city's two most densely populated and least-educated neighborhoods, Pilsen and Little Village, two communities comprised overwhelmingly of poor, Mexican immigrants. Only about 3 percent of young adults in the eight-square-mile area hold a bachelor's degree. Yet from Cristo Rey's humble beginnings in 1996, the school has created an academically rigorous, college-preparatory institution that sends 99 percent of its all-Latino, low-income graduates to college. More than nine in ten go on to four-year colleges and start their college careers with an AP credit in Spanish language or literature.

In several crucial respects, the tale of Cristo Rey departs from that of other successful paternalistic inner-city schools. CRJHS is, of course, a parochial school for low-income students, not a public school. It is also a high school, rather than a middle school—and thus tackles the achievement gap during the intractable teen years. But above all, Cristo Rey is notable more for practicing the paternalism of the workplace than the paternalism of the schoolhouse. Its most distinctive feature is its novel work-study program, which dispatches students one day a week to clerical jobs in downtown Chicago in accounting firms, banks, insurance companies, law firms, and offices of health care providers. Cristo Rey has clearly compiled an impressive record of academic performance. But the school is better known for its "earning curve" than its learning curve. "Cristo Rey is magical," Melinda Gates marveled after a visit to the school in 2007. "What you see is that hope, that optimism. You've got to ask…can [their principles] be embodied at a public school?"[5]

The Roots of Cristo Rey

CRJHS and its signature work-study program have their roots in a slow-moving crisis in inner-city Catholic high schools. Low-income and immigrant children have long turned to Catholic high schools, and these are still the primary alternative to public schools in most cities. But in the last forty years, more than half of the nation's Catholic schools have closed—and their disappearance has been especially acute in big cities like Chicago, Boston, New York, and Detroit. In 1980, the U.S. had 1,540 Catholic secondary schools.[6] Today, the number has dwindled to 1,203, a decline of nearly 25 percent. In 2006-07, just four new Catholic secondary schools opened.[7] Not only has the number of Catholic high schools dropped but their location has shifted to suburbs and rural areas. Nationwide, there were a mere 114 inner-city Catholic high schools in 2005–2006.[8] When Cristo Rey opened in 1996, it was the first new Catholic high school in Chicago in 33 years.[9]

The fading presence of urban Catholic high schools is driven chiefly by the changing economics of parochial education. Unlike a half-century ago, when substantial numbers of priests, nuns, and other religious staff taught in parochial schools, nearly all instructors in Catholic high schools today are laity. Replacing religious staff with lay teachers has sent labor costs spiraling, pricing Catholic schools out of the market for many low-income families. In 2005–2006, the median tuition for freshmen at a parochial school was $5,870;[10] in urban areas, it was often even higher. Catholic high schools not far from Cristo Rey charge between $6,500 and $11,000 a year.

As Irish and Italian Americans have migrated to the suburbs, the one remaining immigrant group particularly disposed to inner-city Catholic high schools is the burgeoning Hispanic population: some 62,000 Hispanic students nationwide attended Catholic secondary schools in 2005–2006, roughly 10 percent of all parochial secondary school enrollment.[11] Hispanic enrollment, however, would almost certainly be higher if parochial high schools weren't so expensive. Meanwhile, the achievement gap between Latino newcomers and their white peers remains wide—in Chicago, about half of high-school dropouts in the metro area are Hispanic.

In the mid-1990s, Father John Foley, Cristo Rey's founder, started wrestling with the conundrum of how to open an inner-city Catholic high school that would be affordable for low-income Hispanic immigrants. Foley quickly seized on an unorthodox idea suggested by friend and consultant Rick Murray, a real estate attorney and developer: Why not have the students work off their tuition costs? Murray's solution to the affordability problem was to send students off to work one day a week, and then use their earnings to defray the cost of their education.

Under Murray's concept, CRJHS would serve as a kind of temp agency that signed up corporate sponsors for clerical positions that four students would share, with each filling the slot one day a week. Cristo Rey would go into the employee leasing business and technically be the students' employer, thus protecting sponsors from legal liability and ensuring that they would not have to offer benefits to the teenage students. Meanwhile, the corporations, banks, and law firms would pay the students' entry-level wages directly to the high school, cutting school costs and giving young people the opportunity to work to pay for a chunk of their own tuition.

In practice, the work-study program has made Cristo Rey affordable for hundreds of poor immigrant families who had never imagined sending their kids to private school. In 2006–2007, the actual costs of Cristo Rey ran about $10,325 per student. But the school recoups 65 percent of the costs from student earnings and raises another $925 per pupil via fundraising. All told, that reduces the price of CRJHS tuition to $2,650, the lowest tuition in the Archdiocese of Chicago. Sixty percent of students also receive financial aid, with the average scholarship award coming to $1,215. Thus, CRJHS's neediest students are paying about an average of $1,500 a year, one of the lowest private high-school tuitions in the country. A hundred percent of CHJHS's 533 students last year were Hispanic, the overwhelming majority of them Mexican. And the average income of CRJHS incoming ninth grade families was $34,531 for a family of five. Nearly nine in ten CRJHS students qualify for the federal subsidized lunch program.

Teachers at Cristo Rey report that the work-study program has also had an invaluable impact in the classroom by helping to boost noncognitive skills like discipline, perseverance, and accountability in formerly timid young people. By sending students into corporate environments, the work-study program has also elevated students' career aims and underscored the imperative of attending college. For the first time in their lives, students are surrounded by white-collar professionals who had to attend college and graduate schools as a prerequisite to landing their jobs. Nonetheless, while CRJHS's founders had hoped the work-study program would prove helpful in the classroom, the program's genesis was almost entirely financially driven.

It was also something of a crapshoot. Cristo Rey today has a $30 million facility with a modern wing connected to the old school building by a suspended walkway. The school has two computer labs, three science labs, two art studios, a large gym, a cafeteria, a library wired with laptops, and 23 classrooms. But the school started in a much humbler setting—a former roller rink.

When CRJHS opened in September 1996, few people outside the school realized how precarious its existence was. Fourteen months before the school's opening, its founder, Father John Foley, was jogging downtown along the shore of Lake Michigan when President Bill Clinton went jogging by the other way with his security detail. Later that night, Foley wrote Clinton and asked the former Jesuit university (Georgetown) graduate to speak at the opening of the school. The Democratic National Convention was in Chicago the following August, and appearing at the opening of a new Catholic high school for low-income Hispanic students held considerable political appeal. Clinton himself didn't make Cristo Rey's opening but Hillary Clinton appeared in his stead. Although Cristo Rey had not yet opened, Hillary effused over the school, saying that it was "committed to providing an unusual combination of education and work experience [by] making it possible for young men and women to find their way through the education system successfully by finding their way in the world of work. For all of us who support children, this is a red-letter day." Clinton added that Cristo Rey was a "bold experiment…which can quickly become a model, not only for Chicago but elsewhere, not only for parochial schools but for public schools." [12]

Meanwhile, Father Foley and other CRJHS administrators—who had to struggle with the realities of opening a brand new high school—were far less certain about Cristo Rey's future. CRJHS was supposed to open in St. Stephen's, an old elementary school that was being closed. But renovations were not finished in time, so CRJHS started with 97 sophomores and juniors in a former roller rink/bingo hall across from the school. Desperate to recruit students, Cristo Rey had accepted virtually any youngster willing to enroll—and had not screened students to see if they could handle going to work at a downtown corporate firm. Many students had failing grades at their previous high schools; others had dropped out or had been expelled. Preston Kendall, the first head of the CRJHS's work-study program, says that "the first year we used to joke that we would take any student with a pulse." By the end of the year, the motley crew of 97 pupils had dwindled to 79 students.

On opening day, Cristo Rey started by divvying the students up and placing them into the four corners of the roller rink. A board member wandered in and heard students in the four corners talking excitedly in English and Spanish under a large bingo board and declared the scene straight out of the Tower of Babel. Shortly thereafter, the first time that students went out to work at their jobs, Father Foley was so anxious that he remembers wanting "to hide under the desk." As he later told CBS *60 Minutes Wednesday*, "I didn't know whether [the employers] would be back in 15 minutes, saying 'what, are you nuts? What are we supposed to do with these kids'?"[13] To Foley's immense relief, employers soon started calling Cristo Rey to express their thanks for the student employees. But Cristo Rey "hadn't really known if the work program was really going to fly," says Preston Kendall. "We thought if you build it, they will come. But we learned we had to do a lot of recruiting in the early years to get families to send their kids to Cristo Rey."

School of Work: Summer boot camp

Many successful inner-city schools require students to attend three to four weeks of summer school. Yet at none of the other five schools profiled here is summer school as critical for incoming students as at Cristo Rey. CRJHS's "business boot camp" for freshmen is unlike any other summer school for high-school students in the country.

Cristo Rey practices paternalism with a capital "P" in its summer school. To appreciate why, it helps to imagine the world of the 14-year-old Latino students who are enrolling. From some classrooms on the upper floors and through the gym windows, summer school students can get a glimpse of downtown Chicago with its gleaming skyscrapers along the Magnificent Mile, the bustling business district in the Loop, and the affluent shopping district and condos that line Lake Michigan and the Gold Coast. But while downtown Chicago is only a few miles away by car, to the school's incoming freshmen, it might as well be located in another country. Pilsen and Little Village are dominated by row houses, small factories and warehouses, bodegas, family restaurants, lavanderias, gas stations, and marginal strip malls. Many freshmen, in fact, have never been downtown. Few of the 14-year-olds have ever set foot in a law office, consulting firm, accounting office, or health service firm — much less worked in one, or worked anywhere else for that matter. Preston Kendall says that "every year we had students arrive who had never been in an elevator, ridden an escalator, been in a revolving door, or seen Lake Michigan." Carlos De La Rosa, who succeeded Kendall as director of the work-study program, says that Cristo Rey has learned "not to assume *anything* about what the kids already know."

Many parents of incoming freshmen work as laborers in factories, construction, and the service industry, and are themselves unfamiliar with the culture of blue-chip business firms. The 106 corporations and firms that provide entry-level clerical positions to Cristo Rey students read like a Who's

Who of the Chicago business world: JP Morgan Chase, Deloitte and Touche, BlueCross BlueShield, McKinsey & Company, Leo Burnett Worldwide Advertising, KPMG, Loyola University Health Systems, Ernst & Young, and law firms like Winston & Strawn and Sidley Austin Brown & Wood. "We treat the workplace as a culture," says De La Rosa. And from the first day of summer school, freshmen get a crash culture course on white-collar mores and business practices, the likes of which would never be introduced at a school in an affluent neighborhood.

When freshmen enter the school, De La Rosa and other instructors, joined by sophomore and junior students, line the hallways to introduce themselves and shake the hands of incoming students. The first lesson freshmen learn is that they don't know how to shake someone's hand. "No, look at me!" De La Rosa tells one student after another. "Shake my hand—don't give me a fish handshake!" The incoming students are initially timid and puzzled. But by the fourth or fifth day when students walk into summer school—with the same routine repeated each morning—they have learned to shake someone's hand. They look De La Rosa squarely in the eye and introduce themselves forthrightly.

The three weeks of boot camp fully flesh out students' introduction to clerical work. In the filing procedures class, students learn that Arabic and Roman numbers are filed sequentially before alphabetic characters, and that Arabic numerals precede Roman numerals. In keyboarding/computer workshops, students practice their touch-typing skills (they have to type at least 20 words per minute) and learn how to open and use e-mail, Microsoft Word, and Excel spreadsheets. In the office machines class, students practice using fax machines, copiers, and scanners.

During map reading class, students learn that the Chicago grid system starts at the intersection of State and Madison in the Loop, with a major street every half-mile or four blocks. Acronyms like HAWK help the students memorize mile-marker streets west of State (Halstead, 800 West; Ashland, 1600 West; Western, 2400 West; and Kedzie, 3200 West). Later during the summer, students take practice runs to their employers to memorize the path from their bus stops to the sponsor's office.

Students also practice the art of taking a phone message—an elusive skill for many 14-year-olds. The telephone skills workshop splits them into business callers and message takers, with four working telephones per classroom.

Business callers read from a prepared transcript while message takers practice writing down an accurate, complete message and sounding professional. Students soon learn that slang like "Huh?" or interjections like "What?" do not fly in a corporate environment. In place of saying "who is this?" De La Rosa drills students to say "May I ask who is calling please?"

While business boot camp builds the job skills of these novice workers, it provides an even larger dose of cultural paternalism in the form of training in professional etiquette. Freshmen, for example, must also complete workshops on hygiene and how to dress. The dress code for CRJHS students is remarkably detailed—and sure not to send teen hearts racing. Boys wear long-sleeved cotton or poplin shirts with collars and buttons and free of lettering and logos. Shirts must be buttoned all the way up and worn over plain white undershirts. A solid black or brown belt must be worn at all times. Trousers must have a crease and hem in the leg, and pants must be worn at the waistline. Leather or leather-like shoes in solid black or brown must hold a shine. A boy's hair cannot be long enough to cover his collar or longer than a #2 clipper attachment. Boys are shown, and practice, how to tie a tie. All the markings of teenhood and teen rebellion—earrings, facial piercings, sun glasses, or corn rows—are flatly forbidden.

The dress code for girls is similarly drab: blouses buttoned all the way up, no white socks, no tight pants, no earrings larger than a quarter, and only soft colors used for eye shadow. Wearing a watch is recommended. But the watches cannot have sports logos or cartoon figures on the timepiece.

The hygiene workshop is equally explicit. It "starts with the toenails and works up to the top of the head," says De La Rosa. "We talk about deodorant, we give them dental floss, and we show them how to use Q-tips to clean their ears. We even talk about the use of toilet paper and not overusing it at work." The instructor's manual for the girls' personal hygiene class has the instructor teaching the female students to use shampoo and conditioner every day, not to pluck the full eyebrow, to wash behind their ears, and to wipe laganas—"eye boogers"—away every morning. Girls are taught always to use a tissue to wipe their nose—and to turn away anytime they have to blow their nose. Lip liner and lipstick application are practiced. During menstrual periods, females are advised to drink warm teas—but not caffeine drinks.

In short, like Amistad Academy, Cristo Rey sweats the small stuff. No detail is too small to worry about—though at Cristo Rey the Emily Post-like preoccupation with etiquette is related more to workplace behavior than classroom conduct. To take one example, many freshmen have never been to a conventional restaurant or seen a formal place setting. What happens if a supervisor takes a student out for lunch at a nice restaurant in the Loop? De La Rosa plans for that possibility, too, by placing students in front of a formal dining setting and making them memorize how to use the various forks and knives.

In addition to sweating the small stuff, summer school provides a dose of cultural imperialism. The instructor's manual for the first impressions workshop illustrates how CRJHS tries to combat Latino traditions by the simple act of teaching students to shake hands. The instructor's lesson plan delineates three components to a successful "business handshake" and explains why they may be alien to freshmen:

> Culturally, our students learn that being very soft spoken and not making eye contact shows respect. In business, it can have just the opposite effect—creating doubts about the student's ability to perform and even generating mistrust if there is no eye contact...Be comfortable with making and demonstrating a proper business handshake with three essential elements: 1) a firm grip (same for boys and girls), 2) making direct eye contact with the recipient, and 3) speaking slowly and clearly...Students should understand that a firm handshake sends strong impressions to business people. A firm grip is friendly and confident. A weak or limp handshake says that you are timid or not interested, or worse, that you do not care about meeting the other person...Women should give a firm grip, too. There is no such thing as a dainty business handshake.

Working Nine to Five

Many high schools, particularly those with vocational tracks, allow students to intern or serve as apprentices. Yet CRJHS's work-study program, or CIP (Corporate Internship Program), differs fundamentally from other high school work experience initiatives. As much as possible, the school's CIP office treats students as real employees who are accountable to their sponsors. Students do not toil in make-work assignments, and they earn $149 a day, or $20 an hour, wages paid directly to Cristo Rey in place of tuition. Every student undergoes three performance reviews from their sponsors, in October, January, and May. Sponsors evaluate student performance on 12 measures, including attendance, professional appearance, initiative, punctuality, accuracy of work, cleanliness, and respect for authority. Then students receive a letter grade from the CIP program that goes on their transcript, based on their job evaluation.

Students who miss work for any reason are fined $100. They can earn back $75 toward their tuition credit by working a make-up day. But any student who ends the school year with more than one absence from work that has not yet been made up receives an automatic F on their report card for their year's work. "No student ends the year without having ever made up missed work days," explains CRJHS principal Pat Garrity. She acknowledges, however, that CRJHS made an exception three years ago "for a student who had open heart surgery. We waived the make-up requirement for him. But if a student is sick with the flu, they are still charged a missed day—and still have to make it up." Similarly, if a student shows up at school in clothing that fails to confirm to dress code, they are sent home to change—or the school provides substitute clothes. "We have a collection of clothes that we will make the kids wear," says Preston Kendall. "One day of that and they never show up out of dress code again."

Despite its strict accountability, the work program is the most popular and memorable part of CRJHS for most students. Many students have never held so much as a summer job when they arrive at Cristo Rey. Going to work one day a week, four or five times a month, becomes a rite of passage. "I was shaking I was so nervous on my first day at the job," recalls sophomore Isabel Gonzalez. "But after the first day it was a great experience because I got to meet people I otherwise would never have met." In part, students appreciate the work-study program because it means one less day in school each week and creates an extra day to catch up on homework. But the attraction of the work-study program runs deeper. Jessica Alcazar, a junior, says "I like the days at work better than at school. You feel like a coworker there and not like a little kid. Dressing up like this makes you feel different—less casual, more adult, more professional."

Alcazar had a very different experience in her middle school, which had no detention system and where she could show up wearing jeans and chewing gum. When she started at Cristo Rey, her former middle school classmates would tease her, saying, "Oh, look at Little Ms. Dress Up!" or "Look at Ms. Serious, look at Ms. Lawyer!" Alcazar soon discovered, however, that Cristo Rey policed violations of white-collar culture quite rigorously. She recalls:

You can't wear tight pants here and I would get detentions for having pants that were too tight. I got detentions for chewing gum, too. I also got detentions for missing two math assignments. If you're [ten] minutes late walking into the building you get detention, or if you are talking to friends and arrive late at class you get detention. If you get five detentions, the school calls home. I got a call home my freshmen year. Ooh, my mom was so mad. I was grounded for a month and couldn't make any phone calls my freshman year.

Alcazar struggled academically as a freshman, earning Cs and Ds. But her grades improved. By the time she was a junior, she was earning As and Bs—and her work experience at Kirkland and Ellis had stirred new career aspirations. "I do want to go to college," says Alcazar. "I want to major in pre-law and business. I'd like to be like the lawyers I have seen." Other students had similar tales to tell about the work-study program.

Unlike most high school work programs, CRJHS students can—and do—get fired. "When a student loses their job," says Principal Pat Garrity, "that is realer than getting an F on a test." Last year, more than 90 percent of the school's 533 students got "outstanding" or "good" overall ratings on performance reviews from their sponsors. But each year, on average, about a dozen students lose their jobs. When students have been fired for serious offenses, such as stealing, lying, or forging a signature on a company check, they are expelled from the school. But for lesser offenses, the pink-slipped students enroll in a five-day "re-employment program" that meets weekly for a month (to compensate for the number of days that students would have been on the job that month).

The no-nonsense re-employment program at Cristo Rey is unambiguously paternalistic. During the five days, student write three letters acknowledging what they did to get fired—one letter to the employer, one letter to their parents, and a third letter to the CIP program. After eating crow and taking ownership of their mistakes, students then read Sean Covey's *Seven Habits of Highly Effective Teens.* Drawing upon Covey's book, they follow up with a three-page book report and a PowerPoint presentation with a mission statement that spells out how they will change their work habits. Students also do typing exercises and practice Excel. De La Rosa says that in an average year, eight out of 12 students successfully complete the re-employment program. "If a student loses a job a second time," says Principal Garrity, "we would ask them to leave. You can't be dubbed unemployable and be a student here."

Typically, the re-employment process straightens out wayward workers. De La Rosa recalls the story of one student who worked in the Sears Tower shortly after 9/11 who was then deep into her "Gothic mode." After doodling Satanic musings and leaving dark poems on her chair, the teenager was fired. But following her re-employment program, she abandoned her Goth persona. "The next year she came back and had dropped the black nail polish," De La Rosa recalls. When he asked the teen why she had abandoned the black painted nails, she responded "Oh, that was so last year." Eventually, the student went to Loyola and enrolled in the university's nursing program. "At one of our school health fairs last year," says De La Rosa, "she was giving our students their flu shots."

A quarter-century ago, liberals and multicultural activists would likely have attacked Cristo Rey's work-study program as "slavefare," an exploitive program tantamount to child labor. Just like welfare mothers who are compelled to "work off" their welfare checks in poorly-paid workfare jobs, CRJHS students are obliged to "work off" their tuition, turning their wages over directly to the school. A precocious underage student cannot enroll as a freshman at Cristo Rey since students below age 14 cannot work without violating child labor laws. It is true, too, that businesses get a sweet deal on their teenage clerical workers. Since the CIP program is technically the students' employer, the work-study office takes care of all the administrative duties that would otherwise fall on businesses, like handling payroll, and filing W-4 forms, I-9's, Workers' Compensation, FICA, and FUTA. Sponsors merely pay the CIP program on a timetable of their choosing—monthly, quarterly, or for the whole year. "We have eliminated all the nuisance factors for the businesses," says Preston Kendall. "They don't have to do any recruitment to fill jobs that ordinarily have a high turnover. And they don't have to pay any benefits."

It is a sign of the acceptability of the new paternalism that no one has attacked the Cristo Rey work-study program for being exploitative. Nor do students themselves feel like employers or school takes advantage of them. Roberto Ochoa, who graduated in 2006, says he felt like "I am getting paid for my work because every time I walk through the door, I am paying for the opportunity to go to this school. And I did real work, too, as a file clerk, opening and posting mail—I had days where the workload was heavy."

Nor do CIP administrators fret about whether their teen charges are being taken advantage of to keep CRJHS afloat. "Considering the benefits that the students get from working at the companies, they should do it even without pay," says CIP director De La Rosa. De La Rosa, who as a first-generation immigrant made the trip north from Mexico with his mother and 12 family members, sees a lot of his own story in the students. "CIP exposes the kids here to white-collar professionals whom they can model themselves after and whom they would not see at home when Mom and Dad work in a factory. You can't pay for that kind of experience," he says.

De La Rosa and Garrity believe that CRJHS's work-study program has two invaluable yet hard-to-quantify impacts on students. First, the experience of working in corporate Chicago speeds up the maturation process and boosts noncognitive skills like discipline and self-confidence that help people advance on the job. English teacher Tim Green reports that "when the freshmen arrive they are quiet and find it hard to talk to an adult. The work program makes them mature faster—in high school they are learning how to prepare their resume." By the time a CRJHS student graduates, his or her resume lists four years of work experience in corporate firms.

The second subtle benefit of the work-study program is that it supports the college-going culture at CRJHS. Students, says principal Garrity, "may not decide to become clerical workers [because of the work-study program] but they do learn the value of work. The CIP program adds motivation for college prep because the kids see what jobs are available to them with and without a college degree." De La Rosa adds that the work-study program has a cumulative impact most visible among twelfth graders. "The seniors here are polished kids—they have put on an adult skin without realizing it," he says. "Working in the corporate world orients them to thinking '*where* will I go to college?' not '*will* I go to college?'"

Character Training, Curriculum, and Catholicism

Like other paternalistic schools, CRJHS embeds the teaching of values and character in its code of student conduct, curriculum, and classrooms. Yet unlike schools such as Amistad or KIPP, CRJHS does not provide rewards for good behavior. CRJHS does not award scholar dollars or special privileges to well-behaved students at the school store. In fact, the Jesuit school purposely limits opportunities to spend money at the school. As the student handbook explains, CRJHS does not promote the sale of clothing or sportswear bearing the school logo because it "reject[s] the environment of consumerism so prevalent in our world." Nor does CRJHS utilize mnemonics in the classroom or constantly monitor students to see if they are slouching in their seats or tracking the teacher with their eyes. CRJHS is at its most paternalistic in the work program, rather than in the classroom.

The academic program at Cristo Rey is authoritarian with a twist: its authority derives from the school's Catholicism and Jesuit roots. CRJHS might be described as a Catholic school with a capital C and a small c. Most other schools that have adopted the Cristo Rey model have more ethnic and religious diversity than Cristo Rey. But at CRJHS, only seven students out of 533 last year were not Catholic. Discipline is plenty strict—but in keeping with that of a traditional parochial school. CRJHS enforces a dress code and hands out detentions for tardiness and misbehavior at the first misstep. School officials also permanently confiscate all cell phones, electronic games, iPods, headphones, and electronic gear whenever a student brings them into school, work, or pulls them out on the bus ride to work. Maintaining decorum—an elusive goal at most inner-city high schools—is a paramount priority at CRJHS. The "Rights and Responsibilities" section of the Cristo Rey student handbook states that

> We will NOT tolerate verbal abuse; inappropriate public display of affection, distasteful language, loud laughter, shouting or whistling in the school building…We will NOT tolerate tardiness, lack of preparation for class, continual absences, and academic expectations that are not met…We will NOT tolerate spitting, chewing gum, littering, and defacing school property.

CRJHS is especially zealous about monitoring gang sympathies and school events for risky behavior. To gain entry to school dances, students and their guests must take breathalyzer tests, and students periodically face random drug testing as part of the work-study program. Most students don't seem to mind the breathalyzer tests because an alcohol-free dance feels safer than one where students have been drinking. But teens who dance suggestively, or bump and grind during a slow dance, are sure to get interrupted by a teacher advising them to "leave some space there for the Holy Spirit." Signs of gang affiliation, graffiti, or gang sympathies common at many inner-city high schools are prohibited. "The moment it becomes acceptable to have gang activity in a school is the moment you lose the school," says Principal Garrity. "If a student even draws gang graffiti on a notebook or piece of paper, we deal with it. They might be suspended for a day the first time. The second time it happened — well, that would be your last day here."

The flip side of being a parochial school is that Cristo Rey, unlike other paternalistic schools, has a significant commitment to religious and social justice. Students take religion class and are required to complete 20 hours of service each year and a daylong retreat run by the campus ministry. The motto of the Jesuit school — Women and Men for Others — is much in keeping with activist student clubs like Fe y Justicia and the Social Action Club. Father John Foley, CRJHS's founder and since 2004 the president of the Cristo Rey Network, talks about the school's mission in expressly religious terms. To cite one example, in the fall 2005 Network newsletter, Foley wrote that "all of us are involved in a supernatural undertaking. We are bringing about the Kingdom."

Spiritual concerns surface in CRJHS's classrooms in ways that would be unthinkable in public schools — and not just in religion class.[14] Some teachers start their classes with prayers. Tim Green began his advanced British literature class last year with a prayer, asking students "if there are any intentions that we want to pray for today?" Half-a-dozen students piped up to say that would like to pray for sisters, aunts, brothers, and grandmothers who were sick or struggling. The class then collectively said the Lord's Prayer — before launching into a discussion of *Beowulf.* In Lauren Gatti's eleventh-grade American literature and poetry class, Gatti pushed students to reflect on the moral quandaries faced by characters in Hawthorne's *The Scarlet Letter.* Drawing from characters in the book, Gatti asked students to "rank the following things from most sinful to least sinful":

— A single person having an affair with a married person.

— A married person having an affair with another married person.

— Becoming obsessed with getting revenge on somebody.

— Publicly criticizing another person for doing something you yourself have also done or partaken in.

— Lying to protect another person.

— Going along with the crowd when they ostracize a person.

— Being insensitive about a parent's life choice (i.e., divorce, adultery, hypocrisy).

Many high-school literature classes discuss the moral controversies raised by the ostracism of Hester Prynne, and teachers at paternalistic schools do not shy away from discussing *The Scarlet Letter* in moral terms. But students at paternalistic public schools are unlikely to rank degrees of "sin" in *The Scarlet Letter*.

In two other respects, CRJHS's curriculum differs significantly from that of other paternalistic schools. First, it is not as carefully prescribed or standards-driven as those of other paternalistic schools. Second, CRJHS provides dual language instruction in English and Spanish. The school seeks to teach students to be able to read and write in both languages.

To be sure, Cristo Rey makes ample use of national standardized tests and assessments to track pupil performance. It is also an academically rigorous school that requires students to take four years of English, Spanish, religion, and the work-study program, and three years apiece of math, science, and social studies. The one-day-a-week work-study program also reduces the number of electives that students take, forcing a focus on core subjects. In its early years, Cristo Rey experimented with group work and nontraditional courses. But after Pat Garrity took over as principal in 2002, the school's curricular content became decidedly more traditional—and now consists, as English teacher Tim Green jokes, "mostly of the old, dead white man's curriculum."

Nonetheless, teachers at the Jesuit school have considerably more leeway than their peers at other paternalistic schools. They do not follow a set of detailed lesson plans or have to teach content based largely on state standards. Unlike public school students, CRJHS students do not take state tests. Nor does Cristo Rey rely on continual assessment to gauge and remedy poor student performance. A large proportion of its students enter college with an AP credit in Spanish, but the school offers few other AP courses. Tim Green's advanced British literature course was the first AP class he had taught. And the school only agreed to develop his AP course after hearing from students who had gone on to Notre Dame and Georgetown that "all the other kids have read Chaucer and *The Canterbury Tales*—and we've never heard of them."

Cristo Rey's bilingual requirement—entering freshmen have to be able to speak Spanish—reflects its desire to serve as a neighborhood school for the surrounding Hispanic community. Unlike most other schools in the Cristo Rey Network, which do not have a bilingual requirement, 100 percent of CRJHS's students are Latino. However, CRJHS is really more of a dual language school than a traditional bilingual school. It does not provide English immersion classes or traditional bilingual instruction in Spanish until students acquire enough English to be taught in English. Instead, from freshman through their sophomore years, students take at least one class in Spanish in addition to Spanish class (e.g., religion, history of the Americas), with homework in Spanish. "To be a student here," says principal Garrity, "you have to be able to speak Spanish. As a freshman, you don't necessarily have to be able to read and write in Spanish. But our goal is to have graduates be bilingual and bi-literate."

Cristo Rey and the Achievement Gap

In the middle-school years, researchers typically track the achievement gap by looking at scores on achievement tests and state assessments. Yet once students reach high school, other measures of the achievement gap take on greater significance, particularly graduating from high school and enrolling in college. Closing the gap in educational attainment, in other words, is arguably even more important in high school than closing the test-score gap. Nationwide, only 31 percent of 18- to 24-year-olds from low-income families in 2000–2001 were in college or had attended college, compared with 75 percent of those from high-income families.[15] Just 6 percent of 24-year-olds from low-income families had a four-year college degree in 2000–2001, while half of 24-year-olds from high-income families had such degrees.[16]

Judged by the metric of educational attainment, Cristo Rey has closed the achievement gap. In 2007, it sent 100 percent of its graduates to college (67 percent to four-year colleges and 33 percent to two-year colleges).[17] Cristo Rey students are far more likely than their Hispanic peers in nearby public schools to complete high school and go on for postsecondary education. Table 5-1 below shows how Cristo Rey compares to the three large nearby high schools where 75 percent or more of the students are Hispanic. At the comparison schools—Benito Juarez Community Academy, David Farragut Career Academy, and Kelly High School—the average student misses four to five weeks of school a year and roughly half of all freshmen fail to graduate within five years. All three are huge, comprehensive high schools—the smallest of them has about 1,500 students. But as the table illustrates, the gulf in educational attainment in 2007 between CRJHS students and their local low-income Hispanic peers is vast.

Table 5-1. Graduation and college-going rates at Cristo Rey Jesuit HS and nearby schools[18]

	Distance from Cristo Rey (miles)	Percentage of 2007 graduates enrolled in college or post-secondary education	High school graduation rate for Hispanic students, 2007 (percentage)
Cristo Rey Jesuit HS		100	99
Juarez Community Academy HS	0.5	27	57
Farragut Career Academy HS	1.9	25	53
Kelly HS	2.5	32	63
District Average (Chicago)		N/A	64
State Average (Illinois)		N/A	73

Sources: Cristo Rey Network Statistical Directory 2007-08, http://www.cristoreynetwork.org/about/ CRN2007-08Directory-FINAL.pdf ; Chicago Public Schools High School Directory, http://www.cps.k12.il.us/ Schools/hsdirectory/HS_Directory.pdf; Illinois Department of Education, 2007 State School Report Cards, http://research.cps.k12.il.us/resweb/schoolqry (all accessed April 1, 2008).

Cristo Rey's towering accomplishment is that it sends virtually all of its graduates on to college, while local public schools with similar demographics send fewer than a third of their graduates on to postsecondary education. After winning admission, virtually all Cristo Rey graduates enroll in college, and the vast majority eventually graduate. (At present, 82 percent of CRJHS graduates are either attending or have completed college.)

Students at Cristo Rey outscore students in the Chicago public schools on the ACT (18.8 compared to 17.6 in 2007). They outscore, too, the average Hispanic public school student in Illinois, 18.8 to 17.9.[19]

Still, the average composite ACT score at Cristo Rey for the class of 2007 (18.8) was significantly below the state average for all students, which was 20.3. (The national average ACT score, 21.2, was even higher. A 36 is a perfect score on the ACT.) If the achievement gap is measured just using test scores, then Cristo Rey has succeeded in narrowing the gap but has failed to close it.

Moreover, a significant portion of Cristo Rey students do not score high enough to meet the ACT's college readiness "benchmark" scores: 18 in English, 22 in math, 21 in reading, and 24 in science. Students who meet the readiness benchmarks have a 50 percent chance of obtaining a B or higher in corresponding credit-bearing college courses and a 75 percent chance of at least

Table 5-2. Academic achievement at Cristo Rey Jesuit HS and nearby schools

	Distance from Cristo Rey (miles)	Mean composite ACT score for class of 2007[20]
Cristo Rey Jesuit HS		**18.8**
Juarez Community Academy HS	0.5	15.4
Farragut Career Academy	1.9	15.7
Kelly HS	2.5	16.7
District Average (Chicago)		17.6
State Average (Illinois)		20.3

Sources: Cristo Rey Jesuit High School (direct communication); Illinois Department of Education, 2007 State School Report Cards, http://research.cps.k12.il.us/resweb/schoolqryCards (accessed April 1, 2008).

obtaining a C or higher. In Cristo Rey's 2006 class, 63 percent of students met the English benchmark on the ACT, roughly the same percent as statewide. But less than a quarter of the class of 2006 met the reading, math, or science benchmarks—well below state averages. Just one student met all four ACT benchmarks, though 20 percent of students did so statewide. Nonetheless, Cristo Rey students were far more college-ready in 2006 than in 2002, when 27 percent of students reached the English readiness benchmark and only 2 percent reached the mathematics benchmark.[21]

Cristo Rey now has an ample modern facility with a new library, spacious gym, and two technology labs. Still, it would be hard to attribute Cristo Rey's success in college admissions to superior resources, class size, or teacher quality. In 2005, district public schools had an average operating expenditure per pupil of $10,409, virtually identical to the $10,326 that CRJHS spent per student. Cristo Rey's classes are slightly larger than those of nearby public schools, averaging 25 to 30 students, due mostly to the logistics of running a rotating work-study program.

The CRJHS day runs from 8:00 A.M. until 3:30 P.M. (On work days, students do not return to Cristo Rey until 5:50 P.M.) However, because students are at work one day a week, they have only 137 days of academic classes, compared to 180 school days at Chicago public schools. Once CRJHS's longer day is factored in, Cristo Rey students got 822 instructional hours in 2006–2007, compared to a minimum of 880 instructional hours in public schools. On the whole, Cristo Rey, unlike most paternalistic schools, does not have significantly extended instructional time or a longer school year—except for ninth grade, when incoming freshmen attend summer boot camp.

Teachers at CRJHS earn much less than their peers in public schools—and are less likely to be certified or to have master degrees. Catholic school teachers are often not unionized. Not surprisingly, they have little job security, and receive far more modest benefits. The average teacher salary in district schools in Chicago is $66,000, more than 50 percent higher than Cristo Rey's average of $41,900. And the Jesuit school's teachers work on annual, renewable contracts.

Yet CRJHS has not had to do serious recruiting for teachers. The Field of Dreams expectations did pan out when it came to attracting teachers. When Father Foley held a press conference in January 1996 to announce the planned opening of the school, the new school's answering machine had three phone messages on it the next morning, one from a Jesuit teacher in Hawaii, a second from a Jesuit teacher in London, and a third from a Jesuit teacher in Chicago—all of whom wanted to teach at the new school. "At Cristo Rey, we tend to attract idealistic teachers who share our vision," says Preston Kendall. "The faith commitment is there, too, though you don't have to be Catholic." CRJHS has benefited as well from the strong informal network of teacher recruitment in Catholic schools. To date, other schools in the Cristo Rey Network have also had to mount just modest efforts to recruit teachers. Some have placed ads for teacher openings on idealist.org or posted openings at Catholic universities like Loyola, DePaul, and Notre Dame. Despite Cristo Rey's modest salaries, the teachers keep coming.

Creaming, Retention, and Parent Involvement

CRJHS is the only one of the six paternalistic schools profiled here with a selective admissions process. While the school does not rigorously screen applicants, its selectivity likely accounts for some of its academic success. When CRJHS first opened in 1996, the school essentially enrolled all comers. But as it established a track record and reputation in Pilsen and Little Village, applications soared. In 2006, 355 eighth graders applied for admission to Cristo Rey, and 153 students enrolled in September, an admissions acceptance rate of just over 40 percent.

Though CRJHS does screen students for admission, it does not do so in the manner of traditional selective schools. It does not, for instance, have an entrance exam or cutoff test score. Rather, the school looks for students who maintained a C average or better in seventh and eighth grades. Students who have a GPA below 2.0 and poor test scores are unlikely to be admitted to Cristo Rey.

CRJHS employs a variety of other filters as well to ensure that it continues to serve low-income Hispanic immigrants from the surrounding neighborhood, most of whom apply from local public schools. Students must be able to speak Spanish, though they don't have to be able to read and write that language. Applicants from Pilsen and Little Village are given preference over those from more distant neighborhoods. And prospective students are disqualified for having too high a family income, or if they have been accepted by another Catholic high school where they can pay the tuition.

The biggest bar to admission to CRJHS is that the school screens applicants for noncognitive skills like hard-work, diligence, and spunk. Cristo Rey students, above all, have to be employable. That means, for instance, that they must be documented workers with Social Security numbers. Yet the requirement to be employable plays out in more subtle ways, too. Jeff Thielman, the original development director for CRJHS and now vice president for development at the Cristo Rey Network, points out that "for a 14-year-old to work at a bank or insurance company they have to be responsible. They have to be willing to do work that can be a grind, like scanning documents eight hours a day." As a result, Thielman says, "we look for kids with desire, with 'ganas' to use the Spanish term. We don't cream academically so much as look for kids with a desire to achieve." Of course, measuring the drive of 14-year-olds is an imprecise art at best. But admissions officers and Principal Garrity use a variety of informal assessments to size up student motivation. "Our admissions interview is really more similar to a job interview than a traditional school interview," says Garrity. "And we give priority to kids and families that have worked to apply on deadline. Classroom performance is more important to us than test scores because it attests to student discipline."

The net result of Cristo Rey's admissions process is that it tends to exclude students at both ends of the bell curve. CRJHS does not recruit the best and brightest from nearby neighborhoods. But it also turns away students with serious learning differences and dismal academic records—in part because these students can be difficult to keep employed. Last year the school had only three English language learners in pull-out classes out of 533 students. Similarly, only three students with learning disabilities received services prescribed under an IEP plan. Principal Pat Garrity says that "an eighth grader with LD issues who applies to Cristo Rey needing more than a half-time pull-out program would be turned down. We just don't have a pull-out capacity like that for LD students." Still, in the 2005–2006 school year, two thirds of Cristo Rey students required academic assistance.

A second factor that may help account for Cristo Rey's impressive college admissions record is the school's mediocre retention rate. CRJHS has a higher retention rate than nearby high schools with large numbers of Latino students. But school officials acknowledge that CRJHS needs to stem the loss of students between ninth and twelfth grade. Cristo Rey's retention rate from freshman year to senior year is 62 percent, a figure that Pat Garrity would like to see rise to 70 and eventually 80 percent. In 2005–2006, Cristo Rey lost 56 students, nearly half of whom left voluntarily and most of whom were sophomores or older. Some students depart because they think the disciplinary procedures, including Saturday detentions, are too strict. Each year, a handful leaves because they do not like the work-study program.

Even so, exit interviews show that academic pressure is the chief reason why students switch schools—which means that Cristo Rey's nearly flawless college-going record may reflect the fact that weaker students are switching back to other schools, mostly public schools, by senior year. "The easy explanation for our low retention number is that it is hard here," says Garrity. "Personally, I think the issue is more that we hold kids accountable. An F here means something and not doing your homework makes a difference in your grade. It's not unusual to hear from a freshman that no one has ever looked at their homework before."

Some skeptics of paternalistic schools contend that their success in closing the achievement gap stems from the involvement of motivated parents. As in most high schools, CRJHS has not systematically studied how its parents compare to other low-income Latino parents in the area who send their children to public schools. Yet the impressionistic evidence that is available belies the claim that parents of CRJHS students are especially engaged in their children's education. In its decade of existence, CRJHS has never had a formal parent organization, including a PTA. Most parents were born in Mexico and are not formally educated, at least not in the United States. Most are ill-equipped to help their children with their math homework by tenth grade. "Our parents look to us with a great level of respect to have us take care of the homework," says Garrity. "Our parents tend to be fairly quiet. In some schools, the parents are calling up the principal to complain but not here. We are both school and church in the eyes of the parents—and that means a lot to them."

Once a month, CRJHS invites parents to come to school to talk about an issue involving adolescents, like gangs or sex. The monthly meetings are well attended, with 100 or more parents always present. But on the whole, CRJHS asks little of parents, apart from having them provide students with a space to do their homework. The poverty and long work hours that many immigrants endure is a formidable bar to parental involvement, too. As work-study director De La Rosa says, "We work hard at Cristo Rey to *not* ask Mom and Dad for any additional [tuition] money—and we don't ask them to sell Christmas wrapping paper to raise money for the school either."

Replication Challenges

The Cristo Rey Network of schools was initially created in 2001 through a $12 million gift from philanthropists B.J. and Bebe Cassin and their Cassin Educational Initiative Foundation. The aim of the Network is to replicate the CRJHS model in high schools in other cities. The Network did not begin full-fledged operations until 2004, when Father John Foley switched from CRJHS to become president of the Network. In addition to the Cassins, the Bill and Melinda Gates Foundation has been a major benefactor of the Cristo Rey Network, providing nearly $16 million in two grants to assist the startup of new high schools. In 2006–2007, the Network had 12 member schools with 2,882 students, and seven additional high schools opened in September 2007. The Cristo Rey Network (CRN) anticipates that 31 high schools with a total of 12,000 students will be operating by 2012–2013.

It is still too early to say how the CRN schools are performing since many of them have only been open for a couple of years. But preliminary results from the copycat schools suggest that their successes and shortcomings are in many respects similar to those of the flagship school in Chicago. By and large, the network high schools have succeeded in offering an affordable parochial education to low-income minority students in inner-city neighborhoods. Close to two-thirds of students at Network schools are Latino, 25 percent are black, and 70 percent of CRN students qualify for the free or reduced price lunch program. CRN schools are mostly located in large cities including New York,

Los Angeles, Chicago, Denver, Kansas City, Portland (Oregon), Sacramento, and Tucson. Several are located in some of the poorest neighborhoods in the country, including St. Martin de Porres on the east side of Cleveland, and Verbum Dei, in Los Angeles' Watts neighborhood near the notorious Nickerson Gardens housing project. Unlike CRJHS, most CRN schools use an admissions test—adding a further element of selectivity. Nine of the first 12 schools in the Network have applicants take the Catholic High School Placement Test.

The preliminary impact of CRN schools on the achievement gap mirrors the pattern established at CRJHS. CRN schools have essentially eliminated the gap in educational attainment, as reflected in their nearly perfect rate of college admission for their graduates. At the same time, CRN schools still have a long way to go to close the test-score gap with non-Hispanic white students.

A whopping 99 percent of CRN graduates in the class of 2007 were accepted at four-year or two-year colleges: 316 of the Network schools' 318 graduating seniors. (The number of graduates is small because many CRN schools are too new or small to have had a significant senior class.) Not all of the CRN classes of 2007 replicated CRJHS's impressive record from 2006 of sending 91 percent of its graduates to four-year colleges. Verbum Dei in Los Angeles, for instance, sent about 60 percent of its 71 graduating seniors to four-year schools. Yet considering that the Los Angeles archdiocese was about to shut down Verbum Dei—an all-boys school that had only 142 students enrolled when it joined the Network in 2002—the school's turnaround under the Cristo Rey model is quite a success story. (By 2006–2007, Verbum Dei enrolled 105 boys in ninth grade alone.)

In general, academic achievement at CRN schools is well above that of most inner-city high schools. However, test scores remain significantly below those of good suburban and urban public schools. On the Iowa Test of Educational Development (ITED), roughly half of students in Network schools scored proficient or above in language arts in 2007 and just under 30 percent were proficient in math.[22]

As CRN schools mature, the Network has set ambitious goals for boosting their academic achievement. On the ITED, the Network goal is to increase the number of students who are proficient or advanced in math and reading by at least 25 percent over the course of four years (i.e., as students advance from their freshman to senior years). At present, Network schools do not have sufficient data to show whether the Cristo Rey model boosts educational achievement the longer students are enrolled. But the current ITED scores of seniors at Network schools are not higher than those of freshmen.

As is the case at CRJHS, Network schools are ill-equipped to handle the neediest students and have serious retention problems, especially with slower learners. In 2006–2007, the 12 schools collectively had only five English language learners in pull-out classes. Network wide, as of 2006–2007, just 61 percent of ninth graders graduate from their school four years later.

Network officials have discovered that replicating CRJHS is doable but challenging. Many traditionalists find the Cristo Rey model instinctively appealing for its emphasis on hard work, religion, and moral character. But they often overlook the practical implications of Cristo Rey's special brand of educational paternalism. As it turns out, running a work-study program obligates a high school to establish and administer a new bureaucracy, rather than reducing school administration.

At each school that adopts the Cristo Rey model, officials have to recruit dozens of sponsors to provide clerical positions in a job-sharing format to inexperienced high-school students. Network schools then have to create a temporary employment agency within the school to handle payroll and employee paperwork like I-9s, W-2s, performance reviews, as well as the re-employment process for students who are fired. Cristo Rey students are also part-time employees who work one day a week. But that means the schedules of all students who work on, say, Tuesday, must be coordinated to create a minimum of classroom disruption inside the school. "Our work program is an incredible matrix and a logistical nightmare," says CRJHS English teacher Tim Green. As Carlos De La Rosa puts it, Cristo Rey "does not just view itself as a high school but as a business. I have five people who work for me in the work-study office. For me, the easiest way to describe our schedule is that we are running four different schools."

To run a successful work-study program, each school must also arrange transportation to and from work for its teenage students. CRJHS, for example, owns four shuttle buses and leases two more school buses that drop off students along a variety of downtown routes in the morning and then bring them back to school at the end of the work day. In 2005–2006, CRJHS spent about $600 per day just transporting students to and from work. Given that CRJHS has 550 students working as part-time employees at some 125 different companies, De La Rosa's five staff-members must inevitably divvy up the monitoring of student performance, too. "Each of my work-study reps manages 25 to 30 companies," say De La Rosa. "They need the I-9s, the W-4 form for the IRS, and W-2s. Somebody has to coordinate make-up day payments, the re-employment process, and performance reviews with the companies." The work-study office also has to keep tabs on the amount of money the school earns from students' work at sponsoring firms and the resulting contribution that students are making to defray the cost of their tuition. In short, Cristo Rey's distinctive work-study program fosters accountability—but at the cost of creating a new labor-intensive bureaucracy inside the school.

Yet the financial viability of the Cristo Rey model depends on the work-study program. If student wages for the work-study program fail to cover most of the cost of educating those students, then Network schools will be unable to provide an affordable parochial school education for low-income minority youngsters—at least not without the help of large grants from private foundations or the Church. When CRN schools are at full enrollment of 300 to 500 students, the revenue from collected student tuition and work-study contracts is supposed to cover 85 percent of their operating expenditures. CRJHS has surpassed the 85 percent benchmark—in 2007–2008, tuition and work-study revenue was slated to cover 86 percent of the school's operating expenses. But most Network schools are still too new to know if they can replicate CRJHS's performance. At present, they are raising just over half of their operating expenses through tuition and work program contracts.

Many Network schools are new schools, which are expensive to launch. New schools can easily cost $3 million a year or more to set up and run. The Cristo Rey Network provides roughly a million dollars a year for start-up costs during the first three to four years, forcing new schools to be aggressive fundraisers. Again, it is too early to say whether Network schools can replicate CRJHS's impressive fund-raising performance. During Father Foley's 1996–2004 tenure as president of Cristo Rey, the charismatic priest raised $26 million for the school—and left CRJHS with a $2 million endowment. To date, the Network has raised close to $30 million from Cassin and Gates, but Network officers and school officials can't expect such large private grants to continue indefinitely. As it is, the Network is a lean nonprofit compared to other ambitious school replication programs like KIPP. (In 2006, the KIPP Foundation had nearly 60 full-time employees to monitor quality and manage its school network. By comparison, the Cristo Rey Network had six employees.)

Even when new schools secure financing, replicating Cristo Rey can be challenging. Each time a school or archdiocese approaches CRN about setting up a Cristo Rey school, the Network conducts a full-scale feasibility study that entails a minimum of 100 interviews, surveys, and focus groups with parents, and 300 interviews, surveys, and focus group meetings with potential students. Typically, a Network feasibility study costs about $75,000. Yet not every interested school is even eligible for a feasibility study. The Network now only considers feasibility study proposals from schools in urban areas with 750,000 people or more, a significant proportion of low-income families, and the economic stability to provide the 125 clerical jobs required to run a school at full capacity. The Network's eligibility guidelines and limits on the size of the work-study program thus effectively preclude any large Catholic high school from joining. At full enrollment, Network schools are still small—with 300 to 525 students.

In the five years since Cristo Rey began its replication efforts, the Network has overseen more than 25 feasibility studies—a quarter of which did not lead to new schools. Why do some parochial schools get rejected? In part, the answer is that CRN officials insist that Cristo Rey schools faithfully replicate the basic model of CRJHS. That does not mean total fealty to the original. Most Network schools, for example, are not bilingual and biliterate. But Network officials have turned down other parochial schools that seemed to drift too far from the CRJHS example. One feasibility study, for example, reviewed the prospects for an all-male and largely black Cristo Rey school in Detroit. Network officials turned down the application because the school's organizers planned to use the work-study program only for juniors and seniors, leaving out sophomores and freshmen.

Other schools interested in joining the Network have lost out because they looked to higher-income families to help cover tuition costs at the school. The only school to date to withdraw from the Network is San Juan Diego Catholic High School in Austin, Texas, which struggled to recruit students poor enough to meet Cristo Rey's guidelines. The Network and the Cassin Educational Initiative Foundation invested $1.2 million in the start-up costs of San Juan Diego. But in its fourth year of operation, the school had just 144 students enrolled, compared to a target of 400 students. In March 2006, the Austin school withdrew from the network.

Much as Achievement First and KIPP have discovered, the Cristo Rey Network has learned that its job doesn't stop when students graduate. Outside the cocoon of Cristo Rey's custodial culture, some students have had trouble adjusting to university life and the academic demands of college, particularly in CRJHS's early graduating classes. "The kids sometimes slipped back after they graduated or they have family financial pressures that oblige them to drop out of school," says Carlos De La Rosa of CRJHS. "We are finding that Brown, Georgetown, and Notre Dame are not always the best fit for students—for some students, smaller liberal arts schools are a better place."

To assist students to make better-informed college choices, the Network hired a full-time director of postsecondary programs in 2006 to start a college relations program. The occupant of that post, Frank Brightwell, has canvassed Cristo Rey alumni to get a better sense of their needs and is seeking to identify universities where graduates are likely to flourish. Like so much about the fledgling Network, the postsecondary program is still a work in progress. But its mere existence underscores that Cristo Rey is determined to close the achievement gap in the long-term—and not just rest on its laurels after seniors have "climbed the mountain" and been accepted into college.

Chapter Six

KIPP Academy — "KIPP-Notizing" through Music

I t is sweltering in the Lou Gehrig Junior High auditorium this June afternoon, and as the thermometer inches up to 90 degrees, the 180 members of the KIPP Academy String and Rhythm Orchestra are tiring. Beads of perspiration begin to dapple the students' shirts as they lift and nestle their violins and violas under their chins during the hour-and-a-half rehearsal after school. In two days, the orchestra will give its commencement concert in this auditorium in the South Bronx to honor the eighth-grade graduates of KIPP Academy, housed in a wing on the fourth floor of Lou Gehrig Junior High. But rehearsal in the stifling auditorium is going poorly. Jesus Concepcion, the dapper conductor and benevolent baton-wielding despot on the podium, is not pleased.

"Sit down!" Concepcion tells a seventh grader playing string bass at the back of the orchestra. The bass player had refused to help a fellow cello player pick up his music when it slid off his music stand, kicking the sheet music back to the student instead. "You want to be nasty?" Concepcion asks rhetorically. "I'll teach you nasty. You don't deserve to play! You let down your teammates. And that music you kicked, I arranged. Get off the stage!" After the student glumly exits the stage, orchestra members keep their eyes glued to Concepcion during a soaring version of "Seasons of Love" from the Broadway show

152

Rent. But as at many rehearsals of the string and rhythm orchestra, the cycle of disruption and discipline continues. A few minutes later, the graduating eighth graders start chatting animatedly in the hallway as they practice lining up. "Unbelievable!" Concepcion exclaims. Mitch Brenner, KIPP Academy's Director of Institutional Solutions and enforcer of all things KIPP, hops up to straighten out the excited eighth graders. "Not a word!" Brenner calls out. "Do not speak! You are our graduates. Do not open your mouth!"

Next it is Quinton Vance's turn to try to inspire the orchestra. Vance, the principal of KIPP Academy, delivers a speech straight out of Knute Rockne. "I hope you recognize the importance of this event," he tells the orchestra. "We could change our songs but the songs that kids at KIPP played 11 years ago we play today. We could change our KIPP shirts and make them in new crazy colors. But we don't. We choose to *honor* tradition. We will still be putting on this [graduation] concert 20 years from now. And it's your responsibility to make this show the best ever—better than Carnegie Hall. You have a responsibility to be perfect on Thursday—this show does honor to the four years of the eighth-grade class."

Slowly, the orchestra settles back into rehearsing—but the tumult is not over, not yet. One girl, and one girl alone, in the 180-member orchestra has looked sullen and bored throughout the rehearsal. Concepcion cannot tolerate having a member of his orchestra be disengaged. "Stand!" he tells the female keyboardist. "Every time I look at you, you challenge me. I will not tolerate disrespect. Everybody stand!" As the orchestra rises to its feet, Concepcion abruptly wheels around and walks out of the auditorium. "Section leaders," says Mr. Brenner quietly, "man your sections. And make sure that everybody stands still and that there is no talking." Thirty seconds pass in silence. A minute passes. Tiny rivulets of sweat are now trickling down the cheeks of the middle school students. Finally, Concepcion walks back down the central aisle of the auditorium, baton in hand. "I did not yell," he announces with a chuckle from the podium. "I just had a pain in my butt. Now, everybody track me at all times and sit straight." And with that, the orchestra breaks into a swinging orchestral version of Shakira's "Hips Don't Lie."

It's just another rehearsal for the KIPP Academy String and Rhythm Orchestra. Yet the battles that afternoon in June 2006 illustrate the charter school's tireless pursuit of excellence. The orchestral regimen is all about the "KIPP-notizing" of middle-school students—from the preoccupation with fostering teamwork to the obsession with cultivating character and discipline. For all of Concepcion's dressing down of his charges at rehearsal, the KIPP Academy orchestra is one of the top middle school orchestras in the country—which is doubly remarkable since less than 1 percent of its members played an instrument or read music when they entered KIPP Academy in fifth grade. "Most of my students have never *seen* a violin or cello before, much less played one," says Concepcion. Unlike performing-arts schools or other middle-school orchestras, the KIPP Academy orchestra is not selective. Students are required to take music classes but no student is obliged to play in the orchestra. Yet for the last five years, every student in the sixth through eighth grade has signed up to play, and every KIPP Academy graduate leaves being able to read music.

It is hard to convey in words the profound impact of watching and hearing 180 African American and Latino middle-school students from the South Bronx intently play violins, violas, cellos, and string basses in unison. But audience members often dissolve into tears and interrupt KIPP concerts with prolonged standing ovations. The KIPP Academy orchestra has an unusually large string section, including 75 violinists and 39 viola players. It primarily performs orchestral arrangements reminiscent of Walter Murphy's 1976 hit, "A Fifth of Beethoven," combining symphonic music with aggressive string-playing and contemporary rhythm. The orchestra does not play dense, demanding Mahler symphonies. But it can play Ravel's "Bolero" and pick up and learn the Brandenburg Concerto No. 5 by Bach in a single rehearsal. When U.S. Secretary of Education Margaret Spellings sat in on an orchestra rehearsal in the spring of 2005 she was astonished. "The KIPP orchestra," she wrote later in a note to Concepcion, "is amazing and truly inspirational."

In the last half-dozen years, the orchestra has performed at Lincoln Center, Carnegie Hall, and the Apollo Theater. During four summer tours, it has given concerts in 18 cities around the country and performed with trumpeter Wynton Marsalis and Al Green, the famed rhythm and blues and gospel singer. Playing at Carnegie Hall is a heady experience for sixth, seventh, and eighth graders from the South Bronx, many of whom had never ventured into Manhattan. But for Concepcion and Dave Levin, the founder of KIPP Academy, the orchestra's appearances in legendary concert halls are less important than the learning that takes place in a lowly rehearsal room in the South Bronx. "Jesus is an incredible teacher—the kids come first for him," says Levin. "He worries first about building the character skills and academic skills and only then about the orchestra." The orchestra, Levin adds, is "such a visual example of what we are trying to teach in every aspect of the school. It demonstrates a type of greatness that is possible when students are willing to work together and sacrifice."

A youth orchestra or other school-wide music and arts programs exist at only a handful of the 57 schools in KIPP's school network in 2008. Even so, the KIPP Academy orchestra is very much in keeping with the commitment to high standards and character education that has made KIPP schools the best-known example of paternalistic, inner-city schooling in the nation. KIPP (Knowledge is Power Program) has been featured twice on *60 Minutes* and championed on *Oprah*, who hailed KIPP as "a revolutionary new school system." In 2005, *USA Today* dubbed KIPP "the most successful charter schools in the U.S." Politicians from both sides of the aisle have joined in the hosannas. Former Democratic senator John Edwards is a fan of KIPP. So, too, is George W. Bush, who visited the first KIPP Academy in Houston a decade ago as governor of Texas. Bush recalled that he came away from his visit "overwhelmed by the spirit of the kids, the involvement of the parents, the dedication of the teachers and the entrepreneurial spirit of the principal." KIPP, said Bush, had "the absolute right attitude for education."[1]

Given its press clippings, it's not altogether surprising that KIPP will soon become the largest charter school organization in the United States. Its 57 schools in 17 states and the District of Columbia currently educate 14,000 students. But in March 2007, the KIPP Foundation announced a dramatic expansion: Private philanthropists and foundations had pledged $65 million to create 34 new KIPP schools in Houston within the next decade, dwarfing all previous gifts in the 16-year history of the charter movement. In Houston, at full enrollment some 21,000 students will attend a total of 42 KIPP schools in 2017, accounting for roughly one out of every ten students in the district and about half of the expected growth in school-age children in Houston over the next decade. KIPP cofounder Mike Feinberg writes that when KIPP reaches full size in Houston, he hopes it will create "a 'tipping point' in public education"[2] in the city. Yet KIPP's visibility as a charter school icon, and the plaudits it receives for closing the achievement gap, have also made KIPP a target for charter critics such as Richard Rothstein of the Economic Policy Institute.

KIPP schools share a common culture that places a premium on academic achievement and building character. All but nine of KIPP's 57 schools are middle schools, serving fifth through eighth graders. Yet no matter what grades a KIPP school serves, students spend roughly 60 percent more time in school than their peers—the result of an extended school day, Saturday morning classes every two weeks, and three weeks of summer school. Teachers frequently use standardized assessments to identify and correct problems. KIPP schools have no admission requirements, and schools with waiting lists select students by lottery. But from the day that kids arrive, they learn what year their class will enroll in college. Classrooms are typically named after the colleges that teachers attended. Students show up at school in uniform or are sent home.

In each KIPP school, students learn the rubric of SLANT in class (Sit up straight, Listen, Answer and ask questions, Nod your head if you understand, and Track the speaker). The curriculum is not uniform from school to school. But mnemonics—chants, claps, rhymes, and finger-snapping—are used in the classroom to teach pupils in every school and to single out students for praise, particularly in the early grades. When youngsters enter a KIPP classroom, the teacher greets them at the door and typically has written on the board a "Do Now" (what students should work on as soon as they sit down), an "Aim" (the lesson objective), and an "Agenda" (the schedule for that day's class). Slogans posted on the walls of KIPP schools—"Work hard. Be nice"; "Team always beats individual"; and "No shortcuts. No excuses"—are the same from school to school. So, generally, is the "paycheck" system for good behavior that is used to parcel out virtual cash rewards, good towards field trips and other privileges.

The String and Rhythm Orchestra is but one more means through which KIPP's flagship school in New York reinforces the culture of achievement. But the middle-school orchestra deserves special attention for two reasons. Most paternalistic inner-city academies—including most schools in the KIPP network—have raised achievement among minority students by stripping away electives like dance or music, while boosting instructional time in math, reading, writing, and science. The KIPP Academy in the Bronx shows that it is possible to do both—to supplement the core curriculum with an elective like orchestra while still boosting instructional time in core subjects. The orchestra also provides a potent example of how a demanding but seemingly nonessential part of the curriculum can be used to enhance vital, noncognitive skills (like persistence and thoroughness) that can help boost student achievement in core areas. Principal Quinton Vance observes that the "orchestra is an anchor of the culture we have in the school—self-exertion, self-control, and high achievement. Orchestra is a place for our students where 100 percent are successful—you can't say that every kid will be 60 percent successful in algebra."

The Unorthodox Roots of KIPP

Like the Cristo Rey work-study program, KIPP has unlikely roots. It was born out of failure—namely, the frustrations of two novice members of Teach for America, Mike Feinberg and Dave Levin, who failed in their initial attempts to teach poor Hispanic and black students in Houston. KIPP's creation was thus not driven by ideological conviction or, say, by expert policy analysts at the liberal Education Trust or the conservative Heritage Foundation, two organizations that later hailed KIPP. In fact, there was little in KIPP's humble beginnings to suggest that it would quickly become a charter juggernaut.

The tale of KIPP's origins has been ably recounted elsewhere, notably by *Washington Post* education columnist Jay Mathews. But it illustrates how urban school reform can take unexpected turns. It begins when Dave Levin and Mike Feinberg met and became friends in 1992 at a summer training institute for Teach for America in Los Angeles. At the time, neither had much experience with the realities confronting students in inner-city schools. Both were recent Ivy League grads (Levin from Yale, Feinberg from the University of Pennsylvania), and Levin had previously attended Riverdale Country School, an exclusive private school in the Bronx.

Yet by the end of their summer training institute, the two friends expected that they would soon be star teachers at their new posts in Houston. Then they started to teach—and realized "they had no idea what they were doing. Levin's class was in chaos. His tires were slashed in the teachers' parking lot. A student sent to the office for throwing a book at Levin's head returned smiling with a Tootsie Pop."[3] Levin's school soon added 17 kids to his starting class of 11 students, but Levin innocently had the two groups of students face each other in the classroom—unaware that they were in rival gangs. An office pool with odds was set up as to whether Levin would last as a teacher past Thanksgiving.[4]

Yet Levin and Feinberg were bone-stubborn. The two men, both 6'3" and basketball fanatics, once played a one-on-one game on a Houston playground for hours because each was too pigheaded to call off the match. They vowed to dedicate themselves to becoming top-notch teachers and soon started spending their hours before and after school visiting surprised students at home, asking parents for help with discipline. Then Levin got a break: Down the hall from his class, a local legend, an African-American woman named Harriett Ball, was teaching. Ball had successfully pioneered the use of mnemonics in her classes—chants, finger snaps, claps, and call-and-response drills—to help disadvantaged students develop math and reading skills. Levin became Ball's protégé and started using many of her teaching techniques. When he had time, Levin sat in on Ball's classes. After school, he would drag her to a nearby club for happy hour drinks and ply her with questions. On weekends, Ball would sometimes stop by Levin and Feinberg's apartment, or they would drop by her house to continue their tutorial.[5]

Feinberg and Levin were fast studies and soon became outstanding teachers themselves. In fact, the faculty at Bastian Elementary School ended up voting Levin "Teacher of the Year" after 96 percent of his students passed either the state math or reading tests and 70 percent passed both.[6] But Levin's and Feinberg's intense passion for teaching did not wear well with school administrators. When Levin's principal directed him to exempt several low-scoring Hispanic students from state tests to boost the school's average scores, Levin refused—and then persuaded parents not to sign a form exempting their children from the test. (The children passed the state tests, as Levin had promised.) At the end of the 1993–1994 school year, Levin was fired for what his principal deemed insubordination.[7]

By then, Levin and Feinberg were already planning to start an academy—or at least a single grade to test their methods. One night in 1993, while listening to U2's "Achtung Baby" on repeat play, the two worked until dawn drawing up a plan for a fifth-grade class in Feinberg's elementary school.[8] The class of 50 students, which they would co-teach in a single classroom, would utilize many of Ball's techniques, embrace high standards, have no-excuses discipline, and provide rewards for good behavior, such as trips to the AstroWorld theme park. "We were not thinking so much 'how can we reform urban education' as 'how can we help these kids?'" says Levin. "It sounds like a cliché, but we kept asking ourselves what more could we do?"

Before Levin and Feinberg could go much farther, they had to find parents of 50 low-income Hispanic and black students willing to take a risk on their child's education with two twenty-something white teachers. The two Ivy League graduates went door to door, trudging through housing projects and apartment complexes in predominantly Hispanic sections of Houston. "When we had no reputation, it was tough," says Levin. "We were setting up a new school that was not familiar to people. There was no way of saying 'this will be just like the school down the street.'"

Despite their own liberal predilections, Levin and Feinberg shared an unflinching commitment to raising achievement scores by any means that worked, even if those means were traditional. They assigned lots of homework to their fifth graders and told students to call them at home with questions, sometimes fielding as many as 20 calls a night on their one phone line.[9]

Once again, Levin and Feinberg had spectacular success. Only about half of their fifth grade class had passed state math and reading tests the previous year; by the end of the year, more than 90 percent passed both the math and English tests. Yet once more, the two reformers roused the ire of the school principal, who wanted them to move their program to another school. At the end of the 1994–1995 school year, Levin relocated back to the Bronx to found KIPP Academy, which opened with 50 fifth-grade students in borrowed space in a public school in September 1995. To recruit students, Levin "had to sneak into a parents' meeting from which he had been barred, and whisper invitations to take a look at KIPP, before he was escorted out."[10]

Back in Houston, Feinberg was getting bumped around from school to school, teaching classes in trailers in a school parking lot, as he slowly expanded to add sixth, seventh, and eighth grades to KIPP Academy Houston. When aides in the Houston superintendent's office stopped him from making his case for more space to then-superintendent Rod Paige, Feinberg went to the district headquarters after school one steaming April day and sat on the rear bumper of Paige's maroon Acura for four hours until Paige left to go home. When Paige (who later became secretary of education) came out of district headquarters, Feinberg confronted him, calling out excitedly "Dr. Paige! I'm in a pickle. You've got to help me. They are trying to take away my babies!"[11] Feinberg got his extra classroom space.

By 1999, five years after their first classes had started, the two founding KIPP academies were the best-performing nonselective middle schools in Houston and the Bronx. Feinberg was still operating KIPP Houston out of a dozen trailers parked just outside the baseball fields of Houston Baptist

University, while KIPP Academy in the South Bronx had graduated to a corridor and a half on the fourth floor of Lou Gehrig Junior High. The success of the two flagship schools led to a glowing *60 Minutes* profile of KIPP. And in 2000, Doris and Donald Fisher, cofounders of The Gap, Inc., formed the KIPP Foundation in San Francisco in partnership with Feinberg and Levin to replicate the two flagship schools elsewhere. Aided by star alumni of Teach for America, whom Feinberg and Levin handpicked to run the first trio of replication schools, the KIPP gospel soon started spreading across the country.

The Acculturation Crash Course

How do newcomers to KIPP "get religion"? Incoming students start learning the KIPP gospel in an acculturation crash course during summer school before fifth grade. New students learn quickly that KIPP schools are different. Their rules governing behavior and appearance are strict, so much so that some critics have sarcastically dubbed KIPP the "Kids in Prison Program."

As part of a 2006 evaluation, a team of researchers observed the first day of summer school for students in Bay Area KIPP schools. Their description, excerpted below, conveys some of the acculturation shock that new "KIPPsters" face. To put the opening day in perspective, imagine being a 10-year-old on his or her first day at summer school:

> At 7:45 a.m. the staff welcomes the new students [in the gym] and immediately recognizes students who are in proper uniform. Throughout the morning, teachers call the parents of students who are not dressed appropriately, e.g., wearing the wrong color pants, a white shirt without a collar, or sneakers, or not wearing a belt. After the staff and returning students are introduced, students learn how to stand properly in line—silently and with a book in their hand. They are taught that lines should be SILENT, STRAIGHT, and SERIOUS. Students then learn how to walk in a straight line, silently. They repeat standing and walking in line a few times, until they get it right, before they walk to the cafeteria for breakfast. At breakfast, students are given a few minutes to eat and then continue their morning work. During breakfast, they are taught how to write a KIPP header on a paper and the "Clap Praise" (a teacher counts 1-2-3 and everyone claps in unison). When students return to the gym, the principal singles out students who were late and reminds students of the value of being on time. Students then learn silent hand signals for yes and no, the clap that teachers use

to get students' attention, and are taught how to use the bathroom and keep it clean. Throughout the morning, students who are off-task or not in proper attire must apologize publicly to their teammates. Working hard, being nice, and following directions are constantly promoted as values that will get them to college. The one academic lesson for the day is that students learn to 'roll their nines' by repeating "9, 18, 27, 36, 45..." over and over, using their fingers to indicate the multiplier (1 times 9, 2 times 9, etc). Before students leave for the day, they receive their first homework assignment. They are told that tomorrow, the second day of summer school, teachers will be checking to see that homework is complete and that "agendas" are signed by parents. Teachers will call the parents of students who do not complete their first homework assignments. [12]

Summer school at KIPP Academy in the Bronx is even tougher because the school has no central air conditioning, forcing students literally to sweat out their three weeks. Once fifth graders start KIPP Academy in the fall, the regimen remains every bit as prescriptive and demanding. George Ramirez, a seventh grader in 2006, remembers his shock when he started fifth grade, even though his older sister had attended KIPP Academy. In Ramirez's grammar school in the South Bronx, students could run around in class without complaint from teachers. At KIPP, students had to walk silently to their lockers. Once, Ramirez spoke to another student on the way to his locker in earshot of a teacher and promptly lost $3 from his $50 weekly virtual KIPP "paycheck." Merely tapping a pen in class, Ramirez discovered, could lead to a paycheck deduction.

At his elementary school, students often failed to pay attention, forcing teachers to repeat the lesson four or five times. KIPP, by contrast, "was very tough at first—it's a very fast way of learning," says Ramirez. "You take all the information down and you are supposed to know it the next day...I needed help in math in fifth grade and called my teacher one week three times a night. That kind of thing didn't happen in my old school." Da'Shawna King, another seventh grader, recalls with dread after-school detention or "AP" for not getting her homework done. "I was in AP four or five times in sixth grade," King recalls. "For AP you had to do homework until 6:00 P.M. and at lunch you had to eat downstairs and sit with the teachers. After lunch, you'd come upstairs and stand on the black [line-up] line [in KIPP's hallway] and wait for the rest of your classmates to come upstairs [to line up]. AP is like being in prison—you can't talk to your friends or go outside."

Yet for all of KIPP's rules and discipline, most students speak fondly about the school, describing it in terms more often applied to a family than a penitentiary. "They are extremely strict here but the teachers strive and strive for you to learn" says Ramirez. "Being at KIPP is like being in your house without your parents—and that's why a lot of kids say KIPP is like a second home." Strictness, in short, goes hand-in-hand with support and encouragement from teachers and staff. KIPP Academy has two fulltime social workers on staff who assist students with personal problems; a third social worker, in the school's KIPP to College program, helps students after they graduate from middle school.

Fifth graders' introduction to the KIPP orchestra powerfully reinforces the acculturation gauntlet. Fifth graders neither play an instrument in the orchestra nor do they play a single note in class or rehearsal for the entire fifth grade. During the first two weeks of music class, fifth graders practice simply walking into the music room, taking their seats, and tracking Concepcion. Concepcion is well aware that KIPP's behavioral training is what makes it possible for him to conduct a 180-person orchestra. "I have 180 kids at practice and they go dead silent when I clap twice," he says. "But I need Dave [Levin's] support and all the support of my fellow teachers. I can stand in a room with 180 kids by myself and command their absolute attention only because teachers don't send me 180 rowdy kids late in the afternoon."

Training for the orchestra is carefully calibrated to allow students to take on more responsibilities as they master basic skills. In fifth grade, after they have learned to sit silently, track Concepcion, and stand, they move on to clapping out rhythms. Soon Concepcion is training them in music theory and sight reading. All the while, he is building an appreciation for music and a reverence for the violins and violas that the students will take home and on which they will practice in sixth grade. Twice a week, whenever a fifth grader walks into music class, they touch the glockenspiel by the door, a sign of respect for the first instrument they will play. By the end of the year, most students are beginning to sight read music and are allowed to take a musical instrument out of its case and name its parts but not to play it. Fifth graders learn to call the instruments they are studying "my baby" to emphasize the instrument's value and need for care.

In sixth grade, every student at KIPP Academy joins the orchestra and finally has the opportunity to study an instrument. At the beginning of the year,

Concepcion assigns the instruments that sixth graders will play—but even then students don't start playing and practicing scales right away. For the first month, they practice opening violin and viola cases and lifting their instruments from the rack. They learn the proper maintenance for their instruments and practice various bow and finger positions on Concepcion's command.

Sixth graders spend significantly more time in the orchestra room than fifth graders. They have three hour-long music classes a week, orchestra practice after school on Monday through Thursday from 3:45 P.M. to 5:00 P.M., and a four-hour rehearsal on Saturday morning. Concepcion arranges all of the orchestra's music—and makes sure to write simpler parts for his novice sixth-grade musicians than for his seventh and eighth graders. Still, by the end of sixth grade, KIPP students are starting to develop a relatively sophisticated ear and knowledge of music notation that is alien to their peers in the South Bronx. They know the difference between an andante and allegro tempo, between playing a note tenuto or a fermata, and between staccato and legato.

By seventh grade, students spend almost as much time in orchestra practice as any core subject. They have music class five times a week and rehearsals after school four days a week plus Saturday morning. Many seventh graders stop by the music room to practice during lunch, and students take their string instruments home to practice. By the close of the year, KIPP seventh graders are becoming accomplished young musicians. The strings play in a confident, aggressive style, and the rhythm section—composed of tympani drums, timbales, congas, bongos, and electric bass—swings.

Seventh and eighth graders at KIPP learn music with stunning speed for a middle-school orchestra, largely because Concepcion has taught every student to sight read and has provided grounding in musical theory and notation. To cite one example, the morning after the orchestra's lackluster rehearsal for the graduation concert, Concepcion improvised a new ending to a song on a D-major chord with his seventh-grade music class. Four times in a row, the orchestra followed Concepcion as he experimented with the D-major resolution. A few minutes later, in his next class, Concepcion told his eighth graders that the orchestra might have to include an intermission in the concert, necessitating the addition of a piece of music at the last moment. "Please get out the Brandenburg Concerto No. 5," Concepcion announced. Without pause, the eighth graders pulled out sheet music for the Brandenburg Concerto and played it easily—though they had not looked at the piece for months.

Even when Concepcion is dealing with his older and more experienced players, he continually emphasizes not just music but character. He leads the orchestra in a kind of affectionate tango, veering back and forth between lectures, intense practice, and shared laughter. After their spotty rehearsal, Concepcion opened class with his seventh graders by announcing, "First, let me tell you what went well yesterday: Nothing! People were not sitting straight, you walked in and out in a sloppy fashion, and the basses were not holding their instruments symmetrically. Let me make clear what I am looking for today. I'm looking for the way you sit and focus. If you can't focus, and you can't handle the heat—which will be worse tomorrow night—you are not playing tomorrow night."

Yet a few minutes later, all is forgiven. A boy asks a question in a voice that breaks between his old tenor register and his newfound baritone, prompting Concepcion to joke "you sound like Barry White." A round of giggles runs through the orchestra. Several students raise their hands with questions, and Concepcion—known universally to his students as "Mr. C"—addresses them warmly, like family. "What is it, my sweetheart?" he asks one girl before calling on a boy by saying "Yes, my son." Katherine Brayan, second chair in the eighth grade violin section, says later that "sometimes Mr. C is like a little kid, like us. But he is always serious when we play." Still, there is a good reason why Concepcion has such a strong paternal bond with the members of the orchestra. For when he looks out at the sea of Hispanic and African-American middle schoolers at rehearsal, he sees himself as a 12-year old, struggling to learn the violin.

Evolution of the KIPP Orchestra

Like KIPP itself, the orchestra started from the humblest of beginnings. When Concepcion first attended a rehearsal in 1999, it had all of 12 members, and it played the same repertoire for years at a time. Concepcion came to KIPP to help music teacher Charlie Randall, Concepcion's former violin teacher and middle-school mentor. During the next five years, Randall helped the orchestra dramatically expand before turning its leadership over entirely to Concepcion. Today, Concepcion is passing on many of the lessons that he initially learned over a decade ago from Randall.

Concepcion grew up just a few blocks away, the son of a father from Puerto Rico and a mother from the Dominican Republic. His father died when

Concepcion was just one year old, and his mother, who worked as a home health aide, never remarried. The family was poor, and Concepcion knew it. His mother would come to school to check on his performance in class first before purchasing a 50-cent tie for his school uniform. Still, Concepcion was fortunate enough to grow up surrounded by music. His sister Petrushka was named after the Stravinsky ballet, and his home was filled with music night and day, from classical to salsa. At first, Concepcion studied the saxophone in his elementary school band. But in sixth grade, he developed a crush on the female violin player who sat first chair in the violin section of the school orchestra and impulsively took up the violin to impress her.

At LaGuardia High School of Music and Art and Performing Arts, Concepcion developed into an outstanding violinist, winning a scholarship to the famed Juilliard School. While at Juilliard, however, Concepcion was in a car accident and cut a tendon in his hand, making it difficult to play with his bow hand. He opted instead to become a conducting major, and was one of only nine students in his class to graduate with a master's degree in conducting. The Juilliard grad then started traveling the world, guest conducting the national symphony orchestras of Venezuela and the Dominican Republic. Finally, when his mother fell ill, Concepcion started looking into more permanent teaching jobs in New York—and eventually found his way to Charlie Randall's door at KIPP Academy in 1999.

No one at KIPP, including Dave Levin—who confesses that he can't "keep a tune, a rhythm, nothing"—anticipated the role the orchestra would assume at the school. But Concepcion soon fell in love with the students at KIPP Academy, despite their lack of musical sophistication. In many respects, their stories were his story. He knew what it meant to grow up poor. He made sure to keep a small stash of toiletries in his office to protect orchestra members from feeling embarrassed for going without. He knew what it was like to walk home to the projects alone at night—and after rehearsals started giving several students rides home when a parent or grandmother could not pick them up. He knew, too, that some single parents had chaotic households or demanding work schedules that led their children to be late for school—and so he started driving students to school in the mornings, too.

Most of all, Concepcion knew that music and the discipline of an orchestra could provide a ticket to the world beyond the barrio. He was awed by Dave Levin's ability and that of other KIPP Academy teachers to command a classroom. "I wasn't born to be a teacher—I went to Juilliard to be a symphony conductor," says Concepcion. "The reason I fell in love with teaching is because of the training that Dave gave me. He didn't have to say anything. Just watching him work with kids that looked like me and lived in the same neighborhood where I grew up—that to me was so real. The fact is I'm just implementing a lot of Dave's ideas."

In many cases, the orchestra's top players are not the school's top students. But just as a great teacher can make a disadvantaged student believe it is cool to be smart, a great conductor can teach an inner-city teenager to appreciate the beauty of Mozart or Mendelssohn. Da'Shawna King admits she had to "work on her attitude" when she started at KIPP and had to stay after school on a number of occasions for failing to do her homework. She says now that she is earning mostly B's and a few C's in class. But as the seventh-grade head of the percussion section, she is a star in the orchestra—and she lights up when she talks about it. "The drums are everything to me," she says. "I love everything about them—like the sound of the high hat opening and closing. I feel like if I wasn't playing the drums, the orchestra would be finished. I don't want to get in trouble and miss a concert." Concepcion sometimes lets King take a snare drum home to practice but she doesn't have her own drum set at home. To compensate, she gets to school early, at 7:00 A.M., to practice the drums before school starts. At the 2006 concert at Lincoln Center, the eighth-grade percussion section leader couldn't play so King headed the orchestra's entire percussion section for the show. "I was afraid of missing my beat in front of a big audience, and I had to make sure my section was sitting upright and paying attention," she says. "But Mr. C said I really stepped up. From now on, I can't let him down."

Most members of the KIPP orchestra learn to play the violin or the viola, two of the most challenging instruments in the orchestra. Holding the neck and bow correctly on the violin, playing a note with the proper intonation, and fingering notes so that they are in tune are no simple feats, even for an experienced violinist, much less for middle-school students. It takes considerable self-control and steady practice for an 11-year-old violin novice to master even the rudiments of playing the instrument—as Concepcion remembers all too well. "By teaching violin we are looking to cultivate the discipline you need to become a good musician and a great orchestra," says principal Quinton Vance. "Our stock phrase is that if you can play a violin, you can read *To Kill a Mockingbird*. If you can play the viola, you can do algebra."

While the orchestra plays an important role in nurturing character skills that help students in core academic courses, the KIPP Academy orchestra has a strikingly different mission than top-flight student orchestras at performing arts schools. "The mistake that most arts teachers make is that they gravitate toward the talented kids," says Concepcion. "That leaves 98 percent of the kids alone." None of Concepcion's students have gone on to play elsewhere or pursued orchestral careers. Concepcion elaborated on the unusual place that the orchestra occupies at KIPP Academy by observing that

> The idea of the orchestra here is not to train musicians — rather it is to use the fact that the orchestra is the one thing that every child at KIPP Academy has in common. At other schools, maybe it's the basketball team that brings students together. But once you have one activity at a school that every student is involved in, you can focus on creating culture and discipline in that activity — and at our school, everyone will rally around the orchestra. I don't penalize a kid if he has trouble with academics. If I can only take 60 students to a concert, I will pick them based on character, not on their grades. I will take the kids who want to challenge other players, who want to be a leader and bring up people in the section. The idea of the KIPP orchestra is not to have a great drummer or violinist. I am very careful in singling out kids for praise. My seventh graders are mighty. But they will tell you that they can't do it without the eighth graders. I need to be able to spread out that feeling of success.

While Concepcion emphasizes teamwork and shared accomplishment, the orchestra also stokes competition among its members. As in many school orchestras, students are arranged in a numerical ranking of chairs by ability, from the concertmaster on down through section heads to the last chair in each section. Students can "challenge" a student in their grade who is in a higher chair to a contest of playing ability, using either a part of a piece in the KIPP repertoire or a series of scales. If the challenger wins, he or she assumes the chair of the fellow musician that was outplayed. But in the KIPP orchestra, students can also lose their chairs for behavioral infractions or a lack of leadership. "Students challenge fiercely — and it happens constantly," says Concepcion.

Section leaders have added responsibilities of maintaining order in their section and teaching parts to their section members. "Mr. C is my teacher, and I'm the teacher to the section," says Ramirez. "But we're only as good as our weakest link. That's why I practice a lot — if you don't know your music well, you can't teach it to the section. And if you don't know your music well, you can be challenged and lose your chair."

Most inner-city schools, paternalistic or not, lack a common unifying activity like the orchestra. But the presence of the orchestra also makes it easier for Concepcion to become a kind of school-wide complaint box for teachers grappling with struggling students. Most mornings, he receives a string of reports from other teachers about students who aren't doing their homework, have acted up in class, or have fallen short of other KIPP goals. To cite one example, the morning after rehearsal for the end-of-year concert, Concepcion refused to let the first chair of the eighth-grade violin section challenge the concertmaster when he learned that she had been slacking off on her school work. Students, meanwhile, constantly call Concepcion on his cell phone when they forget their homework and ask that he put in a word on their behalf with teachers. All told, Concepcion fields about ten phone calls a night at home and is remarkably well-versed in the details of his students' lives.

He once was called at 1:00 A.M. by a student who needed to get let back into his family's apartment after the police locked down his housing project following a shooting. Ramirez used to call Concepcion at night, put him on speaker phone, and ask that he listen to him practice on the violin. "Mr. C would say 'that's good but your C is sharp'," says Ramirez. Ramirez called Concepcion to consult about nonacademic matters, too. In sixth grade, he even phoned to ask what he should get his dad for Father's Day. "He told me to invite him to breakfast and to give him socks because he likes socks," Ramirez recalls. Concepcion says that "a lot of problems come to me, with teachers walking in every morning. I don't particularly like assuming that role. But I do feel like I need to know what is going on in the school."

Concepcion sometimes temporarily serves in loco parentis for students who have single parents that are busy at work, have little schooling, or struggle with their own problems. Yet his parent-like connection with students is typical of many teachers at KIPP schools. As Dacia Toll found at Amistad Academy, Dave Levin and Mike Feinberg believe that KIPP's rigorous model and discipline only work when students believe that teachers care deeply about them. As Feinberg put it in a recent appearance on ABC's *Good Morning America*, "the most important thing [in motivating fifth and sixth graders] is for the children to know that the adults in their life care…The kids should know that the teachers are truly invested in their lives and want to see them go to college." [13]

KIPP asks parents or guardians to show they care, too. Parents sign a "commitment to excellence" contract that says they will get their children to school on time, arrange to pick them up at 5:00 P.M., have them attend school on Saturdays and during the summer, check their homework every night, limit the amount of television they watch, and have them follow the school dress code. Most parents abide by the spirit if not the letter of the KIPP contract, and the school actively encourages parental involvement. KIPP Academy now has a Parents Association of about 15 members, who help chaperone trips and participate in workshops like "Breakfast and Books," which pairs parents with fifth graders to read books and do related art projects.

KIPP Academy has more involved parents than some inner-city schools, though its parents tend to be far less involved than parents at a good suburban school. "Some schools tell parents 'we expect you to spend one day a month in your child's school'," says principal Vance. "We don't say that because it's not realistic for some of our parents who work or who are taking care of kids. But I wouldn't interpret that as a lack of commitment on their part." Still, both Vance and Concepcion acknowledge that a small minority of parents—perhaps ten percent—are actively disengaged from the school and can tie up teachers and school resources. "If you have a small percentage of parents who are not supportive, it can stress you out," says Concepcion. "You can have kids not doing their homework or getting to school late. If I tell a parent to [buzz] off, I have to be ready to be the parent. And I can't be the father to every child."

Rigor without Bells and Whistles

KIPP Academy's decrepit appearance belies its academic quality. The school consists of a corridor and a half on the fourth floor of Independent School (IS) 151, a South Bronx elementary and junior high school (Lou Gehrig Junior High). By no means is it a gilded facility, even by inner-city standards. Its "computer lab" consists of two mobile cart units with 35 laptops. It has no airy library, playing fields, gym, or cafeteria. It leases a mere 15,000 square feet from the district in I.S. 151 for four grades and 250 students—and scrapes by only by borrowing the auditorium, cafeteria, and playground of I.S. 151 for rehearsals, meals, and PE class. Yet despite KIPP's meager facility, visitors are inevitably struck by the difference between the KIPP Academy hallway and the rest of I.S. 151—which is filled with junior high school students from the same neighborhoods and housing projects. One reporter from *U.S. News* described it as a "dingy industrial-style building in New York's bleak South Bronx. In the main lobby, visitors are greeted by two New York City policemen and posted tips on preventing grand larceny. Lined up for lunch, the kids [of I.S. 151] are shouting, shoving, and demonstrably ignoring reprimands from a hall monitor. Upstairs, on the KIPP floor, is a very different scene: In hallways lined with A-grade work and pennants from teachers' alma maters, uniformed students stand silent and still."[14]

As a charter school, KIPP Academy gets only about 80 percent of the funding per student that New York City public schools receive. It makes up the difference through an aggressive fundraising campaign that raised about $2 million in 2006 to help cover operating costs.[15] In addition, the school raises money to run the KIPP to College Program and other programming at KIPP's four middle schools in New York City. Though KIPP Academy lacks the bells and whistles of a comprehensive school, it does have several unusual amenities. With the benefit of privately raised funds, it takes students on year-end trips to Washington, D.C., and California, and to Utah, where they camp and hike in Zion and Bryce Canyons. The orchestra typically tours each summer, too. Purchasing and maintaining instruments for a 180-student orchestra is not cheap. Beginner violins for sixth graders cost about $200 apiece, while eighth graders' violins run about $800. Cellos costs about $1,200, and electric pianos and drum sets are in the $2,500 range. Strings are expensive to maintain, too—Levin reports that KIPP spends about $35,000 a year to keep up the orchestra.

KIPP students also have far more core academic instruction time—over 300 minutes a day—than pupils in typical, urban middle schools, where core instruction time averages only about 185 minutes. Like other KIPP schools, KIPP Academy uses weekly tests and quizzes to assess student progress and weaknesses, sets aside 90-minute blocks for reading and math, and has Saturday classes and summer school. It does not practice social promotion. But as one of KIPP's two flagships, it has gone further than most KIPP schools in providing personal support to students, utilizing what historian Diane Ravitch has called the "social-work concept of schooling." For example, KIPP Academy has two fulltime social workers who meet with the most at-risk students on a daily basis and with all KIPP students regularly.

One of the chief purposes of the school's private fundraising is to recruit and pay talented teachers who share KIPP's mission to close the achievement gap. Sitting in KIPP classrooms, one cannot help but be struck by the unswerving devotion of KIPP's youthful teachers to building character and boosting academic performance. Many are former instructors from Teach for America. As Feinberg has put it, KIPP looks for teachers "with fire in their belly."[16]

KIPP Academy pays instructors 15 to 20 percent more than they would receive at neighborhood schools in the Bronx. Yet the higher salaries are small compensation for the extended school day and school year. As Concepcion puts it, "I don't know what it means to not take my work home." Quinton Vance reports that he calls six students every morning before school to wake them up because their parents work a night shift. Unlike at most KIPP schools, teachers at KIPP Academy are unionized, and all teachers receive nine hours of overtime pay each week in keeping with the union contract. Still, the school's union exists more in name than in reality. "It's laughable, but KIPP Bronx does have a union," says Dacia Toll of Achievement First. Principal Vance allows that "our teachers, by nature of who we are, tend to work outside the constraints of the union. Our teachers are really committed to the educational and character outcomes — versus worrying about how much work they are doing or whether they are helping to serve lunch."

While KIPP is academically rigorous throughout the curriculum, nowhere has the school been more successful than in teaching math. All eighth graders complete a two-year, high-school-level algebra I course and take the New York State Math A Regents exam, a high school exit exam. In 2006, an astonishing 85 percent passed it.

Seventh- and eighth-grade math is taught by Frank Corcoran, an outstanding teacher who has taught math at KIPP for 12 years and won the *New York Post*'s Educator Liberty Medal in 2005. With his shoulder-length, sandy-blonde hair, Corcoran looks more like an aging surfer than an award-winning math instructor. But he has managed to find ways to make math fun as well as rigorous. He built by hand "Corcoran's Math Café," which consists of five booths along the windows of his classroom with various signs and neon-lit café menus that extol the virtues of math. Signs in diploma-sized frames — "Math is Good Food," "Serving Mathematicians since 1995," "Try the π," and "The Math Café serves the best equation in town" — adorn the classroom walls. Next to the café booths is the "The Wall of Honor," which features framed pictures of past students — listing their class, their scores on the Regents exam, their mastery ratings on the algebra standards tests, prep schools that students have gone on to, and, where applicable, the colleges of graduates.

One day in the spring of 2006, the eighth-grade class whistled through factoring the following math expression posted by Corcoran on the blackboard: $24p^3q^7 + 36pq^{10}$.

His class has a one-by-six foot yellow banner opposite the café booths that announces "Team always beats individual!"—and, true to form, Corcoran led his class in a collegial discussion, with different students chipping in to factor the expression. (It reduced to $12pq^7 \times (2p^2+3q^3)$.) At the end of class, Corcoran announced, "Line up please"—only to order students back to their chairs to stand and line up again when they didn't line up properly the first time. Other students quietly used erasers to clean the blackboard and sprayed the café booths with Fantastik to clean them for the next class.

Down the hall, the two sixth-grade classes were hosting their own versions of an English class café, a kind of poetry slam where students served lunch. With help from their teachers, they had organized the two cafés, replete with printed menus and food supplied by parents. Student emcees introduced students before they read their poems, while classmates, teachers, and a few parents munched on hummus with baby carrots, lasagna, and cheese or chicken pastelitos. Though some KIPP critics have suggested that KIPP Academy students do well academically because they come from supportive, intact families, the poetry cafés provided a more complicated picture. One sixth grader read a poem about having no father at the age of 11; another student started crying when she read her poem, "Daddy," about a father who was both distant and critical of her despite doing well at school.

While many of the student works displayed a gift for poetry, none hinted that KIPP Academy students were children of "Buppies," or young black urban professionals. At "Café Colgate," students read poems that showed a sharp appreciation (for 12-year-olds) of life in the ghetto. In his poem "Sometimes," a boy read:

Sometimes I wonder

Why I even try

Because you fly so high

Knowing some day you gonna

Die

Sometimes I wonder

Why even be scared

Because you already know

Death is

Near

Sometimes I wonder

Why I should be good

Because at the end

Of the day you're a boy from

The hood

Getting criticized

By the harsh

Stereotypes that are articulated

In someone's head

Sometimes I wonder

Why I lie

I think to just give it

All a try

Because I can't

Change the fact

That my father

Died

Another sixth grader at Café Colgate wrote about her fierce determination to escape the poverty of the South Bronx in her poem "Where I'm From":

I'm from the crazy streets

I'm from the natural essence

I'm from the streets of tough thieves

I'm from NYC

I'm going places

Doing things

I'm leaving

I'm running from this crazy life

I'm taking my chance to be someone

I'm going away

I'm on track

Staying away from the 'hood'

They say you can take the girl out the ghetto

But you can't take the ghetto out of the girl

The ghetto is leaving this girl

Let me fly

Give me wings

Let me be

'Cause I'm leaving and I ain't coming back

Closing the Achievement Gap

No matter how the numbers are sliced, KIPP Academy's record of academic achievement is impressive. For nine years in a row, it has had the highest math, reading scores, and attendance of any nonselective middle school in the Bronx. It ranks in the top 10 percent of all New York City public schools—and by the time eighth graders graduate, they have eliminated the achievement gap separating white and minority students. On the Stanford-10 tests in 2005–2006, 83 percent of KIPP Academy eighth graders scored above the national average in mathematics, 70 percent did so in language, and 65 percent in reading.

KIPP Academy students make dramatic achievement gains in fifth grade and typically continue to improve as they move through the middle school—indicating that the school itself is boosting student performance rather than just benefiting from having bright incoming students. For the most part, KIPP graduates have gone on to good high schools. Roughly half go to parochial schools, nearly a third attend independent private schools (including many elite prep schools), and about one in five attend specialized public high school programs. Not a single student from KIPP's eight graduating classes has matriculated to a local zoned high school. KIPP Academy middle school students are not quite as likely to later go on to college as their peers at Cristo Rey Jesuit High School in Chicago, but the school still has a very high college matriculation rate—roughly 80 percent in recent years.

The gap in academic performance between KIPP Academy and other public middle schools in the South Bronx is, quite simply, vast. On state tests in 2005–2006, just 16 percent of eighth graders in schools in KIPP's district were proficient in math, and 16 percent in English language arts. KIPP eighth graders were four to five times more likely to be proficient than their South Bronx peers.

Table 6-1 below compares the academic performance of KIPP Academy eighth graders with students at three nearby public middle schools with similar demographic characteristics. All four schools are composed almost exclusively of low-income black and Hispanic students from the same neighborhoods and housing projects. At the three comparison schools, eighth graders failed to make AYP (adequate yearly progress) in every subject while KIPP eighth graders handily made AYP. Note especially the eye-popping disparity in academic achievement between KIPP students and Lou Gehrig eighth graders, who go to school in the same building. While roughly half of Lou Gehrig students have serious academic deficiencies in English language arts or math, about seven in ten KIPP Academy eighth graders have proficient or advanced skills.

Several of the usual demographic suspects fail to explain the superior performance of KIPP students. Like their peers at comparison schools, KIPP students are likely to live in poverty and come from single-parent families. More than 85 percent of them were poor enough to qualify for the federal

Table 6-1. Academic achievement at KIPP Academy and nearby schools

	Distance to KIPP (miles)	2005-06 New York state standards test • Percentage of students meeting or exceeding standards		
		8th grade English Language Arts	8th grade Math	8th grade Science
KIPP Academy		64	87	87
Lou Gehrig (J.H.S. 151)	0	9	5	9
Paul Laurence Dunbar (M.S. 301)	0.7	11	15	12
Theodore Roosevelt Gathings (I.S. 158)	1.1	9	8	7
District Average (District 7 in the South Bronx)		16	16	17
State Average (New York)		49	54	64

Source: New York State School and District Report Cards for School Year 2005–2006, https://www.nystart.gov/ publicweb/ (accessed April 1, 2008). New York State school report cards for 2006-2007 were not available as of April 1, 2008, so data from that year could not be included in this volume.

school lunch program in 2005–2006. KIPP had 17 special education students in 2005–2006 with IEP plans, or 7 percent of its student body (compared with 11.5 percent in New York City public schools that same year). But with about 30 students per class, KIPP Academy does not have small classes — and actually has larger classes on average than Lou Gehrig Junior High.

Teachers at KIPP Academy were more likely to have five years of classroom experience than their peers at nearby schools. But they were significantly less likely to be fully licensed and permanently assigned — in 2005–2006, almost half of KIPP teachers did not have a valid teaching certificate.

Eighth graders' scores at KIPP Academy are not an artifact of a high attrition rate, either.[17] The school has an average yearly attrition rate of 4.5 percent (counting all reasons for student departures, including moves to other boroughs and cities) and hardly ever expels a student. Since arriving in fifth grade, KIPP Academy eighth graders have a total attrition rate of 13 percent, a much lower rate of attrition than at Cristo Rey Jesuit High School in Chicago or at KIPP schools in the Bay Area.

Several demographic factors do, however, appear to contribute to KIPP Academy's success. First, it has significantly fewer Limited English Proficient

(LEP) students than comparison schools in the Bronx (or at least is less likely to classify them as LEP); it also has proportionately more female students (58 percent) who tend to score higher on middle school achievement tests. KIPP does no screening for test scores, grades, behavioral history, or language, with students gaining admission through a random lottery. Nevertheless, for reasons that are unclear, only 2 percent of the KIPP enrollment were LEP students in the 2005–2006 school year (down from 7 percent the year before), while at comparison schools, 11 to 21 percent were English learners.[18]

The Great Creaming Debate

Richard Rothstein, a former education columnist for the *New York Times* and a research associate at the Economic Policy Institute, assessed KIPP's record in two chapters appearing in larger works that argued that schools alone could not close the achievement gap. In his 2004 book, *Class and Schools*, Rothstein argued that the success of KIPP and other no-excuses schools failed to show that "typical" disadvantaged youngsters would overcome social and economic inequalities; KIPP pupils, he wrote "are not typical lower class students. That their parents choose to enroll them in this highly academic program sets them apart...KIPP has [not] shown how to get middle-class results from typical lower-class students without addressing the social and economic causes of failure."[19]

The following year, Rothstein and Rebecca Jacobsen authored a chapter assessing KIPP in an Economic Policy Institute report, *The Charter School Dust-Up*. The volume defended studies by the American Federation of Teachers and the National Center for Education Statistics that found that charter school pupils, on average, lagged behind students in regular public schools. Rothstein and Jacobsen argued that the lower scores of charter students did not stem from their greater disadvantage. For the first time, Rothstein presented data of his own—much of it centered on KIPP Academy in the Bronx—that indicated KIPP students had better academic skills than their inner-city peers. Rothstein and Jacobsen also debunked claims by charter proponents that KIPP had "students who are *more* disadvantaged [my emphasis] than students in comparable regular public schools, yet whose test scores after being in KIPP are typically higher than scores for black and Hispanic children generally."[20]

Rothstein cited several pieces of evidence to document his claim that KIPP Academy attracted superior students from unusually supportive families in the Bronx. As fourth graders entering KIPP Academy, students in 2002 had higher reading scores than all but one of the fourth grade classes at the 31 elementary schools nearest to KIPP. Forty-two percent of them had passed the fourth-grade reading test, but just 28 percent of their peers at the 31 closest schools did so. Rothstein and Jacobsen also interviewed 12 teachers who had referred students to KIPP Academy and KIPP schools in Houston and Washington, D.C., reporting that "a clear pattern to emerge from these interviews was that almost always it was students with unusually supportive parents or intact families who were referred to KIPP and completed the enrollment process."[21] Rothstein's point was not that KIPP was ineffective—he allowed that KIPP schools appear to raise academic achievement and might have laudable practices worth copying. But he insisted that KIPP's record failed to show that the KIPP system could close the achievement gap for typical inner-city students.

Since Rothstein wrote, annual data reported by KIPP Academy have confirmed several of his findings while casting doubt on others. For the last five years, more than 40 percent of entering KIPP Academy students read at or above grade level in fourth grade, while only about 20 percent of fourth graders in KIPP's South Bronx district did so. The gap in pre-KIPP math scores is similar, much like Rothstein's findings from the 2002 school year. KIPP Academy's own data thus confirm a pattern that could be termed creaming, however inadvertent, among entering students. Incoming KIPP students, that is, have significantly stronger academic skills, on average, than most youngsters in the South Bronx.

The fact that KIPP enrolls more skilled pupils is not altogether surprising. After nine years as the top-achieving, nonselective middle school in the Bronx, it stands to reason that KIPP would attract more ambitious students and families. In 2007, 220 applicants were on the school's waiting list. Moreover, KIPP has an extraordinarily high rate of enrollment among younger siblings of students, who are given preferential admission. In 2007–2008, 29 of 70 incoming students at KIPP Academy were siblings. "The sibling dynamic is the kind of transformational change that a school wants to have," Levin asserts.

What are the policy implications of the accidental creaming of students at KIPP Academy? Here the debate gets more complicated. In *The Charter School Dust-Up,* Rothstein focused on demonstrating the superior skills of entering KIPP Academy students in order to debunk claims that he attributed to charter school proponents and KIPP leaders—in particular the idea that KIPP pupils are more educationally disadvantaged than their peers but, nonetheless, do outperform students in comparable public schools.[22] Yet contrary to Rothstein's claims, KIPP leaders such as Dave Levin and Susan Schaeffler (the founding principal of the first KIPP school in Washington, D.C.) make a less far-reaching argument about the representativeness of KIPP students. Levin and Schaeffler's core contention is that KIPP students are roughly comparable to other inner-city students, not that they are worse off.[23]

A better question to ask is whether KIPP students are too dissimilar from average students to serve as useful models for closing the achievement gap. It is true that KIPP Academy in the Bronx attracts students with superior academic skills. As a result, there is no way to know whether it could eliminate the achievement gap if, say, the incoming fifth graders at Lou Gehrig and KIPP switched places. That said, it would also be a mistake to exaggerate the dissimilarity between KIPP students and their peers. Both groups are poor, overwhelmingly black and Hispanic, and come largely from single-parent households. And while Rothstein reported from his teacher interviews that students referred to KIPP "almost always" have "unusually supportive parents or intact families,"[24] KIPP principals and administrators scoffed at such claims. "The parents of students at KIPP Academy are very similar to the parents I worked with when I taught in Newark, New Jersey," says principal Quinton Vance. "We look here for ways to encourage parents to read with their kids because that is not an expectation in many homes."

KIPP Academy lacks figures on the percent of students who come from single-parent families. But Susan Schaeffler of KIPP D.C. KEY Academy sent a letter to Rothstein in February 2005 with data on student family structure after Rothstein sent out the draft of his chapter in *The Charter School Dust-Up* for review—the chapter reporting that teachers in D.C., New York, and Houston almost always referred students with intact or unusually supportive families to KIPP schools. Schaeffler noted that 70 percent of eighth graders in 2004 at KIPP D.C. KEY Academy lived in single-parent families and an additional 10 percent did not live with either parent. Rothstein later thanked KIPP officials for reviewing the chapter.[25] But he did not report the numbers on single-parent families that Schaeffler cited, or otherwise qualify assertions from a lone Washington teacher who claimed that many of the children she referred to KIPP came from two-parent homes.[26]

Mike Feinberg and Dave Levin similarly dispute the notion that KIPP attracts unusually supportive parents. Even at KIPP Academy, incoming students' skills are at best mediocre, with more than half testing below grade level pre-KIPP—leading *Washington Post* education columnist Jay Mathews to point out that KIPP students "had the same great parents when they were getting much lower scores back at their regular public schools."[27] Feinberg noted with sarcasm that all parents had to do to sign up to apply to KIPP was to "answer a knock on the door and listen to us for an hour and sign their name. How difficult."[28] Moreover, before KIPP was well known, Levin and other school leaders recruited families anywhere they could and essentially accepted all comers. Susan Schaeffler recruited her first class of students in part by standing in front of local stores in D.C. and "asking loudly" if anyone wanted to try a new middle school that would keep their kids from 8 A.M. to 5 P.M.[29]

In short, it is easy to overstate the differences between KIPP students and "typical" students in the Bronx. In fact, for most of the last decade KIPP Academy has been required (under the New York State charter law) to accept applications to its admission lottery from residents across the Bronx, not just from the South Bronx, one of the lowest-performing districts in New York. Dave Levin points out that, while KIPP Academy students do have higher entry test scores than their peers in the South Bronx, student incoming test scores are very similar to students in the Bronx at large.

Rothstein and Jacobsen appear to further exaggerate the allegedly atypical nature of KIPP students by likening the Academy to highly selective schools for gifted children. They write:

How to balance the opportunities for more talented children in schools of choice with the harm done to less talented children, remaining in regular schools, where they can no longer benefit from the influence of higher performing peers, is a difficult policy issue in public education today. If KIPP-Bronx (and other KIPP schools) truly do attract the more talented or advantaged fourth-graders in their communities, KIPP resolves this policy dilemma no differently than New York City itself does by operating schools like Stuyvesant High School and the Bronx High School of Science that admit only students with high test scores. Nor is the KIPP solution different from that of New York City and many other urban school districts that create magnet schools to attract children with more motivation and parental support than typical children in disadvantaged communities.[30]

Notwithstanding Rothstein and Jacobsen's claims, a significant number of incoming KIPP students have spotty academic records and disengaged parents. The same cannot be said for Stuyvesant High School and the Bronx High School of Science, two specialized high schools reserved for gifted teens admitted solely on their outstanding test scores. Each year, about 28,000 of New York City's 90,000 eighth graders sit for a special exam to seek admission to a handful of city public high schools for gifted and talented students. Stuyvesant, for example, admits only about 850 applicants, and its 11th and 12th graders racked up a lofty average SAT score of 1414 in 2005.

Less than 6 percent of students at "the Stuy" are black or Hispanic (95 percent are Asian or white). Just one in six qualified for the federal free- and reduced-price lunch program in 2005—though 97 percent of students at KIPP Academy did so that year. And out of 3,000 students at Stuyvesant, a grand total of 2 were special ed pupils. Bronx High School of Science, which boasts six Nobel Laureates among its graduates and is the national all-time leader in the Westinghouse/Intel Science Talent Search competition, also bears little demographic similarity to KIPP. Rothstein and Jacobsen's stretched analogy is doubly puzzling because a year earlier, in *Class and Schools*, Rothstein had cited the failure of KIPP Academy students to pass the admission tests for these schools as evidence that "the distribution of KIPP and middle-class children are still not congruent."[31] (Since Rothstein wrote, three KIPPsters have been accepted at Bronx High School of Science, though all three ended up going to private schools on scholarships.)

It is important to note that while KIPP does tend to attract above-average students from the South Bronx, there is little evidence to indicate that creaming is the norm across the 57 schools in KIPP's network.[32] Rothstein and Jacobsen presented some preliminary evidence in *The Charter School Dust-Up* that students at one other KIPP school, in Baltimore, had higher pre-KIPP fourth-grade test scores in 2002–2003 than their peers elsewhere in the city.

Subsequent longitudinal analysis of the incoming skills of students at the Baltimore KIPP school failed to confirm this pattern of creaming. A June 2007 study by the Center for Social Organization of Schools at Johns Hopkins University examined the fourth-grade reading and math scores of KIPP students in Baltimore and a comparison group of students from KIPP feeder schools who went to other middle schools. In 2002–2003, incoming KIPP fifth graders did not have higher reading and math skills than the comparison group. During the next two years, the incoming KIPP fifth graders in Baltimore did have higher incoming math scores than the comparison group, and the first of the two subsequent fifth-grade classes at KIPP Ujima Village Academy in 2003–2004 also had higher reading scores. But two years later, in 2005–2006, incoming KIPP fifth graders in Baltimore again had essentially the same incoming skills as comparison group students. The Johns Hopkins study concluded that overall "KIPP and comparison students were similar in 4th grade achievement and attendance, as well as on demographic variables."[33]

Nor was there any systematic evidence that entering fifth graders at KIPP D.C. KEY Academy, the third school that Rothstein examined, had higher test scores than students at neighboring schools. In fact, the fourth-grade Stanford 9 reading and math scores of KIPP D.C. KEY Academy fifth graders in 2004 were below the average from ten neighboring feeder schools.[34] In response to Rothstein's study, the KIPP Foundation also undertook a 2005 review of the reading and math scores at KIPP's first three replication schools (in Houston; Gaston, North Carolina; and KIPP D.C. KEY Academy), which failed to find a consistent pattern of students entering KIPP with higher skills. When differences in ability did exist, they were relatively modest.

Unpublished data compiled by the KIPP Foundation for this study also suggest that students at the first few KIPP schools—whose successes received national publicity—had stronger incoming skills than at KIPP schools that opened in later years. Table 6-2 below, detailing the fifth-grade scores of students on nationally normed tests when they arrive at KIPP, shows a large drop between 2001 and 2002, followed by a gradual rise between 2002 and 2006. The numbers below present the national percentile rank (NPR) of KIPP fifth graders in the fall of their entry year.

It is possible, though unlikely, that the poor test scores of entering KIPP fifth graders in 2006 (the 27th percentile in reading, the 35th percentile in math) are artificially low due to summer learning loss between fourth and fifth grades. For KIPP schools in particular, the "summer loss" argument rings hollow since KIPP fifth graders in fact *are* in summer school before they are tested in the fall. At the very least, the unimpressive test scores of entering KIPP

Table 6-2. Test scores of incoming students at KIPP Network schools

	National Percentile Rank, Reading	Number of incoming students tested in Reading	National Percentile Rank, Math	Number of incoming students tested in Math	Number of schools in Network
2001	37	244	52	242	3
2002	21	386	28	385	6
2003	24	2055	31	2055	26
2004	25	2400	34	2399	32
2005	25	2992	34	2971	39
2006	27	3383	35	3384	43

Source: The KIPP Foundation, 2007

fifth graders since 2002 suggest that claims about creaming at KIPP schools throughout its network are substantially exaggerated.

Indeed, there is good reason to think that KIPP students in the Bronx are atypical even in the KIPP network. KIPP Academy has one of the largest gaps among KIPP schools between the year-end scores of its fifth graders and district public school students, wider than in the spring of fourth grade. It could be that this simply reflects the beneficial impact of a year at KIPP Academy. But it also stands to reason that the gap may have widened with unusual speed because incoming KIPP students had more of an educational jump on their peers than incoming KIPP pupils in other cities.

Replicating KIPP

The KIPP model spread rapidly after Doris and Donald Fisher, co-founders of Gap, Inc., established the KIPP Foundation in San Francisco in 2000. By 2008, 57 KIPP schools were spread across 17 states—and the KIPP Foundation anticipates that more than 24,000 students will attend 100 KIPP academies in 2011.

With few exceptions, KIPP schools appear to have been remarkably successful at closing the achievement gap for low-income minority students. At 27 schools where students started KIPP in fifth grade after the fall of 2000 and had completed seventh grade by the spring of 2006, the average youngster entered at the 34th percentile in reading and the 44th percentile in math. After three years at KIPP, those same students had boosted their reading scores to the 58th percentile and their math scores to the 83rd.[35] Since the average student nationally scores at the 50th percentile ("at grade level"), the typical KIPP student at these 27 middle schools arrives below grade level, but by the beginning of eighth grade that student has eliminated the achievement gap and is outperforming the average white student in math. Still, these data are not dispositive for a couple of reasons. At most schools, KIPP lacks previous test scores—and thus cannot flatly rule out the possibility that the entering fifth-grade test scores of KIPP students are artificially low due to summer learning loss between fourth and fifth grade. Also, the sample of KIPP students who have remained at KIPP schools for three years is still relatively small.

In its early years, the KIPP Foundation's efforts to replicate its two flagship schools reflected the idiosyncratic style of founders Levin and Feinberg. Both men lacked managerial experience and were novices when it came to financial planning, fundraising, budgets, and legal affairs. They were cut more from the mold of visionaries—terrific teachers who shared a passion to provide low-income minority youth with a first-rate education. As a result, the co-founders went looking for education entrepreneurs like themselves—gifted teachers and principals who yearned to recruit students and start transformative schools from scratch and who had undergone a pedagogical baptism by fire at an inner-city school, typically with Teach for America (TFA). Even today, KIPP schools are filled with young TFA alums. The average age of principals at KIPP schools is all of 32 years old—and the KIPP Foundation's CEO, Richard Barth, is married to Wendy Kopp, the founder of Teach for America.

Neither Levin nor Feinberg thought much of the training provided by schools of education, and neither did little to hide his disdain for traditional teacher certification. Years earlier, when Feinberg was obliged to take a one-week summer ed school course in Houston to get his credential, he found he could master the course content just by reading the textbook. So he signed in each morning at his seminar—only to head out to the golf course, where he would catch a round on the links before sneaking back in the afternoon to sign out from class.[36] Fortunately, Feinberg and Levin had a knack for sizing up prospective school leaders. Quinton Vance, a TFA product himself, says Levin asked him to take over as principal of KIPP Academy after "a ten-minute interview that consisted of three questions."

Levin and Feinberg's preoccupation with finding topnotch school leaders was reflected in the KIPP Foundation's maiden program, the Fisher Fellows initiative. Typically, Fisher Fellows become future founders of new KIPP schools after taking a year-long program that includes a summer stint at Stanford University's Educational Leadership Institute, followed by residencies at KIPP schools in the fall and start-up work for their new schools in the winter and spring. The KIPP Foundation appoints about 15 Fisher Fellows each year and competition for slots is fierce. In the class of 2002, the KIPP Foundation chose 16 Fisher Fellows from more than 300 applicants. During the course of the next decade, the Foundation anticipates training 15 Fisher Fellows per year.

If recruiting talented principals and teachers was Levin and Feinberg's first priority in replicating the flagship schools, maintaining KIPP's values from school to school was a close second. As a 2005 study from the Bridgespan Group reported, the KIPP Foundation decided that "rather than try to stipulate every aspect of a school's design, the Foundation focused on the element it believed was paramount: the school's culture. Culture was defined through a set of values, norms, and practices, which were spelled out in the 'five pillars' of the KIPP model." The Bridgepan report noted, for example, that "every KIPP school has to have high, clearly defined, measurable expectations for its students' academic performance and conduct. Norms such as parent and student contracts supported this culture of achievement, which was reinforced by a range of formal and informal rewards and consequences as well as a 'no excuses' mindset."[37]

By 2002, the KIPP Foundation was no longer a small group comprised mainly of Feinberg and Levin's friends and colleagues. It had a staff of more than 40 people. But Feinberg was getting restless in his position as executive director—he wanted to return to teaching and starting up new schools in Houston. And the Foundation's search for school leaders was complicated by the fact that it was seeking fiercely independent entrepreneurs at the same time that it wanted school leaders who would remain faithful to KIPP's founding principles. As Feinberg recounted to Howard Husock in a case study for the Kennedy School of Government, "entrepreneurs are just not going to react well if you're told, 'here's the 500-page handbook of how you're going to run this school. And your job is just to oversee it'."[38]

Feinberg's solution was to search for "rock star" school leaders and to eschew prescribing a standardized curriculum for all KIPP schools. The absence of a uniform curriculum made the foundation's replication efforts more decentralized than many replication initiatives. Even so, many school leaders felt pressure to produce dramatic gains in academic achievement—and they soon began turning to headquarters for more guidance on curricula. Today, the KIPP Foundation provides a wide range of optional teaching "tool kits," and the KIPP schools are now more uniform in their curricular content than in the past. So far, only one (in San Lorenzo, California) has copied the concept of the school-wide orchestra to propagate the KIPP pedagogy, but several schools, especially in New York City, have begun using school-wide activities like choir or martial arts to build school unity and speed student acculturation.

Ultimately, the curricular autonomy that the KIPP Foundation provided to new school leaders led to a decentralized model of replication. Separate from the Fisher Fellows program, the KIPP Foundation established a school development division. Its purpose was to free future principals to engage fully in a year of leadership training during their fellowship without being continually distracted by the practical chores of locating funding and facilities and navigating local charter authorizers and school boards. To accelerate the opening of more KIPP schools, Feinberg had the school development staff concentrate their initial efforts in five cities (San Francisco, Chicago, Washington, Atlanta, and New York).[39] This relatively narrow geographic focus enabled school development staff (or "trailblazers," as Feinberg dubbed them) to maximize economies of scale and assured new school leaders that they would not be working alone in cities where KIPP schools were a novel concept.

Each cluster of schools is governed by its own superintendent and board, which help plot the feasibility of school expansion and set policies for school oversight. Dave Levin runs all of KIPP's schools in New York City, Susan Schaeffler runs KIPP's schools in Washington, D.C., and Mike Feinberg oversees KIPP's schools in Houston. (In 2003, Feinberg stepped down as executive director of the KIPP Foundation to return to Houston.) In more recent years, with the aid of a 2003 grant from the Bill and Melinda Gates Foundation, KIPP has also started to branch out beyond middle schools into opening high schools. By 2007, the KIPP Foundation had opened two high schools (in Houston and Gaston, North Carolina) and anticipated opening at least 10 more. In Houston, New York, and Los Angeles, KIPP is also expanding into elementary schools. It has opened a couple of elementary schools in Houston, including one that begins in pre-K; in Los Angeles, KIPP will be adding two new elementary and two new middle schools with the help of a $12 million grant from the Broad Foundation. Five years from now, more than 2,000 students in Los Angeles will be enrolled in KIPP schools in grades K–8.

Stumbling Blocks to Replication

As the KIPP network mushroomed, CEO Richard Barth, previously with Edison Schools, placed new emphasis on business operations—and with good reason. The early versions of the KIPP Foundation's business plans had naively envisioned that KIPP would open more than 100 schools within five years.[40] In practice, replicating the successful KIPP flagship schools turned out to be more complex and expensive. Many of their distinctive features—the extended school day and school year, the bonus year-end field trips, and the higher salaries paid to teachers—cost lots of money. Moreover, as charter schools, KIPP schools typically receive only 60 to 90 percent of the overall public revenue (and usually none of the capital revenues) of regular public schools. All told, the KIPP Foundation estimates that KIPP schools spend an additional $1,100 to $1,500 in privately raised funds per student (beyond what they receive from the state as charter schools) to pay for the KIPP "extras." It is no small feat to raise that kind of money for 57 schools with 14,000 students. Doing so for, say, 200 KIPP schools with 50,000 students, is a daunting prospect.

KIPP's expansion has also forced Foundation leaders to devote more attention to the mundane task of developing financial management systems. In December 2007, Dave Levin had to quell some embarrassing publicity after an audit by the New York State Comptroller found that KIPP Academy could not document that it paid for year-end Caribbean staff retreats in 2005 and 2006 with donated funds, rather than taxpayer dollars.[41] Levin staunchly defended the two five-day getaways as a just reward for his overworked teachers and a valuable occasion to recharge and collectively reassess before the upcoming school year. Yet the *New York Post* ran a lead that declared: "Forget the three R's, staffers at a high-performing Bronx charter school spent nearly $70,000 on the three S's—sun, sand, and surf."[42] Although Levin insisted that the staff retreats were paid for entirely with private dollars, he and his board agreed with the comptroller that KIPP Academy needed to strengthen and formalize some areas of financial oversight, disbursement and procurements, and payroll records—and he reported that the school was in the process of instituting new recordkeeping procedures.[43]

Pressures to develop financial management systems and raise private dollars are only two of the obstacles to KIPP's expansion. As KIPP middle schools matured, school leaders discovered—as Dacia Toll had at Amistad Academy—that some students faltered when they went on to local high schools. "Some of our smartest kids, because of character issues, have not been as successful at they could have been after they graduated from KIPP Academy," says principal Quinton Vance. "They are academically prepared. But they are not ready yet to deal with the pressures of becoming a teenager. And they cannot always get a lot of help at home."

The post-KIPP letdown prompted Levin in 2002 to establish the KIPP to College Program, an extensive initiative that provides parental-like support and guidance to KIPP NYC graduates from the day they leave KIPP to the day they enroll in college. No other paternalistic school network has such a far-ranging program. It consists of four components: A summer internship program; after-school tutoring and counseling; education grants and supplemental tuition aid at parochial and independent private schools; and step-by-step assistance in the college admissions process. In typical KIPP fashion, little is left to chance. KIPP Academy follows all of its graduates and tracks their grades in high school. Struggling students can come in for after-school tutoring or counseling. The program also includes an academic and character building curriculum taught in weekly after-school classes at KIPP Academy. Ninth graders focus on study skills and time management; twelfth graders concentrate on preparing their college applications.

What started out as a small summer internship program in 2003 has expanded substantially, too; more than 110 KIPP Academy alumni/ae worked in paid summer internships in 2007. Interns, however, don't just show up at their jobs. They are required to attend weekly "professional development workshops" sponsored by the KIPP to College program, where they set professional and personal goals for themselves and write about their job experience. As with Cristo Rey's work-study program, KIPP officials have found that monitoring the paid internships creates new administrative responsibilities. Each week, a KIPP to College staff member checks with job site managers and interns to make sure the interns are doing their job and provides weekly feedback on their progress.

When alumni/ae reach their junior and senior years, KIPP to College staff become deeply involved in the college admissions process. As juniors, all KIPP NYC alumni attend a two-day retreat in Rhinebeck, New York where they face rope courses and other outdoor challenges and receive the KIPP College Placement Manual. The manual is a step-by-step guide to the admissions process for low-income students and provides information on financial aid, SAT/ACT test dates, application essays, teacher recommendations, and college comparison worksheets. Throughout the senior year, KIPP to College staff provide help with application essays and admission interviews, network with college admissions officers, and provide traditional college counseling and placement services.

Levin's commitment to ensuring the lasting benefits of a KIPP education is costly. The KIPP to College Program and high school tuition aid for some 400 alumni/ae of KIPP's four New York City middle schools costs several million dollars a year—and the post-KIPP programming will become more expensive as newer KIPP schools send more graduates on to high school and college. Other KIPP schools also aid their graduates, but lack the formal program of extended support found at KIPP Academy. As newer KIPP schools add on grades and expand their roster of alumni/ae, school leaders are already forecasting a need for more programs that will provide a kind of extended warranty for a KIPP education.

The KIPP Foundation also has to serve as a quality control monitor. Not all KIPP schools succeed. In 2006, 41 schools in the network received AYP ratings. Thirty-seven of those schools made AYP but four did not. And while KIPP fifth graders generally tested well above their district peers by the end of the year, they scored below district averages in a handful of KIPP schools. Since KIPP's inception, six schools have quit the network over disputes about performance, management differences, or finances. Still, KIPP overall has an excellent batting average, with more than 90 percent of its new schools still in operation.[44]

By contrast, KIPP's fledgling efforts to take over and transform a few failing public schools has come up short. In August 2005, KIPP opened Cole College Prep in Denver after the former Cole Middle School was closed for poor performance. (Cole Middle School was the first failing school in Colorado to be forcibly converted to a charter school under state law.)[45] The KIPP Foundation planned to run it as a transition school for existing seventh and eighth graders from the old Cole school, opening a new KIPP middle school starting with fifth graders in Cole's building in 2008. But in January 2007, after KIPP was unable to find a strong principal for the new school, KIPP officials announced that they would close Cole College Prep at the end of the school year. "It's almost like joining the priesthood," KIPP spokesman Steve Mancini explained to the *Denver Post*. "It's a challenge to find the right people."[46] KIPP, Mancini reports, has abandoned for now its attempts to run transitional schools. "Our core competency is starting and running new schools," he says.

The fact that several KIPP schools have faltered reinforces the doubts of skeptics who believe that the KIPP model, while worthwhile, cannot or should not be widely replicated across urban America. Like other urban school networks, KIPP lacks the rigorous scientific studies with randomly assigned control groups necessary to demonstrate its impact on academic achievement, after excluding other factors. Recent reports of high student attrition rates at some KIPP schools, notably in the Bay Area, have raised concerns, too, about the robustness of KIPP's reported impact on academic achievement.[47]

An October 2006 review of comprehensive school reform models by the American Institutes for Research (AIR) identified eight quantitative studies of the effects of KIPP on student achievement. But only one of those studies—at a KIPP school in Memphis—had a rigorous design with a matched comparison group. AIR reported that the Memphis study showed KIPP had had a "very strong" effect on reading and math performance, raising student achievement levels by 0.40 of a standard deviation. (By way of comparison, a standard deviation increase of 1.0 is equivalent to an estimated increase of 100 points on the SAT, or enough to move a student from the 20th percentile to above the 50th percentile.) Since KIPP had just one evaluation of this methodological rigor, AIR concluded that the KIPP model overall could only document "limited evidence" of positive effects on student achievement.[48] After the AIR study appeared, KIPP, with funding from the Atlantic Philanthropies Services, commissioned Mathematica in 2007 to carry out a long-term, independent study using random assignment and control groups (at KIPP lottery schools with waiting lists) to assess KIPP's impact on academic achievement.

Ultimately, the biggest potential Achilles heel of the KIPP model may be one of its greatest strengths: Its need for of young, bright, and committed teachers. "No educational model," Richard Rothstein wrote in his 2004 KIPP critique, "can assume that all teachers will be forever young, working extraordinary hours and never expecting salary growth that typically comes with years of experience and that enables teachers to support a middle-class family life. At present, KIPP teachers typically remain at KIPP no more than five years."[49] KIPP currently has a surfeit of teacher applicants and reportedly selects only 6 percent of applicants, about half of them from Teach for America.[50] Yet as KIPP rapidly expands, it faces what Mike Feinberg calls the "Yes, but…" question — namely, are there enough exceptional, committed teachers to go around?

When the KIPP Foundation announced in March 2007 that philanthropists had pledged $65 million to create a total of 42 KIPP schools in Houston over the next decade, Feinberg was the first to acknowledge the recruiting challenge that lay ahead. "We have large boxes of resumes," he told the *New York Times*. "But we do not have large boxes of great resumes."[51] On the other hand, the careers of Feinberg and Levin, and the history of KIPP itself, attest to an impressive ability to adapt, to find "what works." A decade ago, few education experts would have given favorable odds that some 50 KIPP-like schools could recruit hundreds of enthusiastic and talented teachers, much less succeed at closing the achievement gap. Like its tenacious cofounders, who once refused to call it quits in a basketball duel, the KIPP organization is the Energizer Bunny of urban school reform. It continues to push ahead — demonstrating a youthful resolve and single-minded focus on results that other school reformers seek to emulate.

Chapter Seven

The SEED School and the Custodial Culture

We are the SEED   *We can't be stopped*
We are one   *Our minds are too strong*
We won't rest   *We end with knowledge*
Until   *And we don't do wrong*
We've won   *We are working*
People all around us   *Hard everyday*
Wonder who we are   *We are one*
We are the SEED   *And here to stay*
The future star

—The SEED School Pledge, "We Are One"

One mild Saturday afternoon in September 1993, Angelia Smith, 21, strolled down the block from her public housing project in Washington, D.C., with her four-year-old daughter to watch a pickup football game at the nearby elementary school. The Weatherless Elementary School seemed to be one of the few safe havens in the poor, black neighborhood of Greenway in Anacostia, situated in the southeast quadrant of Washington across the Anacostia River. But no sooner had Smith and her little girl sat down with about 70 other spectators when four young men with semiautomatic pistols, one brandishing guns in both hands, walked out of the nearby woods and started firing their weapons across the playing field. The four gang members chased down a rival gang member named Kervin Brown, repeatedly firing off their guns as they ran in the direction of the crowd. After wounding Brown, while Smith and panicked onlookers tried desperately to flee the mayhem, the four gunmen stood over Brown, taunted and killed him.

Smith ran toward her apartment, carrying her little girl Launice in her arms. At first, she thought the two had escaped the shooting unharmed. But then Smith looked down and noticed the blood on her sweater. Launice had been shot after all—in her head and hand. After slipping into a coma, the four-year-old girl, who wore braids and liked to dance to Barney and Baby Bop, died.[1]

In 1993, Washington, D.C. was the murder capital of the nation. But in the midst of a long string of senseless shootings, the murder of Launice Smith stood out. Her death prompted Mayor Sharon Pratt Kelly to petition the White House for the authority to assign the National Guard to patrol crime-infested areas in the District. Syndicated columnists Mary McGrory and E. J. Dionne deplored the shooting and said it exposed the nation's capital as a sordid tale of two cities. One side of the city, McGrory wrote, was composed of "white, affluent, relatively safe enclaves"; the other Washington consisted of "black ghettoes where people are trapped in their homes and children have to learn at an early age to dodge bullets."[2] More than 500 people showed up for Launice's funeral, including Mayor Kelly and Jesse Jackson. "God has sent his angel to give us a warning: 'Nation Beware',"
Jackson said in his eulogy. "He didn't send an old angel with tired wings. He sent a young angel." Jackson admonished the mourners that the plague of black-on-black shootings marked an ominous new turning point. "The murder of this baby," he declared, "represents a new frontier for the civil rights movement. This is a war in which we can have no draft dodgers—everyone must fight."[3]

Before long, however, Launice Smith was largely forgotten. Two years after the shootings, one of the four gunmen was convicted of second-degree murder. But the basketball backboards, still riddled with bullet holes, were left standing on the playground at Weatherless Elementary School. Soon the school itself was shuttered—and then the arsonists took over. Weatherless suffered at least a dozen fires in the five years after Launice's death. By 1998, it looked like a building that had been firebombed in Dresden. Little besides steel girders remained. The school was appraised as having zero value. If ever there was a tragic symbol of urban educational decay, Weatherless Elementary School was it.

Yet one day in 1998, two former management consultants walked around the abandoned shell of Weatherless Elementary and had a vision of a new school that could arise out of the ashes. Eric Adler and Rajiv Vinnakota had an innovative idea. They had just opened what would become the nation's only urban, public, college-preparatory boarding school for low-income students in temporary quarters in downtown Washington, near Union Station. Now they were seeking a permanent campus, where students could be housed in new dormitories, with academic facilities and playing fields. The cofounders of the SEED School believed they could create an Andover for poor kids—but in the students' home community.

As the two men surveyed the site, they sensed that they were expanding into unfamiliar territory. Adler, who had lived in Washington since he was five years old, had never even been east of the Anacostia River until he started working on SEED. Still, they saw potential in the 4.5-acre site. In January 2001—after securing some $26 million in private funding and receiving approval from D.C. Public Schools to take over the site—the SEED School moved into a newly reconstructed four-story, 50,000-square-foot academic center and the first of two new dormitories.

Since then, SEED has received accolades from political leaders, think tanks, and entrepreneurs, based largely on its remarkable record in closing the black-white college enrollment gap. Ninety-seven percent of its first three graduating classes (2004–2006) have been accepted to college and nearly 90 percent are currently enrolled. Secretary of Education Margaret Spellings has hailed SEED as an "inspiring" example of a charter school that is "closing the achievement gap between low-income, minority, and special needs students and their peers."[4] In 2005, the Ash Institute at Harvard's Kennedy School of Government selected SEED for one of its six Innovations in Government Awards, often heralded as the Oscars of public policy entrepreneurship. The Manhattan Institute has singled out SEED, too, naming Adler and Vinnakota as recipients of its Outstanding Social Entrepreneurship Award in 2001.

Celebrities, news anchors, and international statesmen have been just as captivated by the novel college-prep boarding school. Ted Koppel devoted an

ABC *Nightline* special to SEED, describing it as a "notable exception" to failing urban schools that "operates on the premise that inner city youngsters need an entirely new environment."[5] "Perhaps," Koppel observed in closing, "it's time to plant a few more SEEDs." In 2005, Prince Charles, accompanied by Laura Bush, toured the school, sat in on classes, and planted an English oak tree in the school's courtyard.

For all the media hoopla attending Prince Charles's visit, SEED's biggest celebrity booster has been Oprah Winfrey. On her show, Winfrey conferred on Adler and Vinnakota a $100,000 "Use Your Life Award" from her Angel Network, which the school used to build a student center. She also donated 300 computers, and 150 sets of beds, dressers, and desks for SEED dormitories. Winfrey had a personal interest in SEED's success as a boarding school, too. During a visit with Nelson Mandela in December 2000, she had pledged $10 million to create the Oprah Winfrey Leadership Academy for Girls in South Africa. Winfrey's academy—Vinnakota is a member of its advisory council—opened in January 2007 to considerable acclaim.

As a one-of-a-kind urban public boarding school in the U.S., SEED is a uniquely paternalistic institution. Like other no-excuses schools, it places heavy emphasis on developing students' moral character, maintaining order and safety, and providing a rigorous college-prep curriculum. But unlike other such schools, SEED is not like a second home and teachers do not sometimes act like parents. SEED *is* the students' second home. Five days a week, 24 hours a day, the students live at SEED for nearly 10 months of the year. The dorm advisors, or Life Skills Counselors (LSCs) at SEED really are second parents to the students. It is the LSCs that make sure kids don't stay up late, fight with their roommates, or violate house rules. LSCs also insist that students make their beds in the morning, keep their rooms clean, and treat others with respect. SEED thus constantly—not on occasion—acts in loco parentis. The responsibility of taking care of other people's children 24 hours a day is a weighty one—and one that shapes both SEED's strengths and its weaknesses.

The Ambivalence over Paternalism

Boarding schools provide a kind of Rorschach test in the debate over educational paternalism. For decades, Americans have been of two minds about such schools. They believe that boarding schools are stepping stones to privilege for the children of America's elite (and view those schools either as intellectually demanding and character-forming or as repressive dinosaurs and protectors of class privilege). Yet they imagine that residential programs for low-income students are reserved for troubled adolescents and wards of the state. SEED's leaders have been forced to grapple with these negative stereotypes of residential institutions among poor families.

Elite boarding schools initially did help perpetuate upper-class privilege and culture—and for many decades provided an admission ticket to top colleges. In the years prior to World War II, two-thirds of the students from 12 top prep schools attended Harvard, Yale, or Princeton.[6] With their dress codes, honor courts, mandatory athletics, and other fusty rituals, traditional college-prep boarding schools sometimes seem like throwbacks to an earlier era. Yet their graduates continue to have an impact on business and politics that belies their small numbers. Only about 42,500 students are in boarding school.[7] Yet as Stephen G. Smith, the former editor of *U.S. News and World Report*, pointed out in a cover story in 2001, boarding schools produced four of the leading candidates in the 2000 presidential election.

The outsized influence of boarding school graduates in America's leadership class is due in part to inherited privilege. George W. Bush, a relatively indifferent student, went to Andover because his father had gone there. Yet in large measure, boarding schools generate a disproportionate number of leaders because the experience of attending them molds the character of adolescents in ways that day schools usually cannot. The distinctive feature of a boarding school—its 24/7 intensity—forces students to grapple with cultural differences, work out conflicts with roommates and classmates, develop a moral code, and compete academically and athletically. In the apt phrase of Richard Hawley, headmaster of the all-boys University School in Cleveland, boarding schools are "crucibles of character."[8] Long before KIPP and Amistad Academy started teaching students the value of perseverance, self-discipline, generosity, and integrity, elite boarding schools were preoccupied with character training—almost by necessity. They had a parent-like responsibility to care for students from 3:00 P.M. until the lights went out. It was during the after-school hours especially that boarding schools taught their so-called second curriculum, training students how best to lead their lives.

The impact of the boarding school experience can be profound, even for children of privilege. George W. Bush described his time at Andover "as a life-changing experience." John McCain called himself "a victim of Episcopal High School...The principles embodied in the school, and especially in its honor code, are those I've tried to embody in my own life."[9] McCain arrived at Episcopal High School in Virginia in the early 1950s as a self-described rambunctious military brat. But he credits the head of the English Department, a demanding but caring teacher named William B. Ravenel, with turning his life in a new direction. During his first year at Episcopal, McCain got to know Ravenel when McCain had to work off a series of demerits by doing yard work for his teacher. In a talk at Episcopal during the 2008 presidential campaign, McCain told students "I doubt I will ever meet another person who had the impact on my life that my English teacher did."[10] A decade after McCain attended Episcopal, the acclaimed writer John McPhee penned *The Headmaster*, an adoring profile of Deerfield headmaster Frank Boyden that similarly celebrated Deerfield's transformation of teenagers into young men.

Today, it is hard to imagine a writer of McPhee's stature championing the modus operandi of a boarding school. In the post-1960s, novelists who depicted the schools as rigid, soulless institutions held sway. Richard Hawley notes that in novels like J. D. Salinger's *Catcher in the Rye* and John Knowles's *A Separate Peace*, boarding schools were "no longer a crucible of character, but rather a setting for more private, interior crises: sexual adequacy and a highly personal sense of authenticity." In these fictional boarding schools, Hawley observes:

> Schools mainly bruise their students; those in charge are beneath contempt. Indeed, in the recent boys' school film offerings, Dead Poets' Society, Scent of a Woman, and School Ties, the administrations are virtually interchangeable; moreover, they are an adolescent's dream: an adult order so repellent and unworthy of respect that not measuring up to school codes of conduct—indeed remaining adolescent—becomes a positive, even righteous moral stance.[11]

Depictions of elite boarding schools during the last decade frequently portrayed them as places for problem teenagers who were being sent away or as havens of promiscuous sex and surreptitious drinking and drug use. Some specialized schools do, indeed, board troubled adolescents, chiefly from affluent families. Since the 1970s, more than two dozen "therapeutic boarding schools" for difficult teens have sprung up around the nation, as have hundreds of residential treatment options, such as spartan wilderness therapy camps and youth boot camps.[12] However, therapeutic boarding schools, despite their academic components, are designed specifically to assist teens and their dysfunctional families and are not typical college-prep schools. Nor do they much resemble the other residential institutions that parents of inner-city children may be familiar with, such as reform school or rehabilitation facilities for adolescents run by the criminal justice system. It's no wonder that many parents—and especially low-income parents—are confused about boarding schools. As Stephen G. Smith sums up, "boarding schools are little known and little understood in many parts of the country. Even in a cosmopolitan city like Washington, many parents view sending a child away to school as a sign of trouble: They assume either that the youngster is behaving badly or doing poorly in school, or that the family is somehow dysfunctional."[13]

In reality, most college-prep boarding schools provide rich academic challenges and a unique bonding experience that many students prize. A 2005 survey of 1,000 students and alumni/ae of boarding schools found that close to 90 percent of alums in the midst or end of their careers said that they would "repeat the boarding experience" if they had the chance to do it over again. Nearly 90 percent of current students also reported that they were very satisfied or satisfied with their family life.[14] And compared to public school graduates, boarding school graduates were twice as likely to feel that they were ready academically and socially for college.[15]

If the reputation of elite boarding schools took something of a beating after the 1960s, they at least had a long history of being admired and even envied. The same cannot be said of residential institutions for low-income minority children. From orphanages through Indian boarding schools, juvenile detention facilities, and treatment centers for emotionally disturbed children, institutions that house and care for low-income minority children have usually been viewed with deep-seated distrust by black and Hispanic parents. Heidi Goldsmith of the International Center for Residential Education notes that "a common myth is that [disadvantaged] children are placed in residential programs after being ripped from the arms of loving parents and guardians by welfare authorities. This may have been the practice in the 1920s, but it is not the practice today."[16] A survey in the mid-1990s by Goldsmith's organization of residential educational programs for low-income youth—such as Job Corps centers and a smattering of private boarding schools for abused or impoverished kids from single-parent families—found that "the vast majority of young people in these programs were sent by parents who wanted something better for their children."[17]

One of the only boarding programs for low-income children still in existence that bears even a passing resemblance to SEED — and has a positive public image — is Boys Town. Father Flanagan's original Boys Town, a school and home for abused, neglected, and abandoned children outside Omaha, Nebraska, was immortalized in a 1938 film in which Spencer Tracy played the strict but big-hearted Father Flanagan. Like SEED, Boys Town boarding facilities have a strict behavioral management and character development component. But Boys Town was not (and is not) a college-prep school, much less a school for minority, inner-city teens with parents. Most of the boys at Boys Town initially were white and homeless; in later years, Boys Town primarily housed teenagers in foster care.

In the face of the spotty reputation of residential facilities for low-income teens, SEED administrators, particularly in the early years, had to ease parental fears that boarding schools were for bad kids. Eric Adler recalls that "we did encounter the perception that boarding schools were reform schools. Parents would say 'my uncle got locked away.' These parents were not aware that John F. Kennedy went to a boarding school. So it was important for us to tell families that we were a *school* that prepared kids to go to college and we weren't looking to lock anyone up." As Heidi Goldsmith pointed out several years ago, the image of the orphanage continues to dominate public perceptions of residential schools for disadvantaged students. "Why," Goldsmith asked, "is it considered acceptable, if not attractive, to send a young person from a supportive, affluent family away to a residential boarding school, whereas it is considered destructive to send a young person from an unsafe, unhealthy home environment to a nurturing, educational, residential setting? Because of the popular imagery of past orphanage life."[18]

As a college-prep public boarding school, SEED must overcome a double burden. Not only must it assuage fears that it is locking away troubled kids; it also, ironically, must counter perceptions that it is an elite school for a lucky few. SEED's campus and facilities don't begin to compare with those of elite boarding schools. Nonetheless, with its courtyards, white hallways, and modern, tasteful dorm rooms, SEED is a gem in its blighted Greenway neighborhood in Anacostia. A half-million dollars of donated artwork adorns its walls. The library contains about 8,000 volumes and a computer lab. Some neighborhood activists in Washington who have opposed opening a second SEED school in their community have claimed that SEED, in effect, is too nice a public school for a relatively small number of students.[19]

The Roots of SEED

SEED's beginnings differ from those of other paternalistic schools. Its co-founders, Vinnakota and Adler, had no experience teaching in inner-city schools. They were not idealistic Teach for America alumni/ae with a detailed vision and gritty determination to create their schools from the bottom up. Nor were they veteran educators who knew what it meant to be poor and to live in inner-city communities. Compared to other paternalistic schools, SEED's origins were more abstract. The school was effectively dreamed up by two youthful management consultants, neither of whom had attended boarding school himself. The two men shared an entrepreneurial flair, however, an expertise in finance and venture capital, and a commitment to helping disadvantaged students close the achievement gap. But as Vinnakota and Adler might be the first to admit, they would soon receive their own education in the urban-school wars.

Quite by serendipity, Vinnakota first started tinkering with the idea of a college-prep boarding school for low-income students in 1994 after his first reunion at Princeton. He had spent his formative years in Milwaukee but his parents, both teachers, were born in India. His father, a university professor, and his mother, a second-grade teacher, had drummed into him the impor-tance of education and of leaving the world a better place. Yet when Vinnakota graduated from Princeton in 1993 with a degree in molecular biology, opening a school was the furthest thing from his mind. He planned to work for Mercer Management Consulting for several years and then get an M.D. or a Ph.D and go into medical research.

After his first year at Mercer, Vinnakota returned to Princeton for his reunion. Over drinks at the Tower Club, he fell into an animated conversa-tion about urban education with four of his classmates. Vinnakota had long felt that inner-city minority students faced formidable burdens when they left school for the day to return to crime-ridden neighborhoods and sometimes broken families. How could disadvantaged students be assured of a safe place to study or help with their homework? Eventually, Vinnakota recalls, the reunion chat settled on a question: "Why aren't there boarding schools for inner-city children?"[20]

That question stuck with Vinnakota when he returned to his job at Mercer Management Consulting. Although Vinnakota was thriving at Mercer, he had a self-described "crisis of being"[21] in 1996 when he realized that "working 80 hours a week to make Fortune 100 companies more profitable" was not his life's calling. He took a two-month leave of absence and embarked on a listening tour to explore problems in urban education and the boarding school concept. As a well-trained management consultant, he performed a "due diligence and feasibility investigation,"[22] interviewing dozens of educators, donors, social service providers, and the like. It seemed that whenever he asked the experts to identify their biggest concerns about urban education the answer kept coming back that they were worried about "what happens to kids after school lets out." By the time Vinnakota had finished, he had accumulated 500 pages of interview notes. In the midst of his 1996 tour, a mutual acquaintance introduced him to 32-year-old Eric Adler—who had also started to noodle with the idea of starting a college-prep boarding school for low-income students.

Unlike Vinnakota, Adler had spent time as a teacher. But he, too, had no experience in urban public schools. He had attended Washington's Sidwell Friends School, a liberal Quaker private school that Chelsea Clinton would later attend. Although Sidwell had a community service requirement, Adler fulfilled his obligation by coaching soccer. "I was not at all involved in issues of race and poverty in high school," he confesses. Still, Adler opted to continue his Quaker education by enrolling at Swarthmore College. Then he took a job teaching high school physics at St. Paul's School, a prestigious all-boys prep school about ten miles north of Baltimore. St. Paul's had an idyllic rural campus of 95 acres, a rigorous college-prep curriculum, and a championship golf team. It was, says Adler, "pretty much a stereotypical, lily-white prep school." However, on Adler's first day in homeroom, he saw that one of his 14 students was African American. Adler mistakenly assumed that his lone black student was "also a middle class kid."

To his surprise, Adler soon discovered that the boy had no father in his life, that his mother was an alcoholic, and that he took a one-and-a-half hour bus ride every day just to get to school. Afraid that neighborhood kids would taunt or attack him for attending St. Paul's, the boy took his school uniform off every day on the long bus ride home to Baltimore and his family's noisy, chaotic apartment. "I began to realize that maybe it didn't make sense to treat him the same as the other students," Adler recalls. "But it also wasn't a solution to just let him off the hook. I began to wonder, what is the solution?" Adler realized that his student needed to have a quiet place to study. He needed to have his babysitting responsibilities removed and would benefit from tutoring. "If he had all those supports," Adler figured, "he could compete effectively. Otherwise he had to be a superhuman kid to handle all the academic and social pressures."

That was Adler's first inkling that some inner-city students might need a boarding school environment to make their way to college. But during his eight years at St. Paul's, where Adler rose to become dean of students, he was also developing the itch to become an entrepreneur. He enrolled in the Wharton School of Business, thinking he had left his teaching days behind. After Wharton, in 1996, he started work at a management consulting firm. But Adler became restless when he realized there was nothing entrepreneurial about his consulting work. Six months later, Adler started exploring several startups, including the idea of a boarding school for low-income students. "I didn't have any personal experience or sense of boarding schools," says Adler. "But I knew that the children of George Bush and John Kennedy had gone to boarding schools."

Adler and Vinnakota finally met for dinner at a Roy Rogers late in 1996 to discuss the boarding school project and ended up batting ideas around for three hours. The two men, joined by about ten other educators and consultants all under the age of 34, then convened a marathon weekend retreat at Mercer's offices in February 1997 to flesh out a proposal. The following day, the group put together the outlines of a business plan—which called for opening the school in September 1998, just 18 months away. By 5 P.M., everyone except Adler and Vinnakota had left for home. As the two men looked at a white board filled with scribbled ideas, they realized that SEED would never open in time unless they quit their consulting jobs. The two gave notice the next day and started working fulltime on SEED in March 1997. The two management consultants ultimately settled on a progressive-sounding name for their new venture, "SEED," an acronym for Schools for Educational Evolution and Development.

Opening Day: Battling the System

As challenging as the start-ups were for the founders of other paternalistic inner-city academies, launching the SEED School was even more demanding, not just because time was short but also because a public boarding school required far more operations funding and capital support. Like other new schools, SEED had to secure a charter, hire teachers, find classrooms, and recruit students. But it also had to find dormitory space, create a cafeteria that could provide three meals a day, and hire after-school counselors to manage study halls, sports, and evening meals, and sleep on site as dorm advisors.

At least one other college-prep boarding school in the country had provided a free education for low-income students for decades, the Milton S. Hershey School in Hershey, Pennsylvania. But it was a lavish institution with some $6 billion in assets, probably the wealthiest school in the world. SEED, by contrast, was to depend primarily on taxpayer dollars. And a public boarding school in the District would cost roughly three times as much per student as a day school—which meant there was no way SEED could open with the regular per-pupil funding of D.C. charter schools, then around $6,000.

An exception had to be made for SEED, and Vinnakota and Adler started lobbying for one. In short order, they succeeded in pushing through the U.S. Congress and D.C. City Council an amendment to the D.C. charter law that allowed a boarding school to receive more than twice as much funding per pupil as day schools. At the same time, they embarked on a furious fundraising effort to raise capital to buy a site and construct facilities. Like David Levin and Mike Feinberg at KIPP, Vinnakota and Adler were resourceful and relentless. They managed to raise $2 million in private money in little more than a year for their untested school. SEED soon became part of one of the first group of charters granted by the D.C. Public Charter School Board in 1998.

The unique challenge of fundraising for a public boarding school was complicated by the District's woefully inadequate public school system. Twenty years ago, Secretary of Education William Bennett cited Chicago as the worst public school system in the nation. Today, Bennett might well cite the District of Columbia's public schools. A comparison of NAEP scores from 11 big city school districts in 2005 found D.C. students last or tied for last in almost every measure of academic achievement.[23] Three out of four eighth graders in the nation's capital lacked even basic skills in math. Even when cross-city comparisons were limited to poor students, District students were among the worst performers in the country. In 2005–2006, 118 of the city's 146 noncharter public schools failed to make AYP.[24] High school dropout rates were high and college attendance rates low. Just 40 percent of Hispanic ninth graders and 59 percent of black ninth graders graduated four years later.

The one bright spot in the District's dismal record was the test scores of white students, who made up only 6 percent of public school students and were concentrated in the city's affluent northwest neighborhoods. However, the comparatively high test scores of white students made the achievement gap even worse. In a 2007 series, the *Washington Post* reported that Washington, D.C. had "the widest gap between white and minority students among the [11] cities tested" on the NAEP.[25]

District students were not failing because the city was pinching pennies. In fact, its school system was a costly bureaucratic morass. The *Post* reported that "the District spends $12,979 per pupil each year, ranking it third highest among the 100 largest [school] districts in the nation. But most of that money does not go into the classroom. D.C. schools rank first in the share of the budget spent on administration, last in spending on teaching and instruction."[26]

Given the sorry state of D.C. district-operated schools, it is not surprising that Washington has become a mecca for charter schools. Today, 27 percent of public school students are enrolled in more than 50 charter schools. The nation's capital is now tied for the second highest percentage of public school students enrolled in charters in the country, trailing only New Orleans. But at the time SEED obtained its charter in 1998, charter schools were still new. In 1996–1997, the first D.C. charter schools served a mere 160 students.[27]

The poor record of D.C. public schools affected SEED's initial seventh-grade class of 40 students in two ways. First, it made recruiting pupils to an urban boarding school for low-income students easier than would otherwise have been the case. Many parents, particularly working single mothers, were desperate to find an alternative to the public schools. SEED's promise to remove students from the perils of street life and provide a free college-prep education to propel them into college was a potent draw that overcame lingering suspicions about boarding schools. From the start, SEED was able to use a blind lottery to select its students and had two to three applicants for every spot in the entering seventh-grade class. Many parents, in fact, viewed the lottery as a do-or-die opportunity that could determine their child's future. Some mothers jumped for joy, burst into applause, or fell to their knees in prayer to give thanks when their child's number was called at the lottery. Other mothers, who were not lucky enough to have their son or daughter's number called, wept in disappointment.

While the woes of the D.C. public schools helped SEED's recruitment efforts, they also meant that many SEED students arrived with massive educational deficits. Almost all of SEED's 325 students are black (98 percent). Many arrive with skills that are two to three grade-levels behind, and they often come from families where no one has gone to college. Entering students often have poor social skills to boot. And unlike in a day school, those social skills are put to the test immediately at SEED since students are forced to share a bedroom and live side-by-side with their peers for months on end.

SEED's tasteful, orderly campus in Anacostia today belies its early days when Adler and Vinnakota were desperate to find even temporary classroom and dorm space. SEED did manage to open on time in September 1998. But its initial seventh graders met for class in the attic of the Capital Children's Museum, near Union Station. An empty convent lay next door, and Adler and Vinnakota secured a block grant of $350,000 and an additional $300,000 in private donations, which they used to renovate it into nine dorm rooms for the 40 students. Neither facility had a cafeteria, so students ate catered food on trays amid stacks of dusty books. The students dubbed themselves the "Children of the Attic"—and a good part of the academic curriculum and after-school program was fashioned on the fly. SEED's location and the rules governing student behavior changed multiple times in the next several years. It was not until after SEED moved into its permanent facility in 2001 that the school's model, especially its after-school program, began to solidify.

The Custodial Culture

SEED's custodial culture places great emphasis on curbing signs of visible disorder, echoing James Q. Wilson's "broken windows" strategy for promoting public safety. SEED promises parents that their children will be safe, kept off the mean streets, and receive a college-prep education. As a result, the school is zealous about student safety—and not without cause. During 2002–2003, an armed intruder being chased by police ran into one of SEED's dorms while students were in class. After police captured him in the dormitory, SEED finished erecting an iron gate and fence around the campus to prevent unauthorized visitors from entering. SEED also unapologetically expels more students than day schools: 5.6 percent of its pupils each year, on average, compared to 1.8

percent at other charter schools. The school website notes that "as a boarding school, it is critical for us to ensure than any student who is a risk to themselves, to others, or to the boarding campus does not remain at school."

One of the motivations for curbing disorder at a boarding school is simple: No one, least of all the after-school faculty, wants to live in a chaotic home. The Life Skills Counselors (LSCs) inevitably become surrogate parents to the students Monday through Friday. In each grade, students are divided into "houses" named after colleges, and each house has its own LSC. House members form a unit or home away from home; they attend evening study hall together and share community service projects and field trips.

All SEED students understand that they are going to a boarding school, yet the reality of being away from home still takes time to sink in. The privileges and freedoms that many seventh graders treasure are missing at SEED. Televisions, cell phones, boom boxes, pagers, home entertainment or game systems, and portable electronic games are all prohibited. Students can't take a shower or grab meals when they feel like it. Even their bedroom is not their kingdom since they have to share it with a roommate. Patrice Smith Taylor, a senior in 2006, recalls that "what surprised me when I started in 2001 was the whole boarding process. I was actually *living* here—and I realized that I was going to form bonds and be with the same classmates for the next six years of my life." Artiase Brown, a tenth grader who started in 2003, remembers that when she arrived, "I got homesick at first and I was mad, too. I didn't get to talk on the phone. I missed all my favorite TV shows. But once you adapt to it, it feels like a second home."

The fact that SEED becomes a second home, run in loco parentis by the LSC, is a profound change for students—but boarding has important consequences for teachers, too. Laina Diamond, a middle school English teacher, says that she "didn't understand when I came here that if I had an issue with a child I could not just call the mom at home—if I would call her on Tuesday, she would not see her child until the weekend." Before long, Diamond realized that she had to reach out to a student's LSC. "I had to learn," she says, "that during the week the LSCs were going to be the parents. But I still had to keep parents informed, too." Ultimately, Diamond concluded, SEED students actually had *more* contact with adults and adult supervision than if they had lived at home. "When I have to talk to the LSC and the parent, you have three adults committed to helping the student," she observes.

Indeed, for many new students, part of the shock of adjusting to life at SEED is the nearly constant supervision of adults. SEED has small classes of 14 students or less, and overall has a remarkably low 3:1 student-adult ratio. Lesley Poole, the founding principal, points out that "there are many more adults in this community than children are used to—your life-skills counselor wants to make sure your tee-shirt is tucked in and your English teacher asks why your shoes aren't tied." The result, says Poole, is that SEED creates "a circle of caring adults who consistently inquire about how students are doing academically and personally—and that makes students feel safe. But it can be overwhelming for a 12-year-old seventh grader."

From opening day, Adler and Vinnakota were clear that the school had to develop an after-school curriculum that would give structure to the boarding experience and provide character education and social skills training. They did not want SEED to be just a dutiful caretaker, an institution where kids went to school, ate, and slept. "We knew there was a long list of life skills that students needed to learn that they would not pick up in English or math class. But we didn't know what would be on the list," says Adler. When sizing up whether students were ready to move up into the high school, says Adler, administrators "realized that we couldn't promote a student who regularly refused to make his bed or clean up his room."

Besides creating an after-school program of character education and instruction, the new boarding school also needed rules to govern student behavior when the academic-day ended. As Poole notes, the opportunities for misbehavior and disorder at school multiply the longer students are on campus, obliging boarding schools to have more detailed codes of conduct than the typical day school. When SEED opened, there was no existing life-skills curriculum in an urban boarding school setting for low-income students that the school could borrow. Instead, SEED administrators pieced one together from scratch.

The school did not settle on its HALLS curriculum (Habits for Achieving Life Long Success) until 2002, and not until 2005 did SEED articulate a detailed set of standards and benchmarks for measuring student performance in that curriculum. Bill Stevens, who has taught history at SEED since 2000, says that "the longer SEED has been here, the more the core value statements have taken on real value. There hasn't always been a consistent way of teaching respect or compassion." Part of the problem, says Stevens, was "the turnover rate among staff and students. Every year, or every other year, the leadership of the dorm and behavior-management program was changing." By 2005–2006, the faculty had developed more than 200 lessons and activities for the HALLS curriculum. Yet students and some teachers still felt that the lines between acceptable and unacceptable behavior were not always clear. As a supplement to the HALLS curriculum, the school in 2005–2006 adopted a behavior-management program used by Girls and Boys Town (as the Nebraska institution is now known) to reduce disruptive behavior, disciplinary referrals, and expulsions.

As SEED administrators have learned, hundreds of questions arise in boarding schools that never arise in day schools. For example, ninth grader Jelani Gibson was homesick when he came to SEED, but his homesickness was aggravated by the fact that his dorm room smelled because his roommate wet his bed at night. SEED's rules shifted frequently in its earlier years in part because situations would arise that were not covered by existing rules. It was easy to require students to wear uniforms and to specify a dress code. But what happened when a student showed up with her school uniforms for the week on Monday but lacked several days of proper athletic uniforms? At what time during the week would parents be allowed to return to campus to drop off missing uniform items? During the winter, boys were to wear ties. But should ties with cartoon figures be banned from campus? (SEED concluded they should be.) Similarly, students had study hall each evening. If a student chose to study in his room, rather than in a designated study area in the dorm, must he leave the door open so an LSC could check that he is studying? (SEED decided on an open-door requirement.)

Consider the seemingly simple issue of braids, popular among black teens of both sexes. Should a student's LSC be responsible for braiding students' hair during the school week? SEED decided no. Its parent-student handbook informs parents that "students should have their hair done while they are at home on the weekends. Please do not place us in the difficult position of having to call you to attend to your child's hair or having to issue consequences for violations of the dress code. Hair may never be braided during the academic day."

The net result of SEED's effort to codify rules for myriad situations was the development of a remarkably detailed and paternalistic code of conduct. Its 2006–2007 parent-student handbook runs to 61 single-spaced pages, and its HALLS curriculum is every bit as detailed. The handbook warns parents and students that student-life faculty members will perform room and dorm inspections every day that loosely resemble an inspection at an Army barracks. Indeed, the handbook articulates standards for tidiness that many suburban teens would fail miserably.

> Student rooms are to remain clean and in good order at all times. A student can be restricted from extra-curricular activities for having an unclean room.
> Each day prior to going to class or a field/activity trip, each student's room must be in the following condition:
>
> Bed must be properly made with no debris, clothing or shoes on the bed. Bed linen must be changed once a week with freshly laundered sheets.
>
> Linens and other items should be properly folded in the white Yaffa blocks and/or dress drawers.
>
> All clothes must be properly stored. Clothes must be either on hangers or hanging racks, in dresser drawers, or in the laundry bag.
>
> Towels must be hung on a rack.
>
> Shoes must be stored neatly under hanging racks, under the bed, or next to the dresser or the desk.
>
> Personal items on the dresser or on the desk must be arranged in an orderly fashion. Desk and dresser drawers must be closed and chair at desk. Bookshelves, if any, must be arranged neatly.

Like other paternalistic schools, SEED rewards exemplary behavior with "SEED Dollars" that middle school students can use for special privileges like snacks at the school store, staying up late, or additional time on the house phone. It also rewards both student achievement and examples of good character. The Principal's Super Sharp Awards, for example, are given quarterly to four students who have best reflected SEED's core values through their daily attire. A quarterly Academic Honors breakfast recognizes students on the honor roll.

Many aspects of the HALLS curriculum echo the paternalistic instruction provided to students in Cristo Rey Jesuit High School's work-study program. SEED students, for example, take etiquette classes. When meeting someone, they are trained to make eye contact, state their first and last names, and provide a firm handshake. They say "excuse me" before interrupting a conversation. They learn the difference between the salad fork and the dinner fork—and they practice meal time etiquette both at SEED's cafeteria and on excursions to restaurants like Maggiano's.

SEED has an intricate disciplinary code with four levels of increasing severity, but its core premise is that students are obliged to take responsibility for mistakes, much as in other no-excuses schools. Level 1 and 2 infractions are usually managed in class. These may involve unauthorized eating in a classroom or dorm room, being out of one's seat without permission, failing to complete homework, or not having necessary materials in class. For such infractions, teachers first give students a "Redirection," which can consist of a verbal warning, a visual signal, or writing the student's name on the board. When a student has been given two redirections and continues to misbehave, the teacher orders him to do a "reflection." As at KIPP, that means sitting in a designated area where the student is not allowed to talk with anyone. While in "reflection," the student fills out a "MAP" form, short for "My Action Plan." On it, he spells out his infraction, what he will do to improve his behavior, and ways in which adults can assist him to move forward.

More serious student violations (Levels 3 or 4) are typically dealt with by staff, the principal, or the head of school and generally result in detention, suspension, or expulsion. Tenth grader Artiase Brown has been on the honor roll at SEED, provides tours of the school as a SEED ambassador, and is taking Mandarin three days a week so she can go to China in a SEED summer exchange program. But in ninth grade she slipped on one occasion and joined some other girls who were trashing a fellow student's dorm room. It is a mistake she won't forget—or repeat. Along with her friends, Brown was suspended for almost two weeks. During the suspension, Brown had to remain at home and attend counseling sessions. "Having the school call my mom and dad was the worst part," she says with a wince. "When I came back to school, I had a D-Board [Disciplinary Board] hearing, and the school administrators put me on probation for about five months. I had to write a note of apology to the girl and pay her $50 for damage, too. I learned from that to follow my own footsteps—and not to follow other people."

In several respects, the monitoring of student behavior at SEED is even more thoroughgoing than at other paternalistic schools. Like KIPP, Amistad, and

Cristo Rey, SEED has a summer orientation session for incoming students during which new seventh graders live on campus for a week. But when the school year begins, teachers continue to document student conduct in writing in each class. As part of SEED's relatively new behavior management program, each middle school student carries a yellow "School Note" from class to class listing 12 "target behaviors" that can be assigned to one of two columns, "responsible behaviors" or "irresponsible behaviors." At the end of class, teachers assign letter codes in either the "responsible behavior" column or "irresponsible behavior" column for each student on their target behaviors. At the close of the day, Student Life staff tabulates the student's points to determine how many SEED Dollars the student earned that day. Upper school students (grades 9–12) can earn their way out of carrying a School Note during the day by consistently meeting requirements in areas like leadership, character, academics, and school service.

While the HALLS curriculum has a paternalistic cast, it manages to meld progressive elements with traditional values. The student life program requires students to participate in community service projects, teaching each student to "make a commitment to a life of social action." School benchmarks for the HALLS program require students to evaluate their own experiences with prejudice, discrimination, and bullying, and to explore how prejudice undermines diversity and tolerance. As a part of developing a healthy lifestyle, students are obliged to identify the five food groups, explain the impact of a high-fat diet and different exercise regimens, and plan a healthy nutrition and exercise regimen for college. Other subjects include AIDS prevention, abstinence, and condoms. Ninth grader Jelani Gibson says "a lot of HALLS topics deal with African-American culture since we only have three white or Hispanic students in the school. Today we discussed how rap affects culture and whether it is a misogynist culture that hates women."

With its version of left-leaning, life-skills training, SEED—unlike the Indian boarding schools of the turn of the century—seeks to reshape but not eradicate the culture of students' home community. "If we had wanted to 'eradicate' the students' culture we would have placed the school 100 miles away out in the woods," says Eric Adler. "We want the school to be in the neighborhood where the kids come from, and we encourage parents to come on to campus." Part of what SEED is attempting to do is to build up "cultural capital" for low-income students, much in the manner that exclusive boarding schools do for well-to-do students. Internships, travel, and work can all expand students' appreciation and involvement with the world outside their family and neighborhood. SEED has a fulltime staffer who, in addition to fundraising, cultivates partnerships with community institutions such as the Kennedy Center, the Shakespeare Theater, and the D.C. Arts and Humanities Education Collaborative. Such partnerships enable students to attend concerts and plays to which they might not otherwise be exposed. Several years ago, the wife of a former Greek ambassador visited SEED and was so taken by the school that she set up a partnership with the Greek Embassy that allows eight students each summer to visit Greece and stay at the ambassador's family villa on the island of Spetse.

Curriculum and Pedagogy at the SEED School

Many of the trappings of other paternalistic institutions, like their college-directed ethos, are shared by the SEED School. Teachers and principals start talking to students about college as soon as they arrive. Not only are student houses named after colleges, but the hallways are lined with pennants from Agnes Scott College, Oglethorpe University, Ohio University, Berkeley, Ohio Wesleyan, and other schools. Yet there is an important curricular distinction between paternalistic secondary schools that run from seventh to twelfth grade and paternalistic middle schools. Schools such as SEED, Cristo Rey, and University Park have a luxury that stand-alone middle schools lack: time. In all three, the middle school years are primarily taken up with remediation and accelerating students' skills so that they can handle a rigorous college-prep curriculum in grades 9 through 12.

Most entering seventh graders at SEED have the math and reading skills of a fifth grader. During their first two years, teachers work intensively with students to ready them for high school. Small classes ensure that foundering students don't escape attention. They receive hours of assistance in faculty-taught, after-school tutorials each week, and struggling students receive one-on-one tutorials as well. Ninth grader Jelani Gibson says "the academic standards here are way higher than at my old school. Here the teachers will be on you not only about sloppy handwriting but if the quality of your work goes down. The teachers will pull you aside to talk to you—they don't let poor work go by, like in my old school."

SEED does not practice social promotion and has a strict ninth grade "gate" that students must pass to be promoted to high school. Laina Diamond, a middle-school English teacher who previously taught in a working-class neighborhood in Tacoma, Washington, says that gate "is much more difficult than at my old school...The students have to show proficiency in each strand or gate in the core subjects of English and math to pass." Diamond, for example, grades students in six strands in the English gate. They must earn at least a C in all six areas to pass. If a student is not proficient in even one math or English strand, she must repeat eighth grade unless she can make up the course work over the summer. Not surprisingly, SEED retains a large number of students in eighth grade—on average, about 30 percent fail to move on to ninth grade during their first attempt and must repeat eighth grade as a "growth year."

While teachers must prepare students for the ninth-grade gate, instructors at SEED have more pedagogical leeway than at some paternalistic schools. They are responsible for selecting readings and primary sources for core subjects in the academic curriculum. If Diamond's eighth graders do poorly on one strand of the English gate, she has the freedom to alter her course to remedy their weaknesses.

Once admitted into upper school, students take a rigorous college-prep curriculum. To graduate, a senior must have taken four credits in English; three in social studies (in world studies 1 and 2, and U.S. history); four in math (through algebra 2); three in science (including at least two in biology, chemistry, or physics); and three in a modern language. Outside the core curriculum, SEED offers both unusual electives (e.g., financial literacy, youth justice, history of hip hop) and four AP classes, two for juniors and two for seniors. The AP classes are demanding—and few students have so far scored three or higher on AP exams, entitling them to advanced placement at college.

In Bill Stevens's eleventh-grade AP U.S. history class, students discussed a letter that Thomas Jefferson had sent Virginia state senator Joseph Cabell in 1816. In it, Jefferson attacked the idea that the federal, state, or even county governments should have any say over public schools. Jefferson argued that the parents of each "ward" ought to be responsible for creating and overseeing their local school. "When every man is a sharer in the direction of his ward-republic," he wrote, "he will let the heart be torn out of his body sooner than his power be wrested from him by a Caesar or a Bonaparte." Stevens was prepping students for the AP by having them read primary documents and answer hypothetical essay questions. Did Jefferson's letter, Stevens asked, suggest in any way that Jefferson had abandoned his Republican principles?

After a pause, a student pointed out that Jefferson appeared to have crossed the boundaries of his Republican principles 13 years earlier by insisting "that the Louisiana Purchase be controlled by the federal government rather than the state." Stevens nodded in approval.

SEED's AP courses often push students to their limits—and beyond. In 2005–2006, 21 of them (20 percent of high school students) completed 39 AP courses. One student, senior Patrice Smith Taylor had always made the honor roll—except during her junior year, when she took two AP courses. "I was staying up until 1:00 or 2:00 A.M...to get my work done," she recalls. "I feel like SEED should have done more to prep you for the AP courses."

Nevertheless, many students like Taylor take AP courses because of SEED's single-minded focus on preparing students for college-level studies. Diamond, the middle school English teacher, heard about SEED when she saw the Oprah Winfrey show on the school. "I liked Oprah's show but what drew me to the school was that I had never taught in a school that was so centered on every kid going to college. In Seattle, the goal was just to have kids graduate from high school." What "sealed the deal" for Diamond during her recruiting visit to the school was "sitting down at breakfast at the cafeteria and seeing students reading the *Washington Post* and *New York Times*. I couldn't believe it."

As at other paternalistic schools, SEED's teachers are not unionized, and they typically are deeply committed to educating disadvantaged students. Faculty tend to be young, and like many schools in D.C., SEED did not meet the NCLB standard for "highly qualified" teachers. Yet SEED does not recruit most of its teachers from Teach for America. It tends rather to attract teachers with a special interest in teaching low-income students in a boarding school setting. Bill Stevens, the AP history teacher, graduated from Messiah College, a Christian school. He taught first at a school for kids with emotional disabilities before moving on to another charter school in the District and then to SEED. Diamond was so taken with SEED's focus on getting students into college that she moved from Seattle to "the other Washington" to teach in the non-union charter school, even though her mother and brother are public school teachers and her father is a school superintendent.

The intense commitment to students that a boarding school helps promote is evident not just in SEED's after-school tutorials but also in the engagement of teachers in students' personal struggles. Ask Frank Gunn. When he was a junior, his mother was hospitalized for a long stretch. As reported in the *Baltimore Sun*, Gunn's family fell behind on rent and "Gunn was going to drop out to support his siblings. But SEED assembled a team of teachers dubbed 'Team Gunn' that collected enough money to pay the back rent, arranged rides for Gunn to the hospital to visit his mother, and chased him down on Monday mornings if he didn't return to school."[28] Gunn managed to graduate—and went on to attend Tuskegee University.

Academic Achievement

SEED's impact on academic performance and the achievement gap can be interpreted two ways, depending on the measuring stick that is used. Like Cristo Rey, SEED has had enormous success in eliminating the college-entrance gap between white and black students. But also like Cristo Rey, it has not succeeded in coming close to eliminating the test score gap between white and minority students—even though its students are handily outperforming their peers in nearby public schools.

SEED has one of the highest college enrollment rates of any inner-city school in the country. In its first two graduating classes, 100 percent of students went on to college. In year three, 91 percent of seniors went on to college, for an overall three-year enrollment rate of 93 percent. By way of comparison, 56 percent of African-American seniors nationwide enroll in college the fall after graduation and only 48 percent of low-income students do so. SEED's high college attendance rates are all the more impressive because its students have formidable socioeconomic disadvantages. In its first class of graduates, 88 percent came from single-parent or no-parent households, and 93 percent were the first in their families to go to college.[29]

Eric Adler believes that college enrollment is the best metric for measuring SEED's success in closing the achievement gap. "The test that matters more to me than any other," he says, "is whether kids are accepted into college." Adler and former head of school John Ciccone also note that SEED students are more college-ready than many of their inner-city peers, thanks to the boarding school experience. "We have college presidents who visit and say that our students have learned how to live in a dormitory," says Ciccone. "The depth of social preparation here is very valuable—our graduates aren't getting snagged by the independence they have when they go off to college." As of 2008, 85 percent of SEED alumni are on track to graduate from college.

On achievement tests, SEED students are doing far better than their peers at nearby high schools with similar socioeconomic characteristics. At the three comparison schools shown in Table 7-1 below, virtually all the students are black and about 70 percent come from low-income families. SEED ninth graders were significantly more likely to graduate four years later (85 percent), than students at the comparison schools (about 70 percent). The gap in test scores between SEED and the comparison high schools is also large.

Table 7-1. Academic achievement at the SEED school and nearby schools

		2006-07 District of Columbia standards test • Percentage of students scoring Proficient or Advanced	
	Distance to SEED (miles)	10th grade Reading	10th grade Math
SEED		**54**	**45**
H.D. Woodson HS	1.4	11	10
Spingarn HS	1.6	17	16
Anacostia HS	2.3	8	6
District Average (Washington, DC)		34	32

Source: District of Columbia Public Schools, No Child Left Behind Data Reports, http://webb.k12.dc.us/NCLB/ (accessed April 1, 2008).

In both reading and math, SEED students easily outperformed their peers at comparison schools on the District assessment test. Over half (54 percent) of SEED tenth graders were proficient or advanced in reading in 2006–2007, compared to 8 to 17 percent at the comparison schools. Summarized more simply, SEED students were three to six times more likely to be proficient than their inner-city peers. The gulf was equally wide on the math test, with 45 percent of SEED tenth graders having proficient or advanced skills compared to 6 to 16 percent at nearby schools. SEED students similarly outperform the District average.

Still, SEED's test scores fall far short of closing the achievement gap between black and white students. In 2004–2005, SEED was one of just two nonselective public high schools in the District to make AYP. But the following year, the District replaced the ninth edition of the Stanford test with its own citywide test for measuring AYP, the D.C. Comprehensive Assessment System

(DCAS). SEED administrators were shaken and embarrassed when the school failed to make AYP in math on the DCAS in 2005–2006. Though SEED did make AYP in reading (48.4 percent of SEED students tested proficient versus a target of 43.6 percent), it was a few points short in math (37.3 percent versus a target of 40.6 percent). Most troubling, SEED's tenth graders were not more likely to show proficient skills on the DCAS than the school's seventh graders. After nearly four years at SEED, and having cleared the ninth grade gate, SEED's tenth graders should have been outperforming new students.

While the failure to make AYP in 2005–2006 was troubling, changes in D.C.'s testing regime made the results somewhat difficult to interpret. Previously, the District had used the Stanford 9 test for all grades, but the DCAS was only given to seventh, eighth, and tenth graders. Since the seventh graders attending SEED were new to the school in 2005–2006, there was no way to measure whether they were making AYP, and thus their scores were not included in the calculations. That meant that only the test scores for eighth and tenth graders would be used to determine whether SEED would make AYP. It was the low scores of the 30 tenth graders at SEED, a particularly weak class, that caused the school to fail to meet AYP. And while it doesn't explain away the performance of SEED students in 2006, it is worth noting that only a handful of charter schools in the city made AYP under the new test that year. Thirty of 34 charter schools failed to make AYP, as did 118 of 146 district schools.[30] In 2007, SEED returned to form and made AYP in both reading and math.

Nonetheless, the scores of SEED students are mediocre—better than D.C. district school students but far below the national mean. The mean SAT score for SEED's class of 2006 was 851, above the D.C. public school average (814) but a hair under the national African-American mean of 857. And they are well below the national mean of 1026. "When we started SEED," says Eric Adler, "I thought SAT scores would go up 500 points. It is a challenge for to us to figure out why testing has not produced more dramatic gains."

Does SEED's record of superior performance, relative to other D.C. public schools, suggest that it is creaming? The school's mediocre SAT scores and the high proportion of SEED students who are poor and from single-parent families suggest that SEED does not attract especially gifted pupils. Thirteen percent of its 324 students in 2006 were special education students with IEP plans, similar to other D.C. public schools. SEED, moreover, does not impose admission requirements for students entering the lottery for a spot in seventh grade, eliminating any overt creaming. "Student can have straight Ds or straight Fs and still be admitted," says John Ciccone, head of school in 2006–2007.

Yet there is reason to think that part of SEED's impact on academic achievement is attributable to creaming and attrition. Students and families who enter the lottery are likely to be more motivated than other inner-city parents—if only because SEED is asking them to commit to sending a child to boarding school for six years. SEED has worked hard to stimulate parents to become more involved in the school. Contrary to what one might expect of a boarding school, teachers at SEED report that they see parents more often than when they worked at day schools, if only because parents are obliged to come to pick up their children on Friday afternoon. SEED asks parents also to contribute financial support if they can and to volunteer at the school at least once a month. And while its parents don't appear to be extraordinarily involved in their children's education, there is no evidence that parents are disengaged and just packing their kids off to a boarding school.

SEED's impact on academic achievement could also be colored by the fact that the school has a serious attrition problem in middle school, inflating SEED's high college acceptance rate. As noted earlier, SEED's expulsion rate of 5.6 percent is roughly triple that of other D.C. charter schools (1.8 percent). The impact of middle school attrition on high school attainment may be even more significant. Some students drop out of SEED in middle school because their families move or because student and parent ultimately do not want a child to live away from home for six years. But the school also loses substantial numbers of students who fail to pass the ninth grade gate and do not want to repeat eighth grade.

Unlike in neighborhood public schools, when students drop out or are expelled from SEED, they can't be replaced the following year because SEED only accepts students in seventh grade. To give some sense of the scope of middle school attrition, SEED's first graduating class of 2004 had started six years earlier with 40 students. Just 21 of those 40 students graduated on time. (Two more graduated the following year.) The middle school attrition problem wasn't limited to the initial class, either. The class of 2005 had just 13 graduates, and SEED's first three graduating classes had a total of 57 students.

Eric Adler argues that SEED's educational model makes attrition in middle school inevitable. Some students, he says, will depart after failing the school's demanding behavioral standards, while others will fall short of the school's tough academic standards. "We don't do social promotion so kids who would have been retained go elsewhere, to a school that will promote them to the next grade," says Adler. He adds that "a school like ours, with rigorous standards, is almost by definition going to have attrition problems." Even so, SEED's high attrition rate suggests that the school's success stems partly from losing weaker students in the middle school years.

Replicating the SEED

From the outset, Adler and Vinnakota established the SEED Foundation to copy the model of the SEED school in Washington, D.C., and other communities. Over the last decade, it has sought to establish more public boarding schools in poor urban communities, offering both a college-prep and a structured life skills curriculum. But the effort to replicate SEED has gone slowly, due largely to the high cost of boarding school.

One hint of the precariousness of the urban boarding school concept came when the SEED Foundation commissioned a 1999 analysis of boarding schools for inner-city children that looked at SEED and two other schools, one in West Trenton, New Jersey, and another in Granby, Massachusetts. By the time the field research was completed in 2001, the two other schools had closed. The Samuel DeWitt Proctor Academy in West Trenton provided a particularly poignant cautionary tale. Its two cofounders, like Eric Adler, were Wharton M.B.A.'s who wanted to create a boarding school for low-income students that would offer its graduates opportunities similar to those of graduates of elite boarding schools. Students, picked by lottery, wore uniforms and attended life skills classes every morning. But poor student performance on state tests and other issues led the New Jersey Department of Education to put the school on probation in the spring of 2001; by May the state education department informed the school it would not renew its charter. The other school, Boston University Residential Charter School, was developed originally for children in foster care to cut down on their shuttling from placement to placement. But low enrollment and expensive staffing requirements led to the school costing more than $50,000 per student. The University closed the school in 2000—at which point the school had had all of three graduates.[31]

The SEED Foundation has also found it a challenge to raise sufficient funds to establish more public boarding schools—even though Adler and

Vinnakota have shown a flair for fundraising and garnering backers among Washington's elite. Not long after Prince Charles and Laura Bush visited in 2005, the SEED Foundation hosted a benefit dinner at the Kennedy Center attended by Alma Powell (SEED's first commencement speaker in 2004); Boyden Gray, U.S. ambassador to the European Union; Senator Joe Lieberman and his wife, Hadassah (the dinner's honorary cochairmen); Senator Paul Sarbanes; and former Greek ambassador Alexander Philon and his wife. The Philons had been so impressed with SEED that they established a classics program at the school in tandem with the Society for the Preservation of Greek Heritage.

For all its high-profile backers, the cost barriers to opening more SEED schools are formidable. According to a 2006 federal study of eight charter schools that were closing the achievement gap, SEED receives $31,500 per pupil in state and federal funds, with $30,500 coming from the District and $1,000 per pupil from the federal government. That was triple the per-pupil funding of the other seven charter schools.[32] SEED's total cost per student is about $33,000, which leaves the school having to raise $1,500 per student, a manageable sum for a charter school operator. Nonetheless, SEED's generous local and federal support for operating costs still leaves the school with the daunting task of raising private money for facilities. To acquire and build the first SEED school, the SEED Foundation raised more than $26 million in private donations and leveraged more than $14 million in private debt. Estimates suggest that future SEED schools will cost in the neighborhood of $60 million to $70 million.

In short, while it does not take an act of God to fund a public boarding school for low-income students, it does appear to take an act of Congress — or at least of the state legislature. Even then, legislation paving the way for additional revenues is no guarantee of success. After opening its first school in Washington, D.C., the SEED Foundation searched for a second site on which to open a 15-acre, 600-student SEED school. It succeeded in lining up the support of then-mayor Anthony Williams. At the mayor's prompting, Congress enacted legislation in December 2005 that specified that 15 of the 75 acres of federal land being used for a parking lot north of RFK Stadium would be conveyed to a public boarding school, effectively earmarking the parcel for a new SEED school. But neighborhood civic associations and anti-charter groups blasted the plan and protested outside the offices of the SEED Foundation.

One protester went so far as to claim that "SEED is planning to build a gated boarding school, which resembles a prison, for 600 students, most of whom will probably never graduate." Another activist complained that SEED had spent more than $60 million in its eight-year history but then had just 41 graduates to show for its lavish taxpayer and foundation support. When Raj Vinnakota met with the protesters, he said afterwards that he had "never been engaged in a conversation that's so vehement."[33] It is not clear whether the RFK parking lot site will ever become a campus for a SEED school.

The one location besides Washington, D.C. where the SEED Foundation has secured legislation to establish and help fund a public boarding school is Maryland. In January 2007, the Foundation announced that Art and Patricia Modell, former owners of the Baltimore Ravens football team, had pledged $5 million as an "anchor gift" to help start a SEED school in Baltimore. The SEED School of Maryland expects to open in southwest Baltimore on a 52-acre campus in August 2008 with an initial class of 80 sixth graders. Yet the SEED Foundation has to raise a total of roughly $60 million for the school, including $30 million in private donations. Elsewhere, the Foundation has recently secured commitments from donors to provide at least half of the equity down payment for loans for new schools in Cincinnati, Ohio, and Newark, New Jersey. The Foundation has now begun lobbying in Ohio, New Jersey, and Wisconsin for legislation to secure additional funding for public boarding schools. (The school in Wisconsin would be located in Milwaukee, Vinnakota's home town.)

Adler and Vinnakota continue to have grand aspirations for the SEED boarding school model. They don't claim that all or most low-income youngsters in the inner-city need a boarding school, though they believe that many would benefit from it. They acknowledge that SEED is expensive. But they also argue that it is cost-effective once the savings in reduced crime, increased lifetime earnings, and the like are factored in. "SEED is about a movement," Vinnakota told the makers of an independent documentary about the school. "It's about trying to prove to society that we can take any child and we can get them to the point where they are successful."

Adler's faith in the model remains similarly intact. "SEED is small but not as small as people think," he says. "If you look at the number of high school students who are going on to college in the competing neighborhood schools in Anacostia, SEED is producing the same number of college-bound students as the neighborhood school system at large." Would SEED, Adler speculated, "be cost-effective if you created a SEED school for every poor child in America who needed it?" He thinks the answer is yes. "If there is a reasonable chance that SEED does pay for itself, then this is a meaningful social model," he contends. In Adler's view, the worst that happens from the SEED Foundation's replication efforts is that "we end up creating a boutique experiment for a couple of thousand kids. But what if we find that the program pays for itself for tens or hundreds of thousands of kids?" Given the difficulties of quantifying SEED's cost-effectiveness and the schools' steep up-front costs, Adler's question may go unanswered. Yet even when viewed as a boutique experiment, SEED has shown that round-the-clock paternalism in an urban college-prep boarding school can dramatically boost the educational attainment of poor, African-American adolescents—the young people for whom the achievement gap is supposed to be the least bridgeable.

Chapter Eight

University Park's Mission Possible

"The success of the University Park Campus School is not...the story of exorbitant budgets, overstaffing, building luxury, exam-school students, or district favoritism. It is the story of tightening the belt, offering few academic choices, working in an old building with no high school perks, and lottery-acceptances of neighborhood kids. And it is a story of a mission—that every student who entered that school would succeed and that every adult would contribute to that success."

—Donna Rodrigues, founder and principal of the University Park Campus School

After Donna Rodrigues watched one of her students bleed to death following a knife fight outside her Spanish classroom at South High in 1989, she was in shock, grief-stricken, and unsure of her future after twenty years of teaching foreign languages in some of Worcester's biggest, toughest high schools. But in the ensuing months, Rodrigues found she had another unexpected emotion as well: anger. Rodrigues had lived in Worcester's rough Main South neighborhood for years and had taught several generations of neighborhood kids. Yet the public schools to which she had dedicated her life were failing their students. Rodrigues, as she later wrote, was "angry at an educational system that turned its back on kids living in poverty, kids of color, and ELL kids, at the teachers, the schools, and the districts." Not only was she frustrated with "the system," she was upset with her colleagues. She was "angry at the teachers who set low expectations and standards for these students while they spoke of the academic accomplishments of their own children with such pride."[1]

Rodrigues took that anger and channeled it toward a creative end: She helped design and run a new school that proved inner-city students could thrive academically and go on to college. To avoid the mayhem she had witnessed at South High, Rodrigues planned her new neighborhood school with two key features in mind. First, it would create a demanding culture of achievement and enforce a paternalistic code of conduct that barred street talk, swear words, and disrespect. Second, it would have an unrelenting educational mission. As Rodrigues later put it, "the goal of the school was not that [students] graduate from high school, not that they pass the state-mandated MCAS [graduation] test, but that all students, no matter where they were starting from, would leave UPCS prepared to do college-level work. More than a goal, this was the promise I made to every student, every family member, and every teacher."

Rodrigues's promise—essentially that every one of her pupils would get into college—was audacious given the pitiful reading and math skills of students in local public schools. The first class of thirty-five seventh graders at University Park in 1997 included four youngsters who could not read at all. Almost half of the entering students read at or below the third grade level and about a third were special-needs students. More than half spoke English as a second language. Yet three-and-a-half years later, in tenth grade, every one of those seventh graders not only passed the state's demanding Massachusetts Comprehensive Assessment System (MCAS) English and math tests but managed to do so with high scores: more than 80 percent had proficient or advanced skills in both English and math. The MCAS scores of the class of 2003 made UPCS the thirty-fourth ranked high school in Massachusetts (out of 332).[2]

As soon became clear, the MCAS scores of the first class were not a one-year fluke. As Rodrigues vowed, nearly every graduate (95 percent) in UPCS's five senior classes to date has gone on to seek a higher education degree, with 80 percent going to four-year colleges. Tenth graders' MCAS scores actually rose over the next five years until UPCS was outperforming schools in affluent school districts and even some exam schools. By 2003, it was the only public school in Massachusetts where not a single student had failed the tenth grade

MCAS in English or math during the two previous years.[3] For six years running, from 2001 to 2007, no UPCS student failed the English MCAS test on the first attempt. (One tenth grade girl, who did not enter UPCS until ninth grade, failed the math MCAS by one question in 2006, the only blemish on the school's otherwise perfect record. She passed the test in her junior year.) Moreover, unlike some inner-city schools with high test scores and college-acceptance rates, UPCS is an open-admissions neighborhood school with zero attrition. In its ten years to date, just one student has dropped out of UPCS; the high school effectively has a 100 percent graduation rate.

Not surprisingly, UPCS has been showered with accolades. In 2005, *Newsweek* ranked it as the sixty-eighth best high school in the country. When the magazine's ranking was limited to schools where half or more of the students were low-income, UPCS ranked fourth.[4] That same year, the National Association of Secondary School Principals singled it out as one of nine "Breakthrough High Schools" in the country. A 2003 analysis of high-performing urban high schools in Massachusetts found "only one such Massachusetts school in which students consistently performed at high levels—University Park Campus School."[5] Both conservative and liberal luminaries have lauded UPCS. The left-leaning Education Trust first profiled it in 2005 as one of three public schools that had succeeded in narrowing the achievement gap.[6] At the same time, UPCS was praised by Bush appointee Rod Paige, who wrote that when he was the U.S. "secretary of education, and critics were decrying high standards, testing, and high expectations for kids, University [Park] Campus School was proving it could be done."[7]

In several critical respects, UPCS differs from other paternalistic inner-city academies. It shares the academic rigor and paternalistic, character-building code of conduct typical of other successful inner-city schools. But its instruction relies heavily on group work rather than teacher-led instruction. Even more distinctive, UPCS, unlike other outstanding paternalistic schools, is a traditional neighborhood public school, not a charter or parochial school. All its pupils come from Worcester's Main South neighborhood, albeit drawn by lottery. Teachers are part of the Worcester teachers union, and the school receives the same funding per student as every other neighborhood school in the city. Its success thus stands as a rebuke to skeptics who claim that no-excuses schools cannot exist, much less thrive, within the confines of an urban school system and teacher union contract. Indeed, the former superintendent in Worcester who approved and helped design UPCS supported it because he wanted to show that a creative neighborhood school could compete with charter schools in a city that did not have a reputation for fostering educational choice.[8] The fact that UPCS has essentially zero attrition also demonstrates that a demanding paternalistic school need not succeed by having less-gifted students drop out to avoid repeating a grade.

UPCS has one final feature that distinguishes it from other paternalistic schools: its close link to a university. It was conceived out of a partnership between Clark University and the Worcester school district. During its first two years, it was housed on the Clark campus. It subsequently moved into its own building two blocks away, but the university ties have endured. Roughly half of UPCS juniors and seniors take one or more courses at Clark for credit, and each year Clark students serve as mentors and student teachers at UPCS. UPCS pupils routinely use Clark facilities, including the gym and library.

Roughly a dozen UPCS students have gone on to attend Clark tuition-free under a university scholarship program for qualified students from the neighborhood. Still, UPCS is run by the school district and is not a university lab school. Nor is it an "early college" high school. (These typically allow high school seniors to earn a two-year associate's degree along with their diploma or to accumulate enough college credits to enter as a junior.) But by all accounts, UPCS's university-assisted partnership with Clark has proved invaluable in getting students to think about college at a young age.

School with a Promise

With a population of 175,000, Worcester is the second largest city in Massachusetts. Decades ago, it was a manufacturing hub, but over the last half-century, it has gradually lost its industrial base, taking on the air of a fading rust-belt city. No area was hit harder by the loss of manufacturing jobs than the Main South neighborhood, which sits just apart from downtown. Once it was a working-class, Irish neighborhood, dotted with tool-and-die shops and small factories. As shops and homes were shuttered or abandoned, property values dropped. By the 1990's, Main South was the poorest neighborhood in Worcester and a destination for Hispanic immigrants, as well as new arrivals from Vietnam, Cambodia, Albania, Ghana, and Sudan. Today, just over 40 percent of area residents are Hispanic, 10 percent African-American, 10 percent Asian-American, and about 30 percent white, including many

Albanian immigrants. Immigrant families typically live in close quarters in Main South's ubiquitous triple-decker clapboard houses. More than 12,500 people live within the square mile that constitutes Main South.[9]

In the midst of this multiethnic enclave sits Clark, a small, leafy New England research university that had traditionally functioned as a closed campus. Twenty-five years ago, UPCS students likely would not have been allowed even to stroll across the Clark campus. By the mid-1980s, town/gown tensions were getting bad in a hurry. Neighborhood residents resented Clark students for being noisy at night, driving up prices on rental apartments, and reducing street parking. University administrators, meanwhile, worried that the area's high crime rate and poverty would soon start deterring students from applying. Working with neighborhood leaders, the university helped form the Main South Community Development Corporation (CDC) to improve town/gown relations and spur economic development. Clark barred freshmen from bringing cars to campus, built a garage and a new dorm, and spent several million dollars through the Main South CDC to create new low-income housing and rehabilitate decrepit properties. But the Main South neighborhood was not improving fast enough in the early 1990s, at least not to the satisfaction of Clark president Richard Traina. Working with school superintendent James Garvey, Traina set out to create a new secondary school for neighborhood kids that would benefit from Clark's resources but be run by the city. In 1995, Traina and Garvey won a grant from the U.S. Department of Housing and Urban Development to help create the new school and started looking for someone to design and lead it. They found their perfect candidate in Donna Rodrigues.

Rodrigues had resided in the Main South neighborhood since she was a child and still lived and attended church there. Having taught in local schools for two decades, she knew many neighborhood families and was no stranger to the working poor or the immigrant experience. Rodrigues herself was raised in a single-parent family that had struggled with financial problems and illness. In the 1970s, she bought a triple-decker in the neighborhood and occupied one floor with her mother and brother. Fluent in Spanish and French, she was also steeped in school reform philosophy. Following the murder of her student, Rodrigues won a Hiatt Fellowship to attend the Harvard School of Education and took a year off from teaching. She returned to Worcester in the fall of 1995 with her second master's degree in education and a new interest in designing and running her own school.

Rodrigues applied at Clark and soon got the job of planner and founding principal for the new school. But in addition to designing that school, Rodrigues had to recruit its first class of seventh graders. From the school district, Rodrigues secured a list of sixth graders who lived within a mile of the new school. The list contained 115 names, so Rodrigues divided up the neighborhood and started knocking on doors at night unannounced, asking parents and students to enroll in UPCS. Ultimately, she knocked on fifty doors and tried reaching the remaining sixth graders through informational meetings at their elementary schools. Rodrigues was nothing if not tenacious. "When I was making the rounds," she recalls, "the barking guard dogs were intimidating. But so was walking up the back stairs of a triple decker that had no lights on."

Rodrigues's advantage, she says, was her "clarity." Whenever she presented the new school to parents, she put her mission—to get every kid ready for college—in the form of a promise. "I promised the parents not only that their kids would be college-ready but that they wouldn't be tracked," she says. "I knew many of the parents and had taught some of them—and many parents themselves had been tracked when they were in school." Rodrigues also explicitly warned students and their parents that the school would have strict discipline and assign lots of homework. "I told the kids," she says, "that they could be swearing every day in their current school but the rules would be different when they walked through the doors of University Park." Though Rodrigues's school was totally untested, many prospective parents eagerly embraced the opportunity to secure a college-preparatory education for their sons and daughters in the midst of Main South's educational wasteland. "I promised them a safe school," Rodrigues would later recall. "There were parents saying 'Amen, amen.' It was like a revival meeting at points."[10]

Rodrigues secured commitments from thirty-five students to enroll in the new school. But no sooner had she recruited her first class than she requested their test scores from the Worcester public schools and got the bad news. Her first class of students, she says, had "reading and computing skills on the third or fourth grade level. Not one student tested higher than a fourth grade level—and five students couldn't read and were coming out of special ed." Furthermore, about half the students were Hispanic, Vietnamese, or Cambodian; they spoke English as a second language and had parents who spoke little or no English at home.

Many secondary schools in the Worcester area would simply have ignored the adolescents' severe reading deficiencies. "A lot of middle schools don't want to deal with reading anymore, with a kid who can't decode in seventh grade," says Rodrigues. And the incoming test scores, Rodrigues concedes, did "scare me—this was the first class that was going to have to pass the MCAS in tenth grade." Once she realized the depth of the skills gap, Rodrigues took two steps. First, she approached Clark and won funding for a five-week "August Academy" for incoming students to be held at the university. During the afternoons, the seventh graders used the Clark pool, but in the mornings they sat through ninety-minute block classes in math, reading, and writing that provided remedial instruction and intensive diagnostic testing. UPCS's "program works," U.S. Education Secretary Rod Paige later wrote, "because teachers and students are dedicated to testing to find weaknesses and are committed to fixing the areas of weakness."[11] Rodrigues also made a commitment to intensive literacy instruction no matter how basic its beginnings. She hired two gifted veteran teachers to teach the first class, one of whom was June Eressy, a colleague from South High School. Eressy was a whiz at literacy instruction. A few years later, she would be named Worcester's teacher of the year and a Milken National Educator—an award sometimes called the Oscars of teaching. Eressy believed she could teach just about any student to read. With UPCS's first seventh grade class, she started out working with picture books and frequently read aloud to students.

Both the August Academy and the remedial literacy instruction for seventh and eight graders soon became fixtures of the UPCS curriculum. "June [Eressy] and I realized that we might not reach seventh grade standards by the end of seventh grade," says Rodrigues. "But we were determined that we would reach ninth grade standards by the end of ninth grade." In high school, students would then take a rigorous college-preparatory curriculum. With no textbooks or lab equipment, UPCS opened in September 1997. Six years later, thirty-one of the thirty-five members of the original class graduated. (Three had moved out of the area and one returned to a neighborhood school.) All thirty-one were accepted into college.

The "Culture" of University Park

What explains University Park's ability to transform foundering students? A big part is due to the self-described "culture of University Park." Like all paternalistic schools, UPCS creates a no-excuses culture of achievement within its graffiti-free walls that stands in contrast to the culture of the street. But unlike other schools with a no-excuses culture, UPCS does not rely on regular, all-school meetings with chants, awards, and confessionals, field trips, or "UPCS dollars." Nor does it have elaborately codified rules governing student behavior in and out of class, uniforms, or a detailed code of discipline. Instead, UPCS has fairly simple rules: It brooks no disrespect, bullying, street talk, or slang. The principal and teachers also insist that students measure their success first in terms of the collective (e.g., how well the class as a whole performs) and not just by their own individual achievements. The school exudes a can-do attitude. Math teacher Kate Shepard has even posted "The Shepardean Oath" on the walls of her classroom, instructing students that she will treat "the word 'can't' as a swear word." The last part of her oath admonishes students that "we will never say the following phrase, 'I am done,' as there is always something more to learn or someone else to help."

While University Park's paternalism has a kinder, gentler cast than some no-excuses schools, it can be every bit as Big Brotherish — as eighth grader Gabriel Malave discovered. All paternalistic schools forbid students from talking disrespectfully to teachers and principals, but UPCS punishes students who speak disrespectfully to other students as well. Malave, whose parents are Puerto Rican, moved to Worcester from the Bronx in 1999 and soon learned that UPCS was not like his previous schools. Malave had his first brush with UPCS culture as a soft-spoken seventh grader in 2006 when he told a teacher he did not want to switch seats after she caught him talking to another student. The teacher told him that "if I had attitude, I was to get out" and sent Malave to another classroom. Malave had to write a note of apology to the teacher and face the wrath of his mother, who grounded him for a week without television.

The next year, on a fall morning before school started, Malave and several classmates were quietly teasing an overweight student at the back of their classroom. Unbeknownst to them, the custodian overheard the teen banter and reported it to their teacher. The next morning Malave's teacher listened intently before class to the pre-class chatter and heard the student being teased again. "Why don't you do some sit-ups?" one eighth grader asked the overweight boy. Malave, one other boy, and three girls were given an in-house suspension for a day for teasing the boy, though the relatively mild teasing would have gone unnoticed and unpunished in most high schools where, say, "Mean Girls" are allowed to flourish. Malave and his friends all had to write essays explaining why they teased the boy and why they were not supposed to tease another student. Malave recalls that the "other teachers said to me 'we know you're a good kid, but you can't act like that and stay here.'" Malave had to talk about his behavior as well to teacher Ricci Hall, who was then serving as deputy principal. "Mr. Hall made me lift heavy boxes of paper and carry them up to the third floor from the basement," says Malave. He said 'if you don't pay attention in class, you'll be doing menial labor work the rest of your life.' I was like, 'uh, no'—I decided I didn't want to get in trouble again." Malave now does two to two-and-a-half hours of homework a night, and typically comes in to the school's homework center at 7:00 A.M. to finish up.

At UPCS, the culture started with a paternal—or, perhaps in this case, maternal—principal. Donna Rodrigues, a self-described pit bull, was the tireless "keeper of the flame" of the school's culture. Like Ben Chavis at American Indian Public Charter School, she knew all her students by name, knew their parents and many of their grandparents, and often knew their phone numbers. Like Chavis, she walked all twelve classrooms every school day. English teacher Peter Weyler says that Rodrigues was "a very blunt, stubborn woman and she talked very frankly to kids about their family problems and street life. But she married that to the message 'you *will* succeed.' She just would not allow students to fail."

Rodrigues, like Chavis, was not above putting students on the spot to enforce school rules. She expected them to attend every day—and told parents in no uncertain terms that they had to call the school beforehand if for any reason a student would be absent. If a student was late or not at school for the first period, Rodrigues would hop in her 1996 red Taurus station wagon and drive to the student's house. "I would pull up outside the home and honk," Rodrigues recalls with a laugh. "The students thought my car was very uncool, and they would be embarrassed that I was sitting there, honking outside their house for them. When they got in the car, I'd take them to school. But you could see they were thinking 'is there anything this lady won't do to get me to come to school?'" After Rodrigues had shown up a half-dozen times at students' houses during UPCS's first year, the word got around that the principal would embarrass the hell out of them if they didn't get to school on time. Rodrigues never had to make another expedition in her Taurus again.

In 2003, after seven years as principal, Rodrigues left to work on the early college high school initiative at Jobs for the Future in Boston. Her successor, June Eressy, was in many ways set in Rodrigues's mold—and not just because the two had taught at South High together for many years. Eressy, too, would show up unannounced in her car at a student's home if he or she was late. She, too, remembers how one shocked "boy looked at me like he had seen a ghost." UPCS's two principals could also assume a motherly role when needed. In between holding students accountable, Rodrigues or Eressy might hug a student or tell them she loved them.

Teachers at University Park may play an even larger role in maintaining the school's no-excuses culture than at some other paternalistic schools, where instructors are largely responsible only for their own classrooms. Every Wednesday morning, all teachers of core subjects at UPCS meet to discuss the progress and setbacks of their students, possible changes to instruction and schedules, and even potential hires. Teachers at University Park are, thus, unusually aware of what is going on in their colleagues' classrooms and are constantly on students who are acting out in other classrooms. "When a student is being a punk in one class, all the teachers know about it," said Ricci Hall. "You can't go to one class, act up, and then disappear into your next class." Hall says that the faculty consistently "shuns bad behavior—the next day every teacher is going to be asking that student 'why were you acting disrespectfully in after-school yesterday?'"

Many students, in fact, described UPCS teachers and principal as parental figures whom they feared to let down. Monaye Leathers, a seventeen-year-old junior, has faced formidable odds on her path to obtaining a college education. She lives across from the school on the second floor of triple-decker, along with nine siblings. Her mother is on welfare and Monaye says she has not seen her father in more than a decade. Leathers is an enthusiastic student who talks excitedly about "learning something new at University Park every day" and volunteers to help first graders at a local elementary school. But in eighth grade, she got in trouble when she used the cell phone of another student. "I had a suspension in the eighth grade when I took someone's cell phone, a kid I didn't like," she says. "My friend took the cell phone but I used it," Leathers says. She was chastened by the consequences of her actions and went on to become one of University Park's top students. "I never did something like that again," she says. "I had to sit in Mr. Hall's room, and I couldn't bear to see him disappointed in me."

At UPCS, teachers do not just tell students not to use street talk or swear words, they also tell them why they shouldn't use curse words and slang. As tenth grade geometry teacher Jody Bird put it, "we don't just say 'you can't swear because I said so'—we say 'you can't swear because you want to be a professional and you can't do that and use curse words.'" "June and I used to laugh sometimes over the things that we punished students over at University Park because at South that behavior would never have been an issue," says Rodrigues. "At South the slang and street talk was second nature to the students. At University Park, I told them they were going to speak properly and use academic language. When a student goes to interview for an internship, they can't throw out 'yo-yo,' or the n-word—that just drove me crazy."

What is particularly distinctive about the vigilant maintenance of school culture at University Park is that not just teachers but older students and siblings repeatedly enforce the school's code of conduct, too. Many middle school students spoke of juniors, seniors, and older siblings at UPCS who corrected their behavior, telling them "we don't do that here." New seventh graders are required to attend University Park's August Academy but so, too, are UPCS students who will be starting eleventh grade. The UPCS juniors help tutor new students, educate them about their new school, and later serve as their mentors during the school year. Kate Shepard, the eighth grade math teacher, says, "it is really powerful when the older kids tell the younger students, 'you can't tell people to shut up.'"

There is little doubt that University Park teachers, as well as Rodrigues and Eressy, have benefited from having a small school in their quest to maintain the school's culture. After its first two years on the Clark campus, UPCS moved two blocks into a three-story, red-brick schoolhouse built in 1885 that had previously housed an elementary school. The building has four classrooms on each of the three floors for a total of twelve classrooms, or two per grade. Classes average from eighteen to twenty-two students, with each grade having only thirty-five to forty students.

It is no palace. It has no library or auditorium, its internet server is down frequently, and its boiler is erratic. The computer lab doubles as a math class and contains just twenty-two computers, six of which are out on a typical day. The tiny four-table cafeteria is set in a gloomy windowless basement with concrete floors painted a dull gray. Amid stacks of boxes, canned goods, and overhead fluorescent lights, the cafeteria looks more like it belongs in a 1950s bomb shelter than a high school for 230 students. Yet for all its lack of frills, University Park has a hominess and intimacy absent in many comprehensive high schools. Its high ceilings, tall windows, and wide, weathered staircases give the school the feel of an aging mansion where—as in the fabled bar "Cheers"—everybody knows your name.

The net result is that UPCS is the rare inner-city school where learning is cool. Teachers are mostly young and enthusiastic and classes are marked by a visceral engagement on the part of students. They jump to their feet and applaud when the principal announces the latest senior to get into college. "Students see disruptive kids as a distraction from learning here," says Ricci Hall. "The students find that they like to learn and they feel safe at the school—so there is a lot of peer pressure not to cut up." Student engagement is also heightened by early and ongoing exposure to college students and campus life at Clark. Junior Monaye Leathers, the student with nine siblings, will be the first member of her family to attend college—both her mother and older sister dropped out of school in ninth grade. Ever since she started UPCS in seventh grade, Leathers has heard every day "from one or another teacher 'don't you want to go to college?' or 'you *are* going to go to college.'"

In eighth grade, Leathers went with her class to visit the house of the president of Clark University. While there, the students researched various questions on the president's computer and in the books of his library. Being on a college campus is an integral part of being a student at University Park. Leathers, for example, goes to the Clark library to study "because it is quieter" than her house; after she worked in a youth corps that dealt with environmental issues, she got interested in Clark's environmental justice program. "I saw what happened with my sister and my mom [dropping out of high school], and I'm not going to repeat it," Leathers vows. "College is definitely in my head."

Finally, University Park's culture is reinforced by the fact that the principal and teachers also periodically play paternal roles when parental involvement at home is limited. The parents of most UPCS students are not native speakers of English; many are recent immigrants. Though most parents are excited and grateful that University Park promises to ready their child for college and are thrilled at the prospect of sending their child to Clark tuition-free, the vast majority of UPCS students will be the first in their families to attend college, and their parents—many of whom are working one or two jobs—are ill-equipped to help with high school homework. Parental involvement at University Park, says Eressy, does not "look like the ordinary middle-class parental involvement in the PTA." Rodrigues described it by saying "there was no bake sale or Secret Santa because the parents lacked the resources to do that — often the parents were quite young."

Instead, University Park's relationship with parents reaches back to the "social work" model of public schooling that historian Diane Ravitch notes was typical of many schools serving immigrant families a century ago. During its first several years of operation, University Park had an after-school adult education program that ran four evenings a week and enrolled about 200 neighborhood residents. Many of the adult education students were parents of UPCS students — who would hang around and do their homework while they waited for their parents' classes to finish. University Park also joined in opening a health center at the elementary school across the street. "Family involvement at University Park is very different from what you might see at most schools — it's about housing and drug abuse," says Rodrigues. Families become involved with the school because they need the school's help. Parents and students would come to Rodrigues "one step away from tragedy. They were about to be evicted, or they had a kid who hadn't been home in a week." On numerous occasions, Rodrigues called "Section 8 [subsidized housing] landlords on behalf of families threatened with eviction — it was very much in the nature of social work."

Most parents, while not deeply involved with the school, have been supportive of UPCS, but Rodrigues did not hesitate to crack down on immigrant families who put their own needs ahead of their kids' education. "I took at least five parents to court on a 51A, which is pretty much a child abuse form," says Rodrigues. "The parents were depriving their kids by keeping them out of school to do errands for them, or having the kids serve as translators or babysitters. I also filed one 51A on a parent who wouldn't get treatment for their son for drug abuse." As much or more than principals at other paternalistic schools, Rodrigues did not shrink from assuming a paternal role.

University Park's Unorthodox Pedagogy and Orthodox Curriculum

University Park's curriculum resembles those of other successful paternalistic inner-city secondary schools. Yet its pedagogy, particularly the emphasis on group instruction, is different. Much like the SEED School, it uses the middle school years to teach a "catch-up curriculum" that is heavy on remedial instruction but goes beyond skill-and-drill routines. Given the woefully inadequate skills of its incoming seventh graders, University Park's challenge has been to find a way to teach elementary math and reading skills without insulting or embarrassing students. When Rodrigues saw how many students in the first class of seventh graders had tested at the second and third grade level in math, she and her math teacher created a math binder with basic multiplication drills and tables—instead of handing students a second-grade workbook. Meanwhile, June Eressy started by reading picture books out loud to seventh graders and provided instructions in phonics and tutoring for students who could not read.

At Eressy's behest, Rodrigues made University Park classes a "literacy rich" environment: students read and write in all subjects, and teachers and students read out loud in all classes starting in middle school to develop students' ear for language and syntax. In effect, University Park tries to create the kind of literacy-rich environment in school that middle-class students grow up with at home. "We never dumbed down the discourse in the classes," notes Rodrigues. "Even if kids couldn't read in seventh grade, we never assumed that they couldn't hear. June might be reading a picture book. But she would be talking about gender personification at the same time and having the students repeat vocabulary."

As part of the catch-up curriculum, middle school teachers follow specific routines and rituals in every classroom. Math classes, for example, open with a starter problem on the blackboard, which students begin work on before the instructor enters the classroom. UPCS assumes not only that students need remedial help but also that they must be taught how to study and learn. A required seventh and eighth grade class called "Connections" teaches note-taking strategies and study skills that many middle-class students pick up informally. Throughout middle school, all UPCS students take the same courses. They also use identical homework planners and a standard format for their daily agenda—which teachers frequently check to make sure students are recording their homework assignments properly.

University Park fosters an intense focus on a core curriculum in several ways. It offers only three electives in the middle grades (art, music, and health and gym). Sport offerings are meager, too—the school has a track team and girls' and boys' basketball teams but no football team. During its first six years, instructors taught English, math, reading, and Spanish in 90-minute blocks in an extended eight-hour school day, but in 2003, the financially strapped Worcester district cut off funding for all extended school-day programs. As a consequence, UPCS was forced to revert to a traditional 6.5 hour school day and a mix of 60- and 90-minute classes.

Even though more than half its students speak English as a second language, University Park provides no bilingual education and has no pullout classes for English language learners (ELL) or special needs students. ELL students receive full-immersion instruction in English, like everyone else. In recent years, UPCS has hired a fulltime special education teacher, who provided a limited amount of one-on-one instruction for five students with IEPs in 2005–2006, as their plans required. But while special ed students made up 7 percent of the student body in 2005–2006, even those with extensive IEPs rarely spend more than one period a day with the special ed teacher. In fact, up until junior year, when students can opt for an AP course or a course at Clark, disabled students have schedules identical to their classmates' schedules all day long. During the middle grades, teachers usually "loop" with students for two years so that a seventh grade English teacher continues to teach his students when they move on to eighth. The net result of UPCS's continuity and heavy concentration on the core curriculum is that there is no way for students to opt out of a demanding course load.

UPCS makes no secret of the fact that it aligns its curriculum to state standards and the MCAS math and English tests. English and math teachers, for example, use MCAS questions and MCAS-aligned assignments. Students are graded with a common rubric, adopted from MCAS, with scores ranging from zero to four. A 2007 study by the Mass Insight Education and Research Institute reported that "UPCS students use an electronic assessment/feedback system 20 minutes a day to help monitor performance. The program provides individualized progress reports that allow both students and teachers to determine where each student needs helps."[12]

Once students reach high school, they can only take a college-prep curriculum—four years of English, math, history, science, and Spanish. With assistance from Clark, University Park has designed its high school curriculum to match up with college readiness benchmarks so that graduates are prepared to handle freshmen-level work in college. True to Rodrigues's promise, University Park does not allow tracking and teachers treat all students, no matter how poorly skilled, as if they are college-bound. Early on, UPCS tries to make the abstract concept of college real for its inner-city children. Eighth graders, for example, spend a "Groundhog Shadow Day" at Clark where they shadow university employees, including faculty members, IT staffers, physical plant workers, and the president of the university himself.

By tenth grade, students are paired with a Clark University student mentor for the year. Not all Clark mentors take their responsibilities seriously but many do. Edlin Ortiz came to UPCS as a tenth grader speaking almost no English after having moved from the Dominican Republic two years earlier and enrolling in South High's bilingual program. Her friends at South teased her that "University Park is a school for geeks," and Ortiz struggled to keep up during her first year. If not for the after-school tutoring that she received every day from a math teacher, and the aid she received from her Clark mentor, she might not have flourished. "My mentor would work with my teachers," Ortiz recalls. "The teachers would say 'she has an 80 and I'd like to see her get up to an 85,' and she would tell me that and encourage me to work harder." Sometimes Ortiz's Clark mentor would take her to the movies or dinner; she later worked as a student teacher during Ortiz's junior year. By senior year, Ortiz had a 3.6 GPA, was captain of the dance team, and vice-president of her class. But every week her Clark mentor continued to call to see how she was faring. Ortiz went on to enroll at Pace University in New York.

More than half of UPCS juniors and seniors take a course at Clark or at Holy Cross College, and about 15 percent end up enrolling in Clark. But taking a course at Clark is a privilege, not a right. UPCS students must have at least a B+ average and be mature enough to handle a college course. They do not receive high school credit for their courses at Clark—though they may be able to receive college credit once they are enrolled in a postsecondary institution.

A Culture of Collaboration

University Park's distinctive pedagogy relies heavily on group work in almost every classroom. Done well, group work can be academically rigorous and stimulate students' critical thinking. Done poorly, it can be a feel-good farce. Students and teachers often struggle initially to work with groups at UPCS. A noisy class, for example, would ordinarily be a sign of a chaotic classroom. But when students work in groups, a noisy classroom can also be one in which students are animatedly discussing and working out their assignments. For teachers used to being in constant control, group work can feel awkward, since it entails delegating aspects of class discussion and instruction to students. UPCS instructors, for example, are taught to tell students "Ask three and then me"—that is, ask three classmates for help before asking the teacher for assistance.

Rodrigues and Eressy were well-aware of the potential pitfalls of group work. But the veteran teachers knew, too, that well-organized group work could be particularly effective with disadvantaged students. "As a Spanish teacher, I could not just explain the subjunctive once," says Rodrigues. She notes that "in well-structured group work, the kids end up explaining a concept until everyone gets it. But if there isn't control and if there is a lack of accountability, then group work can be an even bigger waste of time than the teacher standing up there and giving the answer."

Rodrigues and Eressy's solution to the shortcomings of group work was to insist that teachers carefully structure all assignments so that group work always resulted in a specific product and was the work of all group members—rather than the work of one student who figured out the answer and passed it on to fellow group members. In practice, that meant that group work, rather than being a day when a teacher could slough off, typically required much more planning, new assignments, and imaginative delegation of responsibilities. One result of the emphasis on group tasks was that University Park developed an abundance of "low-stakes" writing assignments to supplement the "high-stakes" assignments and tests that were part of the college-prep curriculum and MCAS preparation. Students are required to write regularly in and out of class in a variety of formats: Poetry; imaginary dialogues; "double-entry" journals (where students write a quote from the text in one column and a comment on the quote in the second column); writing response groups (where brainstorming and group editing help clarify the fundamentals of good writing); and "Dear Confused" letters, in which students write to a real or imaginary friend who is confused by a concept or assignment. Students are also allowed to rewrite essays as many times as necessary to receive a satisfactory grade, on the theory that stimulating students to rewrite sharpens their skills as writers and maintains their interest in writing.

The key to University Park's group work, apart from the use of creative assignments, is accountability. No matter how simple or difficult the assignment, students are always personally responsible for the group's work. As Rodrigues put it, "the students always had to have a product at the end of the class so they didn't leave saying 'what was that all about?' We never let them off the hook." Teachers reinforce accountability by constantly preaching to students about the school's two preconditions for doing group work: students must treat their peers respectfully, and they must stay on-task. Dan Restuccia, a former math teacher who helps coordinate University Park's involvement with Clark University, says, "there is very little tolerance for students drumming on the desk, looking up at the ceiling, or for being off-task in any way."

If group work at UPCS entails lots of low-stakes tasks, it is also designed to stimulate critical thinking for more demanding assignments. Students are constantly asked in groups to stake out and defend their thinking. In Peter Weyler's eleventh grade English class in the fall of 2006, students held a vigorous debate about fairness in America, using Richard Wright's *Black Boy* as a jumping off point. During the course of his autobiographical novel, Wright described how he came into contact with the Communist Party and how he was attracted by their egalitarian ideals. Weyler divided the class into two sides facing each other across the room and asked them to debate the proposition that America had an unfair distribution of wealth. One student argued that "you get ahead in the U.S. not on how hard you work but based on how well connected you are." A student retorted that hard work "determined whether you get ahead or not." A spirited discussion ensued about whether connections or hard work mattered more to success in America, echoing a modern-day political debate.

One unanticipated side benefit of group work is that it reverses the baleful influence of teen peer pressure evident at many inner-city high schools, stimulating students to collaborate and measure success according to the performance of the collective. Edlin Ortiz, the senior from the Dominican Republic who came to University Park speaking almost no English, says that Spanish-speaking students at the school regularly translated assignments for her. Others in her groups also checked in with her regularly in class to make sure she was mastering material. "The other students were always saying 'Edlin, did you get it?'" she says. "They would remind me when I had a math test coming up and had to study." The net effect of the peer reinforcement, Ortiz says, is that "everybody at University Park is always doing their work—you feel awkward if you are not doing your work." Ortiz's little brother is now in eighth grade at UPCS and hearing much the same message from his older sister that she once heard from her peers. Ortiz stays after school with her brother's math teacher "so I can go home and make sure he got his work done—I tell my little brother to shape up." Another senior, Jorge Ramirez, who will also be the first member of his family to go to college, recalled his class's intense preparation for the MCAS in tenth grade. "I didn't feel like it was about me passing the test but my class passing the test," he says.

The ethic of collaboration extends to teachers as well. Not only do they meet every Wednesday to discuss courses and the performance of individual students, they also spend an unusual amount of time observing each other's classes. The Hiatt Center for Urban Education, a teacher-preparation program at Clark University, provides half-a-dozen master's candidates as student teachers each year. The Hiatt Center has adopted the "medical rounds" model for its student teachers, whereby other master's students and professors discuss a lesson plan before class, observe a student teacher in action, and provide him/her with feedback and criticism during a post-class session. Apart from the Clark student teachers, UPCS does not strictly adhere to a medical rounds model. Nonetheless, the school is no place for thin-skinned teachers. Fellow instructors frequently sit in on other teachers' classes to learn a new instructional technique, a classroom management strategy, or to critique their colleague's performance. Jack Foley, Clark vice president for Government and Community Affairs, says, "the attractive part of the UPCS model is that it is a teacher-driven school. The teachers feel like they own the school and are accountable for the success of the students."

University Park has only 12 teachers for core subjects, two per grade, so the school can ill-afford a sub-par instructor. Rodrigues artfully dissuaded mediocre teachers in the district from transferring to University Park using two stratagems. First, she hired the best Clark student teachers—instructors who already had a strong sense of University Park—straight out of graduate school, keeping openings to a minimum when she could. Second, like Dave Levin at KIPP, Rodrigues devised a series of roadblocks to subtly discourage district teachers from applying to University Park based on seniority, even though she lacked the authority to prevent a transfer.

Worcester has a strong teachers' union, and during Rodrigues's planning year for University Park, she deliberately gave the union a seat on the planning committee. In the years when UPCS had an extended school day, teachers received 19 percent additional pay under the union contract.[13] But Rodrigues also asked the union if she could interview teachers before hiring them at

UPCS, a request the union turned down on grounds that Rodrigues would have to accept the transfer of senior teachers regardless. So Rodrigues went back to the union and asked if she could have "informational meetings" with teachers since the school would be using 90-minute teaching blocks. Eventually, the union acceded.

At those informational meetings, Rodrigues would tell teachers that University Park might not be the right choice for them—before running through a list of extra commitments and constraints that they would operate under at UPCS. She also wrote up a four-page job description that the union let her post. Rodrigues recalls that it "was such a deterrent that not many teachers wanted to be here." In the job description, Rodrigues let aspiring applicants know that

> Young, novice teachers from Clark's education program would be in your room all the time, there was a no-closed door policy, and teachers would be drifting into your room observing you. We were going to have a common planning time every week and talk about student work and rubrics. Some potential teachers didn't want to be responsible for having to hand homework back with comments on it. Others just didn't want the scrutiny—other teachers observing their classes and a principal who would be getting in their face. For many years, no veteran public school teacher applied to teach at University Park.

Free to hire teachers on her own,[14] Rodrigues built a talented and well-credentialed staff—including Eressy, who won her $25,000 Milken award in 2001. All of University Park's teachers are licensed in the subjects that they teach, and more than nine in ten of the core academic teachers are "highly qualified" according to federal standards. Nearly all faculty members have dual certifications, which gives the principal unusual flexibility in deploying them.

After Eressy took over in 2003, a union teacher filed a grievance when he failed to be assigned to University Park despite requesting a transfer and having seniority. The union forced the teacher, a male Latino, onto the school and he flopped. But Eressy didn't have to find a way to get rid of him. As it turned out, students and parents repeatedly complained to the teacher about his performance until he decided to take a "sabbatical."

Academic Achievement

Unlike the two other high schools profiled in previous chapters, University Park has succeeded not only in eliminating the college attendance gap but the achievement test gap as well. An impressive 95 percent of its graduates have gone on to seek a higher education degree, with four out of five of them enrolling in four-year colleges. On the state MCAS test, UPCS students not only far outperform the average student in the state but do as well as students in Massachusetts's most affluent suburbs. Moreover, UPCS students have outperformed others around the state year-after-year—demonstrating that UPCS's success is not a temporary fluke.

University Park's remarkable record of academic achievement cannot be dismissed by rounding up the usual demographic suspects. The case that it is creaming students is a weak one. UPCS has no admission standards—it accepts pupils by lottery, with the only requirement being that they come from the neighborhood. Students that local public schools have sought to expel, including one who assaulted his teacher, have later enrolled at UPCS.[15] When students start at UPCS, many have skills well below grade level. Though the first entering class in 1997 had stunningly poor skills upon arrival, subsequent classes have not been much better. In 2005–2006, two-thirds of incoming students tested below grade level in English as did a quarter of them in math.

Other characteristics of University Park students also undermine the argument that this school succeeds by creaming more skilled or motivated pupils. Roughly three out of four students at UPCS speak English as a second language. And UPCS has roughly the same percentage of students (7 percent) with mild to moderate special needs (who do not require highly specialized, separate classrooms) as nearby public schools. Unlike, say, at some KIPP schools, UPCS obtains the sixth grade test scores of incoming students—that is, their pre-UPCS spring scores—so there is no possibility, even in theory, that their low entry-level scores reflect summer learning loss. Finally, University Park doesn't outperform local schools because students who struggle academically or have behavioral problems drop out or are expelled by the time they enter high school. The school has had one dropout in its ten-year history. Its attrition rate is effectively zero. And its graduation rate is all the more impressive because Hispanic and Asian students in Worcester generally have extraordinarily high dropout rates.[16]

While University Park plainly benefits from its relationship and proximity to Clark University, its accomplishments do not stem from unusual spending or resources either. The school is subject to the same spending caps and cuts as other neighborhood schools. Nor do students come from families with any socioeconomic advantages. In the first three graduating classes, more than 95 percent of students were the first generation in their families to attend college. Three-quarters came from families poor enough to qualify for the free- and reduced-price lunch program, much like nearby schools. The ethnic composition of the student body is similar to that of nearby schools, too, though UPCS has slightly more Vietnamese and Cambodian students.

If UPCS students have any subtle socioeconomic advantage, it may be that they appear to be more likely to come from intact families—a pattern typical of first-generation immigrants.[17] As with KIPP Academy in the Bronx, siblings are also granted preferential admission prior to the lottery, and a significant number of students are siblings. The impact of sibling preference on University Park's academic performance (as at KIPP Academy) is unclear. But it may be that sibling loyalty to the school stems from the presence of families more committed to obtaining a college- preparatory education for their daughters and sons.

To get a sense of how completely University Park eliminated the achievement gap, it helps to know how its students perform in comparison to their peers at nearby neighborhood schools, in the city's public schools, and in the state at large. It is worth noting that the MCAS is one of the more demanding state tests in the country, and that students cannot graduate from Bay State public schools until they pass it. A significant number of students statewide fail the MCAS, including many inner-city students. In Worcester, for example, about a third of all tenth graders fail the MCAS. (They can and do re-take it later.)

Table 8-1 below shows how, in 2006–2007 and over a five-year period (the most recent for which data are available), University Park tenth graders fared on the English and math MCAS compared with tenth graders from South and North High Schools, the city of Worcester, and other students statewide. The differences are stark.

As the table shows, during this five-year period, UPCS students opened up a 13 point advantage in English and a 26 point advantage in math in the advanced and proficient skills categories between UPCS students and the average student in Massachusetts. And in comparison to students from nearby South or North High or those in Worcester at large, UPCS students were veritable superstars. More than one in four tenth graders at South High and citywide failed the English MCAS altogether while not a single UPCS

Table 8-1. Academic achievement at University Park Campus School and nearby schools

	Distance from UPCS (miles)	2006-07 MCAS test • Percentage of students scoring Proficient or Advanced		2003-2007 MCAS tests (Five-Year Average) • Percentage of students scoring Proficient or Advanced	
		10th grade ELA	10th grade Math	10th grade ELA	10th grade Math
UPCS		**76**	**91**	**79**	**87**
South High	2	52	44	41	31
North High	3.1	43	46	43	38
District Average (Worcester)		52	48	43	37
State Average (Massachusetts)		71	69	66	61

Source: Massachusetts Department of Education School and District Profiles, http://profiles.doe.mass.edu Profiles (accessed April 1, 2008).

tenth grader failed. Even more students at South and citywide failed the math MCAS—close to half at South over five years. One tenth grader at UPCS failed the math MCAS during the five-year period—and she was only at UPCS half as long as other students who took the test. In fact, in recent years University Park has ranked among the top public schools in Massachusetts on several occasions, even when the comparison was not limited to other open-admission, urban high schools. In 2003, UPCS tenth graders had the fifth-highest MCAS scores in the state. That year, a whopping 97 percent of UPCS sophomores were advanced or proficient in math and 87 percent in English. The scores were not far below those of students at Boston Latin, a well-known exam school.

The only blemish in University Park's otherwise stellar record of achievement occurred on the 2006 MCAS when UPCS's sophomores recorded scores merely equivalent to the average Bay State student. Instead of having 80 to 90 percent of students score advanced or proficient, as UPCS students had done in previous years, about two-thirds scored at this level. However, the dip in scores in 2006 appears to be an anomaly. University Park's veteran tenth grade English teacher, who had considerable experience preparing and coaching students for the MCAS, retired at the end of the 2005 school year. At the same time, the tenth grade's geometry teacher went on maternity leave in March 2006, leaving the class with a long-term substitute who was a new teacher unfamiliar with the curriculum. In 2007, UPCS's scores rebounded to their previous range, with 76 percent of tenth graders scoring advanced or proficient on the English MCAS and 91 percent showing advanced or proficient skills on the Math MCAS.

University Park's rigor and academic achievement also show up in student participation in Advanced Placement courses and enrollment in four-year colleges. More than three out of five UPCS high school students take AP courses, and students have generally far outperformed their inner-city peers on the demanding AP exams. As sophomores, a significant number of students score a 3 or higher on AP tests, even though their SAT scores may not be particularly high. In the class of 2003 (whose average SAT score failed to break 800), 30 percent of sophomores who took an AP U.S. history course scored 3 or better on the AP exam. The following year, 60 percent of sophomores who took a world history AP course scored a three or better.

Table 8-2 below, detailing the record of the five graduating classes at University Park from 2003 through 2007, shows heavy participation in AP courses, despite modest SAT scores. It also illustrates the school's impressive record of sending graduates on to four-year colleges.

Replicating the Model

As noted above, nearly all students (95 percent) in UPCS's five graduating classes have gone on to attend college and about 80 percent of graduates have enrolled at four-year institutions. The vast majority of UPCS students from the school's first four graduating classes—76 percent—are on track to gain a bachelor's degree in six years. Those numbers far exceed the norm: In 2001, only 6 percent of low-income students nationwide attained their bachelor degree in the six years after high school. (About half of middle- and high-income students earn their diploma in six years.)[18] Yet like other paternalistic secondary schools, UPCS administrators have discovered that once students depart the school cocoon, they sometimes struggle in college, notwithstanding their early exposure to Clark University. "We found that when kids left us, they were often unfamiliar with how to navigate college," says June Eressy.

Table 8-2. SAT and AP test scores and college-going rates at University Park Campus School

	UPCS Class of 2003	UPCS Class of 2004	UPCS Class of 2005	UPCS Class of 2006	UPCS Class of 2007	**All UPCS Graduates**
Number of graduates	31	25	30	31	36	**153**
% taking AP classes	39	71	80	61	44	**58**
SAT Verbal	374	487	436	478	475	**449**
SAT Math	400	503	464	525	525	**484**
SAT Total	774	990	900	1003	1000	**933**
% enrolling in 4-year colleges	71	88	73	81	81	**79**

Source: UPCS

Not surprisingly, a potential downside of paternal-like involvement and leadership by principals and teachers is that high school graduates may not be as independent as they might otherwise be. Tenth grade geometry teacher Jody Bird notes that "the teachers here take on a lot of parental roles, especially for seventh and eight graders, asking questions like 'where is your homework?' And it's hard not to fall in love with these kids." The hitch, says Bird, is "that when the students become seniors, it is also harder to cut the umbilical cord. And we're working at being better at that." In the last couple of years, University Park has instituted several reforms to orient seniors toward college life. During the first semester of senior year, a college counselor teaches a course designed to help students fill out their college applications. Seniors also follow a college semester schedule and have course syllabi that mimic those of college, with reading assignments by the week. If a senior has not already taken a college course at Clark or Holy Cross, he or she is now required at least to audit a college course for three weeks during twelfth grade. In June 2007, UPCS hired a half-time alumni/ae coordinator to track and assist graduates and gather data that might help improve the college readiness of juniors and seniors.

While University Park is committed to spreading its model, its replication effort is more informal than those of other paternalistic schools. In 2004, with funding from the Bill and Melinda Gates Foundation, University Park formed a partnership with Clark University and the Boston-based non-profit Jobs for the Future to propagate the UPCS model in small schools. But the UPCS/

Clark University Institute for Student Success does not aim to create copycat versions of University Park. Rather, the Institute hosts visits and workshops at UPCS for teachers and principals interested in observing the school and adapting its principles of curricular instruction and school culture. Dan Restuccia, the Institute's training director, notes that nearly 500 educators have attended the Institute's weeklong summer and/or the two-day residency since 2004.

The Institute has worked particularly closely with several school reform efforts, including the City University of New York's (CUNY) early college project, the National Council of La Raza's charter school network, and a public/private partnership that is reforming high schools in North Carolina. CUNY adopted parts of the UPCS model, particularly its middle school "catch up curriculum," in the design of six early-college high schools in New York City. Most teachers and principals at those new schools participated in training at the Institute as part of their orientation. The North Carolina New Schools Project is both opening new schools and redesigning old ones. Last year, 30 to 40 North Carolina schools sent teachers and leaders to UPCS for training. [19]

Closer to home, University Park's model has played a powerful role in the overhaul of two neighborhood secondary schools in Main South: Claremont Academy (previously known as the Accelerated Learning Laboratory) and South High, Rodrigues and Eressy's former school. UPCS is part of the Hiatt-Main South Secondary School Collaborative, which assists with the overhaul of the two schools. Claremont Academy began years ago as a magnet school. But after three years of failing to make AYP, it fell into corrective action and was reconstituted as two schools, an elementary school and a secondary school.

The superintendent of Worcester's public schools, James Caradonio, asked June Eressy to step in as the principal of the secondary school at Claremont in 2006, in addition to serving as principal at UPCS. Eressy agreed. Claremont is a comparatively small school, with 400 pupils in grades seven through twelve. Meanwhile, at South High, Rodrigues and Eressy's former teaching colleague Maureen Ciccone has taken over as principal. She is presiding over a large-scale conversion effort, breaking up South into three smaller learning communities.

If University Park is not seeking to create replicas, its attempt to spread its principles into existing schools is, in some ways, as ambitious as the replication efforts of other paternalistic schools. Almost all attempts at replication by other outstanding paternalistic inner-city schools entail starting new, small schools. Yet reforming existing schools, with their entrenched faculty and school traditions, can be even more challenging. Overhauling an existing school can be especially daunting when it is a large, comprehensive institution like South High with 1,500 students. It may also be easier to launch school reform from the confines of a private foundation—built upon the success of a group of charter or parochial schools—than to spur change in a neighborhood public school, subject to the whims of the district bureaucracy.

At Claremont Academy, Eressy says she is not trying to turn the secondary school "into another UPCS." Claremont had a long tradition of project-based learning that was thematically driven—students, for example, might study pioneers for a quarter. But Eressy is seeking to build a stronger sense of community at Claremont by steering all students toward college and promoting a UPCS-like culture of high expectations, with no swearing, street talk, bullying, or disrespect allowed. "The students are shocked when I stop them in the hallway and tell them you can't use street talk or talk disrespectfully," she reported in the fall of 2006. Her first week of school, Eressy adds, "one kid pulled his pants down on the way back from lunch and I suspended him for five days. He seemed surprised—so I think that kind of behavior was let go in the past."

At South High, principal Maureen Ciccone also has not formally adopted the UPCS model. But she is borrowing liberally from it, pushing the development of a literacy-rich curriculum, high academic expectations, and post-secondary education for all. Ciccone has hired student teachers from Clark who did their internships at University Park, and in 2005 she signed an agreement with the New England Institute of Technology (NEIT) that allows South students taking courses in automotive technology to earn college credits while in high school through the Advanced Tech Program at NEIT. Ciccone openly admires what Rodrigues and Eressy accomplished at UPCS. "Everyone has benefited from the results that University Park has achieved," she says. "What they've done is what everyone should be able to do if we just dig a little deeper. They've shown us what's possible."[20]

Chapter Nine

The Habits of Highly Effective Schools—
and How to Create More of Them

T he examples of successful inner-city secondary schools in the preceding chapters speak to the central civil rights issue of our century: closing the pernicious achievement gulf between white and minority students.

The most successful of these new schools do not merely narrow the achievement gap but eliminate it altogether. The middle school students at American Indian Public Charter School, Amistad Academy, and KIPP Academy test well above white students; in some cases they even outperform affluent white students from the top schools in their state. Similarly, in Cristo Rey Jesuit Academy, the SEED School, and the University Park Campus School, students are more likely to matriculate to college than their white peers, with more than 95 percent of graduates winning college admission.

The record of these schools in closing the achievement gap is remarkable. Yet their performance is not just a matter of numbers. The most impressive accomplishment of these no-excuses schools is their ability to transform the lives of their students. Armante Washington was receiving Ds and Fs at his grade school before coming to Oakland's American Indian Public Charter School (AIPCS), where principal Ben Chavis informed him he would have to repeat seventh grade. By spring, Washington had the highest GPA in his class and had qualified for the summer program at the Johns Hopkins University Center for Talented Youth. Dean Vargas, a Lakota Sioux, was also racking up Ds and Fs in his Oakland grammar school, all the while earning a reputation as a troublemaker. Vargas got into brawls at his elementary school and broke into cars to steal money and jewelry. His mother, who supported five children on welfare, was so financially strapped that she sent Vargas to live with his aunt. But after suffering a string of detentions at AIPCS—and the indignity of having his principal drive him to school when he was late—Vargas buckled down and left the streets behind. He, too, qualified for the math program at the Johns Hopkins summer session for gifted students.

Such tales of transformation are not unusual. Students who arrived at KIPP Academy in the South Bronx without ever having played a note on an instrument can reel off the exact dates when they played with the KIPP youth orchestra in Carnegie Hall or Lincoln Center. Da'Shawna King gets to KIPP Academy early to practice the drums before school because she doesn't have a drum set at home. "The drums are everything to me," she says, adding that one of her most memorable moments was when she had to "step up" and lead the percussion section during its performance at Lincoln Center. In Washington, D.C., the SEED School rose literally out of the ashes of an abandoned elementary school after four-year-old Launice Smith was gunned down by a group of young black males firing semiautomatic weapons at a rival gang member. Today, more than 95 percent of SEED's first three classes of graduates have been accepted into college and nearly 90 percent are currently enrolled.

While the power of the new paternalistic schools to transform students gives new hope to the cause of urban school reform, the success of these schools also puts to rest several shibboleths about inner-city schools. For starters, the performance of these schools belies the claim that secondary schools alone are unable to close achievement gaps between white and minority adolescents. At the same time, the superior performance of students at these schools undermines skeptics who argue that they succeed only because they skim off students who are the cream of the crop. The schools described here, with the exception of Cristo Rey, have open admission procedures, with admission often determined by lottery. Achievement First, the parent organization of schools modeled after Amistad Academy, specifies that none of its schools may have more than a 7 percent variance between its student body and the population of the local public school district in terms of minority representation, English language learners, and special education students. Some creaming of motivated families occurs at paternalistic schools, simply because parents have to choose to sign up; one renowned school with a lottery, the KIPP Academy in the Bronx, clearly attracts students with stronger average incoming academic skills.

Yet claims that these schools succeed because their students are different do not withstand closer scrutiny. Students often arrive with reading and math skills that are two to three grades below grade level. The student body is overwhelmingly black and Hispanic, from low-income families usually headed by a single mother—just like their peers at neighborhood schools. Yet despite these burdens, students graduate not only performing at grade level but doing better, in most cases, than their white peers.

The record of these new paternalistic schools challenges other elements of the conventional wisdom about urban school reform, too. Cultural pessimists, on both the left and the right, have long argued that inner-city adolescent culture is so polluted by violence, video games, television, and racial inequality that minority teenagers are mired in an oppositional culture that belittles studiousness and mocks a love for learning. Yet that oppositional culture is not all-powerful. High-performing minority students are celebrated by their peers in paternalistic schools, not jeered for "acting white."

The schools' success does not, of course, mean that socioeconomic differences are irrelevant to the achievement gap. As Coleman reported more than 40 years ago, poverty, broken families, and the cultural deficits of lower-class neighborhoods remain important obstacles to school success for many minority adolescents. But the new paternalistic schools show that such barriers need not be determinative—demography, that is, need not be destiny. Schools matter, and the best schools matter a great deal for low-income minority students.

Much the same point might be made about the perennial dispute over school resources. With few exceptions, successful paternalistic secondary schools spend either less or the same amount per student as failing neighborhood schools. Fiscal equity lawsuits, which ensure that states like New York, New Jersey, and Arkansas spend as much on inner-city students as on their suburban peers, may make moral and legal sense. But the performance of under-funded paternalistic schools suggests that fiscal equity should not be mistaken for a true solution to the achievement gap.

Most high-achieving paternalistic schools have limited course offerings and modest facilities. The American Indian Public Charter School has such a run-down facility that it was cited by California governor Arnold Schwarzenegger as evidence of the need for a statewide school bond issue. Nor does reduced class size seem to figure in boosting academic achievement. The SEED school has smaller classes than neighborhood schools, but at most no-excuses schools, classes are comparable in size to neighborhood schools. At Amistad, Cristo Rey, and KIPP, class sizes are slightly larger than in-zoned schools.

To be sure, the record of these schools is not without flaws. In particular, several schools—notably Cristo Rey, SEED, and some schools in the KIPP network—lose substantial numbers of students to attrition. At Cristo Rey, roughly 40 percent of students who start ninth grade fail to finish twelfth grade at the school. Students who flunk grades and face repeating a year, and those intimidated by the academic demands of rigorous schools, exit to neighborhood schools that practice social promotion.

Attrition could become a problem at paternalistic schools for two reasons. Student attrition undermines principals who want to build a school culture and sense of mission. But attrition also can diminish the apparent achievements of high-performing schools since it suggests that successful schools may do well only after ridding themselves of struggling students.

Another shortcoming of no-excuses schools is that they are generally ill-prepared to handle large numbers of disabled students, such as youngsters with IEP's who require pull-out classes. These schools truly do subscribe to the view that no child should be left behind, and they tend to assign special-ed designations as a last resort, preferring to provide additional instructional support to struggling students. A few schools, like Amistad Academy, make valiant efforts to recruit and teach special-ed students, and most of the new paternalistic schools have a significant population of learning-disabled students (on the order of 7 to 11 percent), though nearby neighborhood schools may have 12 to 15 percent special-needs students. Cristo Rey Jesuit High School lacks the capacity altogether to teach students with learning differences in full-time pull-out classes. Only 3 of its 533 students in 2006 with learning disabilities had an IEP plan and received special services.

The Critique of Paternalistic Schools, Revisited

Today's foremost skeptic of no-excuses schools is Richard Rothstein of the Economic Policy Institute, a former education columnist for the *New York*

Times. Rothstein is not opposed to these schools per se—in fact he believes these schools may use practices that other inner-city schools could emulate. But in 2005 he coauthored an early analysis of the KIPP school network, relying heavily on data from KIPP Academy in the Bronx, in which he contended that KIPP had failed to demonstrate it could close the achievement gap for "typical" inner-city students.[1] In subsequent years, some aspects of Rothstein's preliminary analysis proved correct. However, his core claim that KIPP schools in general succeed by creaming off skilled students, often from intact families, has not been borne out by more recent data. It's true that the much publicized Bronx school attracts students to its lottery who have stronger math and language skills than their peers in the South Bronx. But that skills gap does not appear to be the norm at KIPP schools. At Baltimore's KIPP Ujima Village Academy, for example, one of the schools cited for creaming by Rothstein, a 2007 study by Johns Hopkins University found that students had incoming math and reading skills similar to a comparison group of students from neighborhood feeder schools who did not go on to attend the Baltimore KIPP school.[2]

The most serious charge leveled by Rothstein against proponents of no-excuses schools is not simply that they have exaggerated the accomplishments of these schools but rather that they have given false hope to reformers, driving away from other schools good teachers who despair of ever living up to the purported record of their peers at these highly touted establishments. In his first look at KIPP in 2004, Rothstein warned:

> In American education today, policy makers and educators frequently invoke slogans like "no excuses" or "all students can learn to the same high standards."...Some say that these incantations are harmless, and, even if they are hyperbolic, serve the useful purpose of spurring teachers, principals, and other school officials to greater efforts to raise the achievement levels of minority and other disadvantaged students. Such whips can serve this useful purpose. But they can also do great damage. They de-legitimize good and great teachers who dedicate themselves to raising minority student achievement in realistic increments. They drive out of the teaching profession decent teachers who feel inadequate to the task of reaching utopian goals, or who resent the cynicism of politicians and administrators who demand that such goals be attained. If this disconnect continues between what is realistically possible and the goals we

establish for educators, the nation risks abandoning public education only to those willing to pander to political fashion by promising to achieve in schools what they know, in their hearts, is not possible.[3]

A closer look at the new paternalistic schools suggests that his warnings have proved wide of the mark. Rothstein offers no evidence that advocates of no-excuses schools have ever actually driven good teachers away from urban schools; if anything, the record suggests that such schools serve as magnets for young, bright teachers who might not otherwise be hired in the public schools. At the same time, Rothstein's caution that inflated expectations of school reform might cause the nation to risk "abandoning public education only to those willing to pander to political fashion" is far from fruition. Many of the founders of the new paternalistic academies are anything but conservative curmudgeons plotting to undermine public education by holding inner-city schools to hopelessly utopian standards. Instead, these school founders tend to be young, white, political liberals who earnestly believe that students can reach standards that may seem impossibly high to others. It is true, of course, that a number of Republicans have hailed schools like KIPP and Amistad. Yet the supporters of the new paternalistic schools cannot simply be characterized by their political ideology or an alleged animus to public schools. Such prominent Democrats as Hillary Clinton and John Edwards have singled out paternalistic schools for praise, too.

One of Rothstein's more pointed criticisms was that proponents of no-excuses schools were "promising to achieve in schools what they know, in their hearts, is not possible" — suggesting, in effect, that supporters of the new paternalistic schools were either intellectually dishonest or political opportunists. Yet far from being "pander bears," the new generation of school leaders at paternalistic schools sets and attains concrete goals for student achievement and character development — as the stories in this book attest. And when paternalistic school leaders reevaluate their goals, more often than not they conclude that they need to be *more* ambitious. At Amistad, for example, school officials vowed initially to close the achievement gap between minority and white students in Connecticut; now they aim to close the achievement gap between minority and *affluent* white students in Connecticut. At American Indian Public Charter School, Ben Chavis initially wanted to have the highest-performing middle school in the Oakland area, beating out Piedmont Middle School. After

AIPCS surpassed Piedmont, however, Chavis announced that his new goal was to have the highest test scores of any middle school in California.

While much of Rothstein's critique is overblown, more rigorous evaluations of the new schools would help to definitively dispel lingering questions about the size of their impact on the achievement gap. How much is due to an unconscious self-screening of families that allows more motivated families to apply for admission? What explains the significant attrition rate at some schools and what impact does attrition have on student achievement? Fortunately, a number of the new academies are better situated than traditional schools to carry out randomized studies in the years ahead. Because schools like KIPP Academy, Amistad Academy, the SEED School, and University Park Campus School enroll students through blind lotteries, researchers should be able to compare the post-lottery academic performance of students who entered the lottery but did not gain a spot in the school with students who did attend a no-excuses school. The KIPP Foundation, with funding from Atlantic Philanthropies, began the process in 2007 by commissioning Mathematica to carry out just such a long-term study of KIPPs impact utilizing random assignment and control groups.

As Rothstein notes, the average achievement of black and white students typically differs by about a full standard deviation, or about 30 percentile points on most standardized tests. A school that had an effect size of half a standard deviation would increase the test scores of black students by a bit more than 15 percentile points. In Rothstein's view, schools that raise achievement by half a standard deviation would "truly be extraordinary—my guess (without evidence) is that the best school reform…might aspire to an effect size of 0.3, or about 10 percentile points."[4] Is Rothstein right that even the best schools can only increase minority test scores by 10 percentile points, thus leaving a large achievement gap? The new paternalist schools certainly appear to have a far more profound impact than Rothstein has allowed. But without, as he says, methodologically rigorous "evidence" that this is the case, the debate can and does and will continue.

The Habits of Highly Effective Urban Schools

The paternalistic inner-city schools that have had great success in closing the achievement gap share certain common elements, suggesting that their formulas for success may be replicated elsewhere. Unlike earlier generations of exemplary inner-city schools, today's no-excuses institutions follow a replicable school model and do not depend heavily on charismatic principals whose leadership cannot be copied elsewhere.

Many traits of successful inner-city schools are not surprising. They are academically rigorous, have high expectations, and provide extra core instructional time, either by extending the school day or year (or both) or by reducing electives, assemblies, announcements, and other diversions during the school day. Yet these characteristics are necessary but not sufficient conditions to narrow achievement gaps during the teen years.

In fact, the record of today's paternalistic schools suggests not only that the devil is in the details of urban education reform but also that these schools succeed because they follow a series of interconnected reforms, tied together by common themes. A top 20 list of successful reform practices at these schools—one might think of it as a distillation of the habits of highly effective urban schools—would look something like this:

1. Tell students exactly how to behave and tolerate no disorder.
2. Require a rigorous, college-prep curriculum.
3. Align curriculum with state standards and specify performance outcomes.
4. Assess students regularly and use the results to target struggling students.
5. Keep students busy in class with a clear plan and a variety of assignments.
6. Build a collective culture of achievement and college-going.
7. Reject the culture of the streets.
8. Be vigilant about maintaining school culture.
9. Extend the school day and/or year.
10. Monitor and enforce attendance.
11. Welcome accountability for adults and embrace constant reassessment.
12. Give principals and teachers more autonomy—think "charter school."
13. Eliminate (or at least disempower) local teacher unions.
14. Use unconventional channels to recruit committed teachers.
15. Don't demand much from parents.
16. Escape the constraints hobbling traditional district schools.
17. Don't waste resources on fancy facilities or technology.
18. Keep the school small.
19. Track and support students after they graduate.
20. Help create additional schools following your model.

Spelled out in more detail, here is the annotated version of that same list.

1. Tell students exactly how to behave and tolerate no disorder.

The overarching trait of successful paternalistic schools is that they are, well, paternalistic. They are highly prescriptive institutions that assert their moral authority both to define good character and to teach adolescents how to behave, much like a firm but loving father. These schools go several steps further than the many schools that purport to teach "values"; they unapologetically preempt misbehavior by obliging students to live up to a detailed code of conduct based on middle-class values and the Protestant work ethic. Unlike most inner-city schools, the new paternalistic schools have little tolerance for disorder—they sweat the small stuff.

A core animating concept of the new paternalistic institutions, adopted from James Q. Wilson's "broken windows theory," is that urban schools suffer primarily from disorder. Stop the visible signs of disorder—fix the broken window, in Wilson's terms—and teachers and students will regain a sense of safety and involvement. Conversely, evidence of disorder left unattended—graffiti on toilet stalls, rowdy hallways, dirty cafeterias, students walking about with their shirts not tucked in—only breeds more disorder.

As a result, these schools supervise students' lives in ways that even strict Catholic schools or authoritarian public schools do not. Like many urban schools, paternalistic secondary schools typically have uniforms and dress codes. They have rules against students running in hallways and impose detentions for being tardy or talking disrespectfully to a teacher. But they go much farther: from specifying that hoop earrings can be no larger than a quarter to deducting "school dollars" from a student's "paycheck" for tapping his or her pen in class. At the SEED School, boys must have ties—but they can't have cartoon figures on them. If SEED students opt to do their homework in their dorm rooms during study hall time, they must leave their doors open.

No detail of appearance or hygiene is too small to teach students at Cristo Rey's summer boot camp. When female students head to their jobs on their work study day, they are encouraged to wear a watch—just not a watch with a sports logo on the timepiece. In their personal hygiene class, girls learn to pluck the full eye brow, to wipe away laganas ("eye boogers") every morning, to turn away when they blow their nose, and to practice applying lip liner. In an after-school program, SEED students take etiquette classes, too. They learn to make direct eye contact during an introduction, state their first and last names, and provide a firm handshake. They are taught to say "excuse me" before interrupting a conversation—and they learn the difference between the salad fork and the dinner fork.

The second distinctive aspect of educational paternalism is that these schools both define responsible behavior for students and then compel students to act responsibly, much like a morally authoritative parent. Indeed, it is no coincidence that students often liken a principal or teacher to "another parent" or say that the school is like a "second home." This monitoring of students for compliance with rules is visible and explicit. At SEED, each middle-school student carries a "school note" listing 12 "responsible behaviors" and 12 "irresponsible behaviors" on which teachers evaluate his or her conduct after every class. At the end of the day, Student Life staff tabulate the students' points on the School Note to determine how many "SEED Dollars" the student earned that day. If students act up in class, they are sent to a designated "reflection" area where they have to fill out a MAP form—short for "My Action Plan"—specifying what they will do to improve their behavior and ways that adults can assist them to move forward.

Similarly, Cristo Rey goes further than traditional urban schools in barring and monitoring displays of gang sympathies. It enforces intrusive rules to prevent school functions from being disrupted by gang activity. Both students and their guests, for example, have to take breathalyzer tests to gain entry to a Cristo Rey school dance. When students do violate school rules, the principal or teachers don't just mete out punishments—much like parents do, they also force students to take responsibility for their actions before allowing them to return to class. When a seventh-grade boy at Amistad Academy taunted fifth grader Lauren Okafor about her mother on the ride home from school, Okafor got in a fight with the older boy after the two got off the school bus. Both students were suspended. But they were only permitted to return to school after they both stood up at Amistad's morning circle and apologized to the entire school for their actions.

The third distinctive feature of paternalism at these schools is that they unabashedly instruct and oblige students to act according to middle-class mores. In effect, paternalistic educators help students adapt to a new culture by teaching them how to shake hands properly or by insisting that they not wear ties displaying cartoon characters. Teachers at KIPP and Amistad frequently tell students to "correct your SLANT"—short for Sit up, Listen, Ask and answer questions, Nod your head so people know you are listening, and Track your speaker by keeping your eyes on whoever is talking. The acculturation to the work ethic and value system is not always draconian—the new paternalistic schools also promote traditional values through a variety of rewards and public recognition.

No-excuses schools insist relentlessly that students take responsibility for their lives and school work. While many high schools have work experience programs, for example, Cristo Rey has a unique combination of behavioral acculturation and strict accountability. It strives to treat students as real employees responsible to their sponsors. Students undergo reviews from their sponsors in October, January, and March on 12 different measures of work performance, ranging from professional appearance and punctuality to the accuracy of their work and their respect for authority. If students miss work for any reason, they are fined $100; at the end of the year, if they have more than one absence from work that has not yet been made up, they receive an automatic F on their report cards. Each year about a dozen of the school's 530 students also get fired from their jobs—and have to attend Cristo Rey's no-nonsense re-employment program.

The new paternalistic schools, in short, are not just rigorous about academics but about character development as well. They drill into students the importance of traditional virtues like hard work, politeness, diligence, respect for their elders, and good citizenship. KIPP Academy conductor Jesus Concepcion had every student in his 180-pupil orchestra stand silently for two minutes in a sweltering auditorium during an after-school rehearsal because one member of his orchestra looked at him disrespectfully. And under the watchful eye of a University Park teacher, student Gabriel Malave was reprimanded for speaking disrespectfully to another student. After the soft-spoken Malave and some of his fellow eighth graders chided a boy one morning before school about being overweight, Malave received an in-school suspension for the day. He was obliged to write an essay explaining why he had teased the boy and why he shouldn't tease another student.

2. Require a rigorous, college-prep curriculum.

The structure and rigor of the curriculum are similar at high-achieving inner-city schools: All high school students take a college-prep curriculum, supplemented with honors and Advanced Placement courses. Paternalistic schools provide no bilingual instruction, do not track students, and offer little formal multicultural instruction or full-time pull-out instruction for special-needs students.

The curricular requirements of paternalistic high schools are generally similar: four credits in English, four credits of math through at least Algebra II, and three or more credits (each) of science and modern language. No paternalistic school offers vocational or life adjustment courses. There is some narrowing of the curriculum at most paternalistic schools since core subjects receive additional instructional time—though a few schools offer certain exceptional electives and after-school activities like the KIPP Academy youth orchestra.

Schools that start in seventh grade provide considerable remedial instruction in the form of a "catch-up curriculum" to seventh and eighth graders to ready them for a college-prep curriculum in grades 9–12. Stand-alone middle schools do not have the time or resources to provide remedial instruction to entire classes if their goal is to bring students to grade level and beyond in just three years. Even so, middle schools typically provide intensive tutoring and other assistance to struggling students before, during, and after school. At American Indian Public Charter School in Oakland, students who are lagging receive two to four hours of additional instructional time each week. Amistad assigns its best teachers to students with the weakest academic skills and has a "Whatever It Takes Team" of teachers who tutor students who are struggling with reading.

3. Align curriculum with state standards and specify performance outcomes.

Paternalistic schools align a demanding curriculum with state standards and specify performance outcomes.

Successful paternalistic schools establish explicit benchmarks for students. As Samuel Casey Carter observed in his 2001 monograph on no-excuses schools, "high expectations are one thing—the relentless pursuit of excellence is another. Tangible and unyielding goals are the focus of high-performing schools."[5] Achievement First, for example, has specified that the primary "outcome metric" at successor schools to Amistad Academy will be dramatically raising achievement on state assessments until the achievement gap is closed (not just narrowed). At minimum, Achievement First expects all of its schools to make progress toward eliminating the achievement gap by having test scores that surpass state averages for full-price lunch students or by having "student achievement [gains] that increase at least five national percentiles (i.e., from the 65th to the 70th) in every subject at every grade level each school year." After one year at an Achievement First school, at least half the students are expected to be proficient on the state assessment in all subject areas; after two years, the bar is 75 percent, on up to 95 percent proficiency for students at an AF school for four years.

Surprisingly, pegging performance measures to state standards tends to make the curricular content of the new paternalistic schools more demanding instead of reducing it to a narrow curriculum propelled by state tests. For example, middle schools such as American Indian, Oakland Charter Academy, and KIPP Academy in the Bronx require all students to take Algebra I in eighth grade — though few students at inner-city schools traditionally do so.

4. Assess students regularly and use the results to target struggling students.

Paternalistic schools assess pupil progress regularly and use the test results to target struggling students and alter classroom instruction.

With few exceptions, paternalistic secondary schools assess student performance at regular intervals throughout the school year and then use the performance data to improve instruction — a technique that researchers have dubbed the "cycle of continuous instructional improvement."[6] At Amistad Academy, teachers test students every six weeks to see how they are faring in mastering essential material and to gauge their readiness for the state's year-end standards test. Teachers at Amistad brief the principal on the status of each student in each subject every six weeks and also use the assessment data to correct problem areas for students and teachers alike. When Matt Taylor was teaching seventh graders at Amistad, he learned from one interim assessment that 72 percent of his language arts class didn't know how to write a proper summary, so Taylor taught his unit on writing summaries a second time.

One encounters no sense at these schools that frequent testing is unfair to poor black and Hispanic students. Paternalistic schools do devote considerable class time to assessment and preparing students for state tests, yet they do not just "teach to the test." In the aftermath of the 2002 No Child Left Behind law, a number of journalists and academics have claimed that urban schools that assess students regularly and align their curricula with state standards are sterile institutions that practice "drill-and-kill" instruction. But no-excuses schools bear little resemblance to the mechanistic, zombie-like institutions that critics deride.

Rather, they show that secondary schools can prepare their pupils for tests, assess them regularly, and still have a stimulating core curriculum. American Indian (AIPCS) is renowned for carefully aligning its instruction with state standards. But when Isaac Berniker's seventh grade AIPCS class was studying Leonardo Da Vinci, the students didn't just spit back facts. They discussed how Da Vinci had used scientific studies of hydraulics and bird flight to try to better humanity. When the discussion turned to Da Vinci's famous painting, the *"Mona Lisa,"* Berniker explained how chiaroscuro gave an illusion of depth to the portrait that contributed to her famously enigmatic smile.

5. Keep students busy in class with a clear plan and a variety of assignments.
Classroom methods and instruction vary somewhat from school to school but typically include a clear lesson plan for each class, a variety of pedagogic formats, and a mix of high-stakes and low-stakes assignments—all designed to create a literacy-rich and writing-rich environment.

There is no single method of classroom instruction at the new paternalistic institutions, though most schools use a variation of teacher-led direct instruction. The University Park Campus School relies heavily on group work and group assignments. Instruction at AIPCS is distinguished by the fact that the school has self-contained classrooms in which the same instructor teaches all core subjects rather than having students move from room to room. At University Park, too, teachers loop with their students during their first few years.

Despite some differences, the pedagogical routines at today's paternalistic institutions have much in common. When students enter class, teachers have already written a series of "quick questions" on the board to which students silently write answers when they sit down. Lesson plans for the day, including the ideas to be covered and subjects for discussion, are often loosely outlined on the board, along with homework assignments. Many schools require students to have identical homework binders and planners. At KIPP and Amistad, teachers use unconventional classroom mnemonic techniques to teach students in younger grades, such as chants, claps, and snaps, as well as countdowns and timers to keep classes moving along. Paternalistic schools prefer longer block classes for core subjects, often covering math and English during morning hours when students are fresh.

A rigorous curriculum can also include frequent "low-stakes" assignments, such as requiring students to write regularly in journals, draft poems, or read aloud. Pupils aren't expected necessarily to get it right the first time — indeed, UPCS, SEED, and KIPP Academy encourage students to raise their grades by correcting assignments and rewriting papers. Paternalistic schools believe that low-income students benefit from literacy-rich and writing-rich environments where they are required to read and write each day, even if in low-stakes assignments. A literacy-rich environment at school is intended to help students compensate for growing up in homes with meager literary and writing resources.

6. Build a collective culture of achievement and college-going.

The schools create a collective culture of achievement and college-bound expectations, while bucking the oppositional culture found in many inner-city schools.

At the three high schools featured in these pages (Cristo Rey, SEED, and UPCS), 95 percent or more of the students are accepted into college, effectively eliminating any college-acceptance gap with white students. That remarkable record is no accident. From day one, these schools create a college-going culture. Students at SEED board in dorm houses named after colleges, and teachers and administrators start talking to students about getting into college as soon as they arrive. At Amistad and KIPP, each class is named after a college, and all students learn upon arrival the year they are supposed to graduate from a four-year college. When Amistad students get ready to go to their next class, their instructor will call out "Tufts, line up!" — rather than "Mr. Sudmyer's class, line up!"

It is cool to do well in school. When Connecticut governor M. Jodi Rell came to visit Amistad in 2006, she announced afterwards: "I have never been in a school where there has been so much enthusiasm." At University Park, students face plenty of peer pressure — but it is pressure not to be disruptive so that they won't reflect poorly on their classmates. Teachers don't voice the conviction, often heard in inner-city schools, that they will have done their job well if they reach "only one kid" and steer him/her to college. The expectation is that every student will succeed—and an ethos of teamwork makes it hard to slip through the cracks. Edlin Ortiz, an immigrant from the Dominican Republic, arrived at UPCS, fresh from a bilingual-ed program and speaking almost no English. But other students in her class reminded her when she had an upcoming math test and constantly translated questions for her, asking afterwards "did you get it?" Ortiz found that because "everybody at University Park is always doing their work, you feel awkward if you are not doing your work."

At these schools, students come to take great pride in their academic triumphs, including youngsters who rebel at first. Shamont Wright started fifth grade at Amistad reading at a third-grade level and performing math at a second-grade level. When Wright subsequently earned a 95 percent score on the textual analysis section of the practice test for Connecticut's mastery test, he called it "the happiest day of my life."

7. Reject the culture of the streets.

Schools have a clear mission and code of conduct, both designed to provide a cultural booster to protect students from the call of the streets and the negative culture of lower-class neighborhoods.

As Paul Tough pointed out in a November 2006 cover story in the *New York Times Magazine*, no-excuses secondary schools "reject the notion that all these struggling students need are high expectations; they do need those, of course, but they also need specific types and amounts of instruction, both in academics and attitude, to compensate for everything they did not receive in their first decade of life."[7] Typically, the schools forge their culture and establish their mission by recognizing exemplary behavior among students. At some schools, well-behaved students are celebrated with chants, snaps, and claps. Thus, Amistad's Morning Circle meeting feels more like a Protestant-virtue revival rally than a routine assembly. The opening call-and-response chant at one morning circle in May 2006 succinctly summarized the school's expectations that students would devote themselves to their education:

People, people do you see?

Education is the key.

We work hard all day long

Our REACH values keep us strong

Amistad reaching! Amistad achieving! Amistad succeeding!

In many instances, these schools literally rebuff the culture of the street by banning street language, swearing, gang insignia, and "tagging" school property with graffiti. If students so much as doodle gang graffiti on a notebook or piece of paper at Cristo Rey, they are suspended. And if they doodle a gang symbol a second time, principal Pat Garrity expels them.

8. Be vigilant about maintaining school culture.

Principals are obsessively vigilant about school culture and are a constant, visible presence.

No excuses schools have active principals who frequently visit classrooms, query students, and enforce school rules. They are the "keepers of the flame." University Park founding principal Donna Rodrigues walked all 12 classrooms in her school each day, knew all her 230 students by name, and knew many of their parents and grandparents—much like Ben Chavis at AIPCS. Chavis even fined himself on two occasions when he used profanities in earshot of students. Principals, moreover, often have a surprising familiarity with students' personal lives—and aren't afraid to intervene if necessary. Donna Rodrigues took half-a-dozen parents to court on child neglect charges for keeping their kids out of school to do errands or serve as translators and babysitters. When one parent wouldn't get treatment for her son's drug abuse problem, Rodrigues took that mother to court, too.

Principals also serve as watchdogs, warning teachers and students when school traditions are in danger of eroding. At Amistad, director Matt Taylor made a sixth-grade class step forward a second time at Morning Circle after they "didn't step forward clearly enough for your recognition."

9. Extend the school day and/or year.

The schools typically have an extended day and/or school year, periodic Saturday classes, and mandatory summer school, particularly for incoming students.

School founders view extended time as a vital tool to compensate for their students' cultural deficits. Extra instructional time gives students a foot up academically, but it also reduces the amount of after-school time spent at home or hanging out on the corner. The most extreme example is the SEED School, where students board five days a week throughout the school year. But at most high-performing urban schools, students spend far more time at school than their peers. At KIPP, they spend roughly 60 percent more time than average in school due to the extended day, Saturday morning classes every two weeks, and three weeks of summer school. At KIPP in the Bronx, a middle-school student has over 300 minutes a day of core academic instruction time compared to 185 minutes at a typical urban middle school. American Indian, Amistad, and Oakland Charter Academy all use a similar schedule. At University Park, principal Donna Rodrigues was sorely disappointed when district funding cutbacks forced UPCS in 2003 to revert to a normal 6.5-hour school day.

The only paternalistic school that does not provide significant additional instructional time is Cristo Rey, where students toil at their work-study jobs one day a week. But Cristo Rey does require incoming freshman to attend a month-long summer school "boot camp." At most urban secondary schools, summer school is reserved for failing students who have to make up course work. At no-excuses schools, summer school serves two different purposes. First, it orients new students to school rules, uniforms, codes of conduct, and classroom routines. On their first day at summer school, incoming KIPP fifth graders learn how to stand properly in line—silently, and with a book in their hand. For returning students, summer school serves a different purpose: it extends the school year, accelerating learning and protecting against summer learning loss.

10. Monitor and enforce attendance.

Paternalistic schools monitor and enforce attendance scrupulously and consistently have 95 percent or more of students in class.

Perfect or nearly perfect attendance is important at high-performing secondary schools because having all students present minimizes wasted instructional time and reinforces the school's mission of academic rigor. As a result, principals often go to extraordinary lengths to make sure students don't miss school. University Park principal Donna Rodrigues would park outside tardy students' homes in her uncool 1996 red Taurus station wagon and lay on the horn until they came out. AIPCS's Ben Chavis paid to change a student's plane ticket so her class could maintain a perfect record of attendance for a full school year. At Amistad, Dacia Toll handed out alarm clocks to students with mediocre attendance records—and sent taxis out to pick them up. KIPP Academy principal Quinton Vance personally calls six students every morning before school to wake them up because their parents work a night shift. As Leah Rose, a sixth-grade teacher at American Indian summarized, "It makes a huge difference to always have the class present. You don't have to constantly retrace steps for kids who missed class."

11. Welcome accountability for adults and embrace constant reassessment.

Principals welcome accountability and strive to foster a school-wide ethos of accountability and constant reassessment to accompany their ambitious goals for academic excellence.

For principals at many urban secondary schools, the buck stops—just not necessarily on their desks. When students and inner-city schools founder, principals often explain away their failures by blaming the kids' socioeconomic and cultural deficits, insufficient school resources, or lack of support from the central office. These factors may indeed contribute to a school's shortcomings. But principals at no-excuses schools don't excuse poor performance. The few slips recorded in this book (e.g., when University Park had its first student fail the math MCAS on her first attempt in 2006, or when SEED failed to make AYP in math in 2006) forced searching reappraisals of classroom instruction.

In general, these schools are marked by a kind of intellectual restlessness. They regularly engage in self-criticism and reexamination of teaching methods and curriculum. Despite their accomplishments, they spend surprisingly little time resting on their laurels. Their leaders are competitive, too, and want to best other high-performing schools (even if they are not as public about it as is American Indian's former principal, Ben Chavis, who confesses he loves "taking low-income kids and just kicking butt on the state exams and the SATs—and kicking the ass of the rich kids"). If other high-achieving inner-city schools have instructional or behavioral strategies that work, principals are happy to adopt them. At Amistad, Dacia Toll borrowed liberally from KIPP,

North Star Academy, and Calgary Academy. As Matt Taylor, Amistad's current director, puts it, "We have a culture of overachievers here—and of never being satisfied with our accomplishments."

12. Give principals and teachers more autonomy—think "charter school."

These schools generally afford principals and teachers unusual autonomy. Not surprisingly, they are likely to be charter schools.

Not all of the schools featured in preceding chapters are charter schools—Cristo Rey, of course, is a parochial school, and University Park is a neighborhood public school. Nevertheless, most high-achieving paternalistic schools are charter schools—and even Cristo Rey and University Park have more authority than traditional public schools over curriculum and character development.

Typically, charter schools are at a considerable financial disadvantage compared to neighborhood schools. But the flip side of less funding is that school founders have more freedom to design and run their own schools. As a result, the charter schools profiled in this volume (AIPCS, Amistad, KIPP, and SEED) can experiment in ways that would be unimaginable in many neighborhood schools. Unlike principals of neighborhood schools, the principals of charters do not answer to the superintendent and school board. It is hard to imagine that a controversial, hot-headed, and profanity-spouting principal like Ben Chavis could long survive at a neighborhood school in Oakland.

As the chapters on AIPCS, Amistad, KIPP, and SEED illustrate, principals at charter schools can handpick the instructors they want, rather than have teachers foisted on them by district headquarters. In most instances, they can hire non-union teachers, set their own pay scales, or recruit teachers through unconventional means like Craigslist. They can require teachers to work Saturdays and during the summer and can provide them with cell phones to answer student queries after hours. They can evaluate teachers based on their record of improving student performance, rather than their seniority—and can fire those who perform poorly. They can have teachers oversee the character development of their students in ways that are exceedingly rare in zoned schools, from barring the use of slang, street talk, and gang insignia, to insisting that students clean dirty bathrooms and tuck in their shirts.

These charter schools also provide teachers with unusual freedoms, beginning with less paperwork and "administrivia" hassle from district headquarters and teacher unions. They are free to teach academically demanding material. They can collaborate with colleagues who share their enthusiasm for raising student achievement and work together to assist pupils who are struggling academically or acting out in class. They can work for committed principals, who pay them more than they would have earned at the neighborhood school. Best of all, they get to show up each morning at a school where students, for the most part, are ready if not eager to learn.

13. Eliminate (or at least disempower) local teacher unions.

The schools either have no teacher unions or unions in name only.

It is no secret that teacher unions are a part of the problem of poorly performing inner-city schools. However, no-excuses schools have either a pliant union or no teacher union at all. Two of the six schools featured here—KIPP and University Park—do have unionized teachers but mostly in name only. Dacia Toll described the union at KIPP Academy as a "joke," and teachers similarly paid no heed to safeguarding their union rights and observing union work rules at UPCS. In informational meetings and job postings, University Park's Donna Rodrigues deliberately set out to deter veteran union teachers from applying by describing how they would be under constant scrutiny from the principal, other teachers, and Clark University student teachers. The one teacher who filed a seniority grievance to get transferred to UPCS left after parents and students complained about his performance.

14. Use unconventional channels to recruit committed teachers.

Principals find gifted, committed teachers through a variety of unconventional channels. They tend to look first for teachers who did well in school themselves and second for individuals who are willing to go the "extra mile" to educate disadvantaged teenagers.

Freed from the obligation to employ teachers assigned by district headquarters, principals at the new paternalistic schools use idiosyncratic methods and networks to recruit their teams. Instead of turning primarily to education schools, they seek bright college graduates, and they recruit heavily among

Teach for America alumni/ae, especially at KIPP and Achievement First schools. Fully half of the teachers at Achievement First's new schools in Brooklyn were TFA products. At American Indian and Oakland Charter Academy, principals Ben Chavis and Jorge Lopez recruited teachers by posting job openings on Craigslist. They looked primarily for book smarts in their applicants, not teaching credentials. During the 2005–2006 school year, AIPCS's eight teachers in core subjects included three graduates of Wesleyan, and one each from Harvard, Brown, Berkeley, Columbia, and Dartmouth. Just one of the eight instructors had a teaching credential.

Typically, school founders search for teachers who—as KIPP's Mike Feinberg put it—have a "fire in the belly," a passion for teaching disadvantaged teens. Indeed, the record of paternalistic schools underscores the well-documented importance of high quality teachers to closing the achievement gap, from KIPP Academy's award-winning math teacher Frank Corcoran to University Park's literacy guru and Milken Educator June Eressy. Yet the record also suggests that the traditional certification system and formal alternative certification programs—now often run by education schools, too—offer little help in ferreting out outstanding teachers.

A few no-excuses schools, like Amistad Academy, are obligated by state law to hire certified teachers. But even at Amistad, school leaders have been able to screen teachers for their personal commitment to closing the achievement gap. Applicants first have to pen six short essays about their teaching philosophy and explain how they would handle hypothetical classroom situations. If applicants pass that initial screen, Amistad invites them to guest teach a class and receive feedback on their performance. When the school identifies a promising rookie teacher, it puts him through a two-year professional development program to accelerate his training.

15. Don't demand much from parents.

While principals at most paternalistic schools encourage parental involvement, parental involvement is not of paramount importance and no successful paternalistic academy is a parent-driven school.

Many school reformers treat parent involvement as a kind of sword in the stone that, once unsheathed, will liberate disadvantaged students. School leaders at no-excuses schools take a far more modest view of parental participation.

With the exception of Ben Chavis at AIPCS, principals think that parent involvement benefits students, and most principals try to encourage it. But these school leaders anticipate that inner-city parents will not be involved to the same degree as they would at say, a high-performing suburban school. Parent Teacher Associations at paternalistic academies are weak or nonexistent. Parents don't do bakes sales and Secret Santa rituals. On the contrary, school leaders assume that teachers and principals will periodically serve as surrogate parents. Even at University Park, a neighborhood school, teachers and the principal sometimes assume parental roles.

The SEED boarding school is certainly the most graphic example of surrogate parenting. But students at other schools frequently described their school as a "second home" and consulted trusted teachers about personal or family matters. KIPP student George Ramirez called orchestra conductor Jesus Concepcion to ask what he should buy his father for his birthday (socks, Concepcion advised). At American Indian, the opening line of the school's credo is "The Family: We are a family at AIPCS."

AIPCS's Ben Chavis argues that "in schools for poor kids, 'parental involvement' has become an excuse to blame somebody—Johnny can't read because his momma didn't work with him." But other school leaders were more intent on working with parents. KIPP and Amistad have parents sign nonbinding contracts, spelling out how they will support their children by providing a quiet study space at home, getting their kids to school on time, and checking to see that students did their homework. But the contracts are largely symbolic. Principals anticipate that few low-income parents are going to be seriously involved in the school. Many single parents, burdened by raising children or working low-wage jobs, are unlikely to commit to spending a minimum number of hours per month at the school. At the same time, many cannot help their children with homework, either because they do not speak English or because they themselves were high school dropouts.

Amistad initially asked parents to contribute 10 hours of volunteer time to the school each year, but eventually abandoned the requirement once it became clear that it was creating make-work and administrative headaches. The vast majority of parents at these schools are disengaged, yet loosely supportive.

16. Escape the constraints hobbling traditional district schools.

The new paternalistic secondary schools are rarely traditional district schools; their operating principles are too different.

Only one of the six schools featured in this volume is a neighborhood school, and even it has community resources and administrative flexibility atypical of most such schools. Owing to its close partnership with and proximity to Clark University, UPCS students are able to use Clark's library, athletic facilities, and auditoriums. Juniors and seniors take classes at Clark and Holy Cross, and Clark students work as student teachers and mentors at UPCS. The school's small size allows its teachers to provide one-on-one assistance to struggling students that would be difficult at comprehensive, urban high schools. And principals Donna Rodrigues and June Eressy have deftly deterred veteran teachers who do not share the school's mission from applying to teach there.

At most neighborhood schools in big cities, the rules are quite different. Their principals typically have to accept whichever teachers are assigned. School leaders usually have limited ability to set curriculum, pick textbooks, mandate longer days, or free teachers from burdensome paperwork.

It is revealing that persistent efforts by the Education Trust and The Achievement Alliance to identify high-achieving, high-poverty district schools have turned up few secondary schools in big cities. Karin Chenoweth's 2007 book for The Achievement Alliance, *It's Being Done: Academic Success in Unexpected Schools* profiled 16 high-performing, high-poverty neighborhood schools. But they included just three high schools and one middle school — and only one of those was in a big city. What was the one high-performing, high-poverty urban high school in Chenoweth's study? University Park Campus School.

17. Don't waste resources on fancy facilities or technology.

Extra funding and well-equipped facilities are not central to the success of paternalistic schools, which succeed despite generally spending the same or less per student as nearby district schools, and whose students thrive despite modest physical plants.

Most no-excuses schools spend less per student than nearby district schools, though University Park receives the same funding per student as other zoned schools in Worcester. SEED is the only paternalistic school that spends more per student than district public schools — more than twice as much. However, SEED's high costs are almost entirely a function of the fact that it is a boarding school.

Of the schools profiled here, SEED may also have the best-appointed campus, though even its facilities are modest compared to those of elite boarding schools. Amistad and Cristo Rey, which opened a large addition several years ago, are modern, cheerful facilities with ample gymnasiums. But a newcomer cannot help be struck by the meager facilities and resources of most no-excuses schools. AIPCS has no technology lab or student computers, and its small library, propped up on a stage, is supplemented by a biweekly bookmobile visit. Cristo Rey opened in a roller rink in Chicago, and students spent their first few years in an old Catholic elementary school on the verge of closing. When University Park opened in 1997, it had no textbooks or lab equipment. Today, UPCS still has no library or auditorium and just 22 computers, six of which are down on a typical day. The renowned KIPP Academy in the Bronx consists of a corridor and a half on the fourth floor of Independent School 151. Despite its outstanding record, it has no computer lab, library, playing fields, gym, or cafeteria. The school scrapes by, borrowing the auditorium, cafeteria, and playground of I.S. 151 for rehearsals, meals, and PE class.

18. Keep the school small.
Successful paternalistic schools are small, which enables their principals and teachers to make personal connections with students, tailor assistance for struggling students, and create a sense of community.

By far the largest of the six schools featured in preceding chapters is Cristo Rey—which, at 530 students, is still less than half the size of an average urban high school. Most of the schools here have 250 to 325 students. Their small size is no accident. Such schools work most effectively when principals and teachers can build personal ties to students. It is far more difficult to create a culture of achievement and character in a faceless 2,000-pupil high school than in one where, to borrow the *Cheers* tagline, everybody knows your name.

Students at no-excuses schools tend to think of their schools as communities and believe that their own successes are tied to those of their classmates. That sense of community breeds a collaborative ethic largely absent from big schools, where rooting for the team is largely confined to cheering at athletic events and Spirit Week. University Park Senior Jorge Ramirez explained that during the intense preparation of his tenth-grade class for Massachusetts's demanding MCAS test, "I didn't feel like it was about me passing the test but my class passing the test. When we got our scores, everyone was walking around saying 'did you get proficient?'"

19. Track and support students after they graduate.

Successful paternalistic schools are establishing programs to support and track students after they leave—reflecting the concern that hard-won gains may otherwise be lost.

At Amistad, Cristo Rey, and KIPP, school administrators all knew of students who had slipped academically or fallen in with a "bad crowd" after they graduated. Paternalistic schools are responding to this post-graduation letdown in two ways. First, several middle schools, including AIPCS, Oakland Charter Academy, and Amistad Academy, have added high schools for their graduates. These high schools are still small and usually start with a single grade. But they do provide an alternative for students who want to go on to a school that adheres to the same model as their middle school.

Second, Cristo Rey and KIPP have both developed counseling and support programs for students as they move into high school and college. The Cristo Rey Network has just begun a one-man college relations program to better target colleges where Cristo Rey alumni will flourish. By contrast, KIPP Academy in the Bronx has an extensive post-graduation support program, open since 2002. It now tracks 100 percent of its graduates and obtains copies of their grades throughout high school. In addition, the school's KIPP to College program provides a weekly after-school academic and character-building curriculum, plus tutoring and counseling, and oversees more than 100 paid, summer internships in closely-monitored jobs for KIPP alumni. During graduates' junior and senior years in high school, the KIPP to College staff becomes deeply involved in guiding them through the college applications process. Among other support activities, alumni attend a two-day college-application prep retreat at Camp Ramapo in Rhinebeck, New York. KIPP to College staff also assist alumni with writing application essays and preparing for admission interviews.

20. Help create additional schools following your model.

Finally, school founders are devoting substantial resources to replicating their flagship school(s). They are not content to create one successful inner-city school but aim, over time, to help reshape inner-city education across the country.

Some school leaders are well along in their replication efforts while others are just getting underway. In Oakland, Ben Chavis and Jorge Lopez are starting with local ambitions, to remake schools in their hometown. By contrast, KIPP and Cristo Rey have created multimillion-dollar networks of schools around the nation. But all six schools have set up distinct entities to help spread their gospel. Many of the foundations and nonprofits overseeing replication efforts, particularly the parent organizations of Amistad and KIPP, are concentrating on replicating their programs in new schools willing to hew faithfully to the model of the flagship schools—as opposed to trying to modify existing schools.

It is too soon to say that all of the copycat schools will succeed. But the early results are encouraging and underscore the idea that these schools operate successful models of education, which can be replicated and do not depend on the efforts of one heroic individual (though the schools certainly require committed and talented leaders). In fact, one of the guiding principles of Achievement First's replication efforts in Connecticut and Brooklyn is that mere mortals can successfully eliminate the achievement gap. Successful schools don't demand superhuman principals.

Lessons for Reformers

The new paternalistic schools are different from other K–12 reform efforts because they truly transform the lives of inner-city students. Standards-based reform and school choice have both helped modestly to narrow the achievement gap. Yet these popular reforms and the schools that have implemented them have failed to equalize the performance of minority and white students. By contrast, successful no-excuses schools effectively eliminate the achievement gap such that minority students are as likely as white students to graduate from high school and gain admission to college. The new paternalistic school is a break-the-mold institution, a wholesale shift from the traditional industrial model of education—which has prevailed in urban education for the last century—to a more directive and tailored form of schooling.

What lessons can be drawn from these breakthrough schools? Their record demonstrates that reformers bent on closing the achievement gap are likely to have their greatest impact if they concentrate on expanding the replication efforts of existing no-excuses schools, rather than pursuing elements of paternalism in incremental fashion. It is possible that these schools, so radically different from traditional public schools, could one day educate not just several thousand inner-city youngsters but tens or even hundreds of thousands of students in cities across the nation.

At education reform conferences, advocates sometimes claim that the nation currently has about 200 true "achievement gap-closing" charter schools. (The derivation of this number is a mystery, but it seems to have taken on a life of its own.) Yet there is no reason that the paternalistic model cannot spread to hundreds of additional secondary schools in the inner city, and eventually, perhaps, to more than a thousand urban schools.

The prospects for such replication are far more promising today than a decade ago when exceptional schools seemed to be just that—exceptions. In a 2006 study of the replication efforts of high-performing schools, Kimberly Wicoff and her colleagues at the Bridgespan Group noted that

> unlike a decade ago, when it was hard to find more than a handful of high performing public schools, today many such schools exist. As a result, the goal posts have shifted. The question is no longer, "Can we create schools that achieve outstanding results for all their students?" but rather, "How can we replicate schools that we know can work, without sacrificing quality outcomes and within the constraints of the existing funding environment?"[8]

The replication efforts to date help provide some answers. KIPP currently has 57 schools in 17 states, educating over 14,000 students. Those numbers attest to the charter network's impressive growth during the last decade, as do KIPP's plans to dramatically expand operations in Houston to serve 21,000 students a decade hence—about 10 percent of all public school students in the district. The second largest network, Cristo Rey, has 12 member schools at present with about 2,900 students. It hopes by 2012–2013 to have 31 high schools with a total enrollment of 12,000 students. These are ambitious growth plans for any school model. Yet at the current rate of replication, the new paternalistic schools will still be educating a relatively small percentage of the millions of inner-city secondary school students a decade from now.

The great challenge to speeding up the replication process is that hurried efforts could go awry. Indeed, if there is a lesson to date in the replication efforts of model no-excuses schools, it is that successor schools perform best when they faithfully copy the essential elements of the flagship schools and have parent organizations with strong managerial capacities.

Every successful inner-city school that seeks to replicate itself faces a basic tactical quandary. If they wish to spread their model quickly to numerous schools, they must forfeit some quality control, meaning they cannot be sure that successor schools will carefully reproduce all of the core elements of the flagship schools. On the other hand, if they choose quality over quantity, it will obviously take longer to multiply their educational model.

Most of the new paternalist schools were founded by education rebels with little background in finance and management. In their early years, these mavericks placed a high premium on commitment and recruiting like-minded school leaders, as opposed to focusing on budgeting and administration. By temperament, the founders of no-excuses schools are disposed to be free-wheeling entrepreneurs. They have sometimes had to learn the hard way that financing, administration, legal issues, and careful replication are more important than they originally realized.

As the KIPP network has mushroomed, Dave Levin, Mike Feinberg, and the KIPP Foundation have hired executives who know the *business* of schools. Cristo Rey Network officials similarly decided that they had to be more scrupulous about replicating their flagship school after a parochial school in Austin, Texas, had to drop out of the network because it wanted higher-income families to help cover tuition costs. Cristo Rey executives commissioned 25 feasibility studies after the network began its replication efforts five years ago — and a quarter of those did not lead to the opening of new schools. The network turned down an application for one all-male and largely black Cristo Rey school in Detroit because school leaders planned to use the model's work-study program only for juniors and seniors, leaving out sophomores and freshmen.

A key issue in the debate over how to build on the success of high-performing inner-city schools is whether schools can successfully apply the new paternalism in piecemeal fashion, or if all the core elements need to be copied to ensure success. The weight of the evidence suggests that piecemeal paternalism is unlikely to dramatically narrow the achievement gap. To take one example, urban secondary schools that have an extended day or year do not necessarily outperform neighborhood schools with a traditional school day and year. At the same time, University Park Campus School lost its extended school day due to district budget cuts—but UPCS students managed to continue outperforming white students from affluent districts. Other paternalistic-style reforms that have been tested in urban high schools in piecemeal fashion (e.g., expanding college preparatory offerings, providing enrichment courses for remedial students, giving youngsters adult mentors) have usually failed to make an appreciable dent in the achievement gap.[9]

In short, transformative "gap-closing" schools are likely to flourish only when they implement most, if not all, of the 20 habits of highly effective schools. The record also attests to the importance of tenacity and mission. Time and again, the founders of successful no-excuses schools have had to buck the education establishment. They battle with district headquarters to protect their autonomy and struggle with unions to keep them out of their schools. They seek to work outside the traditional system in recruiting and compensating teachers. And they often train principals and teachers on their own, rather than relying on education schools.

One obvious step to accelerate the spread of paternalistic schools is to have foundations, philanthropists, venture capitalists, and government offer financial support to the organizations that are responsible for the success stories chronicled in this book and that are now trying to ramp up the number of schools they run. To cite but one example, the Cristo Rey Network, which is seeking to open 25 new schools, currently has only six employees to oversee this challenging assignment. With more funds, the organization might be able to expand more rapidly.

A number of school reform "incubators" already provide funding to support the expansion of paternalistic school networks such as KIPP (e.g., the NewSchools Venture Fund and New Profit Inc.) and SEED (Venture for Philanthropy Partners). Nonprofits and venture capitalists who support these incubators and others like them (the Charter School Growth Fund, for instance) help strengthen and expand the managerial infrastructure that sustains the growth of paternalistic schools. As more incubators form, the number of schools modeled along the lines described here will also grow.

Districts and superintendents committed to transformational reform might similarly create separately empowered "turnaround" offices, with charter-like freedoms, to oversee the restructuring of persistently low-performing schools. Some 5,000 schools, or about 5 percent of the nation's public schools, are already slated for restructuring by 2009–2010 under the No Child Left

Behind law. Several major school districts, including New York City, Chicago, Philadelphia, and Miami-Dade, have started to experiment with local "turnaround zones" to boost the chances for transformational change in their worst schools.[10]

Incubators can also have a multiplier effect on school reform efforts. One successful innovator can spur more. Teach for America's mission is not to recruit career teachers (corps members are asked to serve two-year stints) but rather to enlist a future generation of leaders in the "movement to end educational inequity." TFA alum-turned reformers now include not only Mike Feinberg and Dave Levin of KIPP, but also the founders of the successful YES Prep Public Schools (Chris Barbic), Generation Schools (Furman Brown), Idea Schools (Tom Torkelson), and the new schools chancellor in Washington, D.C., Michelle Rhee.

The multiplier effect of good incubators is particularly important because the direct provision of venture capital in secondary education is likely to remain modest. K–12 education currently does not provide the kind of financial return that venture capitalists can find in other fields. By contrast, philanthropies can and do invest significant sums in school start-ups, incubators, and urban school reform. In 2005, venture capital investors funneled only $64 million into pre-K–12 businesses, according to the market research firm Eduventures. That same year, philanthropic support of K–12 education totaled $1.5 billion.[11]

Finally, advocates seeking to expand the managerial infrastructure to support transformational reform should recognize that they will often be supporting unconventional organizations. The new networks of no-excuses schools are distinguished not just by their unusual degree of autonomy but also by their agility and adaptability. It is no coincidence that paternalistic schools have adopted the no excuses slogan. They adapt to overcome obstacles even while clinging to a single-minded focus on raising academic achievement and elevating student behavior. At most traditional public schools, principals and teachers are concerned with first satisfying the demands of adults, not those of children. District regulations must be followed, forms must be filled out, prescribed textbooks must be purchased, parents and community leaders must be placated, and union work rules must be heeded. And yes, children are to be educated.

By contrast, paternalistic schools are hyper-focused on academic achievement. They place all-out emphasis on the educational and developmental needs of students. Yes, they go through the paces, as necessary, to comply with district regulations. But so long as students continue to rack up impressive gains in achievement and character, school leaders don't much care if teachers file grievances or sue the school (as was the case at University Park Campus School and Oakland Charter Academy) or if the district only provides a few rooms in a public school to educate students (as with KIPP Academy in the Bronx). At paternalistic secondary schools, education truly is all about the kids.

This radical reorientation — this rethinking of the relationship between an inner-city school and its students — is yet one more reason why replicating successful paternalistic schools is a demanding task. It can be done, probably in hundreds of schools with tens of thousands of students. But that important piece of good news is tempered by the fact that radically expanding paternalistic schooling to, say, half-a-million students may take longer than advocates would like. Building the organizational capacity to support reform is painstaking work. Rushing the launch of new schools, or opening copycat schools without ensuring that the crucial elements of the school model are present, could prove disappointing. And failing to manage the financial nuts and bolts of school replication can also retard efforts. In short, copying successful no-excuses schools requires a relentless tenacity and dedication. A bit like the little engine that could, paternalistic schools can scale the peak of urban school reform. But to keep on chugging, their engineers have to maintain an unflagging pursuit of their educational mission.

Chapter Ten

Obstacles and Alternatives to Radical Paternalistic Reform

I n theory, everyone is in favor of radically reforming failing urban schools. Every president wants to be the "education president," every governor wants to be the "education governor." Teacher unions, too, are "pro-reform." Yet everyone is also in favor of world peace and justice for all. Real-world, urban school reform and the particulars of implementing a paternalistic overhaul in cities across the nation face formidable obstacles.

The new paternalistic schools hold rich implications for reform of inner-city secondary schools. But for all the evidence of their effectiveness, a sweeping makeover of inner-city schools to resemble paternalistic schools is unlikely anytime soon.

The Peculiar Politics of the New Paternalism

The successful paternalistic schools profiled here do not easily wear a liberal or conservative label, and radical reform via paternalism differs in many ways from the programs and strategies generally promoted by those on the left and right. In reviewing the top twenty Habits of Highly Effective Urban Schools in the preceding chapter, one soon observes that many school reforms beloved by liberals or conservatives did not make the list. Conservative favorites—including providing low-income families with vouchers to attend private and religious schools, turning over public schools to private managers like Edison Schools, home schooling, and expanded parent participation—bear no role in closing the gap at these high-performing urban schools. At the same time, liberal reform tenets, like pushing greater resources into urban schools, do not seem critical to closing the achievement gap either. Other prominent progressive solutions, including reduced class size, greater parent involvement, deploying teachers who reflect the ethnicity of their pupils, and providing bilingual instruction and multicultural courses for immigrants, all play little role in successful no-excuses schools.

The new paternalistic schools might be described as schools of obligation, not express-yourself "Schools of Rock." They are squarely at odds with deeply held views of progressive educators—who oppose universal academic standards, think frequent testing of minority students is discriminatory, and favor experiential learning over direct instruction. Whereas progressive educators believe that disadvantaged adolescents should be free to explore and develop their critical-thinking skills, paternalistic educators believe students need first to drill to build basic skills in reading, writing, and math before they are ready to handle a college-prep curriculum.

That philosophical gap between progressivism and paternalism does not prevent other liberals from embracing the new schools. The virtues they teach—perseverance, discipline, politeness—can also be thought of as noncognitive skills. A number of liberal education reformers, including Richard Rothstein and economist James Heckman, argue that inner-city schools must boost these very skills in order to raise academic achievement and compensate for students' deep seated cultural deficits.

Left-leaning school founders like SEED's Eric Adler, Amistad's Dacia Toll, and KIPP Academy's Dave Levin also ascribe a liberal tint to their school's paternalistic practices. They point out that though their teachers sometimes assume parent-like roles, those same instructors are expanding students' cultural horizons and building up their social capital through educational partnerships, job internships, and field trips to concerts, plays, colleges, and national parks.

Today's paternalistic schools are also more palatable to liberals than earlier models because their curricula for character development promote not only traditional virtues but also social activism. SEED, for example, explicitly encourages community involvement in progressive causes, as do KIPP Academy,

Cristo Rey, and University Park. SEED requires students to participate in community service projects and teaches each student to "make a commitment to a life of social action." Students are urged to reflect upon their own experiences with prejudice, discrimination, and bullying.

Dacia Toll and Dave Levin believe that their schools' paternalistic elements help pave the yellow brick road to college and liberate the potential of students. Like political scientist Lawrence Mead, they also believe that careful monitoring of student conduct, over time, *preempts* misbehavior, so that the longer students are in school, the less they require constant supervision. One of the great accomplishments of their schools, they contend, is permanently altering how students think and feel—not just changing the way they act.

In contrast to Indian boarding schools and large orphanages, today's paternalistic schools do not seek to supplant parents or wipe out all cultural ties, only to reshape the culture of the poor and boost family support. As SEED cofounder Eric Adler put it, "if we had wanted to 'eradicate' the students' culture we would have placed the school 100 miles away out in the woods... [rather than place] it in the neighborhood where the kids come from." One recent sign of the defanging of paternalism is that liberal commentator Bob Herbert of the *New York Times* urged policymakers in 2007 to study KIPP schools and "mine [them] for potentially transformative effects"[1] on inner-city education.

If those schools are winning the affection of new bedfellows on the left, they may yet engender wariness on the right. No-excuses schools were first publicized by the Heritage Foundation, and for much of the last decade conservatives have lauded paternalistic schools for their academic rigor, strict behavioral regimen, commitment to accountability, and success in closing the achievement gap—without spending additional money. But a closer look at today's paternalistic schools reveals elements that could make some conservatives uneasy.

It's true that most no-excuses schools are charters and, thus, schools of choice, which conservatives welcome. Yet they are hardly free-market icons. They exert a supervisory authority over student lives that would make libertarians squirm if adults rather than teens sat in students' seats. Eric Hanushek of the Hoover Institution winced when I referred to KIPP and Amistad as "paternalistic" schools. "I prefer to think of them as highly structured." Columnist Andrew Ferguson scoffs at the idea that meddling in schools alone can do much to close the achievement gap. In a September 2007 cover essay in the *Weekly Standard* that attacked NCLB and the "BGC" crowd (Big Government Conservatives), Ferguson wrote that "No research has ever established that the quality of individual schools is a cause of the gap in test scores among groups of students—especially compared with the other facts in a student's life." Sounding a bit like Richard Rothstein, Ferguson concluded that what really causes the achievement gap is "the safety of [a student's] neighborhood, the income of his family, the presence of books in his home, the amount of television he's allowed to watch, or whether he's being raised by a mother and a father: facts, every one of them, beyond the manipulation of any education reformer."[2]

Like other paternalistic institutions, these schools also display a strong strain of social work that many conservatives find intrusive and nanny-like. Staffers devote many hours to helping fix problems in the home lives of students. Donna Rodrigues of University Park tracked down landlords in the Section 8 housing voucher program to help families threatened with eviction. KIPP Academy in the Bronx has two full-time social workers on staff who assist at-risk students on an almost daily basis; a third social worker in the KIPP to College program aids them after middle school.

In his 2006 *New York Times Magazine* article on urban schools that close the achievement gap, Paul Tough cautioned against assuming that schools like Amistad and KIPP can be run on the cheap:

> [W]hen educators do succeed at educating poor minority students up to national standards of proficiency, they invariably use methods that are radically different and more intensive than those employed in most American public schools…The message inherent in the success of their schools is that if poor students are going to catch up, they will require not the same education that middle-class children receive but one that is considerably better; they need more time in class than middle-class students; better-trained teachers and a curriculum that prepares them psychologically and emotionally, as well as intellectually, for the challenges ahead of them.[3]

The New Paternalism and the Field of Dreams Syndrome

Since the new paternalist schools contain both conservative and liberal elements, one might wonder if they lay the groundwork for a grand compromise between the left and the right on urban education. On first impression, they do seem to provide a roadmap towards such a compromise, not unlike that which emerged in the landmark welfare reform law of 1996. Following up on Bill Clinton's campaign promise to "end welfare as we know it," the new law limited receipt of public assistance to two years. In the decade that followed, welfare rolls dropped by about 60 percent, and work among welfare recipients soared. Once the government had slashed the number of families on the dole, it became permissible for conservatives to join liberals in supporting an expanded earned income tax credit and additional spending for child care, child support enforcement, and training for welfare mothers who were looking for work or filling low-wage jobs.

The new paternalistic schools could similarly appeal to both conservatives and liberals. The former can cheer them for teaching the work ethic and traditional virtues; liberals could applaud them for placing poor kids on the path toward college—and out of poverty. A grand bargain might be in the offing: If inner-city schools across the nation successfully adopt a no-excuses model, would conservatives be willing to support spending increases for longer school days, an extended school year, and additional tutoring? Would liberals be willing to grant principals and teachers of these schools a great deal of autonomy, allowing these schools to circumvent state and district regulations and union contracts?

Alas, this scenario is so improbable that the question is likely to go unanswered. Public education is far more decentralized than welfare. Policy and spending are dictated largely at the state and local level, and teacher unions play a far more powerful role in schools than the American Federation of State, County, and Municipal Employees plays in welfare offices.

The three legs of the education establishment tripod—teacher unions, education schools, and the district bureaucracy—are all unlikely to embrace key elements that make paternalistic schools work. Requiring teachers to work longer days and years would violate union contracts. So would allowing principals to handpick teachers (who may or may not be certified), evaluate and pay instructors based on their effectiveness, and fire those who are not successful in the classroom. Frequent testing, teacher-directed instruction, and flunking students who fail to meet academic standards are all unpopular at schools of education. District bureaucrats, meanwhile, are loath to grant individual schools the freedom to do things differently, especially when it comes to curriculum and budget. These forces of stasis are powerful indeed. In a 2005 C-SPAN interview, Dave Levin lamented that not a single official from J.H.S. 151 or P.S. 131 had ever come by to visit KIPP Academy in the Bronx during the previous six years to seek ideas for reform—never mind that KIPP Academy was located in the same building as the middle school and elementary school.[4] As John Chubb and Terry Moe have summed up, "existing institutions cannot solve the problem [of low-performing students], because they *are* the problem."[5]

Yet the tantalizing prospect of transforming urban schools persists. The first book to popularize the concept of no-excuses schools, Samuel Casey Carter's 2001 Heritage monograph, *No Excuses: Lessons from 21 High-Performing, High-Poverty Schools*, devoted little analysis to the real-world limitations of taking such schools to scale. "Nothing these [principals] do," Carter baldly asserted, "is beyond the reach of any school in the country."[6] In fact, advocates of transformational change in urban schools have consistently overestimated the power of example—or what Ed Kirby of the Walton Family Foundation has dubbed "reform by enlightenment." Too many education reformers, Kirby argues, mistakenly fall prey to a kind of Field of Dreams syndrome, believing that "if you build a high performing [*insert your favorite supply side initiative here*], policy makers will flock to it, take notes, and duly change the rules and incentives so that the rest of the sector can follow suit. In theory, the concept sounds great. In reality, it consistently fails."[7]

Urban Schools and the Tipping Point Theory

More sophisticated proponents of sweeping inner-city education reform acknowledge the intractability of the public school establishment. They believe that a radical remake of urban schools will not come about all at once but by gradually crossing a "tipping point." The early hope of charter school advocates was that once high-quality charters spread across urban areas, school districts would either "feel compelled to make changes in response to a massive outflow of students and staff to the superior charter schools, refuse to change and go out of business, or be replaced with a system of charter schools by legislators."[8]

To date, however, the tipping point concept has had scant impact on schools—and there is good reason to think that it won't anytime soon. In 1996, the nation had about 250 charter schools; today, more than one million students attend some 4,000 of them. In six cities, charter schools account for more than 20 percent of all students; in 19 cities, more than 10 percent of students are in charters.[9] Yet for all their growth, charter schools simply enroll far too few students—about 2 percent of all K–12 students—to truly alter the public school establishment. Several years ago, Frederick Hess of the American Enterprise Institute calculated that 2,000 new charter schools would have to open each year through 2015 before charter school students would account for as much as 10 percent of public school enrollment nationwide.[10] As it happens, the number of new charter schools started each year since 2001 has leveled off or even fallen.[11] Meanwhile, the prospect for rapid growth in the decade ahead is starting to fade. Half of the states, plus the District of Columbia, still cap the number of charter schools in some manner. And even in states where these schools flourish, they typically receive 20 to 33 percent less funding per student than surrounding district schools. The charter school tipping point keeps receding, like a distant shore once glimpsed but never reached. "Nobody knows what the tipping point is," writes Paul T. Hill of the National Charter School Research Project. "[It] surely [is] not at 20 percent of public schools as schools of choice, as some first thought. Maybe, as a cynic recently guessed, the tipping point comes at 99 percent."[12]

The roadblocks to reaching a tipping point in favor of paternalistic schools include educational philosophy. As it turns out, few charter schools are thoroughgoing, paternalistic inner-city secondary schools. In fact, a good case can be made that charter schools are doing more to spread progressive pedagogy than paternalistic instruction. Charter school experts Sara Mead and Andrew Rotherham have concluded that "Overall, in the major charter states of Arizona, California, Florida, Michigan, and Texas, charter schools appear to favor 'progressive' approaches over traditional educational ones."[13]

At the same time, the vast majority of charter schools are idiosyncratic, community-driven institutions or "mom and pop" charters, not faithful replications of proven models. Only 9 percent of charter schools are run by CMOs(charter management organizations, like the KIPP Foundation) or EMOs (for-profit education management organizations, like Edison Schools). Fifteen years after its founding, Edison Schools, the largest EMO in the nation, is running only about 85 out of nearly 95,000 public schools in the United States.[14]

Missed Opportunities: New Orleans; Restructured Schools; and Small Schools

Imagine what would happen if the traditional education establishment was effectively disarmed. Given a blank slate, could reformers close the achievement gap with a far-reaching remake of inner-city schools? As it happens, Hurricane Katrina created a natural experiment in New Orleans. Katrina swept away not just thousands of structures but the dysfunctional New Orleans school system itself. Shortly after the hurricane, the Louisiana legislature designated 107 of 128 city-run schools as "failing" and took control of them for five years, effectively stripping the Orleans Parish School Board of most of its funding and authority. The school board turned around and promptly fired all of its 7,500 teachers and support staff—making New Orleans perhaps the only big city in the nation without a viable teacher union.

This educational breach was filled largely by an explosion of new charter schools. Federal and state governments committed tens of millions of dollars to expanding charters in New Orleans. Many of the nation's best known charter school and education reform groups rushed to the city, including KIPP, Edison Schools, Teach for America, the Bill and Melinda Gates Foundation, and New Leaders for New Schools (which recruits and trains principals). By June 2007, nearly 60 percent of the city's public school students were attending charter schools, by far the highest proportion in the United States. "The result," as Amy Waldman observed in *The Atlantic*, "was the fastest makeover of an urban school system in American history…Most radical of all, the neighborhood school had been banished—parents would have total freedom to choose which school their children would attend."[15] The cause of comprehensive reform was further strengthened when Paul Vallas, Philadelphia's well-regarded superintendent of schools, took over as head of New Orleans's new Recovery School District in July 2007. Vallas, too, saw this as a once-in-a-lifetime shot at radical school reform. He pledged that New Orleans' school makeover would "be the greatest opportunity for educational entrepreneurs, charter schools, competition and parental choice in America."[16]

Yet many struggles lay ahead. Before Vallas got there, acting superintendent Robin Jarvis favored a number of elements of paternalistic reform. She strove to create a culture of high expectations and extended the school day. She insisted that all principal and teacher applicants take and pass a skills assessment and job interview, and she helped handpick principals and teachers, hiring them

291

on one-year contracts, forcing them to be more accountable for their performance. But Jarvis's ambitious reform agenda made uneven progress, at best. The tasks of restoring and opening several dozen school facilities all at once, and the search for new teachers, were simply too overwhelming in a city rife with poverty, property damage, and a crippling shortage of affordable housing. When the schools opened, they suffered from teacher shortages, missing textbooks, nonfunctioning cafeterias, and more. By year's end, fewer than half the students were even showing up at school.[17]

Vallas himself believed in some aspects of paternalistic reform and had successfully implemented a number of prescriptive changes in previous stints in Chicago and Philadelphia. In Philadelphia, for example, Vallas aligned school curricula with state standards and assessments and required schools to tests students every two weeks to assess student and teacher weaknesses. He also ordered that teachers receive a guide detailing the lessons they were to teach each week and doubled the daily periods for math and reading to 90 minutes.[18]

In New Orleans, Vallas went further, announcing his intention to try to transform public schools into a kind of substitute family. District schools would have an extended school day and year and would provide services such as three meals each day and eye and dental care. "You begin to provide the type of services you would normally expect to be provided at home," Vallas told the *New York Times*. "You begin to make the schools community centers. The whole objective here is to keep the school open through the dinner hour, and keep schools open 11 months out of the year."[19] Under Vallas' plan, summer school will no longer be voluntary for district students who fail the state exam, repeatedly miss school, or have poor grades. He anticipates that more than half of district students will require the more intensive, 11-month program.

It is still too early to pass judgment on the New Orleans experiment, though the initial returns suggest again how difficult it is for reform-minded superintendents to transform an entire school district, even without the presence of teacher unions and a district bureaucracy. Nor does New Orleans provide an entirely fair test of radical reform. In the aftermath of the hurricane, students are far more impoverished and traumatized there than in other big cities. A 2006 Louisiana State University mental health survey found that one in seven of the city's children had friends or relatives who died in the storm and more than 20 percent had friends or relatives who were injured. Nearly 10 percent were still separated from their primary caregivers.[20] Thousands had lost their homes or been forced to relocate to temporary housing, too.

Yet even should reformers ultimately succeed in shrinking the achievement gap in New Orleans, proponents of a paternalistic-style overhaul of inner-city schools cannot expect to institute similar reforms in other cities without running into bitter opposition — and, somewhat surprisingly, a lack of interest from charter operators. One logical target of opportunity in coming years will be the thousands of inner-city schools that fail to make AYP five years in a row and are required under NCLB to "restructure." A 2007 report by the Mass Insight Education and Research Institute projects that 3,200 public schools will be restructuring due to NCLB in 2008–2009. Roughly 90 percent of these schools are in large urban districts.[21]

Under NCLB, a state can take over schools slated for restructuring, or the district can replace all or most of the school staff, reopen the school as a charter school, or do "other major restructuring." The latter "wild card" category can entail changes as mundane as alterations to curriculum and professional development programs. The early results of restructuring efforts are in from 2005–2006 (when about 600 schools entered restructuring) and the results are not encouraging to advocates of transformational reform. Almost without exception, states have declined to take over failing schools and school restructurings by districts have taken the most minimalist path. In Chicago, where 200 schools started the restructuring process in 2005–2006 under NCLB, *not one* of the schools chose chartering. Just 5 of the 200 schools opted for some form of staff replacement.

Why such tepid reforms at avowedly awful urban schools? A recalcitrant district bureaucracy is not the only barrier to school restructuring. Part of the answer is that charter management organizations overwhelmingly prefer to start new schools rather than try to fix ailing ones. The 2007 study from Mass Insight surveyed 47 school support organizations and management organizations (including KIPP, Achievement First, the SEED Foundation, and Edison Schools) in six large urban school districts. Roughly one in five providers in the six cities said they weren't interested in getting involved in school restructuring under any conditions; half said — with perfect reasonableness — that they would only be interested if the district was willing to cede control over issues like staffing, curriculum, admission policies, finances, and collective bargaining.

Urban districts are unlikely to part easily with these prerogatives—but even if they were, charter management organizations are not prepared to take over a slew of failing schools. Thus Mass Insight found a "profound mismatch" between supply and demand in the school restructuring market:

Collectively, these six districts are likely to restructure 500 to 700 schools in the next three to five years. Twenty SMOs [school management organizations, like Achievement First or Edison Schools] would each have to be willing to restructure five schools annually for five years even to reach the bottom of this range. In fact, many of the SMOs in this study are planning to grow annually by fewer than five schools of any kind, including start-ups. So even under the best of circumstances, it is unlikely that the current cohort of SMOs could be involved in restructuring more than a fraction of the schools that need it.[22]

The founders of no-excuses charter schools show much the same preference for autonomy and a "fresh start" in opening new schools, ideally starting with a single grade. None of KIPP's current 57 schools is a conversion school, and in 2007 KIPP abandoned its attempt to reconstitute Cole College Prep in Denver as a new KIPP middle school after the KIPP Foundation was unable to recruit a top-notch principal for the foundering school.[23] When KIPP closed it, the school had only 49 eighth graders. The KIPP Foundation has since opted to forego restructuring failing schools in favor of starting up new KIPP schools. "Our core competency is starting and running new schools and we are going to stick to that for now," says KIPP spokesman Steve Mancini. In Oakland, Ben Chavis and Jorge Lopez both turned around low-performing schools before starting new paternalistic academies. But when Chavis arrived at American Indian Public Charter School in 2000, the student body had dwindled to a mere 27 students—hardly a test of what it would mean to take over and transform a failing inner-city high school with 2,000 students.

New schools are inevitably expensive and demanding to start. An alternative way to remake inner-city schooling would be to break up giant comprehensive secondary schools into smaller schools. To date, all of the successful no-excuses schools are small because they benefit from establishing a paternal-like bond and trust between teachers and students. Under the small-is-beautiful credo, failing high schools would be broken up into smaller "learning communities," in many cases creating opportunities to craft new schools.

Such a movement is underway in a number of cities, such as New York and Los Angeles. As Thomas Toch reported in his 2003 book, *High Schools on a Human Scale*, small high schools—with, say, 400 students or less—generally have less violence, classroom disorder, truancy, and gang problems than comprehensive urban high schools. Student achievement among poor and minority students is as high or higher in small urban high schools, and they employ less tracking of students.

Breaking up larger schools does not have to be costly, but it can necessitate new capital and staff expenditures, and it often runs counter to a district's funding incentives. Because school revenues are based largely on government per-pupil funding, administrators in many districts have an incentive to increase class size modestly or even add an additional section to each grade to boost school funding. Newly reconstituted small high schools can also fall prey to pedagogical humbug. New York City, for example, now has at least 15 new, smaller higher schools that are "social justice" schools, adhering to a social justice-centric curriculum that in some cases appears to hold little educational value.[24]

The slow growth of the charter movement, the difficulty of building a truly different school system in New Orleans, and the inability of districts to restructure failing schools along paternalistic lines all represent missed opportunities for transformational reform, the kind of paternalistic-style reform that closes the achievement gap. Whether it is hampered by burdensome regulations (like charter caps blocking would-be entrepreneurs from opening new schools) or the limited capacity of organizations equipped to advance radical reform (who cannot handle all the schools in need of restructuring), the paternalistic model has made only modest inroads.

The Teaching Supply Problem

Some of the obstacles to transformational change are political problems that can be tackled by reformers. If the growth of charter schools has been limited by charter caps, then activists can fight to lift the caps—as they have with some success in recent years. If union contracts and bureaucratic procedures limit principal autonomy, then districts can establish specially empowered turnaround offices with charter-like freedoms to overhaul lousy schools. If there are too few school management organizations to take over failing schools, this shortfall can be partly remedied by raising the per-student payments made to groups who can turn around schools.

Other obstacles to transformational reform seem less susceptible to political solutions. Ultimately, for any large-scale reform of inner-city schools to be effective, teachers will have to buy into it. But there are serious questions as to whether there is adequate talent in the current teacher and principal pool to expand the new paternalism to scale. At present, high-poverty urban schools generally attract less qualified teachers than other schools. Teachers in inner-city schools are significantly more likely than their peers to be teaching out-of-field, lack experience, or have failed their licensing exam. By contrast, the new paternalistic schools place far greater demands on teachers than even the current faltering system.

No-excuses schools seek teachers with a personal commitment to closing the achievement gap, teachers willing to work an extended school day and school year, teachers who want to instruct teens both about traditional course matter and character development—and who will make themselves available to students whenever needed. Moreover, teachers are expected to fulfill all these extra roles without the assurance of tenure or other union protections. It is no coincidence that most teachers in the new paternalistic schools are young, single, idealistic, and relatively inexperienced. Will they remain in these roles when they turn 35, get married, have children, and have a mortgage? Jesus Concepcion, the 34-year-old KIPP Academy youth orchestra conductor, was one of the few teachers at these schools who was married with children. But after 10 years at KIPP Academy, Concepcion left in November 2007 to set up a consulting business working with school orchestras. "I loved every minute at KIPP," Concepcion says, "but after ten years of six-day weeks at school and always bringing my work home with me, I needed a break from the classroom." Many teachers who are older and married lack his intense commitment to teaching. In fact, no one really knows yet if most of the twenty-something instructors at the new paternalistic schools will spend their careers there or burn out after five years and call it quits.

Mike Feinberg is worried about finding enough good teachers to fill 34 new KIPP schools in Houston over the next decade, the largest charter school expansion in the country. At full enrollment, KIPP's expanded Houston network would account for about one of every ten students in the district. But that requires a massive teacher recruitment effort. As Feinberg fretted to the *New*

York Times, "We have large boxes of resumes. But we do not have large boxes of great resumes."[25] And even though KIPP runs its own training program for future school leaders, it struggles at times to find outstanding principals. "It's almost like joining the priesthood," KIPP spokesman Steve Mancini explained to the Denver Post. "It's a challenge to find the right people."[26]

KIPP and Achievement First currently recruit heavily from the ranks of Teach for America, which provides about half of their teachers. Teach for America now has a corps of about 5,000 teachers in 26 regions; it aims to double in size to 10,000 teachers by 2010. Still, the United States has about three million teachers in public schools alone. The overwhelming majority of them were trained in education schools—which show little interest in studying the new paternalistic schools or in training teachers to meet their more intensive instructional demands. In his foreword to Samuel Casey Carter's 2001 monograph, *No Excuses,* Adam Meyerson noted that

> The principals in this study sharply criticize the teaching philosophies that have dominated education schools for the past generation. They reject whole language, whole math, developmentally appropriate education, and other teaching theories that deemphasize the acquisition of skills. They teach science, music, and history, not self-esteem…No Excuses schools have a superb track record of training teachers on site. But most of the high-performing, high-poverty schools profiled in this book have never been studied by leading educational journals or teachers' colleges. Business schools study successful business practice. Medical schools study successful medical practice. It's time for education schools to study systematically the principals and teachers who know how to improve the academic performance of their students, regardless of their race or family background.[27]

Little has changed since then.

The Price Tag

Last, but not least, the cost of transformational reforms could present serious stumbling blocks to taking no-excuses schools to scale. To date, the new paternalistic schools have generally succeeded while spending the same amount (or slightly less) per student as traditional district schools. But as charter schools, most also receive less per pupil than neighborhood schools. They have dealt with these disparities by vigorously soliciting money from foundations, philanthropists, and venture capitalists. In effect, no-excuses schools have cut back on expensive but popular school amenities (e.g., modern facilities and computers) and then used their private-sector funding to provide expensive "add ons" like extra tutoring and an extended school day and/or year. But it is not clear that this impressive management feat—coupling rigorous cost control with aggressive private fundraising—can be sustained on a much larger scale.

Leaders at paternalistic schools ruthlessly eliminate services and programs that they believe are not central to the school's mission. They shorten lunch hours, shut down computer labs, cut out electives and after-school sports, and ask teachers to work extra hours with little extra compensation. All of these steps are doubly difficult to achieve in neighborhood schools handcuffed by district regulations, union work rules, and community supervision.

In addition, many of these no-excuses schools have had to launch Herculean fundraising efforts to raise the wherewithal to open new schools, eliminate the funding gaps characteristic of charter schools, and provide "extras" like an extended-time schedule. Many of these schools have already received multi-million dollar replication grants from such major education philanthropies as the Bill & Melinda Gates Foundation, the Walton Family Foundation, and the Pisces Foundation. (Several school networks have also secured significant investment from a growing array of education venture capital funds.) It is not clear that hundreds more paternalistic schools could rouse the same level of financial support from the private sector.

Consider the seemingly simple example of extending the school year and/or school day. It is extremely expensive since teachers have to be paid for extra months on the job. Diana Jean Schemo of the *New York Times* reports that "of all the steps schools districts take to try to improve student achievement, lengthening the day is generally the costliest—an extra $1,300 a student annually here in Massachusetts."[28] School superintendents in Minnesota recently abandoned a proposal to lengthen the year by 25 days after discovering that to do so would cost $750 million. Most states and districts have responded to the steep price tag of extending school time by targeting just a few failing schools or struggling pupils. New Mexico is spending $2.3 million to extend the school day by one hour for 2,100 students in four districts who failed state achievement tests; providing the extra hour of math and reading tutorials costs about $1,000 a student.[29] Massachusetts, a leader in the extended-time movement, has spent about $20 million to date to support a public-private partnership to lengthen the school day at 19 schools in eight districts.[30] In Murfreesboro, Tennessee, school officials experimented with a longer day but dropped the program after their financing ran out.[31]

Charter schools can ultimately raise funds more easily than neighborhood schools to pay for an extended schedule. For the nation's far more numerous neighborhood schools, it is next to impossible to independently raise hundreds of thousands of dollars to extend the school year, to provide intensive tutoring for all struggling students, or to break a school into smaller schools. University Park Campus School, the lone neighborhood school profiled in this volume, was unusual in that it obtained financial start-up support from a federal grant, from Clark University, and from foundations. Yet after the financially strapped Worcester school district cut back funding for its extended-day programming in 2003, UPCS was forced to revert to a traditional school day.

Even when the dollars can be found, an extended-time program in inner-city schools is likely to face formidable opposition from teachers, district administrators, students, and some parents. After all, one attraction to becoming a teacher is that it allows time off in the summer and enables teachers to spend after-school hours with their families. Some teachers don't mind spending extra time in the classroom, as long as they are compensated for it. But in Lowell, Massachusetts, teachers "balked at the district's original plan to participate [in the extended-time program], saying they were too tired at the end of the day for extra work and had their own obligations at home."[32] When Edison Schools began 15 years ago, it, too, stipulated that its schools would have both a longer school day (by one to two hours) and an extended year. (It added two weeks to the school calendar at the start of school and two additional weeks into the summer.) But during the additional weeks, student absenteeism jumped, undermining the value of extending the school year. Teachers didn't much like having to stay in the classroom for an additional month either. Eventually, Edison abandoned the longer school year and now sticks to an extended-day schedule.[33]

Nor is it a simple matter to navigate the school bureaucracy to implement an extended-time schedule. As former New York City education chancellor Rudy Crew once told a reporter from *Time*, "If I want to get things done, like instituting a longer school day, I have to go get the Governor's signature, the mayor's signature, the commissioner's signature, the board of regents' signature.

Do you understand how much of my life I could spend here just getting those stars in alignment?"[34]

The obstacles encountered by those who wish to spread paternalistic reform on a large scale are thus both political and practical. The difficulty of funding an extended school day and year, the challenge of finding the excellent teachers needed to work an extended schedule, the reluctance of districts to grant autonomy to innovative school leaders, the limited ranks of those with the skills to turn schools around, and the flawed charter laws and union contracts that tie the hands of entrepreneurs are just some of the factors that make it difficult to imagine radical reform succeeding on a large scale anytime soon.

One final challenge looms ahead as well: the conundrum created by the role of paternalism in the success of no-excuses schools. The idea that principals and teachers should rigorously supervise the education and acculturation of inner-city teenagers is too alien to the education establishment to be adopted on a comprehensive scale at present. Instigating educational paternalism writ large would require reversing the powerful tides of progressive education, multicultural and bilingual education, and the teacher training regimen of most education schools. More fundamentally, adopting the no-excuses model would obligate educators to rethink their knee-jerk antipathy to educational paternalism and rebuff the reigning Romantic philosophy of Jean-Jacques Rousseau and John Dewey. Educators and those who train them will need to overcome their prejudices and open their minds to the possibility that Rousseau and Dewey were wrong to believe that adolescents—at least disadvantaged ones—should be granted as much freedom as possible to evolve naturally. Instead, it appears that many poor adolescents benefit from being told exactly what to learn and how to conduct themselves in middle-class society.

Incorporating "Paternalism Lite" into Urban School Reform

Given the political and philosophical obstacles to an en-masse restructuring of inner-city schools in the mold of paternalistic schools, reformers could also opt to pursue a "paternalism lite" agenda in the near-term. An array of less prescriptive school reforms implicitly adopt the guiding principles of no-excuses schools, primarily the idea that the best way to foster achievement is to specify precisely what students should learn and how they should behave and then back up academic expectations and school rules with consequences.

Urban school reform can be pursued at either the micro level (e.g., by school principals and teachers) or the macro level (by districts, the mayor's office, the state education department). For micro-reformers of individual schools, the record suggests a paternalism-lite agenda of at least five steps that stops well short of truly transformative school reform but that helps create more high-performing, secondary schools in the inner city—and perhaps paves the way for a more sweeping overhaul of inner-city schooling to the paternalistic model. The paternalism-lite agenda would include:

- Replace the curricular smorgasbord of comprehensive secondary schools with a demanding college-prep curriculum, minimizing tracking, bilingual instruction, and multicultural courses.

- Use regular assessments, aligned with state standards, to target students and teachers who need help—and provide intensive remedial assistance and tutoring support to pupils with below grade-level skills.

- Provide teachers with more on-site training and new opportunities to review student progress and discipline problems, and to observe other teachers' classrooms.

- Principals, with assistance from teachers, need to create a sense of mission and concern for student character. They should enlist all staff in attaining their goals, including the secretaries and janitors.

- Finally, hire principals and teachers who like—and celebrate—their students.

As this list suggests, paternalistic educators advocate a number of measures that are unpopular, even thought to be counterproductive, in some quarters of the education establishment. Frequent testing, for example, is not embraced by progressive circles. But educators who have bought into paternalism know that regular assessments are a rich source of information that enables them to target student weaknesses and correct gaps in classroom instruction, not a state-imposed burden that leads to deadening "drill and kill" instruction. In their view, frequent assessments are all the more critical because many inner-city students are far behind when they enter secondary school. Hence, these educators believe it is unrealistic to expect students to handle a college-prep curriculum without intensive remedial help and tutoring in the form of a "catch-up curriculum" at the start of middle school. Interim assessments are one means by which teachers can identify the specific weaknesses of faltering students.

Paternalistic educators also resist the idea that union protections and work rules are good for students—or even for teachers. One of the invaluable compensations for teachers at the new paternalist schools is that they can develop a far more robust connection to their colleagues. Several of these schools schedule an entire grade to have "specials" once a week (e.g., electives like P.E. or art), so as to allow core teachers to meet to go over the status of their students. The faculty review sessions ensure that students don't fall through cracks, but they also build a sense of personal investment in the school. As Jack Foley, a vice president at Clark University put it, "the teachers [at UPCS] feel like they own the school and are accountable for the success of the students." Teacher collaboration, and a school ethic of one-for-all and all-for-one, provides a critical non-monetary reward for the long hours that non-union teachers put in at no-excuses schools.

A second theme of the paternalism-lite agenda is that school leaders need to relentlessly keep their eyes on the prize—narrowing the achievement gap—and not get distracted. Many inner-city secondary schools lack a palpable sense of mission. Their hallways are not proudly festooned with outstanding student work or photos of students on the dean's list. Even when inner-city schools have some of these trappings, the support staff often seems disconnected from any sense of the school's academic purpose. The secretaries may be surly to students. Jaded janitors leave the bathrooms unkempt. Broken windows, backed-up toilets, and leaky pipes go unfixed. Security guards may screen incoming visitors but do little to intervene in the school unless a student is flagrantly breaking the law or engaged in a fight on school property.

Principals who want to instill a culture of achievement in inner-city high schools need to enlist *all* support staff in their cause. Molding school culture is a tricky and elusive assignment, and there is little doubt that the fragile sense of community is easily fractured at large urban high schools. But at the new paternalist schools, it is striking how often the support staff helps to reinforce school culture.

A subtle yet essential element of paternalistic schools is hiring principals and teachers who celebrate their students. In his 1965 classic *Dark Ghetto*, Kenneth Clark observed that "the dominant and disturbing fact about ghetto schools is that the teachers and students regard each other as adversaries.

Under these conditions the teachers are reluctant to teach and the students resist learning."[35] Since Clark wrote about the blackboard jungle, not much has changed in ghetto schools—many teachers and students still view each other as adversaries. As Karin Chenoweth reports in her 2007 book, *It's Being Done*, one of the defining features of successful high-poverty neighborhood schools is that "They like kids. This characteristic seems almost too simple to include in a list but the fact is that in too many schools…the dominant emotion among teachers and administrators seems to be a kind of contempt for students—and their parents—that can only grow out of dislike."[36]

It doesn't take a pedagogical prodigy to recognize that urban high schools that breed contempt can never succeed academically. The ethos at the new paternalist schools could not be more different. Students treat teachers and principals with respect, and teachers and principals return it, with affection. All of the paternalistic schools conspicuously display testaments to student achievement and character in their hallways. Yet these schools don't artificially puff up students' self-esteem for trivial accomplishments; they work hard to earn recognition. Here again, a high-performing school acts much like a good parent. Principals and teachers don't crow over every step that adolescents make in the manner, say, of a helicopter mom. Yet they celebrate and honor hard-won accomplishments. Principals and teachers at these schools get a kick out of their teenage charges, even though the students sometimes exasperate or worry them as well.

Even as reformers pursue paternalism-lite at the school level, superintendents, school boards, district administrators, lawmakers, and philanthropists can also take a cue from no-excuses schools in designing macro or district-wide reforms. Most of these seven measures are politically viable, though several could prove expensive:

- Reduce barriers to opening charter schools and converting failing neighborhood schools into charters.

- Break up comprehensive high schools into smaller units of 400 or so students, concentrating such efforts on failing schools.

- Lengthen the school day, and, when possible, the school year, by adding quality instructional time at poorly performing schools.

- Put an end to social promotion and require students to pass a graduation exam.

- Cast a wider net to recruit high-quality principals in high-poverty
  schools. Instead of recruiting principals based on paper credentials,
  superintendents should seek activist principals who prowl the halls and
  demonstrate a capacity for instructional leadership, especially when it
  comes to school culture and student performance.

- Give principals more freedom to hire teachers based on their cognitive
  ability, commitment, and classroom record, rather than basing staffing
  decisions on seniority and paper credentials.

- Allow principals to evaluate teachers based on the performance of their
  students, and make it easier to fire incompetent teachers and transfer
  mediocre ones.

A number of the elements in this paternalism-lite agenda, such as ending social promotion, are familiar. They have been tried before—and failed
to transform urban schools. Even so, the steps on this agenda are necessary
prerequisites to expanding the potential for transformational reform in inner-
city schools.

To cite one example, it is true that charter schooling is no silver bullet;
indeed, many urban charters have failed miserably. Yet for all their shortcomings, charter schools find it easier to create a culture of achievement and
character than do district schools. Charters find it easier to maintain safety
and order, too, and their principals have much more freedom to hire teachers
of their choosing, determine curriculum, and establish a code of conduct.[37]
That enhanced authority is critical to remaking inner-city education and holding schools accountable. It is not necessary that every urban school become a
charter school, as Stephan and Abigail Thernstrom recommend in their 2003
book, *No Excuses*.[38] Yet the Thernstroms raise an important point: Poorly
performing inner-city schools cannot be transformed into high-performing
educational institutions without being freed from most of the constraints of
big-city school bureaucracies.

A good place to start is to reduce the many handicaps that states impose
on charter schools. Roughly one in five states do not have any charter schools
and half impose some kind of cap on their growth. State laws that stack the

deck against charter schools—such as statutes that prohibit charter schools from receiving capital funds or stipulate that charters must operate with less funding per pupil—are ripe targets for elimination. There is ample public support; three out of four Americans believe that charter schools should be given at least as many dollars per child as district-operated schools. [39]

Some charter advocates still believe that they should be able to outperform public schools even with less funding per pupil. But reduced financing continues to discourage educational entrepreneurs from opening charters. At the same time, the federal government could also dramatically expand funding for charter school start-ups and tune-ups. In 2007, the federal government allotted just $250 million to charter schools, a disproportionately tiny share of the U.S. Department of Education's K–12 budget. [40]

In much the same vein, social promotion must be eliminated because creating a culture of achievement within inner-city schools is all but impossible when students can flunk their courses yet still advance to the next grade. At present, social promotion is widespread in urban schools, though a few cities (e.g., Chicago and New York) and states (Florida) require students to pass a test to move on to specified grades. [41] Just over half the states currently require students to pass an exam to graduate from high school. Once again, doing away with social promotion and requiring students to pass a graduation exam draw considerable public support, even if the reforms remain unpopular among many educators. A 2007 survey by *Education Next* and Harvard University found that four in five Americans support requiring students in certain grades to pass an exam before being promoted to the next grade and nearly 90 percent favor high school graduation exams. African Americans and Hispanics also strongly support the abolition of social promotion, with 82 percent of blacks and 79 percent of Latinos saying that students should be required to pass an exam in certain grades before moving on. [42]

While parts of the paternalism-lite agenda are popular with the public but unpopular with many educators, all sides to the reform debate agree on one reform element: having more high-quality teachers in urban schools is one of the only sure ways to boost achievement among low-income adolescents. Using data on teachers gathered in Tennessee, researchers found that a student who has three very high-quality teachers in a row will gain 50 percentile points more on achievement tests than a student who has three teachers in a row of average ability. [43]

While everyone agrees on the importance of topnotch teachers, it seems almost impossible to reach a common sense agreement between school districts and unions to grant principals more authority to evaluate the impact of teachers on student learning and to dismiss incompetent instructors. It is here that paternalistic educators are most apt to part ways with progressives and union officials about boosting teacher quality. Without granting principals greater leeway, it is hard to imagine that inner-city schools can copy the successful recruitment record of paternalistic schools.

Well under 1 percent of urban teachers nationwide are let go for cause each year. In a typical year in New York City, one-hundredth of one percent of tenured teachers lose their jobs for being ineffective.[44] In the face of bitter union opposition, Chancellor Joel Klein's fledgling effort to weed out incompetent teachers has yet to bring about the revolution. Last year (2006–2007), New York City terminated a total of 28 teachers out of the city's 80,000 public school teachers.[45] These numbers suggest that 996 teachers out of every 1,000 were competent last year—a preposterous number that even die-hard union advocates would not claim approximates reality.

Even at failing inner-city schools, principals almost never terminate an incompetent teacher. In Chicago, in a striking demonstration of the Lake Wobegon effect, nearly all teachers miraculously appear to have above-average abilities. Principals in that city's public schools gave 93 percent of teachers "superior" or "excellent" ratings from 2003 to 2006. At 87 failing schools in Chicago—schools with below-average test scores that dropped from 2003 to 2005—principals still rated their teachers as superior or excellent. At 69 of these schools, principals did not issue a single unsatisfactory teacher rating for three years running. Asked why they were inflating teacher ratings, principals cited the failure of the performance evaluation tool to assess teacher performance meaningfully, union contract restrictions against lowering teacher ratings, the threat of lengthy grievance processes, and the fact that tenured teachers would not be dismissed anyway.[46]

Establishing an equitable, district-wide methodology for evaluating teacher impact on student achievement is a challenge. Yet at the school level, researchers have also found that principals are able to identify their most and least effective teachers.[47] At no-excuses schools, principals also believe that the identities of their strongest teachers are not a mystery. They carefully and regularly evaluate the impact that teachers are having on student performance. They sit in on classes and send master teachers to watch junior teachers in action. The record suggests that providing principals with more leeway to assess teachers honestly in inner-city schools can be done—and is a necessary first step to making teachers more accountable for closing the achievement gap.

Along with improving the quality of teachers, the other universal recommendation for improving inner-city schools is to staff more of them with first-rate principals. One might think that reformers would, therefore, agree that districts, states, and Washington should devote substantial resources to boosting the quality of leadership in inner-city schools. But one would be wrong. The School Leadership program—the only federal initiative that explicitly addresses the problem of attracting quality principals to high-need districts—received a paltry $14.7 million in 2006.[48] Every year, districts are turned down for grant money because the under-funded federal program has run out of money.

Across the country, inner-city schools face a severe shortage of high-quality applicants to assume the principal's mantle. If anything, the existing system for preparing principals to lead urban secondary schools is even weaker than the teacher preparatory system. A series of reports from the National Staff Development Council, the Southern Regional Education Board, the RAND Corporation, the Thomas B. Fordham Institute, the Institute for Educational Leadership (IEL), and Arthur Levine of Colombia Teachers College have all attacked principal certification programs for being too theoretical and lacking any real-world clinical training. "Few disagree about what is wrong with how our nation recruits and prepares school principals," the Institute for Educational Leadership reported. And principals themselves, the IEL noted, "agree that training programs deserve an 'F.' In a survey of educational leaders conducted by Public Agenda, 69 percent of the principals responding indicated that traditional leadership programs were 'out of touch with the realities of what it takes to run today's schools.'"[49]

As states and cities rethink the recruitment and training of urban principals, they can steal a page from the paternalistic-school playbook. The record of these schools attests not only to the need for forceful principals but also to their singular importance as instructional leaders and molders of character. At paternalistic schools, the principal is the "keeper of the flame," as University Park's Donna Rodrigues puts it. The principal is constantly roaming the halls, sitting in on classes, and checking with teachers about the progress of individual students. Like a good parent, principals at no-excuses schools are alternately demanding and supportive. Trust characterizes their interactions with teachers and students, and they don't shirk from being held accountable for the performance of their staff teams and their pupils.

While shortages of high-quality principals in inner-city schools are acute, the new paternalistic schools are helping to lead the effort to revamp the recruitment and training system for principals. The KIPP Foundation places so much value on selecting top school leaders that it developed its own training institute (the Fisher Fellows program) at Stanford. A second KIPP Foundation initiative, the summer Leaders in Training program, also helps develop future school leaders for like-minded charter school networks, such as Achievement First, Uncommon Schools, and the Noble Network.

Superintendents are also beginning to look toward other alternative leadership sources for support in screening urban school leaders. New Leaders for New Schools (NLNS), the Broad Residency in Urban Education, and the Academy for Urban School Leadership are just a few of the promising principal preparation and professional development programs that have provided hundreds of new principals to urban schools in the last five years. In a handful of cities, NLNS trainees will soon constitute about half of district school leaders. By 2008, NLNS anticipates that 55 percent of principals in Washington, D.C., will be NLNS trainees, with Memphis (45 percent) and Oakland (40 percent) close behind.[50] Meanwhile, The New Teacher Project (TNTP)—founded by TFA alum Michelle Rhee, prior to her appointment as chancellor in Washington, D.C.—has successfully cast a wider net for teachers, too. To date, TNTP has recruited, prepared, and/or certified approximately 23,000 mid-career professionals and recent college graduates to teach in public schools. In 2006, more than 80 percent of TNTP teachers filled openings in subject areas with chronic shortages in inner-city schools, such as math, science, and special education. Roughly a quarter of New York City's math teachers are now hired through TNTP's NYC Teaching Fellows program.[51]

Some paternalism-lite reforms, like lengthening the school year or providing more tailored tutoring for struggling students, could prove costly if applied across the board. Numerous states and districts are now exploring extending the school day or school year, largely because thousands of schools—perhaps as many as 10,000—are likely to be designated by NCLB as underperforming during the next few years.[52] Extended days would help enable these schools to tutor students and prepare them for state tests.

Still, shifting urban schools to an extended schedule throughout the nation, or even in a single big-city district, would be expensive. And that's not all. As Elena Silva pointed out in a 2007 report from Education Sector, students who spend more time in school do not necessarily do better. What matters is *how* low-income students spend the extra time—and particularly if the expanded time increases quality instructional time.[53] When it comes to time in school, studies repeatedly show that quality trumps quantity.

It is easy to foresee that weak schools with inexperienced teachers could fail to raise academic achievement if they required students to hang around longer in poorly taught classes and unfocused study halls. Extending the school year into summer could prove similarly fruitless, since traditional summer programs have poor attendance and little connection to the regular curriculum. In short, any school district that switches to an extended schedule will have to ensure that the additional instruction provided is of high quality.

The cost of paternalistic-lite reforms can be reduced substantially by targeting interventions toward the worst performing inner-city schools and students—perhaps concentrating on school-wide Title I secondary schools (i.e., high-poverty schools). The 100 largest districts in the country contain some 7,900 school-wide Title I schools, but roughly three-fourths of the students in those schools are in elementary school. It appears that the nation's 100 biggest school districts contain fewer than 2,000 school-wide Title I secondary schools—a far more manageable target. Similarly, most states and districts experimenting with lengthening the school day or school year are sensibly limiting their programs to high-poverty schools that repeatedly fail to make AYP, or targeting low-income students who lag well behind their peers. It is not easy for school officials to find sufficient funding to expand the school day or school year. But it can be done. Schools can use Title I funds to help pay for extra time, or they can seek grants from the federal Twenty-First Century Community Learning Center program and from local philanthropists.

Paternalism and Transformational Reform Revisited

Paternalism-lite is not apt to lead directly to transformational reform of inner-city schools, but many of its elements would set the stage for more radical reforms. Supporting the expansion of charter schooling, creating more small schools, extending the school day and year, hiring innovative principals and giving them autonomy—these are all steps that make a larger revolution in inner-city schooling more conceivable.

Note that the barriers to transformational reform at inner-city schools are chiefly political. District bureaucracies, unions, and education schools would oppose radical reform as a threat to their self-interests, whether the model was applied throughout a single district or in urban schools more broadly. But to paraphrase the cliché, when there is a political will in America there is a way. The no-excuses schools chronicled in these pages have already shown the way, demonstrating how school improvement alone can dramatically narrow or close the achievement gap. Yet the political will to radically overhaul urban education, while stronger than before, is still fairly weak. What might strengthen it?

The growing sense of public disillusionment and outrage over the inferior education of inner-city minority students is surely one critical spur. Reformers need constantly to highlight that injustice to make their case to policymakers. Reformers also need to appeal to the education establishment. My hope is that the record of the remarkable inner-city schools chronicled here will help prod district bureaucrats, union officials, school superintendents, and mayors to rethink their instinctual wariness toward radical reform and their perpetual, piecemeal tinkering with inner-city schools.

The paternalism-lite agenda would open the door to creation of new schools with innovative, autonomous principals and motivated teachers, schools focused on preparing all of their pupils for college. But the lesson of the schools profiled in this book is that truly transformational schools offer something more: a benevolent paternalism.

If these schools succeed in no small part because they closely supervise the education and acculturation of teenagers, that development has far-reaching ramifications. Educators will need to rethink their deep personal attachment to the progressive idea that all adolescents will flourish if they are given the freedom and support to grow naturally. And policymakers need to consider whether what inner city schools really need is not more money or higher standards or better teachers or more autonomous principals but more paternalism—which may involve all of those other things but includes so much more.

For all of the enduring barriers to transformational change, no excuses schools do provide the outlines of a new educational covenant. Their overarching lesson is that inner-city teens thrive when two linked conditions are met: schools must create more freedom for principals and teachers to enforce a culture of accountability, but they also must oblige students to take on new responsibilities to regulate their behavior. As the new paternalistic schools demonstrate, principals and teachers need the authority to turn inner-city schools into institutions that minimize disorder. These high-performing secondary schools create an all-important atmosphere of respect and safety by ceding authority to principals and teachers, while saddling teenage students with new obligations. Only after disorder and disrespect have been minimized will principals and teachers be able to do more to build a culture of achievement in the classroom.

In the end, the new paternalistic schools are institutions that provide optimism about the future, a rare commodity in many ghettos and barrios. They illuminate how urban schools might begin to put an end to the enduring legacy of racial discrimination, even while narrowing, if not eradicating, race-linked achievement gaps. And while the promise of these schools is new, it is worth remembering there is little that is glamorous or wholly without precedent about them.

Indeed, they call to mind a famous commercial from the 1980s that the classic British actor John Houseman made for Smith Barney, the investment house. The aging Houseman, who once won an Academy Award for his portrayal of a crusty Harvard law professor in *The Paper Chase*, dryly explains the secret of Smith Barney's success. "They make money the old-fashioned way," Houseman intones. "They *earn* it." Paternalistic schools have earned their successes, too, and much of the time the old-fashioned way.

Endnotes

Unless otherwise indicated, all quotations from students, teachers, and principals come from interviews with the author. Their cooperation, time, and patience are much appreciated.

Introduction

1   Chester E. Finn Jr., "Paternalism Goes to School," in *The New Paternalism: Supervisory Approaches to Poverty*, ed. Lawrence M. Mead (Washington, D.C.: Brookings Institution Press, 1997), 243.

2   In New Haven, home to Amistad Academy, Aspire broadened its list of comparison schools to include several magnet schools because the New Haven school district has shifted in recent years to a theme- and magnet-school system.

3   The Comprehensive School Reform Quality Center, "CSRQ Center Report on Middle and High School Comprehensive School Reform Models," American Institutes for Research, Washington, D.C., October 2006, 2, 20.

4   Andrew Calkins, William Guenther, Grace Belfiore, and Dave Lash, "The Turnaround Challenge: Why America's Best Opportunity to Dramatically Improve Student Achievement Lies in Our Worst-Performing Schools. Supplement to the Main Report" (Mass Insight and Education Research Institute, Boston, Mass., 2007), 64. The

supplemental report to "The Turnaround Challenge" study presents Mass. Insight's analysis of five high-performing, high-poverty high schools in Massachusetts, one of which is University Park Campus School.

5   Richard Rothstein, *Class and Schools* (Washington, D.C.: Economic Policy Institute, 2004), 61–83; Richard Rothstein and Rebecca Jacobsen, "Are Charter School Students More Disadvantaged Than Regular Public School Students, and Does This Explain Charter Schools' Unexpectedly Low NAEP Scores?" in *The Charter School Dust-Up* (Washington, D.C.: Economic Policy Institute, 2005), 51–65.

6   David J. Armor, *"No Excuses:* Simplistic Solution for the Achievement Gap?" *Teachers College Record*, February 12, 2004; "Can NCLB Close Achievement Gaps?" *Teachers College Record*, August 16, 2006. For a more recent iteration of this critique, see Walter P. Coombs and Ralph E. Shaffer, "The Myth of Charter School Success," *Los Angeles Times*, Feb. 12, 2008.

Chapter One

1   Gunnar Myrdal, *An American Dilemma,* cited in David Tyack and Elisabeth Hansot, *Managers of Virtue: Public School Leadership in America, 1820-1980* (New York: Basic Books, 1982), 224.

2   Richard Rothstein and Tamara Wilder, "The Many Dimensions of Racial Inequality" (paper prepared for The Social Costs of Inadequate Education Symposium, Teachers College, Columbia University, October 24, 2005), 1.

3   "Secretary Spellings Praised Urban Schools for Raising Scores, Narrowing Achievement Gap," U.S. Department of Education press release, March 20, 2006.

4   David J. Armor, e-mail message to author, January 8, 2007.

5   Richard Rothstein, *Class and Schools* (Washington, D.C.: Economic Policy Institute, 2004), 53.

6   Christopher Jencks and Meredith Phillips, "The Black-White Test Score Gap: An Introduction," *The Black-White Test Score Gap*, eds. Jencks and Phillips (Washington, D.C.: Brooking Institution Press, 1998), 45.

7   Emily Sachar, an education reporter for *New York Newsday,* recounted her experiences teaching for a year in Brooklyn in her book, *Shut Up and Let the Lady Teach* (New York: Simon and Schuster, 1991), 67, 69, 75, 148.

8   Christina Asquith, "A Real Education," *Columbia Journalism Review* (March-April 2002): 14. Cited in Abigail and Stephan Thernstrom, *No Excuses: Closing the Racial Gap in Learning* (New York: Simon and Schuster, 2003), 209.

9   Brian A. Jacob, "The Challenges of Staffing Urban Schools with Effective Teach-
    ers," *The Future of Children: Excellence in the Classroom* 17, no. 1 (Spring 2007):
    135; Heather G. Peske and Kati Haycock, "Teaching Inequality: How Poor and
    Minority Students Are Shortchanged on Teacher Quality," *The Education Trust*
    (June 2006): 2, 3, 6.

10 "Hiring, Assignment, and Transfer in Chicago Public Schools," *New Teacher Project*
    (July 2007): 44, 53, 46. The Thernstroms recount how Milwaukee superintendent
    Howard Fuller was unable to fire three incompetent teachers, despite the fact that one
    of the three teachers was caught on tape playing craps with his students. See Thern-
    strom, *No Excuses*, 260.

11 Jacob, "The Challenges of Staffing Urban Schools with Effective Teachers," 131.
    Jacob's data are drawn from the U.S. Department of Education's 2003–2004 Schools
    and Staffing Survey.

12 Ibid., 131. Also see the discussion in Abigail and Stephan Thernstrom, *No Excuses,*
    152–56, 166–68.

13 Jacob, "The Challenges of Staffing Urban Schools with Effective Teachers," 131. For
    data from the Council of the Great City Schools, see Michael Casserly, "Beating the
    Odds: A City-by-City Analysis of Students Performance and Achievement Gaps on
    State Assessments," Council of the Great City Schools, Washington, D.C., March
    2006, vi, vii, 25. Casserly reports slightly higher student-teacher ratios than Jacob. But
    his figures also indicate student-teacher ratios among the Great City school members
    were only slightly higher than the national average — 17 students per teacher in the
    major city schools in 2003–2004, compared with 16 nationally.

14 Table 162, "Total and current expenditure per pupil in public elementary and second-
    ary schools: Selected years, 1919–1920 through 2002–2003," in *Digest of Education
    Statistics: 2005*, National Center for Education Statistics, NCES 2006-030, June
    2006. In 1970–1971, the nation was expending $4,065 per pupil in constant dollars,
    compared to $8,468 in 2002–2003. Data on the dramatic decline in class size since
    the 1950s is cited in Richard J. Murnane and Jennifer L. Steele, "What is the Problem?
    The Challenge of Providing Effective Teachers for All Children," *The Future of Chil-
    dren: Excellence in the Classroom* 17, no. 1: 22.

15 Table B1.1a, "Annual expenditure on educational institutions per student for all
    services [2003]," *Education at a Glance 2006 — Tables*, Organization for Economic
    Co-operation and Development. Available at www.oecd.org.

16 Paul Tough, "What It Takes to Make a Student," *New York Times Magazine*, Nov. 26,
    2006, 69.

17   Christopher Jencks et al., *Inequality: A Reassessment of the Effect of Family and Schooling in America* (New York: Harper Colophon Books, 1972), 134, 176–246. Jencks et al. concluded that "the noncognitive effects of schooling are likely to be more important than the cognitive effects. But we do not know what these noncognitive effects are likely to be" (page 134).

18   James J. Heckman and Flavio Cunha, "Investing in Our Young People" (paper funded by National Institutes of Health grant RO1HD43411. University of Chicago, November 6, 2006). Also see Richard Rothstein, Rebecca Jacobsen, and Tamara Wilder, "A Report Card on Comprehensive Equity: Racial Gaps in the Nation's Youth Outcomes," Economic Policy Institute, Washington, D.C., Feb. 21, 2008; and John Deke and Joshua Haimson, "Expanding Beyond Academics: Who Benefits and How?" *Mathematica Policy Research, Issue Brief,* no. 2 (Sept. 2006): 1–4.

19   Tough, "What It Takes to Make a Student," 69.

20   Angela L. Duckworth and Martin E. P. Seligman, "Self-Discipline Outdoes IQ in Predicting Academic Performance of Adolescents," *Psychological Science* 16, no. 12: 939–44.

21   David Whitman, *The Optimism Gap: The I'm OK-They're Not Syndrome and the Myth of American Decline* (New York: Walker and Company, 1998), 17–21.

22   Ibid., 20–21.

23   National data on the paucity of school transfers among students at Title I schools under NCLB come from a report, "Title I Accountability and School Improvement, from 2001 to 2004" in *SRI International,* prepared for the U.S. Department of Education (2006), xii, xvi, 7–9, 15–16. State data are cited in the Appleseed Foundation's report, "It Takes a Parent: Transforming Education in the Wake of the No Child Left Behind Act" (Washington, D.C.: Appleseed Foundation September 2006), 23.

24   See the public opinion polls cited in "Title I Accountability and School Improvement, From 2001 to 2004,"in *SRI International,* prepared for the U.S. Department of Education (2006), 25–26.

25   Daniel De Vise, "Failing Schools Fighting Back in Pr. George's," *Washington Post,* Oct. 25, 2006.

26   While a raft of studies documents that parental involvement boosts academic achievement in elementary school, parental involvement declines significantly once students reach middle school and high school. One large-scale survey of California elementary schools serving low-income students found that parental involvement was significantly less important than other factors in boosting academic achievement. See Trish Williams et al., "Similar Students, Different Results: Why Do Some Schools Do Better?

Initial Report of Findings," *EdSource* (Mountain View, Calif.), Oct. 26, 2005; and Jay Mathews, "Parents' Effect on Achievement Shaky," *Washington Post*, Nov. 22, 2005.

27 Bill Cosby and Alvin F. Poussaint, *Come On People* (Nashville, Tenn.: Thomas Nelson, 2007), 119. Cosby and Poussaint add a paragraph later: "All these misguided souls, poor or not, saunter through school imitating the rappers and ignoring Standard English because it is 'white.' Unfortunately for them, gangsta rappers don't design the standardized tests or do the hiring for jobs. And no translator at the UN can tell you what 'fo' shizzle, ma nizzle' means. Hanging on to such styles in school can spell doom for these kids."

28 Text of Barack Obama comments at Selma Voting Rights March Commemoration, Selma, Alabama, March 4, 2007. Available at www.BarackObama.com.

29 See the discussion in Abigail and Stephan Thernstrom, *No Excuses*, 144–45.

30 From the Manhattan Institute, see Abigail and Stephan Thernstrom, *No Excuses*, 12–121, 133–47; from the Economic Policy Institute, see Richard Rothstein, *Class and Schools*, 19–37, 47–51, 95–127.

31 Herman Badillo, *One Nation, One Standard* (New York: Sentinel, 2006), 196.

32 Henry Louis Gates Jr., "Forty Acres and a Gap in Wealth," *New York Times*, Nov. 18, 2007.

33 Richard Rothstein, "Lessons; Poverty and Achievement, and Great Misconceptions," *New York Times*, Jan. 3, 2001; Rothstein, *Class and Schools*, 71–75.

34 School-wide programs operate only in schools where 40 percent or more of the students are low-income. Title I "eligible" schools have lower poverty rates, and Title I services, such as pull-out instruction, are only provided for at-risk, low-income students who have been identified as Title I students.

35 Rothstein, "Lessons; Poverty and Achievement, and Great Misconceptions," *New York Times*, Jan. 3, 2001; Rothstein, *Class and Schools,* 71–75.

36 The Comprehensive School Reform Quality Center, "CSRQ Center Report on Middle and High School Comprehensive School Reform Models," American Institutes for Research, Washington, D.C., October 2006, 20.

37 Robin J. Lake and Paul T. Hill, eds., *Hopes, Fears, and Reality: A Balanced Look at American Charter Schools in 2006* (Seattle: University of Washington, Dec. 2006), vii.

38 The Comprehensive School Reform Quality Center, "CSRQ Center Report on Middle and High School Comprehensive School Reform Models," 17, 115, 190.

39 Robert Bifulco, William Duncombe, John Yinger, "Does Whole-School Reform Boost Student Performance? The Case of New York City," *Journal of Policy Analysis and Management* 24, no. 1 (2005): 47–72.

Chapter Two

Epigraph: Thomas C. Schelling, *Choice and Consequence* (Cambridge, Mass.: Harvard University Press, 1984), 81.

1   Lawrence M. Mead, "The Rise of Paternalism," in *The New Paternalism: Supervisory Approaches to Poverty*, ed. Lawrence M. Mead (Washington, D.C.: Brookings Institution Press, 1997), 5.

2   Ibid., 61–64.

3   Ibid., 11.

4   James Q. Wilson, "Paternalism, Democracy, and Bureaucracy," in *The New Paternalism*, 337.

5   Ibid., 330.

6   Quoted in "The Avuncular State: A Smarter, Softer Kind of Paternalism Is Coming into Style," *The Economist*, April 6, 2006.

7   E. D. Hirsch Jr., *The Schools We Need and Why We Don't Have Them* (New York: Doubleday, 1996), 214.

8   David Brooks, "Teaching the Elephant," *New York Times*, Dec. 3, 2006.

9   Colin Powell and Joseph E. Persico, *My American Journey* (New York: Ballantine Books, 1996), 541.

10 See Thomas M. McCloy and William H. Clover, "Value Formation at the Air Force Academy," in *The Military: More Than Just a Job?* eds. Charles C. Moskos and Frank R. Wood (Washington, D.C.: Pergamon-Brassey, 1998), 135–38. For an excellent review of successful education programs initiated by the military for disadvantaged teens, see Hugh B. Price, "Demilitarizing What the Pentagon Knows about Developing Young People: A New Paradigm for Educating Students Who Are Struggling in School and in Life," working paper, Brookings Institution, Center on Children and Families, Washington, D.C., May 2007, 13–35. Price's study cites 12 attributes of successful quasi-militaristic education initiatives worth emulating. These programs typically: 1) Create a sense of belonging among teenagers; 2) Instill an ethic of teamwork; 3) Build motivation and self-discipline; 4) Assume that every teen can succeed; 5) Educate and develop the whole adolescent; 6) Use a prescriptive curriculum and catch-up instruction; 7) Provide structure and routine; 8) Offer mentoring and require monitoring; 9) Provide rewards and recognition; 10) Require accountability and consequences; 11) Provide safety and security; and 12) Follow a demanding, extended

schedule. Also see Hugh B. Price, "Demilitarizing What the Pentagon Knows about Educating Young People," *Education Week* 27, no. 6 (Oct. 3, 2007): 32, 40.

11 I am indebted to the psychoanalyst Harvey L. Rich for bringing the "good-enough father" void to my attention. Michael J. Diamond, a clinical professor of psychiatry at UCLA, also explores the concept of the good-enough father in his book, *My Father Before Me: How Fathers and Sons Influence Each Other Throughout Their Lives* (New York: W.W. Norton and Company, 2007), 26–30.

12 Bill Cosby and Alvin F. Poussaint, *Come On People: On the Path from Victims to Victors* (Nashville, Tenn.: Thomas Nelson, 2007), 2–3.

13 Ibid., 119.

14 Michael B. Katz, *In the Shadow of the Poorhouse* (New York: Basic Books, 1986), 121.

15 Quoted by Ross D. London, "The 1994 Orphanage Debate: A Study in the Politics of Annihilation," in *Rethinking Orphanages for the 21st Century*, ed. Richard B. McKenzie (Thousand Oaks, Calif.: Sage, 1999), 95.

16 Ibid., 89.

17 Ibid., 91.

18 David Wallace Adams, *Education for Extinction: American Indians and the Boarding School Experience* (Lawrence, Kansas: University Press of Kansas, 1995), 210.

19 Ibid., 15.

20 Ibid., 215.

21 Ibid., 132.

22 Ibid., 228.

23 Ibid., 168–70.

24 Ibid., 301.

25 Diane Ravitch, *The Great School Wars: A History of the New York City Public Schools* (Baltimore, Md.: Johns Hopkins University Press, 2000), 167.

26 Ibid., 171.

27 David B. Tyack, *The One Best System: A History of American Urban Education* (Cambridge, Ma.: Harvard University Press, 1974), 235.

28 Jonathan Zimmerman, "Ethnics against Ethnicity: European Immigrants and Foreign-Language Instruction, 1890–1940," *The Journal of American History* 88, no. 4 (March 2002): 1403.

29 Letter from Theodore Roosevelt to Richard K Hurd, president of the American Defense Society, January 3, 1919. Available online from the Theodore Roosevelt Association, *The Theodore Roosevelt Web Book*, page 243 at www.theodoreroosevelt.org.

30 See bilingual advocate James Crawford's paper, "Anatomy of the English-Only Movement" (paper first presented at a Conference University of Illinois at Urbana-Champaign, March 21, 1996), 12–14. Available online at: http://ourworld.compuserve. com/homepages/JWCRAWFORD.

31 Quoted in *New York Times,* Sept. 10, 1917; also available online from the Theodore Roosevelt Association, *The Theodore Roosevelt Web Book*, page 243.

32 Diane Ravitch, *The Great School Wars,* 171

33 Ibid., 191.

34 Quoted in Joel Schwartz, *Fighting Poverty with Virtue: Moral Reform and America's Urban Poor, 1825–2000* (Bloomington, Ind.: Indiana University Press, 2000), 167. Barack Obama made a similar point in a recent speech commemorating the anniversary of the 1965 Selma voting rights marches. "One of the signature aspects of the civil rights movement was the degree of discipline and fortitude that was instilled in all the people who participated," Obama said. "Imagine young people, [aged] 16, 17, 20, 21, backs straight, eyes clear, suit and tie, sitting down at a lunch counter knowing somebody is going to spill milk on you but you have the discipline to understand that you are not going to retaliate because in showing the world how disciplined we were as a people, we were able to win the conscience of a nation. I can't say for certain that we have instilled that same sense of moral clarity and purpose in this generation." Text of Barack Obama's speech at the Selma Voting Rights March Commemoration, Selma, Alabama, March 4, 2007, available at www.BarackObama.com.

35 Daniel Patrick Moynihan, "The Negro Family: The Case for National Action," Office of Policy Planning and Research, U.S. Department of Labor, March 1965, 30.

36 Ibid., 47.

37 Quoted in Kay S. Hymowitz, "The Black Family: 40 Years of Lies," *City Journal,* Summer 2005.

38 David Whitman, *The Mad, Mad World of Textbook Adoption* (Washington, D.C.: Thomas B. Fordham Institute, Sept. 2004), 7–12. Also see Diane Ravitch's definitive account, *The Language Police* (New York: Knopf, 2003).

39 Cited in Abigail and Stephan Thernstrom, *No Excuses: Closing the Racial Gap in Learning* (New York: Simon and Schuster, 2003), 137.

40 Diane Ravitch, *The Schools We Deserve: Reflections on the Educational Crises of Our Times* (New York: BasicBooks, 1985), 81–82.

41 Chester E. Finn Jr., "Paternalism Goes to School," in *The New Paternalism,* ed. Lawrence M. Mead, 230.

42 Ibid., 231.

43 See, for example, the excerpt from Jonathan Kozol's book, *The Shame of the Nation: The Restoration of Apartheid Schooling in America* (New York: Crown, 2005) in *Harper's* magazine. Jonathan Kozol, "Still Separate, Still Unequal: America's Educational Apartheid," *Harper's* 311, no. 1864 (Sept. 2005)

44 Richard L. Zweigenhaft and G. William Domhoff, *Blacks in the White Establishment? A Study of Race and Class in America* (New Haven, Conn.: Yale University Press, 1991), 4–5.

45 Ibid., 17–19.

46 Ibid., 20.

47 Ibid., 23.

48 Vanessa Gezari, "More Perfect Unions," *St. Petersburg Times*, Jan. 7, 2007. Robert Lerman of the Urban Institute reports that "If the Bush-sponsored initiative succeeds, federal and state governments could spend more than $200 million a year for five years on marriage education, training, mentoring, and public advertising, as well as on reducing financial disincentives to marry. An additional $100 million per year would fund research and demonstration projects promoting healthy marriages." Robert Lerman, "Should Government Promote Healthy Marriages?" *Short Takes on Welfare Policy, no. 5, Assessing the New Federalism Project* (Washington, D.C.: Urban Institute, 2006).

49 Avis Jones-DeWeever, "Marriage Promotion and Low-Income Communities: An Examination of Real Needs and Real Solutions," Institute for Women's Policy Research, IWPR Publication D450 (June 2002), 1.

50 Gezari, "More Perfect Unions."

51 McKenzie, "Orphanage Alumni: How They Have Done and How They Evaluate Their Experience," in *Rethinking Orphanages for the 21st Century*, 117–19.

52 Ibid., 110–21.

53 Richard J. Gelles, "Family Preservation and Child Maltreatment," in *Rethinking Orphanages for the 21st Century*, 60.

54 Quoted in Peter J. Boyer, "The Deliverer," *The New Yorker*, Feb. 19 and 26, 2007, 90.

55 Christopher Lee, "Simple Question Defines Complex Health Debate," *Washington Post*, Feb. 24, 2008. Lee quotes Obama saying that Clinton would "have the government force you to buy health insurance, and she said that she'd consider 'going after your wages' if you don't." On the paternalistic aspects of individual health insurance mandates, see Jonathan Cohn, "Mandate Overboard," *New Republic*, Dec. 7, 2007; for a critique from the right, see William Murchison's syndicated column, "The Comeback of Paternalism," Oct. 2, 2007, available at www.realclearpolitics.com.

56 "The Avuncular State: A Smarter, Softer Kind of Paternalism Is Coming into Style," *The Economist*, April 6, 2006.

57 Jim Holt, "The New Soft Paternalism," *New York Times Magazine*, Dec. 3, 2006, 15.

58 Glen Whitman, "Against the New Paternalism: Internalities and the Economics of Self-Control," Cato Institute, Policy Analysis No. 563 (Feb. 22, 2006), 2.

59 Cass R. Sunstein and Richard H. Thaler, "Libertarian Paternalism Is Not an Oxymoron," *The University of Chicago Law Review* 70, no. 4 (Fall 2003): 1162, 1202.

60 Robert E. Goodin, "Permissible Paternalism: In Defense of the Nanny State," *The Responsive Community* (Summer 1991): 50–51.

61 In 2003–2004, California had 24.5 percent of the nation's four million LEP students. See Christine Rossell, "Making Uneven Strides: States Standards for Achieving English Language Proficiency under the No Child Left Behind Act," Lexington Institute (Sept. 2005), Appendix I: State LEP Populations Served by Title III, 2003–2004, page 33.

62 Charles C. Moskos and John Sibley Butler, *All That We Can Be: Black Leadership and Racial Integration the Army Way* (New York: BasicBooks, Twentieth Century Fund Book, 1996), 126–27.

63 Hugh Price, foreword to *Reconnecting Disadvantaged Young Men*, eds. Peter Edelman, Harry J. Holzer, and Paul Offner (Washington, D.C.: Urban Institute Press, 2006), xiv.

64 Moskos and Butler, *All That We Can Be*, 2. Robert Wright, a fellow at the left-leaning New America Foundation and guest columnist at the *New York Times* has written that "the whole, larger stereotype — that the military is a right-wing institution, best viewed with skepticism if not cynicism by the left — is way off. Growing up in, or least amid, the Army helped make me a liberal — not because I reacted against my environment, but because I absorbed its values. If all of America were more like the Army, it would be a better country." Robert Wright, "My Life in the Army," *New York Times*, April 3, 2007.

65 Moskos and Butler, *All That We Can Be*, 6.

66 Ibid., 13.

67 Ibid., 127.

68 See Price, "Demilitarizing What the Pentagon Knows about Developing Young People," 16.

69 Ibid., 25.

70 Colman McCarthy, "Colin Powell Just One More Warlord," *National Catholic Reporter*, Oct. 15, 1993.

71 The "Military Area Office Fact Sheet," available at www.chicagojrotc.com shows that in 2005–2006, Chicago public schools had 9,572 high school cadets enrolled in

JROTC at 43 schools. Thirty-one of those schools hosted traditional JROTC programs; an additional 12 high schools with JROTC programs were military academies or had military academies within a school. One surprising figure: More girls (5,364) in high school enrolled in JROTC in Chicago than boys (4,208).

72 Hugh Price, foreword to *Reconnecting Disadvantaged Young Men*, xv–xvi.

73 See PowerPoint presentation by Daniel Donohue, founder of the National Guard Youth ChalleNGe Program and asst. to the Chief of the National Guard Bureau at the Brookings Institution policy forum, "Quasi-Military Approaches to Educating Students Who Are Struggling in School and in Life," Center for Children and Families, Washington, D.C., Brookings Institution, Oct. 31, 2007.

74 Amanda Poulson, "Push to Win Back Dropouts," *Christian Science Monitor*, Sept. 5, 2006. Data on the National Guard Youth ChalleNGe Program is available at www.ngycp.org.

75 "Table 29. Percentage of public schools that had specified safety policies to regulate school climate, by selected school, 1999–2000," School Survey on Crime and Safety (SSOCS), National Center for Education Statistics, U.S. Department of Education.

76 Ibid.

77 Paul T. Hill and Jon Christensen, "Safety and Order in Charter and Traditional Public Schools," in *Hope, Fears, & Reality: A Balanced Look at American Charter Schools in 2007*, ed. Robin J. Lake (National Charter School Research Project, Center on Reinventing Public Education, Daniel J. Evans School of Public Affairs, Seattle: University of Washington, Dec. 2007), 59. Hill and Christensen's data is taken from the U.S. Department of Education's 2003–2004 School and Staffing Survey. Only 19 percent of principals at traditional public schools reported requiring student uniforms.

78 Lawrence M. Mead, "The Rise of Paternalism," 22.

Chapter Three

79 Lolly Lee, "Native American Charter School Coming to Oakland," Golden Gater Jr., July 1996. Posted online at www.journalism.sfsu.edu/www/pubs/ggjr/ggjr96/INDIAN.html.

80 Ibid.

81 The Academic Performance Index measures the performance of California schools on a variety of measures. A school's API score summarizes the results of various statewide tests, including California Standards Tests (CSTs), the California Achievement Test,

the California High School Exit Examination, and the California Alternate Performance Assessment (CAPA) for English language learners.

82 Josh Richman, "Governor Touts School Spending," *Oakland (Calif.) Tribune*, March 23, 2006.

83 Dropout rates in Oakland schools (from a 2002 Urban Institute and Harvard Civil Rights Project study) are cited in Joe Williams, "National Model or Temporary Opportunity? The Oakland Education Reform Story," Center for Education Reform (Washington, D.C., Sept. 2007), 2.

84 Robert Gammon, "The Caustic Reformer," *East Bay Express*, May 3, 2005, 16–17.

85 Quoted in Williams, "National Model or Temporary Opportunity?" 5.

86 Todd Ziebarth, "Top 10 Charter Communities by Market Share, Second Annual Edition," National Alliance for Public Charter Schools, Washington, D.C., October 2007, 1–2.

87 Office of the Governor, State of California, "Governor Spotlights California's Need for New School Facilities," March 23, 2006, press release, 1.

88 A Charter School's Unconventional Success, Day to Day program, hosts Alex Chadwick and Madeline Brand, National Public Radio, August 23, 2006.

89 Ibid.

90 Simone Sebastian, "Hard Line, Top School," *San Francisco Chronicle*, Dec. 16, 2005.

91 Governor, Remarks, "Governor Schwarzenegger Visits American Indian Public Charter School in Oakland," Office of the Governor of the State of California (Oct. 24, 2006), 2.

92 Bret Harte and East Oakland were included in the comparison because they are located close to American Indian Public Charter School. Roosevelt was added as a comparison school because it closely matched AIPCS in demographics. The latter selection was performed by Aspire Consulting.

93 The API, or Academic Performance Index, score for ninth and tenth graders is a weighted average of student performance on California Standards Tests (CST), the California High School Exit Examination (CAHSEE), and the California Alternate Performance Assessment (CAPA) (which is taken by a small number of English-language learners.).

94 See "State's Highest-Scoring Schools: California Department of Education," *San Jose Mercury News*, Sept. 1, 2007.

95 Katy Murphy, "Madman, Genius, or Both?" *Oakland (Calif.) Tribune*, June 15, 2007.

96 Katy Murphy, "Charter's Notorious Chief Quits," *Oakland (Calif.) Tribune*, July 27, 2007.

97   Ibid.

98   Cited in Lance T. Izumi and Xiaochin Claire Yan, *Free to Learn: Lessons from Model Charter Schools* (San Francisco, California: Pacific Research Institute, 2005), 140. Chapter one of *Free to Learn* is devoted to American Indian Public Charter School, 11–24; Chapter nine is devoted to Oakland Charter Academy, 135–47.

99   Ibid., 141.

100 Rod Paige, *The War Against Hope: How Teachers' Unions Hurt Children, Hinder Teachers, and Endanger Public Education* (Nashville, Tenn.: Thomas Nelson, 2006), 162–64.

Chapter Four

1   Marc Porter Magee, introduction to *The State of Connecticut Public Education: A 2006 Report Card for Elementary and Middle Schools*, ConnCAN, Sept. 2006, New Haven, Conn., 5. Also see ConnCAN's summary of the 2007 NAEP test score gaps between poor and non-poor students in all 50 states, which can be found at www.conncan. org, "Connecticut Dead Last in Achievement Gap on 2007 'Nation's Report Card'," ConnCAN press release, Sept. 25, 2007. Connecticut had the widest achievement gap in the country between poor and non-poor students in both fourth-grade reading and math and in eighth-grade reading and math. Poor eighth-grade students in Connecticut were 3.2 years in grade level behind their non-poor peers in reading and 3.6 years in grade level behind in math.

2   White eighth-graders in Connecticut outscored Hispanic eighth-graders by 39 points on the 2007 Math NAEP. (The average score of white eight-graders was 293; for black students, the average score was 255. Hispanics scored an average of 254). National Center for Education Statistics, "Mathematics 2007, State Snapshot Report, Connecticut, Grade 8, Public Schools," The Nation's Report Card, U.S. Department of Education, Sept. 25, 2007

3   Magee, introduction, 8, 12.

4   ConnCAN, *The State of Connecticut Public Education*, 18; ConnCAN, "Success Stories, Amistad Academy, New Haven," available at www.conncan.org.

5   Quoted in Julia Levy, "Charter School's Formula of Longer Hours, Higher Expectations 'Works'," *New York Sun*, July 23, 2004.

6   Paul Tough, "What It Takes To Make a Student," *New York Times Magazine*, Nov. 26, 2006, 71.

7   Maria Garriga, "Amistad Academy Pupils Show Their Spirit to Delight of Rell," *New Haven Register*, Sept. 8, 2006.

8   To meet the federal definition of "highly qualified," public school teachers of core subjects must have at least a bachelor's degree and be state-certified for and demonstrate subject matter competency in the core subject(s) they teach.

9   East Rock Global Studies Magnet and John S. Martinez schools were included because they are located close to Amistad: 0.4 miles and 0.6 miles away, respectively. The other schools were added as comparison schools because they more closely matched Amistad in terms of the percentage of minority students enrolled in the school, the percentage of students eligible for free and reduced lunch, and the percentage of Limited English Proficient students. This latter selection process based on student demographics was performed by Aspire Consulting.

Chapter Five

1   Quoted in Carolyn Alessio, "Sergio's Words," *Chicago Tribune*, magazine, Nov. 30, 2003.

2   G. R. Kearney, *More Than A Dream: The Cristo Rey Story* (Chicago: Loyola Press, 2008), 338.

3   H. Gregory Meyer, "Motive Unknown in Teen's Slaying," *Chicago Tribune*, March 24, 2003.

4   Robert Pigott, "The Jesuits' School Experiment," BBC News, August 20, 2006.

5   Claudia Wallis, "On a Listening Tour with Melinda Gates," *Time*, May 8, 2007.

6   Cristo Rey Network, "Strategic Business Plan: 12,000 Students by 2012," Chicago, Ill., August 2005, 5; Dale McDonald, "Annual Report of Catholic Elementary and Secondary Schools, United States Catholic Elementary and Secondary School Statistics, 2005–2006; Synopsis of the Annual Statistical Report on Schools, Enrollment, and Staffing," National Catholic Educational Association, 1.

7   Michelle Boorstein, "Buzzworthy Sisters in Habits Headed to Virginia School," *Washington Post*, Nov. 25, 2007.

8   McDonald, "Annual Report of Catholic Elementary and Secondary Schools," 10.

9   Kearney, *More Than a Dream*, 120.

10   McDonald, "Annual Report of Catholic Elementary and Secondary Schools," exhibit 22.

11   Ibid., exhibits 15 and 24.

12   Text of August 1996 speech delivered by Hillary Rodham Clinton for the opening of Cristo Rey Jesuit High School, courtesy of Cristo Rey Jesuit High School, Chicago, Ill.

13 "The School That Works," a segment on CBS's *60 Minutes Wednesday*, correspondent Vicki Mabrey, aired on October 27, 2004. The travails of Cristo Rey during its first year are carefully recounted in G. R. Kearney's, *More Than a Dream,* chapters 13–15. In the school's first year, lunch consisted of pizza from two nearby pizzerias—three, and occasionally four, classes would meet simultaneously in the roller rink.

14 A handful of female students who have gotten pregnant while at Cristo Rey have been supported by school officials and helped to stay in school. But when a popular Mexican-American teacher got pregnant out-of-wedlock in the 1999–2000 school year, Cristo Rey administrators refused to rehire her the following year when she declined to move up her wedding date before the start of the school year. The dismissal of the teacher—who was let go on the grounds that she was promoting a practice contrary to the teachings of the Catholic Church—proved bitterly divisive among the faculty. See Kearney, 274–75.

15 Colleen O'Brien, "Indicators of Opportunity in Higher Education: 2005 Status Report," Pell Institute, Washington, D.C., 2005, 6.

16 Ibid., 11.

17 Mary L. Gautier and Anna C. Buck, "2007–2008 Statistical Directory," Cristo Rey Network, Chicago, Ill., Dec. 2007, table 8.

18 Farragut, Juarez, and Kelly were included as comparison schools because they closely matched Cristo Rey in terms of the percentage of minority students enrolled in the school, the percentage of students eligible for free and reduced lunch, and the percentage of Limited English Proficient students. This selection process based on student demographics was performed by Aspire Consulting.

19 ACT High School Profile Report, The Graduating Class of 2007, Illinois, http://www.act.org/news/data/07/pdf/states/Illinois.pdf

20 All students attending Chicago Public Schools take the ACT as 11th graders. Some take the ACT as 12th graders as well. The mean composite scores reported here for students at Juarez, Farragut, and Kelly High Schools are the most recent scores available for students in the class of 2007. All students at Cristo Rey take the ACT as 11th graders and again as 12th graders. The mean composite score reported here for students at Cristo Rey are also the most recent scores available for students in the class of 2007, which means their scores as 12th graders. When the students in the class of 2007 at Cristo Rey took the ACT as 11th graders, their mean composite ACT score was 18.1.

21 Data for Cristo Rey students provided by Pat Garrity of Cristo Rey Jesuit High School, direct communication.

22 See Gautier and Buck, "2007–2008 Statistical Directory," tables 28, 29.

Chapter Six

1 President, George W. Bush, Remarks at KIPP D.C. KEY Academy, "President Discusses Education Reform in D.C.,"Office of the Press Secretary, The White House (July 1, 2003), 1.

2 Mike Feinberg, "Commentary: Mike Feinberg," *Forbes*, Jan. 23, 2008.

3 Jay Mathews, "School of Hard Choices," *Washington Post*, August 24, 2004.

4 Susan Headden, "Two Guys…and a Dream," *U.S. News and World Report*, Feb. 20, 2006.

5 Mathews, "School of Hard Choices.".

6 Ibid.

7 Ibid.

8 Headden, "Two Guys…and a Dream."

9 Mathews, "School of Hard Choices."

10 Ibid.

11 Ibid.

12 Jane L. David, Katrina Woodworth, et. al, "San Francisco Bay Area KIPP Schools: A Study of Early Implementation, First Year Report, 2004–2005," SRI International, Menlo Park, Calif., March 2006, 11, exhibit 3.

13 Mike Feinberg, interview by Bill Weir, *Good Morning America*, ABC News, Oct. 21, 2007 (transcript).

14 Headden, "Two Guys…and a Dream."

15 Office of the New York State Comptroller, "KIPP Academy Charter School: Financial Management Practices," Division of State Government Accountability, Report 2006-N-15, Dec. 2007, 3.

16 Susan Horsburgh, "Second-Chance School," *People* 59, no. 17 (May 5, 2003), 114.

17 For data on high attrition rates at several KIPP schools, see KIPP Foundation, "Fact Sheet on Student Mobility at KIPP Schools," and "Q & A—Student Mobility at KIPP," June 7, 2007; Martha Abele Mac Iver and Elizabeth Farley-Ripple, "The Baltimore KIPP Ujima Village Academy, 2002–2006: A Longitudinal Analysis of Student Outcomes," The Center for Social Organization of Schools, Johns Hopkins University, June 2007, 20–23; and Erik W. Robelen, "KIPP Student-Attrition Patterns Eyed," *Education Week*, June 13, 2007.

18 Larry Maloney, Table of KIPP Academy comparison schools, based on New York State card report data, 2004–2005, Aspire Consulting, Washington, D.C. Prepared for the Thomas B. Fordham Foundation, 2006.

19 Richard Rothstein, *Class and Schools* (Washington, D.C.: Economic Policy Institute, 2004), 74.

20 Richard Rothstein and Rebecca Jacobsen, "Are Charter School Students More Disadvantaged Than Regular Public School Students, and Does This Explain Charter Schools' Unexpectedly Low NAEP Scores?" in Martin Carnoy, Rebecca Jacobsen, Lawrence Mishel, and Richard Rothstein, *The Charter School Dust-Up* (Washington, D.C.: Economic Policy Institute, 2005), 51.

21 Ibid., 58.

22 Ibid., 55, 58.

23 In *The Charter School Dust-Up,* Rothstein reports Dave Levin's speculation to him that elementary school teachers and principals were likely to refer their more disruptive and academically unsuccessful students to KIPP Academy as a way of ridding their schools of troublesome students before the students enter fifth grade. Rothstein and co-author Rebecca Jacobsen also quote Susan Schaeffler telling Jacobsen that principals at regular D.C. public schools recommend to parents that they send children to KIPP in cases where the children "aren't doing well in public schools" (55). Rothstein and Jacobsen concluded that they could not confirm Levin and Schaeffler's "claims that schools were systematically referring their more troublesome or lower-performing students to KIPP" (58). Dave Levin recalls his interview with Rothstein differently. Instead of asserting that KIPP Academy systematically gets the most troublesome or lowest-performing students referred to the school, Levin says that he was responding to Rothstein's statement that teachers had told him and Rebecca Jacobsen that they referred only their best students to KIPP Academy. "He talked to three or four anonymous teachers who refer students to KIPP Academy," says Levin. "He concluded from that the [feeder] schools were sending their top kids and I found that really infuriating. I told him I could give him the name of three principals who were sending their more disadvantaged and troubled kids to us, too. I'm sure there are some teachers who send us their better kids. But that wouldn't show that the [feeder] schools systematically send us their best kids." After reviewing the draft of Rothstein's chapter, Susan Schaeffler, the founding principal of KIPP D.C. KEY Academy, made much the same point in a February 14, 2005 letter to Rothstein. She wrote that "While I did say that some of my students struggled before coming to KIPP, I did not say that KIPP DC students were 'more disadvantaged' than DC students. I simply said that we have the 'same kids' as regular DC public schools. In the interview [with Rebecca Jacobsen], I explicitly said that students of low and high ability levels enter KIPP DC." Rothstein

and Jacobsen, however, opted not to make changes to the passages quoting Schaeffler and Levin about the weak skills of students referred to KIPP.

24 Ibid., 58.

25 Ibid., 177–78.

26 Susan Schaeffler, letter to Richard Rothstein, Feb. 14, 2005; Rothstein et. al, *The Charter School Dust-Up*, 59.

27 Jay Mathews, "Assessing the KIPP Schools—A New Perspective," *Washington Post*, March 29, 2005.

28 Headden, "Two Guys…and a Dream."

29 Mathews, "Assessing the KIPP Schools—A New Perspective."

30 Rothstein and Jacobsen, in *The Charter School Dust-Up, 64.*

31 Rothstein, *Class and Schools, 82–83.*

32 In an August 30, 2006, rejoinder to a posting by Chester Finn of the Thomas B. Fordham Foundation about no-excuses schools, Rothstein appeared to broaden his claims about creaming at KIPP schools to extend beyond the two schools he originally examined in the Bronx and Baltimore. Referring to his previous research, Rothstein wrote that he had "demonstrated that KIPP schools enroll students whose incoming capacity was better than the average capacity of the students in the schools from which they transferred." Richard Rothstein, "Response to 'March of the Pessimists'," August 30, 2006, 6–7. Available at the Economic Policy Institute website at: http://www.epi.org/webfeatures/viewpoints/200608_rothstein_finn/ rothstein-response_to_finn.pdf

33 Martha Abele Mac Iver and Elizabeth Farley-Ripple, "The Baltimore KIPP Ujima Village Academy, 2002–2006: A Longitudinal Analysis of Student Outcomes" (The Center for Social Organization of Schools, Johns Hopkins University June 2007), 1–2. The Abell Foundation, which funded the Johns Hopkins study, has also provided funding for KIPP schools. Liz Bowie, "City Charter School Shines; Study Shows KIPP Ujima Students Leading Math, Reading," *Baltimore Sun*, June 24, 2007.

34 Susan Schaeffler, letter to Richard Rothstein, Feb. 14, 2005. Also see KIPP Foundation, "Who Chooses KIPP? An Analysis of Student Demographic and Achievement Data for the Original Three KIPP 'Replication' Schools," March 24, 2005.

35 KIPP Foundation, "KIPP: 2006 Report Card," May 2007, San Francisco, Calif., May 2007, 4–5.

36 Jay Mathews, "Maverick Teachers' Key D.C. Moment," *Washington Post*, June 18, 2007.

37   Susan Colby, Kim Smith, and Jim Shelton, "Expanding the Supply of High-Quality Public Schools," *The Bridgespan Group*, Sept. 2005: 10–11.

38   Howard Husock, "The KIPP Schools: Deciding How to Go to Scale," Case Program, C16-06-1847.0, Kennedy School of Government, Harvard University, 2006, 6.

39   Matt Candler, New Schools for New Orleans, "Supply-Side Reform on the Ground" (paper presented at the American Enterprise Institute, conference on The Supply Side of School Reform and the Future of Educational Entrepreneurship, Oct. 25, 2007), 2–5.

40   Ibid., 2.

41   Office of the New York State Comptroller, "KIPP Academy Charter School: Financial Management Practices," Report 2006-N-15, Dec. 2007, 5–7. The Comptroller's audit found that KIPP Academy paid $67,951 for the two five-day retreats to the Caribbean—a relatively small portion of the $2 million in donations that the school raised in FY 2006 and an even smaller percentage of the $4.1 million operating surplus that the school had accumulated over the previous decade. Twenty-one staff members attended the June 2005 trip to the Dominican Republic, and 49 staff went on the June 2006 retreat to the Bahamas. Also see Office of the New York State Comptroller, "DiNapoli: KIPP Implements Additional Internal Controls as a Result of Audit," press release, Dec. 6, 2007.

42   Julia Dahl and Yoav Gonen, "Furor Over 'Class' Trip—To Bahamas," *New York Post*, Dec. 7, 2007.

43   Ibid., Also see Letter from David B. Massey and David Levin to Steven E. Sossei, Audit Director, Office of the State Comptroller, Sept. 28, 2007, reprinted in Office of the New York State Comptroller, "KIPP Academy Charter School: Financial Management Practices," Report 2006-N-15, Dec. 2007, Appendix A, 14–19.

44   Jay Mathews, "Looking at KIPP, Coolly and Carefully," *Washington Post*, April 24, 2007.

45   Alan Gottlieb, "Earlier, Smarter Intervention Could Have Saved Cole, Insiders Say," *The Term Paper, The Piton Foundation* 4, no. 1 (Jan. 2005): 1–3. See also Amy Berk Anderson and Dale DeCesare, "Opening Closed Doors: Lessons from Colorado's First Independent Charter School," Augenblick, Palaich and Associates, Inc., a report prepared for the Donnell-Kay Foundation and Piton Foundation, Sept. 5, 2006, 3–25.

46   Allison Sherry, "Cole Charter School Set for Closure," *Denver Post*, January 11, 2007.

47   KIPP Foundation, "Fact Sheet on Student Mobility at KIPP Schools," and "Q & A—Student Mobility at KIPP," June 7, 2007; Erik W. Robelen, "KIPP Student-Attrition Patterns Eyed," *Education Week*, June 13, 2007.

48 The Comprehensive School Reform Quality Center, "CSRQ Center Report on Middle and High School Comprehensive School Reform Models," American Institutes for Research, Washington, D.C., Oct. 2006, 17, 114–15.

49 Rothstein, *Class and Schools*, 75.

50 Robert Maranto and April Gresham Maranto, "Markets, Bureaucracies, and Clans: The Role of Organizational Culture," in *Educational Entrepreneurship*, ed. Frederick M. Hess (Cambridge, Mass.: Harvard Educational Press, 2006), 160.

51 Tamar Lewin, "Charter Group Will Enroll More Pupils in Houston," *New York Times*, March 21, 2007.

Chapter Seven

1 Cindy Loose, "A Mother Waits for Answers," *Washington Post*, Sept. 29, 1993; Cindy Loose, "A Life Just Started Is Taken Away," *Washington Post*, Sept. 30, 1993; Bill Miller, "Girl's Slaying: A Case of Frustration," *Washington Post*, July 7, 1995.

2 Mary McGrory, "Reasons for Grief and Shame," *Washington Post*, Oct. 5, 1993.

3 Cindy Loose, "A Child Is Leading Us Out of This Destruction," *Washington Post*, Oct. 5, 1993.

4 U.S. Dept. of Education, Office of Innovation and Improvement, "Charter Schools: Closing the Achievement Gap," prepared by WestEd, October 2006. See Secretary Margaret Spellings' foreword, page v, and 55–58.

5 A special on ABC's *Nightline*, aired on June 28, 2002.

6 Richard L. Zweigenhaft and G. William Domhoff, *Blacks in the White Establishment?* (New Haven, Conn.: Yale University Press, 1991), 68–69.

7 Stephen G. Smith, "The Appeal of Boarding Schools," *U.S. News and World Report* 130, no. 19 (May 14, 2001).

8 Richard A. Hawley, "The Romance of Boys' Schools," (Hunting Valley, Oh.: University School Press, 1994), International Boys' School Coalition (IBSC), 10.

9 Quoted in Smith, "The Appeal of Boarding Schools."

10 Transcript of U.S. Senator John McCain's remarks at Episcopal High School, Alexandria, Va., April 1, 2008, available at www.JohnMcCain.com.

11 Hawley, "The Romance of Boys' Schools," 10. For a more recent account of a sex scandal at Milton Academy, see Abigail Jones and Marissa Miley, *Restless Virgins* (New York: William Morrow, 2007).

12 On therapeutic boarding schools, see David L. Marcus' deft account, *What It Takes to Pull Me Through: Why Teenagers Get in Trouble and How Four of Them Got Out* (Bos-

ton, Mass.: Houghton Mifflin, 2005). Diana Jean Schemo cites problems in youth boot camps in "Report Recounts Horror of Youth Booth Camps," *New York Times*, Oct. 11, 2007.

13 Smith, "The Appeal of Boarding Schools."

14 Art and Science Group, "The Truth About Boarding School: A Comparative Study of Education Options," prepared for The Association of Boarding Schools (TABS), 2005, 5, 14.

15 Ibid., 11.

16 Heidi Goldsmith, foreword to *Rethinking Orphanages for the 21ˢᵗ Century*, ed. Richard B. McKenzie (Thousand Oaks, Ca.: Sage Publications, 1999), xii.

17 Ibid.

18 Ibid., ix.

19 Oprah Winfrey has had to respond to similar charges that her Oprah Winfrey Leadership Academy for Girls in South Africa is elitist. The 152 girls in the first class of seventh- and eighth-graders at Winfrey's academy were Third World dirt-poor and many students had lost family members to AIDS. Even so, the *Washington Post* reported that Winfrey had to defend herself against "suggestions that the school was elitist and unnecessarily luxurious." Celean Jacobson, "Oprah Winfrey, Fulfilling Pledge to Mandela, Opens South African School for Girls," *Washington Post*, Jan. 3, 2007. Winfrey's academy shared a number of similarities to SEED, including strict policies for limiting phone contact between students and their parents during the school week. But Winfrey and her school were rocked during its first year by an abuse scandal that entailed allegations of sexual and physical abuse by a dorm parent. "Nothing is more serious or devastating to me than an allegation of misconduct by an adult against any girl at the academy," a heartbroken Winfrey told the press. See Michelle Tauber, "I'm So Sorry," *People*, Nov. 12, 2007, 83–84.

20 Cason Crosby, "An Educational Experience," The (*Princeton University, N.J.*) *Daily Princetonian*, Oct. 24, 2000.

21 Rajiv Vinnakota, Guest Columnist, "Living Deliberately During Your College Years," The (*Princeton University, N.J.*) *Daily Princetonian*, , Oct. 17, 2005.

22 William DeVane Logue, "Residential Charter Schools: The Road Behind, The Path Ahead," study commissioned by The SEED Foundation, Feb. 2002, 10.

23 The NAEP results are summarized in Dan Keating and V. Dion Haynes, "Can D.C. Schools Be Fixed?" *Washington Post*, June 10, 2007. Also see the original NAEP reports, Anthony D. Lutkus, Bobby D. Rampey, and Patricia L. Donahue, *The Nation's Report Card: Trial Urban District Assessment Reading, 2005,* National Assessment of

Educational Progress, National Center for Education Statistics, Feb. 2006, and Bobby D. Rampey, Anthony D. Lutkus, and Gloria S. Dion, *The Nation's Report Card: Trial Urban District Assessment Mathematics, 2005*, National Assessment of Educational Progress, National Center for Education Statistics, Feb. 2006.

24   See Keating and Haynes, "Can D.C. Schools Be Fixed?"

25   Ibid.

26   Ibid.

27   Gregg Vanourek, "State of the District of Columbia Charter School Sector: 2006, A Ten-Year Review," Fight for Children, Oct. 2006, 1.

28   Liz Bowie, "Live and Learn," *Baltimore Sun*, Jan. 27, 2006.

29   Danna Harman, "The Little Class That Could," *Christian Science Monitor*, June 15, 2004.

30   Theola Labbe and V. Dion Haynes, "Charter Schools Largely Miss Benchmarks," *Washington Post*, Sept. 27, 2006.

31   Logue, "Residential Charter Schools: The Road Behind, The Path Ahead," 8–13.

32   U.S. Dept. of Education, "Charter Schools: Closing the Achievement Gap," 4–5, 28.

33   Petula Dvorak, "Kingman Park Fights a School Many Praise," *Washington Post*, May 7, 2006.

Chapter Eight

Epigraph: Donna Rodrigues, "The School with a Promise: University Park Campus School, A Guide for School Reform in an Urban Community" (*Boston, Mass.*) *Jobs for the Future*, Nov. 2003: 15.

1   "The School with a Promise: University Park Campus School, A Guide for School Reform in an Urban Community (*Boston, Mass.*) *Jobs for the Future*, Nov. 2003, 7–8

2   Ibid., 9.

3   Ibid., 12.

4   Barbara Kantrowitz, "The 100 Best High Schools in America," *Newsweek*, May 16, 2005.

5   Center for Education Research and Policy at MassINC, "Head of Class: Characteristics of Higher Performing Urban High Schools in Massachusetts," Boston, Mass., Fall 2003, 4.

6   Karin Chenoweth, "The Power to Change: High Schools That Help All Students Achieve," The Education Trust, Nov. 2005, 11–16. Chenoweth expanded and updated

her profile of the University Park Campus School in Karin Chenoweth, *It's Being Done* (Cambridge, Mass.: Harvard Education Press, 2007), 23–34. Other left-leaning writers have praised UPCS's model as well. See Joy G. Dryfoos and Carol Barkin, *Adolescence: Growing Up in America Today* (Oxford, UK: Oxford University Press, 2006), 175–77.

7   Rod Paige, *The War Against Hope: How Teachers' Unions Hurt Children, Hinder Teachers, and Endanger Public Education* (Nashville, Tenn.: Thomas Nelson, 2006), 165–66.

8   Worcester did a poor job of initially implementing the choice provisions of NCLB. In the fall of 2003, nearly 4,700 students in failing schools in Worcester were eligible to transfer to higher-performing schools under NCLB but only one student did so. Cited in Paul T. Hill, "NCLB School Choice and Children in Poverty," in *Standards-Based Reform and the Poverty Gap: Lessons for No Child Left Behind*, ed. Adam Gamoran (Washington, D.C.: Brookings Institution Press, 2007), chapter 8, 232.

9   Rodrigues, "The School with a Promise," 10.

10   Katie Zezima, "Hard Work Opens College Door for Whole Class," *New York Times*, June 4, 2003.

11   Paige, *The War Against Hope,*166.

12   Andrew Calkins, William Guenther, Grace Belfiore, and Dave Lash, "The Turnaround Challenge: Supplement to the Main Report" (Massachusetts Insight Education and Research Institute, Boston, Mass. November 2007), 69.

13   Ibid., 72

14   The Mass Insight Education & Research Institute also reported that a clause in the UPCS-teacher union contract states that "changes to the contract could be made with a two-thirds faculty vote. This allowed the principal to choose staff based on more than just seniority in the Worcester Public Schools." Ibid., 73.

15   Chenoweth, *It's Being Done*, 32

16   Roughly 3 out of 4 Hispanic and Asian-American students in Worcester's class of 2003 did not earn a high school diploma on time. See Rodrigues, "The School with a Promise," 14.

17   Ibid., p.10.

18   Colleen O'Brien, "Indicators of Opportunity in Higher Education: 2005 Status Report," The Pell Institute, Washington, D.C., Fall 2005, 11.

19   Anne Gibson, "One School at a Time: The Jacob Hiatt Center for Urban Education Leads the Universal Call to 'Leave No Child Behind'" (Clark University alumni magazine, *Clark University, Worcester, Mass.*) *Clarknews*, Spring 2007.

20 Quoted in Michelle Bates Deakin, "Worcester's Wonder: An Inner-City High School Sets a New Standard for Public Education," *CommonWealth*, Spring 2004: 69.

Chapter Nine

1 Richard Rothstein and Rebecca Jacobsen, "Are Charter School Students More Disadvantaged Than Regular Public School Students, and Does This Explain Charter Schools' Unexpectedly Low NAEP Scores?" in *The Charter School Dust-Up* (Washington, D.C.: Economic Policy Institute, 2005), 51–65.

2 Martha Abele MacIver and Elizabeth Farley-Ripple, "The Baltimore KIPP Ujima Village Academy, 2002–2006: A Longitudinal Analysis of Student Outcomes" (The Center for Social Organization of Schools, John Hopkins University, June 2007), 2, 4–8.

3 Richard Rothstein, *Class and Schools* (Washington, D.C.: Economic Policy Institute, 2004), 146–47. Jonathan Kozol similarly claims that high-performing inner-city schools are "the heroic exceptions…highlighted in the media, not with the serious notion that they represent replicable models, but in order to humiliate the others." Paul Houston, "A Conversation with Kozol," *School Administrator*, Nov. 2000.

4 Richard Rothstein, "Response to 'March of the Pessimists'," August 30, 2006, 3–4. Available on the Economic Policy Institute website at: http://www.epi.org/webfeatures/viewpoints/200608_rothstein_finn/rothstein-response_to_finn.pdf.

5 Samuel Casey Carter, *No Excuses: Lessons from 21 High-Performing, High-Poverty Schools* (Washington, D.C.: Heritage Foundation, 2001), 9.

6 Joanne Weiss, NewSchools Venture Fund, "Conditions for Student Success: The Cycle of Continuous Instructional Improvement," working paper 4, School Finance Redesign Project, Center on Reinventing Public Education, Daniel J. Evans School of Public Affairs, University of Washington, Seattle, March 14, 2007.

7 Paul Tough, "What It Takes to Make a Student," *New York Times Sunday Magazine*, Nov. 26, 2006, 50.

8 Kimberly Wicoff, Don Howard, Jon Huggett, "Replicating High-Performing Public Schools: Lessons from the Field," (The Bridgespan Group, August 2006), 3.

9 See Flavio Cunha and James J. Heckman, "Investing in Our Young People" (paper funded by a grant from the National Institutes of Health, prepared for America's Promise—The Alliance for Youth, Nov. 6, 2006), 25–28. Also see Dr. Heckman's comments at "Every Child, Every Promise" symposium, America's Promise Alliance, Washington, D.C., Nov. 15, 2006. On the limited impact of after-school programs on

academic achievement for middle-school students, see Mark Dynarski, Susanne James-Burdumy et al., "When Schools Stay Open Late: The National Evaluation of the 21ˢᵗ Century Community Learning Centers Program, New Findings," *Mathematica Policy Research, Inc.*, prepared for the U.S. Department of Education, National Center for Education Evaluation and Regional Assistance (Washington, D.C.: U.S. Government Printing Office, Oct. 2004), xv, xvii, xx–xxii.

10   Andrew Calkins, William Guenther, Grace Belfiore, and Dave Lash, "The Turnaround Challenge," Supplement to the Main Report (Boston, Mass.: Mass Insight Education and Research Institute, November 2007), 32–54.

11   Kim Smith and Julie Petersen, NewSchools Venture Fund, "Social Purpose Capital Markets: Financial Capital for Social Entrepreneurs in Education" (paper presented at the American Enterprise Institute, prepared for the conference on The Supply Side of School Reform and the Future of Educational Entrepreneurship, Washington, D.C., Oct. 25, 2007), 14–15.

Chapter Ten

1   Bob Herbert, "Our Schools Must Do Better," *New York Times*, Oct. 2, 2007.

2   Andrew Ferguson, "No Child Left Alone: An Education Reform Run Amok," *The Weekly Standard* 13, no. 2 (Sept. 24, 2007). Professor Jay P. Greene has also noted that Charles Murray and Richard Rothstein share a similar pessimism about the impossibility of closing the achievement gap through school improvement. See Jay P. Greene, "The Odd Couple: Murray and Rothstein find some unexpected common ground," *Education Next* 7, no. 4 (Fall 2007).

3   Paul Tough, "What It Takes to Make a Student," *New York Times Sunday Magazine*, Nov. 26, 2006, 47.

4   Cited in Robert Maranto and April Gresham Maranto, "Markets, Bureaucracies, and Clans: The Role of Organizational Culture," in *Educational Entrepreneurship*, ed. Frederick M. Hess (Cambridge, Mass.: Harvard Educational Press, 2006), 161. The Marantos's report that Levin's interview with Brian Lamb ran on CSPAN in 2005.

5   Quoted in Abigail and Stephan Thernstrom, *No Excuses: Closing the Racial Gap in Learning* (New York: Simon and Schuster, 2003), 267.

6   Samuel Casey Carter, *No Excuses: Lessons from 21 High-Performing, High-Poverty Schools* (Washington, D.C.: Heritage Foundation, 2001), 8.

7   Ed Kirby, The Walton Family Foundation, "Break the Rules: How Supply-Side Investors and Entrepreneurs Can Sustain Their Work through Regulatory Advocacy" (paper

presented at the American Enterprise Institute, conference on The Supply Side of School Reform and the Future of Educational Entrepreneurship, Washington, D.C., Oct. 25, 2007), 13.

8   National Charter School Research Project, "Quantity Counts: The Growth of Charter School Management Organizations" (Seattle, Washington: Center on Reinventing Public Education, Daniel J. Evans School of Public Affairs, University of Washington, August 2007), 11. As Paul T. Hill has written, "special surprises were in store for scholars and philanthropists who thought that good schools could be replicated quickly in large numbers, and that public education would soon reach a 'tipping point' beyond which choice would become universal. As it turns out, replicating success is hard, and organizations trying to run many schools of choice struggle with costs and quality and can end up resembling inefficient district central offices." Paul T. Hill, "Waiting for the 'Tipping Point': Why School Choice Is Proving to Be So Hard," *Education Week* 27, no. 2 (Sept. 5, 2007), 26–27.

9   Sara Mead and Andrew J. Rotherham, "A Sum Greater Than the Parts: What States Can Teach Each Other about Charter Schooling," *Education Sector*, Sept. 2007, 1. In 1996, the nation had an estimated 253 charter schools, a statistic cited in Patrick McGuinn, "The Policy Landscape," in *Educational Entrepreneurship*, ed. Frederick M. Hess, 70.

10   Cited in Thernstrom, *No Excuses,* 263.

11   National Charter School Research Project, "Quantity Counts: The Growth of Charter School Management Organizations," 15, Figure 1. Also see Jon Christensen and Robin J. Lake, "The National Charter School Landscape in 2007," in *Hopes, Fears, and Reality: A Balanced Look at American Charter Schools in 2007*, ed. Robin J. Lake (Seattle: University of Washington, Dec. 2007), 2–3.

12   Hill, "Waiting for the 'Tipping Point',"26–27.

13   Mead and Rotherham, "A Sum Greater Than the Parts," 16.

14   Michael Serpe, Edison Schools, New York, e-mail message to author, Feb. 24, 2008. The Edison-managed schools were located in 17 states.

15   Amy Waldman, "Reading, Writing, Resurrection," *The Atlantic*, January/February 2007, 89.

16   Quoted in Walter Isaacson, "The Greatest Educational Lab," *Time*, Sept. 6, 2007.

17   Adam Nossiter, "A Tamer of Schools Has Plan in New Orleans," *New York Times*, Sept. 24, 2007.

18   Ibid.

19   Ibid.

20 Survey data are cited in Julia Cass, "For Many of Katrina's Young Victims, The Scars Are More Than Skin Deep," *Washington Post*, June 13, 2006.

21 Mass Insight Education and Research Institute, "Considering School Turnarounds: Market Research and Analysis" (report prepared for the NewSchools Venture Fund, March 2007), 7.

22 Ibid., 36.

23 On the tortured history of KIPP's ultimately unsuccessful effort to reconstitute Cole Middle School in Denver, see Allison Sherry, "New Start at Cole Ends This Spring," *Denver Post*, March 15, 2007; Sherry, "Cole Charter School Set for Closure," *Denver Post*, Jan. 11, 2007; Dale DeCesare and Amy Berk Anderson, "Charter Law 'Fix' a Mistake," *Denver Post*, Sept. 9, 2006. The Piton Foundation's January 2005 newsletter, *The Term Paper*, is devoted primarily to the restructuring of Cole Middle School — see vol. 4, no. 1 (Jan. 2005), 1–3, 5, 8–9, 11.

24 Sol Stern, "The Ed Schools' Latest — and Worst — Humbug," *City Journal*, Summer 2006, 50.

25 Tamar Lewin, "Charter Group Will Enroll More Pupils in Houston," *New York Times*, March 21, 2007.

26 Sherry, "Cole Charter School Set for Closure."

27 Adam Meyerson, foreword to Samuel Casey Carter, *No Excuses*, 5.

28 Diana Jean Schemo, "Failing Schools See a Solution in Longer Day," *New York Times*, March 26, 2007.

29 Ibid.

30 Debra Viadero, "Massachusetts. Initiative: Does More Time Equal More Learning?" *Education Week* 27, no. 15 (Dec. 12, 2007), 10–11.

31 Schemo, "Failing Schools See a Solution in Longer Day."

32 Ibid.

33 Elena Silva, "On the Clock: Rethinking the Way Schools Use Time," (*Washington, D.C.*) *Education Sector*, Jan. 2007, 7.

34 Quoted in Thernstrom, *No Excuses*, 257.

35 Kenneth Clark, *Dark Ghetto* (New York: Harper and Row, 1965), 137.

36 Karin Chenoweth, *It's Being Done: Academic Success in Unexpected Schools* (Cambridge, Mass.: Harvard Education Press, 2007), 221.

37 See Paul T. Hill and Jon Christensen, "Safety and Order in Charter and Traditional Public Schools," in *Hopes, Fears, and Reality: A Balanced Look at American Charter Schools in 2007*, ed. Robin J. Lake (Seattle: University of Washington, Dec. 2007), 53–63.

38 Thernstrom, *No Excuses,* 267–69.

39 William G. Howell, Martin R. West, and Paul E. Peterson, "What Americans Think About Their Schools," *Education Next* 7, no. 4 (Fall 2007), page 7 of printout.

40 Kim Smith and Julie Petersen, NewSchools Venture Fund, "Social Purpose Capital Markets: Financial Capital for Social Entrepreneurs in Education" (paper presented at the American Enterprise Institute, prepared for the conference on The Supply Side of School Reform and the Future of Educational Entrepreneurship, Washington, D.C., Oct. 25, 2007), 18.

41 Howell, West, and Peterson, "What Americans Think About Their Schools," page 3 of printout.

42 Ibid.

43 Brian A. Jacob, "The Challenges of Staffing Urban Schools with Effective Teachers," *The Future of Children: Excellence in the Classroom* 17, no. 1 (Spring 2007), 138.

44 Elissa Gootman, "A New Effort to Remove Bad Teachers," *New York Times,* Nov. 15, 2007.

45 Comments by Laura Smith, Director of Market Maker, New York City Department of Education, at American Enterprise Institute (panel at the conference on The Supply Side of School Reform and The Future of Educational Entrepreneurship, Washington, D.C., Oct. 25, 2007). Though Smith cited a figure of 28 teachers who were let go in 2006–2007, Chancellor Joel Klein's Nov. 16, 2007, letter to principals stated that only 10 tenured teachers were fired for incompetence the previous year (in a city with 55,000 tenured teachers). See Vaishali Honawar, "Lawyers' Squad to Weed Out Bad Teachers in N.Y.C.," *Education Week* 27, no. 14 (Dec. 5, 2007). Smith's comments suggest that 18 of the teachers who were let go in 2006–2007 did not have tenure.

46 The New Teacher Project, "Hiring, Assignment, and Transfer in Chicago Public Schools," July 2007, 44–46, 48–49, 53–55.

47 Ibid, see research cited in footnote 31 at page 86.

48 Column by Gail Connelly and Gerald N. Tirozzi, "Principals' Perspective: Additional Funds Imperative for Principal Training Programs," National Association of Secondary School Principals, Reston, Va.

49 Elizabeth L. Hale and Hunter N. Moorman, "Preparing School Principals: A National Perspective on Policy and Program Innovations," Institute for Educational Leadership, Washington, D.C. and Illinois Education Research Council, Edwardsville, Il., 2003, 5.

50 Figures cited in Christine Campbell, "Building A Pipeline of New School Leaders," in *Hopes, Fears, and Reality: A Balanced Look at American Charter Schools in 2007,* ed. Robin J. Lake (Seattle: University of Washington, Dec. 2007), 38.

51 Bryan C. Hassel, Public Impact, "Human Capital: Looking Inside the Sector" (paper presented at the American Enterprise Institute, prepared for the conference on The Supply Side of School Reform and the Future of Educational Entrepreneurship, Washington, D.C., October 25, 2007), 26.

52 Diana Jean Schemo, "Failing Schools See a Solution in Longer Day," *New York Times*, March 26, 2007.

53 Elena Silva, "On the Clock: Rethinking the Way Schools Use Time," *Education Sector*, January 2007: 2–4.

Index

A

ABC (A Better Chance) program, 55–56

Academy for Urban School Leadership, 308

Achievement First (AF), 99, 100, 108, 297, 308. *See also* Amistad Academy

    AF Crown Heights Charter Elementary School, 118, 119

    AF Crown Heights Middle Academy, 118

    AF East New York Charter School, 118

    Elm City College Preparatory schools, 118

    Elm City middle school

        academic achievement, 118

        existing achievement gap, 118

    performance benchmarks, 119–120

    school growth plans, 117

    teacher recruitment, 112, 113

achievement gap

    closing

        in secondary schools, 7

        No Child Left Behind Act, 8, 12-13, 54

        successful reform practices, 258–259, 260–278

cost of, 15

cultural differences and, 27

history of, 28-32

in Connecticut, 98

in Washington, D.C., 204

National Assessment of Educational Progress (NAEP) findings, 11, 13

Phi Delta Kappa/Gallup Poll findings, 12

pre-kindergarten, 14

size of, 11

Adams, David Wallace, 47

adequate yearly progress (AYP), 13, 25, 175, 189, 217, 293

Adler, Eric, 40, 66, 194, 195, 199, 200, 201, 202, 207, 211, 215, 218, 219, 221, 222, 285, 286

AF Crown Heights Charter Elementary School, 118, 119

AF Crown Heights Middle Academy, 118

AF East New York Charter School, 118

American Enterprise Institute, 290

American Federation of Teachers, 177

American Indian Public Charter School (AIPCS). *See also* American Indian Public High School; Oakland Charter Academy.

    academic achievement, 81–84

    attendance records, 75, 86–87

    Berniker, Isaac, 75, 85–86, 87, 88, 265

    Chavis, Ben, 40, 69–71, 73–79, 81, 82–83, 84, 86–87, 88–90, 94, 232, 252, 257, 258, 268, 270, 271, 273, 274, 278, 294

    disciplinary approach, 70, 74, 76–79

    existing achievement gap, 69

    facilities, 72–73

    history of, 68–71

    looping, 85, 86, 87

    Mishkin, Jerry, 88

    replicating the model, 90-94

    Rose, Leah, 87

    self-contained classrooms, 85, 86, 87

    teacher recruitment, 70–71, 87–88

    test scores, 71, 81–82, 83

American Indian Public High School (AIPHS), 88, 89

American Institutes for Research (AIR), 7, 190

Amistad Academy. *See also* Achievement First (AF)

    academic achievement, 113–117

    disciplinary approach, 102–103

    existing achievement gap, 98

    facilities, 115

    history of, 99–101

    instructional methods, 99

    McCurry, Doug, 100, 117

    mnemonics, 108

    morning circle, 97–98

    Orput, Tamara, 109–110

    parental involvement, 115–116, 117, 120–121

    pedagogy, 107–113

    REACH, 102, 103–104

    replicating the model, 117-121

    Sloat, Joshua, 108

    student incentives, 105–106

    Sudmyer, Jeff, 110

    summer program, 112

    Taylor, Matt, 40, 51, 97, 105, 107, 111, 112, 120, 264, 268, 271

    teacher

        evaluation, 111

        recruitment, 112–113

    test scores, 98, 113

    Toll, Dacia, 22, 66, 100–101, 105, 107, 111, 112, 114, 116–117, 120, 270, 272, 285, 286

Anacostia High School, 216

Armor, David, 7, 13

Ash Institute, Harvard's Kennedy School of Government, 194

Aspire Consulting, 6

Aspire Public Schools, 61

Association for Effective Schools, 29, 31

Atlantic Philanthropies Services, 190

B

Badillo, Herman, 27

Ball, Harriett, 109, 158

Barbic, Chris, 282

Barth, Richard, 184, 187

Benito Juarez Community Academy, 139, 141

Bennett, William, 24, 203

Berniker, Isaac, 75, 85–86, 87, 88, 265

bilingual instruction, 48, 49, 50, 53, 61

Bill and Melinda Gates Foundation, 145, 186, 248, 291, 298

Billingsley, Andrew, 52

Bird, Jody, 234, 248

black males

    Army education, 62

    incarceration statistics, 11, 15

    need for role models, 121

    "oppositional identity" culture, 26–27

boarding schools, 195–199

    college-prep, 198

    elite reputation, 196

    private, 55-56

    therapeutic, 197–198

Borges, Francisco, 56

Boston University Residential Charter School, 219

Boyden, Frank, 197

Boys Town, 199

Brenner, Mitch, 153

Bridgespan Group, 185, 279

Brightwell, Frank, 150

Broad Residency in Urban Education, 308

"broken windows" theory, 21, 101, 205, 260

Bronx High School of Science, 181

Brooks, David, 41–42

Brown, Furman, 282

Brown, Jerry, 72

Bush, George W., 4, 155, 196

Bush, Laura, 195, 220

Butler, John Sibley, 62, 63

C

Calgary Academy, 101

Caradonio, James, 249

Carter, Samuel Casey, 30, 289, 297

Cassin, B.J. and Bebe, 145

Cassin Educational Initiative Foundation, 145, 149

Cato Institute, 60

Center for Social Organization of Schools, 181–182

Chafin, Ann, 26

charter management organizations (CMOs), 290, 293, 294

Charter School Growth Fund, 281

charter schools, 31, 177, 289–290, 291, 304–305

Chavis, Ben, 40, 69–71, 73–79, 81, 82–83, 84, 86–87, 88–90, 94, 232, 252, 257, 258, 268, 270, 271, 273, 274, 278, 294

Chenoweth, Karin, 275, 303

Chicago public schools, 24–25, 293

Chubb, John, 289

Ciccone, John, 215, 218

Ciccone, Maureen, 249, 250

City University of New York (CUNY), 249

Claremont Academy, 249

Clark University, 227, 228

    Foley, Jack, 242, 302

    Traina, Richard, 228

Clark, Joe, 8

Clark, Kenneth, 302–303

Clemente Leadership Academy, 113

Clinton, Bill, 45, 127, 288

Clinton, Hillary, 45, 59, 127

Coalition of Essential Schools, 29, 31

Cole College Prep, 189–190, 294

Coleman Report, 22, 29, 50, 254

Columbia Teachers College, 307

Comer, James, 29

Comprehensive School Reform Demonstration (CSRD) program, 31

Concepcion, Jesus, 152, 153, 154, 162–169, 171, 262, 274, 296

Contract with America, 45

Corcoran, Frank, 171, 172

Corporate Internship Program (CIP), 131–135

Cosby, Bill, 27, 28, 43

Council of the Great City Schools, 18

Craigslist, 70, 88

creaming, 7, 177–183, 217–218, 253–254

Crew, Rudy, 299

crime reduction, 21

Cristo Rey Jesuit High School (CRJHS). *See also* Cristo Rey Network (CRN)

    academic achievement, 140–141

    bilingual instruction, 138–139

    business boot camp, 128–131

    college admission rates, 140

    Corporate Internship Program (CIP), 131–135

    curriculum, 138–139

    De La Rosa, Carlos, 128, 129, 130, 131, 133, 134, 135, 145, 147, 148, 150

    disciplinary approach, 136, 144

    dress code, 130

    existing achievement gap, 139

    facilities, 141

    Foley, Father John, 125, 126, 127–128, 137

    Garrity, Pat, 132, 133, 135, 136, 138, 139, 143, 144, 268

    Gartland, Father Jim, 123

    Garvey, James, 228

    Gatti, Lauren, 137

    Green, Tim, 135, 137, 138, 147

    history of, 126–128

    Kendall, Preston, 127, 128, 132, 134, 142

    Murray, Rick, 125

    parental involvement, 144–145

    re-employment program, 133–134

    replication challenges, 145–150

teacher recruitment, 142

test scores, 140–141

Thielman, Jeff, 143

work-study program, 124, 126, 127, 131–135

Cristo Rey Network (CRN). *See also* Cristo Rey Jesuit High School (CRJHS)

academic achievement, 146

Brightwell, Frank, 150

college admission rates, 146

feasibility studies, 149

financing new schools, 148–149

Foley, Father John, 145

Iowa Test of Educational Development (ITED), 146–147

test scores, 146

Verbum Dei, 146

work-study program, 147–148

D

D.C. Comprehensive Assessment System (DCAS), 216–217

Daley, Richard, 64

David Farragut Career Academy, 139, 141

De La Rosa, Carlos, 128, 129, 130, 131, 133, 134, 135, 145, 147, 148, 150

Dewey, John, 41, 300

Diamond, Laina, 206, 212–213, 214

Dionne, E. J., 193

disorder

"broken windows" theory, 21, 101, 205, 260

curbing, 21, 37, 260–262

inner-city schools and, 16

paternalism and, 21, 37, 260–261

Domhoff, G. William, 56

DuBois, W.E.B., 10, 50

Duckworth, Angela, 23

E

East Rock Global Studies Magnet, 113

Economic Policy Institute, 22, 155, 177

Edison Schools, 31, 285, 290, 291

Edmonds, Ronald, 29–30

education management organizations (EMOs), 290

Education Next, 305

Education Sector, 309

Education Trust, 226

Educational Leadership Institute, 185

Eduventures, 282

Edwards, John, 59, 155

Elm City College Preparatory schools, 118

Episcopal High School, 197

Eressy, June, 230, 233, 236, 237, 240, 243, 247, 249, 250, 273, 275

Escalante, Jaime, 8, 92

extended-time program
    cost factor, 298–299
    in Massachusetts, 298–299
    in New Mexico, 298
    opposition to, 299

F

Fair Haven Middle School, 113

Feinberg, Mike, 109, 155, 157, 158, 159, 160, 168, 171, 180, 184, 185, 186, 191, 282, 296–297

Ferguson, Andrew, 286–287

Ferguson, Ronald, 53

Field of Dreams syndrome, 287–289

Finn Jr., Chester E., 4, 54

Fisher, Doris and Donald, 160, 183

Fisher Fellows program, 185, 308

Foley, Father John, 125, 126, 127–128, 137, 145

Foley, Jack, 242, 302

G

Gap, Inc., 160, 183

Garrity, Pat, 132, 133, 135, 136, 138, 139, 143, 144, 268

Gartland, Father Jim, 123

Garvey, James, 228

Gates Jr., Henry Louis, 28

Gates, Melinda, 124

Gatti, Lauren, 137

Gelles, Richard, 58

Generation Schools, 282

Gingrich, Newt, 45–46

Girls and Boys Town, 208

Gladwell, Malcolm, 101

Goldsmith, Heidi, 198, 199

Goodin, Robert E., 60–61

Gray, Boyden, 220

Green, Tim, 135, 137, 138, 147

Gruwell, Erin, 8

Guaspari, Roberta, 8

H

Hall, Ricci, 232, 233, 235

Hanushek, Eric, 286

Harrington, Michael, 51

Harvard University, 305

Hawley, Richard, 196, 197

H.D. Woodson High School, 216

Heckman, James, 22, 285

Herbert, Bob, 286

Heritage Foundation, 30, 286

Hess, Frederick, 290

Hiatt Center for Urban Education, 242

Hiatt-Main South Secondary School Collaborative, 249

Hill, Paul T., 290

Hirsch, E. D., 41

Hoover Institution, 286

Houseman, John, 311

Hurricane Katrina, 291

Husock, Howard, 185

I

Idea Schools, 282
Indian boarding schools, 46–47
Institute for Educational Leadership (IEL), 307
Institute for Student Success (UPCS/Clark University), 249
Institute for Women's Policy Research, 57
International Center for Residential Education, 198
Iowa Test of Educational Development (ITED), 146–147
Ivins, Molly, 45

J

Jackson, Jesse, 193
Jacobsen, Rebecca, 177, 180, 181
Jarvis, Robin, 291–292
Jencks, Christopher, 14, 22, 51
Jobs for the Future, 248
John S. Martinez School, 113
Johns Hopkins University
    Center for Social Organization of Schools, 181–182
    Center for Talented Youth (CTY), 71, 94
Johnson, LouAnne, 8
Johnson, Lyndon B., 51
Jones-DeWeever, Avis, 57
JROTC program, 42, 63–66
Junior ROTC. See JROTC

K

Katz, Michael, 44
Kelling, George L., 21
Kelly High School, 139, 141
Kelly, Sharon Pratt, 193
Kendall, Preston, 127, 128, 132, 134, 142
Kennedy School of Government, 185
Kennedy, John F., 51
King, Martin Luther, 50–51
King/Robinson Magnet School, 113

KIPP (Knowledge is Power Program), 155. *See also* KIPP Academy;
    KIPP Foundation
    acculturation crash course, 160–164
    Cole College Prep, 189–190, 294
    existing achievement gap, 183–184
    Feinberg, Mike, 155
    history of, 157–160
    Mancini, Steve, 190, 294, 297
    mnemonics, 156
    parental involvement, 179–180
    replicating schools, 183–191
    Schaeffler, Susan, 179, 180, 186
    school culture, 155–157
    SLANT, 156
    student incentives, 156
    teacher recruitment, 190–191
    test scores, 183
KIPP Academy. *See also* KIPP (Knowledge is Power Program); KIPP Foundation
    academic achievement, 174–177
    amenities, 170
    attrition, 176
    Brenner, Mitch, 153
    Concepcion, Jesus, 152, 153, 154, 162–169, 171, 262, 274, 296
    Corcoran, Frank, 171, 172
    creaming, 177–183
    curriculum, 171
    existing achievement gap, 175
    facilities, 169–170
    Feinberg, Mike, 109, 157, 158, 159, 160, 171, 180, 184, 185, 186, 191, 282,
        296–297
    fundraising, 170
    history of, 159–160
    KIPP Academy String and Rhythm Orchestra, 152, 153, 156–157, 162–164,
        164–167
    KIPP to College Program, 188–189
    "KIPP-notizing," 153–154

Levin, Dave, 23, 40, 42, 66, 98, 109, 154–155, 157, 158, 159, 160, 165, 178, 179, 180, 184, 185, 186, 187, 188, 203, 242, 280, 282, 285, 286, 289, 328n23

  parental involvement, 169

  Randall, Charlie, 164, 165

  replicating the model, 183–191

  teachers, 170–171, 176

  test scores, 171, 174–175, 176

  Vance, Quinton, 153, 157, 171, 179, 184, 270

KIPP Academy String and Rhythm Orchestra, 152, 153, 156–157, 162–164

  history of, 164–167

KIPP Bridge College Preparatory Academy, 93

KIPP D.C. KEY Academy, 179, 182

KIPP Foundation, 72, 160, 291

  Barth, Richard, 184, 187

  Bridgespan Group report, 185

  curricular autonomy, 186

  financial management, 187–188

  Fisher Fellows program, 185, 308

  Leaders in Training program, 308

  future schools, 155, 183, 186–187

KIPP to College Program, 188–189

KIPP Ujima Village Academy, 182, 256

Kirby, Ed, 289

Klein, Joel, 99, 306

Kopp, Wendy, 111, 184

Koppel, Ted, 194–195

Kozol, Jonathan, 54

L

Ladner, Joyce, 52

Lamar, Lucius Q., 46

Leaders in Training program, 308

Levin, Dave, 23, 40, 42, 66, 98, 109, 154–155, 157, 158, 159, 160, 165, 178, 179, 180, 184, 185, 186, 187, 188, 203, 242, 280, 282, 285, 286, 289, 328n23

Levine, Arthur, 307

Lewis, Dan, 24, 25

Lewis, Oscar, 51

Lieberman, Joe, 220

Locke, John, 41

looping, 85, 86, 87, 238

Lopez, Jorge, 90–94, 273, 278, 294

Lou Gehrig (J.H.S. 151), 175, 176

Lowell High, 88, 89

M

magnet schools, 29

Main South Community Development Corporation (CDC), 228

Malcolm X, 50

Mancini, Steve, 190, 294, 297

Mandela, Nelson, 195

Mass Insight Education and Research Institute, 7, 238, 293, 294

Massachusetts Comprehensive Assessment System (MCAS), 225, 226

Mathematica, 190

Mathews, Jay, 157, 180

Maxwell, William Henry, 49

McCain, John, 59, 197

McCarthy, Colman, 64

McCurry, Doug, 100, 117

McGrory, Mary, 193

McKenzie, Richard, 57–58

McPhee, John, 197

Mead, Lawrence, 35–36, 60, 67, 286

Mead, Sara, 290

Meyerson, Adam, 297

military schools, 42

Mill, John Stuart, 40–41

Milton S. Hershey School, 203

Mishkin, Jerry, 88

mnemonics, 108, 156, 158

Modell, Art and Patricia, 221

Moe, Terry, 289

Monaghan, Tom, 58

More Effective Schools (MES) movement, 29, 31
    Edmonds, Ronald, 29–30

Moskos, Charles, 62, 63

Moynihan report, 50, 51, 52

Moynihan, Daniel Patrick, 51–52

multiculturalism, 50, 52, 53

Murray, Rick, 125

Myrdal, Gunnar, 11

N

Nakagawa, Kathryn, 24

National Assessment of Educational Progress (NAEP), 11, 13

National Association of Secondary School Principals, 226

National Center for Education Statistics, 177

National Charter School Research Project, 290

National Council of La Raza, 249

National Staff Development Council, 307

National Urban League, 62

neighborhood schools, 23–26

New American Schools Development Corporation, 31

New England Institute of Technology (NEIT), 250

New Leaders for New Schools (NLNS), 291, 308

New Orleans
    comprehensive school reform, 291–295
    Hurricane Katrina, 291
    Orleans Parish School Board, 291
    Recovery School District, 291

New Profit Inc., 281

New York State Math A Regents exam, 171

NewSchools Venture Fund, 281

No Child Left Behind Act (NCLB), 8, 12–13, 54
    adequate yearly progress (AYP), 13, 25, 175, 189, 217, 293
    restructuring requirement, 281–282, 293
    Title I choice provision, 25
    Title I schools, 25, 26, 31, 62, 309

universal proficiency requirement, 12–13, 25

no-excuses schools, 4, 9, 30, 286

Noble Network, 308

noncognitive skills, 22, 156–157, 285

North Carolina New Schools Project, 249

North Star Academy Charter School of Newark, 61, 101

O

Oakland Charter Academy (OCA)
    academic achievement, 93–94
    existing achievement gap, 91–92
    history of, 90–93
    Lopez, Jorge, 90–94, 273, 278, 294
    test scores, 93

Oakland public schools, 71–72

Obama, Barack, 27, 59

Oprah Winfrey Leadership Academy for Girls, 195, 332n19

Organization for Economic Cooperation and Development (OECD), 19

Orleans Parish School Board, 291

orphanages, 44–46, 57–58

Orput, Tamara, 109–110

P

Paige, Rod, 98, 159, 226, 230

parental involvement
    Amistad Academy, 115–116, 117, 120–121
    Cristo Rey Jesuit High School (CRJHS), 144–145
    in low-income communities, 26
    KIPP (Knowledge is Power Program), 179–180
    KIPP Academy, 169
    neighborhood schools, 24–26

parochial schools, 124–125

paternalism. *See also* paternalistic school reform
    cultural aversion, 40–44
    defined, 34
    governmental, 34, 40, 56

avuncular state, 59

health insurance, 58–59

marriage-promotion programs, 57

pension reform law, 59–60

welfare reform, 56–57, 288

history of

ABC (A Better Chance) program, 55–56

"Americanization," 48–49

boarding schools

Indian, 46–47

private, 55–56

decline, 50

orphanages, 44–46

post-Civil War, 44

revival, 56–61

new, 35, 60

politics of, 35–36

transformational reform, 309–311

v. progressivism, 285

paternalistic school reform, 3–4, 37-39

core elements, 258–278

accountability, 270–271

attendance monitoring, 269–270

character development, 262

culture, 266–267, 268

curriculum, 262–263

curbing disorder, 21, 37, 260–261

extended day/year, 268–269

facility spending, 275–276

learning environment, 265–266

middle-class mores, 21–22, 261–262

nontraditional district schools, 274–275

parental involvement, extent of, 273–274

performance outcome specification, 263–264

principal autonomy, 271–272

replicating school model, 277–278

school size, 276–277

street culture rejection, 267–268

student assessment, 264–265

student behavior, 261–262

teacher recruitment methods, 272–273

teacher union disempowerment, 272

tracking students post-graduation, 277

cost of, 297–300, 309

incubators, 281–282

incremental, 300–309

politics of, 284–288

replicating existing models, 278–283

paternalistic schools

attrition, 255

comparison schools, methodology, 6

creaming, 7

disabled students, 255

"good-enough father" concept, 43–44

middle-class values and, 50

noncognitive skills, 22–23, 156–157, 285

skepticism about, 7

social activism, 285–286

unions, 302

Paul Laurence Dunbar (M.S. 301), 176

Phi Delta Kappa/Gallup Poll, 12

Philon, Alexander, 220

Piedmont Middle School, 71, 81–82

Pisces Foundation, 298

Poole, Lesley, 207

Poussaint, Alvin, 27, 43

Powell, Alma, 220

Powell, Colin, 63, 64

Price, Hugh, 62, 64

Prince Charles, 195, 220

principals

shortage of, 307

training and development of, 308
progressivism
    disadvantaged students and, 41–42
    in charter schools, 290
    pedagogy, 50
    tenets described, 53
    v. paternalism, 285
Public Agenda, 307
public schools
    Chicago, 24–25, 293
    District of Columbia, 203–204
    neighborhood, 23–26
    New Haven, 98
    Oakland, 71–72

R

RAND Corporation, 307
Randall, Charlie, 164, 165
Ravenel, William B., 197
Ravitch, Diane, 48, 49, 53, 170, 236
REACH, 102, 103–104
Recovery School District, 291
Reich, Robert, 56
Rell, M. Jodi, 107
Restuccia, Dan, 241, 249
Rhee, Michelle, 282, 308
Rodrigues, Donna, 1, 2, 224–225, 228, 229, 230, 232, 233, 234, 236, 237, 240,
    242–243, 287, 307
Romney, Mitt, 59
Roosevelt, Theodore, 49
Rose, Leah, 87
Rotherham, Andrew, 290
Rothstein, Richard, 7, 11, 14, 22, 155, 285, 287
    on KIPP Academy, 177–182
Rousseau, Jean-Jacques, 41, 300
Ryan, William, 52

S

Samuel DeWitt Proctor Academy, 219

scaling up

    comprehensive reform in New Orleans, 291

    cost, 297–300

    incremental reform, 31, 280–281, 300–309

    limitations, 287–289

    replicating model schools, 90-94, 117-121, 145-150, 183-191, 219-222, 247-250

    secondary schools, 31

    whole-school reform, 31-32

Schaeffler, Susan, 179, 180, 186

Schemo, Diana Jean, 298

School Development Program, 29

School Leadership Program, 307

school management organizations (SMOs), 294

Schools for Educational Evolution and Development (SEED), 202

Schurz, Carl, 46

Schwarzenegger, Arnold, 71, 73, 78, 255

SEED Foundation, 219, 220, 221, 222, 293. *See also* SEED School

SEED School. *See also* SEED Foundation

    academic achievement, 215–219

    accolades, 194

    Adler, Eric, 40, 66, 194, 195, 199, 200, 201, 202, 207, 211, 215, 218, 219, 221, 222, 285, 286

    attrition, 218–219

    Ciccone, John, 215, 218

    college enrollment rates, 215

    creaming, 217–218

    curbing disorder, 205–206

    curriculum, 213, 214

    custodial culture, 205–212

    Diamond, Laina, 206, 212–213, 214

    disciplinary code, 210

    existing achievement gap, 203–204, 205

    facilities, 199

    HALLS (Habits for Achieving Life Long Success), 207–208, 211 history of, 194, 200–205

Life Skill Counselors (LSCs), 195, 206, 208

pedagogy, 212–214

Poole, Lesley, 207

replicating the model, 219–222

SEED Dollars, 209, 211

SEED School of Maryland, 221

Stevens, Bill, 207–208, 213–214

teacher recruitment, 214

test scores, 216–217

Vinnakota, Rajiv, 194, 195, 200, 201, 202, 219, 221

SEED School of Maryland, 221

Seligman, Martin, 23

Shepard, Kate, 231, 234

Shoeman, Janet, 88

Silva, Elena, 309

Sizer, Theodore, 29

SLANT, 102

Sloat, Joshua, 108

Smith, Steven G., 196, 198

social promotion, 3, 305

South High, 249, 250

Southern Regional Education Board, 307

Spellings, Margaret, 13, 99, 154, 194

Spingarn High School, 216

Stack, Carol, 52

Stanford University Educational Leadership Institute, 185

Stephanopolous, George, 45

Stevens, Bill, 207–208, 213–214

Stuyvesant High School, 181

Success for All Foundation, 29, 31

Sudmyer, Jeff, 110

Sunstein, Cass, 60

T

Taylor, Matt, 40, 51, 97, 105, 107, 111, 112, 120, 264, 268, 271

Teach for America (TFA), 111, 112, 184, 191, 282, 291, 297

teacher evaluation, 17, 306–307

teacher recruitment

    American Indian Public Charter School, 70–71, 87–88

    Amistad Academy, 112-113

    Cristo Rey Jesuit High School, 142

    in paternalistic schools, 295–297

    KIPP, 190–191

    KIPP Academy, 170–171

    SEED School, 214

    University Park Campus School, 242–243

    via Craigslist, 70, 88

Thaler, Richard, 60

The New Teacher Project (TNTP), 308

Theodore Roosevelt Gathings (I.S. 158), 176

Thernstrom, Abigail, 12, 30, 304

Thernstrom, Stephan, 12, 30, 304

Thielman, Jeff, 143

Thomas B. Fordham Foundation, 6

Thomas B. Fordham Institute, 307

tipping point, 289–290

Title I choice provision, 25

Title I schools, 25, 26, 31, 62, 309

Toch, Thomas, 295

Toll, Dacia, 22, 66, 100–101, 105, 107, 111, 112, 114, 116–117, 120, 270, 272, 285, 286

Torkelson, Tom, 282

Tough, Paul, 20, 22, 287

traditional instruction, 53–54

Traina, Richard, 228

Troup Magnet Academy of Science, 113

Twenty-First Century Community Learning Center program, 309

Tyack, David, 48

U

U.S. Army, 62–63

Uncommon Schools, 61, 308

unions, 171, 242, 243, 302

universal proficiency, 13, 25

University Park Campus School (UPCS), 2

    academic achievement, 243–247

    accolades, 226

    August Academy, 230, 234

    Bird, Jody, 234, 248

    Clark University and, 227

    culture of, 230–236

    curriculum, 236–239

    disciplinary approach, 231

    Eressy, June, 230, 233, 236, 237, 240, 243, 247, 249, 250, 273, 275

    existing achievement gap, 225, 229, 244, 245

    facilities, 234–235

    group instruction, 239–242

    Hall, Ricci, 232, 233, 235

    history of, 224–225, 228

    Institute for Student Success, 249

    Mass Insight Education and Research Institute report, 238

    pedagogy, 236–239

    replicating the model, 247–250

        Claremont Academy, 249

        South High, 249, 250

    Restuccia, Dan, 241, 249

    Rodrigues, Donna, 1, 2, 224–225, 228, 229, 230, 232, 233, 234, 236, 237, 240, 242–243, 287, 307

    Shepard, Kate, 231, 234

    teacher recruitment, 242–243

    test scores, 225, 226, 245–247, 248

    union, 242–243

    Weyler, Peter, 232, 241

University School, 196

university-assisted partnership, 227

urban school reform

    comprehensive, 291

core elements, 259, 260–278

incremental, 31, 280–281, 300–309

neighborhood schools, 24–25

obstacles to, 284–300

teacher recruitment, 295–297

tipping point theory, 289–290

transformational change, 309–311

V

Vallas, Paul, 64, 291, 292

Vance, Quinton, 153, 157, 171, 179, 184, 270

Verbum Dei, 146

Vinnakota, Rajiv, 194, 195, 200, 201, 202, 219, 221

W

Waldman, Amy, 291

Walton Family Foundation, 289, 298

Ward, Randy, 72

Washington, Booker T., 50, 51

Weatherless Elementary School, 192, 193–194

Weyler, Peter, 232, 241

Whitman, Glen, 60

Whittle, Chris, 31

Wicoff, Kimberly, 279

Wilder, Tamara, 11

Williams, Anthony, 220

Wilson, James Q., 21, 36–37, 40, 45, 101, 260

Wilson, Woodrow, 33

Winfrey, Oprah, 195, 214, 332n19

Winnicott, Donald, 43

work-study program, 124, 126, 127, 131–135, 147–148

Y

YES Prep Public Schools, 61, 282

Z

Zimmerman, Jonathan, 49
Zirkel, Sabrina, 89
Zweigenhaft, Richard, 56